Laywomen and the Crusade in England
1150–1300

Crusading in Context

Series Editor
William J. Purkis

The crusading movement was a defining feature of the history of Europe, the Mediterranean and the Near East during the central and later Middle Ages. Ideas and practices associated with it touched the lives of people within and beyond Christendom and the Islamicate world, regardless whether they were ever directly engaged in, witnesses to, or victims of acts of crusading violence themselves.

This series aims to situate the medieval experience of the crusades and crusading societies in the broader social, cultural and intellectual contexts of the Middle Ages as a whole. Chronologically, its scope extends from the eleventh to the sixteenth century, and contributions from a range of disciplines are encouraged. Monographs and edited collections are both welcome; critical editions and translations of medieval texts will also be considered.

Proposals and queries should be sent in the first instance to the series editor or to Boydell and Brewer, at the addresses below.

Prof. William J. Purkis, School of History and Cultures, University of Birmingham, Edgbaston, Birmingham, B15 2TT
w.j.purkis@bham.ac.uk

Boydell and Brewer Ltd, PO Box 9, Woodbridge, Suffolk, IP12 3DF
editorial@boydell.co.uk

Previous titles in the series are
listed at the back of the volume.

Laywomen and the Crusade in England 1150–1300

Gordon M. Reynolds

THE BOYDELL PRESS

© Gordon M. Reynolds 2024

All Rights Reserved. Except as permitted under current legislation no part of this work may be photocopied, stored in a retrieval system, published, performed in public, adapted, broadcast, transmitted, recorded or reproduced in any form or by any means, without the prior permission of the copyright owner

The right of Gordon M. Reynolds to be identified as the author of this work has been asserted in accordance with sections 77 and 78 of the Copyright, Designs and Patents Act 1988

First published 2024
The Boydell Press, Woodbridge

ISBN 978 1 83765 224 2

The Boydell Press is an imprint of Boydell & Brewer Ltd
PO Box 9, Woodbridge, Suffolk IP12 3DF, UK
and of Boydell & Brewer Inc.
668 Mt Hope Avenue, Rochester, NY 14620–2731, USA
website: www.boydellandbrewer.com

A CIP catalogue record for this book is available from the British Library

The publisher has no responsibility for the continued existence or accuracy of URLs for external or third-party internet websites referred to in this book, and does not guarantee that any content on such websites is, or will remain, accurate or appropriate

Contents

List of Illustrations	vi
List of Abbreviations	viii
Conventions	ix
Timeline of Relevant Events	x
Introduction	1

PART I – PROPAGANDA

1.	Crusade and Culture in England	23
2.	The Papacy and Incentives to Support	45
3.	Preaching Patronage	59

PART II – SUPPORT

4.	Encouraging Crusaders	83
5.	Backing the Expeditions	101
6.	Trends and Motivations	121

PART III – MEMORY

7.	Commemoration and Creating Identity	145
	Conclusion: Identities Beyond the Battlefield	173

APPENDICES

Appendix 1: Crusade-Support Activity	179
Appendix 2: Known Round Churches in England	187
Appendix 3: Patronage of English Hospitaller Houses	189
Bibliography	191
Acknowledgements	229
Index	231

Illustrations

Tables

1. Dower lands sought by Emma of Meauton [Great Malton], 1223–4.   99

Figures

1. St George intervenes in the Battle of Antioch (1099), on a twelfth-century tympanum in St George's Church, Damerham (Hampshire). (Photographed with kind permission of Rev Mark Hayter and the parish of Damerham – Photograph: Author).   33

2. Twelfth-century wall paintings on the north wall of St Botolph's Church, Hardham (Sussex), featuring the life of St George. In the bottom-left panel, the saint intervenes in the Battle of Antioch (1099). (Photographed with kind permission of the Parish of Bury, Coldwaltham, Hardham and Houghton – Photograph: Author).   34

3. Thirteenth-century frieze of knights in combat, north wall of the nave of St Mary's Church, Claverley (Shropshire). (Photographed with kind permission of Rev Gary Ward and the parish of Claverley – Photograph: Author).   37

4. Detail of Knights in the Claverley Frieze. (Photographed with kind permission of Rev Gary Ward and the parish of Claverley – Photograph: Author).   38

5. The twelfth-century Church of the Holy Sepulchre, Cambridge, a well preserved example of a 'round church'. (Reproduced by kind permission of Round Church Cambridge. © Christian Heritage Cambridge).   41

6. A thirteenth-century 'Crusade Chest' originally from St Mary's Church, Climping (Sussex). (Photographed with kind permission of the Dean and Chapter of Chichester Cathedral, and Rev Richard Hayes and the parish of Climping – Photograph: Author).   107

7. A charter drawn up by Sybil of Icklesham and her husband Nicholas Haringod around the time of crusade preparations, with both their seals attached. (Huntington Library, BA v.41/1236 – Reproduced by kind permission of the Huntington Library, San Marino, California).   117

Illustrations

8. A thirteenth-century imagining of a departure scene in which two women, an elderly man and two children look distraught as they bid farewell to a group of Crusaders. (Vienna, Österreichische Nationalbibliothek, Bible Moralisée, Codex Vindobonensis 2554, f.4r. – Reproduced by kind permission of Österreichische Nationalbibliothek).   147

9. The Seven-Headed Dragon of the Apocalypse battles with 'the Elect', including two women, in the *Trinity Apocalypse*. (Cambridge Trinity College, MS R.16.2, f.14r. © Trinity College Cambridge, University of Cambridge).   162

10. A reconstruction of the painted scene on the north base of Eleanor of Castile's tomb in Westminster Abbey. (London, Westminster Abbey Library, WA 3682. Reproduced here by kind permission of the Dean and Chapter. © Dean and Chapter of Westminster).   171

The author and publisher are grateful to all the institutions and individuals listed for permission to reproduce the materials in which they hold copyright. Every effort has been made to trace the copyright holders; apologies are offered for any omission, and the publisher will be pleased to add any necessary acknowledgement in subsequent editions.

Abbreviations

Carisbrooke	S.F. Hockey (ed.), *The Cartulary of Carisbrooke Priory* (Southampton, 1981)
CCR	*Calendar of Close Rolls, Henry III – Edward I, 1227–1302*, 19 vols (London, 1902–75)
Chronica Majora	Matthew Paris, *Chronica Majora*, 7 vols, H.R. Luard (ed.) (London, 1872–83)
CIPM	*Calendar of Inquisitions Post Mortem, Henry III – Edward II*, 6 vols (London, 1904–10)
CPR	*Calendar of Patent Rolls*, 66 vols (London, 1891–1986)
CRR	*Curia Regis Rolls*, 20 vols (London, 1922–61)
EYC	W. Farrer and C.T. Clay (eds), *Early Yorkshire Charters*, 14 vols (Edinburgh, 1914–65)
Frideswide	S.R. Wigram (ed.), *The Cartulary of the Monastery of St. Frideswide at Oxford*, 2 vols (Oxford, 1895–6)
HMC	Historical Manuscripts Commission
Lacock	K.H. Rogers (ed. and trans.), *Lacock Abbey Charters* (Stoke-on-Trent, 1979)
SAC	Sussex Archaeological Collections
SHC	Somerset Heritage Centre

Conventions

Money

The finances of medieval England, like much of western Europe, operated around the unit of the *libra* or 'pound' of silver. One *libra* (*l*) was equivalent to twenty *solidi* (*s*) or shillings, and each *solidus* was worth twelve *denarii* (*d*) or pence. Silver pennies formed the basic unit for transactions. However, in many fiscal accounts of the era, *marcae* (*m*), or 'marks', were frequently referred to as a unit of currency. These may be valued at 13*s* 4*d*, that is 160*d*. Although inflation, silver quality and coin weight could all affect the value of money across the 150-year period that will be discussed, these given values will offer the reader some understanding of the finances that the medieval records refer to.

Land

Medieval people were practical to a fault. They did not measure land in standard sizes, instead they judged it by its use, value or taxability, and their definitions could subtly vary from region to region. I have tended to use the exact units of land that our sources specify, rather than translate into modern equivalents. An *acre* in this period generally referred to the area one ox could plough in a day. Above that, an *oxgang* or *bovate* was the area that the same ox could plough in a season. This was usually something like fifteen to twenty *acres*, depending on the terrain. A *virgate* referred to two *oxgangs/bovates* and a *carucate* measured four *virgates*. Thinking on this rough terminology will help the reader get an idea of the sizes of land discussed.

Placenames and Personal Names

Throughout the text I have rendered placenames in England, the British Isles and beyond, in their modern form. Latin placenames, such as *Eboracorum*, for example, are offered in their modern English form, which in this case would be 'York'. Some placenames, particularly rural ones, or small patches of land with local bynames, which cannot be identified or have no modern equivalent, are rendered as they are in their original text and in *italics*. Individuals' personal names are also rendered in their modern equivalent, where there is reasonable cognate.

Timeline of Relevant Events

1095	Pope Urban II preaches at Clermont (France), calling for a Christian expedition to assist the Byzantine Empire and take Jerusalem – the beginnings of the First Crusade.
1099	Jerusalem is stormed by the armies of the First Crusade.
1100	Henry I becomes king of England.
1102	Edgar Ætheling – a Saxon prince in exile who was elected (though never crowned) king of England following the Norman Conquest – arrives in the Holy Land with a fleet of his followers.
c.1100–15	Simon I de Senlis (?) orders construction of a round church in Northampton, in imitation of the Holy Sepulchre of Jerusalem.
1128	Hugh de Payns, master of the Knights Templar, tours the British Isles to gain donations and support for his newly-formed Order.
c.1130s	The Knights Templar begin construction of their chapel in Holborn (London), later moving closer to the Thames, erecting their round church at modern-day Temple.
1135	Stephen of Blois becomes king of England, causing a conflict known as The Anarchy as he vies for power with Empress Matilda.
c.1144	The Knights Hospitaller begin construction of their church at Clerkenwell, London.
1145	Responding to the fall of Christian-held Edessa, Pope Eugenius III calls upon western Christians to mount an expedition to the Holy Land – the beginnings of the Second Crusade.
1147	A combined fleet of English and Flemish crusaders sail from Dartmouth to Iberia and lay siege to Muslim-held Lisbon, capturing the city by October.
1154	Henry II becomes king of England.
1157	Pope Adrian IV, the only pope from England, encourages people in the West to donate arms and equipment to crusaders, in return for spiritual rewards.
1166	Tax levied in England for the maintenance of the so-called Crusader States within the Holy Land.
1170	Henry the Young King is crowned as a co-ruler by his father, Henry II.

Timeline of Relevant Events

1177	The count of Flanders leads a private crusade and numerous participants from England depart to join him.
1187	Saladin, sultan of Egypt, Damascus and Aleppo captures Christian-held Jerusalem.
1188	King Henry II of England takes the cross and levies the Saladin Tithe – a widely unpopular tax to fund his crusade.
1189	Richard I becomes king of England. Jewish Communities in England are soon attacked and many of the assailants are crusaders.
1190	King Richard I departs for the Holy Land, leading his contingent on the Third Crusade.
1199	John becomes king of England.
1201	Pope Innocent III's encyclical *Ex multa* nullifies the need for spousal consent if a married individual wishes to go on crusade.
1202	The Fourth Crusade is launched, though it attracts relatively little interest from landholders in England.
1213	Pope Innocent III calls for the Fifth Crusade in his encyclical *Quia maior* – explicitly requesting support from women.
1215	King John takes the cross and the First Barons' War begins – many of the rebel leaders are themselves crusaders.
1216	Henry III becomes king of England.
	Margaret de Lacy founds a Hospitaller nunnery at Aconbury (Herefordshire).
1217	The Fifth Crusade begins, aimed at Damietta in Egypt. The First Barons' War ends the same year, freeing up recruits and resources in England.
1227	Peter des Roches, bishop of Winchester, and nobleman William Briwere lead contingents from England on the Sixth Crusade. Preachers in England convince many women and men to take the cross and then redeem their vows for cash.
1235	Crusade preachers in England explicitly direct their sermons towards women and men, and encourage donations.
1240	Richard earl of Cornwall and Simon de Montfort earl of Leicester lead contingents from England on the Barons' Crusade.
1244	Christian-held Jerusalem falls to a Khwarazmian army.
1249	William II Longespée leads a contingent from England on the Seventh Crusade and the venture is blessed by his mother abbess Ela of Salisbury.

Timeline of Relevant Events

1264	Second Barons' War begins. The rebels and royalists harness the culture of crusade, using crosses as insignia.
1270	Lord Edward (later King Edward I) leads crusaders from England to join King Louis IX of France on crusade in Tunis.
1272	Edward I becomes king of England.
1274	Edward returns from the Holy Land and is crowned.
1287	King Edward I and, probably also, his wife Eleanor of Castile take the cross a second time.
1290	Otto de Grandson – perhaps acting as a crusade-proxy for Eleanor of Castile – departs England with a small contingent of crusaders.
1291	Acre, the last vestige of the Crusader States on the Levantine mainland, falls to the forces of the Mamluk Sultanate.
1300	King Edward I and his accompanying knights invoke crusading culture by wearing crosses while on campaign against the Scots in Annandale and Galloway.
1307	Edward II becomes king of England.
1308	The Knights Templar are first put on trial in the British Isles – the beginnings of the dissolution of the order.
1309	A Hospitaller-led contingent of crusaders departs England to aid Christian Armenia and help in the capture of Rhodes.

Introduction

As to the monies that you ought to have of the Crusade [fund], the legate, thanks be to him, has granted that he will let us have them if we can discover where they are. But little have we found, except that they are in the hands of those who *would* go into the Holy Land. But what we shall be able to obtain for you from that and elsewhere, between this and the passage of St John, we will then send you by the messengers of the Temple, who will carry their monies. And for God's sake, dear son, keep yourself another time from making such a bond as you have made with Sir Ingram de Umfravile for I doubt that it will fall on your demesne to have to pay it. And dear sweet son, I earnestly pray you that you do not send to us because you have had so much relief of my commanding.

(Hawisa de Nevill writing to her son, c.1266–9).[1]

This frank letter is as full of concern as it contains pragmatic, salt-of-the-earth advice on finances. Hawisa de Nevill, a noblewoman in Essex, wrote this message to her son Hugh while he was in the port city of Acre in the Holy Land, sometime between 1266 and 1269. She is clear about the support she has been offering, if a little exasperated with her fiscally cavalier son. This exchange between a crusader and his mother has been described as a "unique" survival of correspondence.[2] Here, we get a fleeting glimpse of a noblewoman's thoughts, in her own words no less, on crusade and its effects on her family (and their wealth).

Hugh had left some lands with his mother and brother before he departed for that crusade, perhaps so the property would not be mismanaged, maybe so his family would give him some cash in exchange.[3] However, Hugh's preparations had not gone entirely to plan. He had been forced to embark on his journey without receiving the 500*m* of silver that the papacy had allocated to him from huge collection drives made in England.[4] Hawisa's letter is brimming with frustration. She believed that people claiming that they would go on crusade had instead squandered the funds. She told Hugh that she would do her utmost to raise more capital herself:

---

[1] My emphasis. M.S. Giuseppi, 'XIX – On the Testament of Sir Hugh de Nevill Written at Acre, 1267', *Archaeologia*, vol. 56 (1899), pp. 351–70, at 360. For Old French, see p. 358.
[2] C.R. Young, *The Making of the Neville Family in England, 1166–1400* (Woodbridge, 1996), p. 57.
[3] *CCR, 1264–68*, p. 254.
[4] Giuseppi, 'XIX – On the Testament of Sir Hugh de Nevill', p. 354.

William FitzSimon brought me news that you are so poorly provided with monies. But God Almighty if it please Him bring speedy amendment there! And I will do it with all my power.[5]

We do not know if Hugh saw this particular letter, but he knew that his mother was supporting him. As he lay dying in Acre in 1267, he had time to draft his testament. In it, he referred to a lump sum (other than the papal subsidy) that was on its way to him.[6] Undoubtedly, Hawisa had consistently backed her son. There is a clear sense that she felt a genuine responsibility for Hugh's crusade. Although the letter may be unique, the actions she alluded to were not, and Hawisa's candour suggests that she did not consider what she was doing to be unusual.

In order for the many thousands of crusaders and hangers-on to make their journey, even greater numbers of people had to offer up their support. Parents, spouses, friends and more, all across Christendom, must have felt an overwhelming affinity with crusade despite never physically taking part. So much so, that they poured their time and wealth into sending their family to holy war. Those people living in western Europe during the twelfth and thirteenth centuries inhabited a world that celebrated crusade – it formed a backdrop to a complex spectrum of medieval concerns about pageantry, chivalry, largesse, family tradition and internal spiritual struggle, as much as it could be about far-flung religious warfare. This is not to say that the whole of Latin Christendom was poised to mobilise *en masse*, with everyone willing to personally join crusading expeditions, but rather, their society generally expected that every Christian could, and should, do *something* to help the movement. This book examines that culture and the people who never went on crusade, yet strived to connect with it.

... yet why do I speak of staying?

(William of Malmesbury [d.c.1143])[7]

It may seem odd that this, a book about crusade, does not investigate crusades *per se*, but instead examines individuals who, at first glance, may seem to have sat on the periphery of one of the great struggles of the medieval world. However, no one made the decision to go on crusade in isolation; understanding the people

---

[5] Giuseppi, 'XIX – On the Testament of Sir Hugh de Nevill', p. 360, for Old French, see p. 358, "... Will le fiz Simun me porta les noueles ke uus estes si pouremēt estore de dens. Mes deu ke tut put imette si li plest hastif amendemēt. e io le frai a tut mon poer".

[6] Giuseppi, 'XIX – On the Testament of Sir Hugh de Nevill', p. 354.

[7] William of Malmesbury, *Gesta Regum Anglorum*, 2 vols, R.A.B. Mynors, R.M. Thomson and M. Winterbottom (eds and trans.) (Oxford, 1998–9), at vol. 1, bk. iv, cpt. 348, p. 609. For Latin, see p. 608, "Quid dico de remanentibus?".

Introduction

who encouraged crusade is key to understanding the wider movement. Around 1125, William of Malmesbury described the events of the First Crusade (1095–9).[8] In his hyperbolic prose, the expedition was so attractive that whole cities emptied, and fields became bereft of farmers as people rushed to the Holy Land. Yet, the chronicler took a moment to point out that not everyone went – "yet why do I speak of staying?" – William quickly changed the topic back to the crusaders (presuming it was the more interesting subject for his elite lay and monastic readers). For many people today, the thought of crusade is dominated by a picture of cross-emblazoned knights and the chilling violence that transpired in the Holy Land and beyond. However, vast numbers of people in Christendom were encouraged to remain in their homelands and support crusade through prayer, financial donations, and pressuring those suited for battle into going instead: for them, this was crusade.

Papal letters and preachers' sermons routinely discouraged people from joining expeditions, if they considered them to be a hindrance to the campaigns.[9] Infirm or elderly men, and children were all thought to cause logistical problems. Clerics often performed spiritual care on the march, but many of them were discouraged from joining crusades to limit non-combatants. Women, however, were often distrusted on moral grounds. The sources give the distinct impression that sexual licentiousness was considered a source of sin that could bring God's disfavour upon a campaign, and women (rarely men) were blamed.[10] Despite the reservations of monastic chroniclers and preachers, people from all walks of life consistently joined crusades, from small private ventures to large-scale expeditions.[11]

---

[8] William of Malmesbury, *Gesta Regum Anglorum*, vol. 1, bk. iv, cpt. 348, pp. 606–9. For more on this chronicler, see: R.M. Thomson, E. Dolmans and E.A. Winkler (eds), *Discovering William of Malmesbury* (Woodbridge, 2017).

[9] C.T. Maier, *Preaching the Crusades: Mendicant Friars and the Cross in the thirteenth Century* (Cambridge, 1994), pp. 135–40; P.J. Cole, *The Preaching of the Crusades to the Holy Land, 1095–1270* (Cambridge, 1991), pp. 160–5.

[10] M. Lower, *The Barons' Crusade, A Call to Arms and its Consequences* (Philadelphia, 2005), pp. 13–36; H.J. Nicholson, 'Women's Involvement in the Crusades', in A. Boas (ed.), *The Crusader World* (London, 2016), pp. 54–67, at 55; M.E. Parker, '*Papa et pecunia:* Innocent III's Combination of Reform and Fiscal Policy to Finance the Crusades', *Mediterranean Historical Review*, vol. 32, no. 1 (2017), pp. 1–23, at 8 and 15; J.A. Brundage, 'Prostitution, Miscegenation and Sexual Purity in the First Crusade', in P.W. Edbury (ed.), *Crusade and Settlement, Papers Read at the First Conference of the Society for the Study of the Crusades and the Latin East and Presented to R.C. Smail* (Cardiff, 1985), pp. 57–65; H.J. Nicholson, *Women and the Crusades* (Oxford, 2023), pp. 1–5.

[11] The corpus on this topic is very large, see especially: B.Z. Kedar, 'The Passenger List of a Crusader Ship, 1250: Towards the History of the Popular Element on the Seventh Crusade', *Studi Medievali*, vol. 13, no. 1 (1972), pp. 267–79; R. Mazeika, '"Nowhere was the Fragility of their Sex Apparent": Women Warriors in the Baltic Crusade Chronicles', in A.V. Murray (ed.), *From Clermont to Jerusalem: The Crusades and Crusader Societies 1095–1500* (Turnhout, 1998), pp. 229–48; C.T. Maier, 'The Roles of Women in the Crusade Movement: a Survey', *Journal of Medieval History*, vol.

Perhaps frustrated by this, by the end of the twelfth century, the papacy began offering indulgences – the spiritual reward of crusade – to these groups, and women in particular, who refrained from travelling to theatres of crusading warfare and instead helped the cause in supportive roles.[12] These activities included: recruitment, financing crusaders, prayer, participation in liturgical processions and acting as regents or custodians of property while crusaders were away, as well as various roles within the Military Orders – such as the Knights Templar and the Hospitallers. There was huge variety in the ways people could perform crusade, connect with the movement and strive for ideals other than that of the archetypal crusade warrior or pilgrim. This was the majority of Latin Christians' experience. Without critically considering their perspective, we will never understand medieval crusading.

This book aims to broaden our view on these aspects of the crusading world, by focusing on laywomen, much like Hawisa de Nevill, and their experience of holy war from within England. It uses this kingdom as a regional case study to explore how and why these women engaged with the crusade without leaving the Latin West. The discussion centres on the aims and actions of laywomen who supported people bound for the Holy Land, considering how their involvement helped them to influence identify with the crusading movement during the twelfth and thirteenth centuries.

Who were the 'Supporters' and 'Crusaders'?

To be able to identify crusaders and supporters, we have to be able to define crusade itself. This, however, is a surprisingly difficult thing to distil. A huge amount of scholarship has been dedicated to characterising this medieval movement. There is no easy answer, and with that comes a raft of problems. To be as broad as possible, the general consensus is that a crusade was an armed pilgrimage. Yet, contemporaries and historians alike approached that idea in radically different ways. It is crucial to explore how a crusader can be identified before we can investigate who supported them and why.

30, no. 1 (2004), pp. 61–82; N.R. Hodgson, *Women, Crusading and the Holy Land in Historical Narrative* (Woodbridge, 2007); S.G. Heller, 'Surprisingly Historical Women in the Old French Crusade Cycle', in S.S. Poor and J.K. Schulman (eds), *Women and Medieval Epic: Gender, Genre, and the Limits of Epic Masculinity* (Basingstoke, 2007), pp. 41–66; N. Christie, 'Fighting Women in the Crusading Period through Muslim Eyes', in N.R. Hodgson, K.J. Lewis and M.M. Mesley (eds), *Crusading and Masculinities* (London, 2019), pp. 183–95; Nicholson, *Women and the Crusades*.

12 C.M. Rousseau, 'Home Front and Battlefield: The Gendering of Papal Crusading Policy (1095–1221)', in S. Edgington and S. Lambert (eds), *Gendering the Crusades* (Cardiff, 2001), pp. 31–44; C.T. Maier, 'Propaganda and Masculinity: Gendering the Crusades in Thirteenth-Century Sermons', in N.R. Hodgson, K.J. Lewis and M.M. Mesley (eds), *Crusading and Masculinities* (London, 2019), pp. 21–35.

Introduction

Various academic schools of thought have sprung up as people have struggled to describe the crusades and who the crusaders were, all of which have their merits and caveats in helping us develop a clearer picture of the past. In the eighteenth and nineteenth centuries, two major approaches gained currency: Traditionalist views and Materialist motivations. Writers focusing on a Traditionalist interpretation (as we now call it) stressed that Latin Christian campaigns, aimed at the Holy Land from the eleventh to the thirteenth centuries, were the only true crusades; nonetheless many acknowledged later expeditions or alternative destinations, such as in the Baltic, Iberia or the territories of the Cathars in southern France. Other writers zeroed in on what they believed were the motivations of the crusaders, considering that Materialism and proto-colonial attitudes defined the aims of medieval holy war. By the twentieth century, these views had hardly disappeared, but historians began adding to our definitions of crusade with Generalist and Pluralist interpretations, while also debating Popularist motivations. Generalism takes a sweeping look at Christian, religiously motivated wars, during the Middle Ages (and into the early modern era), situating the crusades within them. Pluralism is subtly different, since this school considers the mechanics of crusade to be the key definer, asking how the papacy initiated crusades, and how contemporaries perceived the legal definitions of crusading. Likewise, Popularist views of crusading investigate the myriad motivations that people had for going, by paying close attention to the participation of the masses and their eschatological concerns.[13]

In truth, relatively few modern historians would say that they are strict adherents to a single school of thinking – there are credible elements to each. With no clear-cut consensus on how to approach crusading history in broad terms, we must turn to our source material in England for a regional approach.

Medieval authors tended to use quite ambiguous terminology when discussing the nature of a person's journey to the Holy Land or elsewhere. The modern word *crusader* derives from the Medieval Latin term *crucesignatus*, a formation of two Latin words meaning "signed with the cross".[14] This referred to the vow that some individuals made before going on crusade and the subsequent sewing of a cross on their garments, which contemporaries increasingly treated as separate from a regular pilgrimage over the course of the twelfth century.[15] The term *crucesignatus*

---

[13] For more on these schools, see: J. Riley-Smith and S.A. Throop, *The Crusades: A History*, 4th edn (London, 2023), pp. 5–23; N. Housley, *Contesting the Crusades* (Oxford, 2006), pp. 2–23; G. Constable, 'The Historiography of the Crusades', in A.E. Laiou and R.T. Mottahedeh (eds), *The Crusades from the Perspective of Byzantium and the Muslim World* (Washington DC, 2001), pp. 1–22, at 10–8.

[14] M. Markowski, '*Crucesignatus*: Its Origins and Early Usage', *Journal of Medieval History*, vol. 10, no. 3 (1984), pp. 157–65, at 157.

[15] Mark Blincoe notes that as early as the 1120s William the Huntsman and count Fulk V of Anjou both composed charters in which they described themselves respectively as wearing the cross "in the custom of" and "for this type" of pilgrimage, see: M.E.

5

was used in medieval England from the thirteenth century onward, and sometimes very pointedly. One record left by an English crusader named William de Muntford stated: "let it be known that I make my journey to the Holy Land Jerusalem *as I am a crucesignatus*".[16]

Although some people made a distinction, *crucesignatus* was just one of a variety of terms, and not necessarily the most popular, that denoted a person participating in holy war. The term pilgrim, or *peregrinus* in its Latin form, was preferred throughout the High Middle Ages.[17] This often leads scholars to define crusade by the physical journey that was undertaken, and the visiting of shrines or holy sites. Yet, defining crusaders simply as those who made an *iter* or 'journey' to Jerusalem, say, is also problematic because some crusaders went to other places, and some never even left their homelands.[18] Not all who went armed to the East actually took part in fighting, nor did all combatants take crusade vows.[19] From the outset of the crusade movement, members of the clergy, women and children took crusade vows, some of whom intended to fulfil the vow through acts of violence, while others not. Indeed, the wealth of studies on Latin Christian women's exploits and settlement in the Near East and beyond has helped considerably to redefine crusade as a movement in which both sexes actively took part.[20]

Blincoe, 'Angevin Society and the Early Crusades, 1095–1145', 3 vols (Unpublished PhD Thesis, University of Minnesota, 2008), at vol. 1, p. 129. My thanks to Dr James Doherty for drawing my attention to this source.

16 My emphasis, see: E.O. Blake (ed.), *The Cartulary of the Priory of St Denys Near Southampton*, 2 vols (Southampton, 1981), at vol. 1, p. 26, no. 39, "scilicet ad iter meum faciendum ad Terram Sanctam Ierusalem eo quod sum crucesignatus".

17 W.R. Cosgrove, '*Crucesignatus*: A Refinement or Merely One More Term among Many?', in T.F. Madden, J.L. Naus and V. Ryan (eds), *Crusades – Medieval Worlds in Conflict* (London, 2010), pp. 95–107, at 101–2; C. Tyerman, *England and the Crusades, 1095–1588* (Chicago, 1988), p. 3. See also: M. Tamminen, *Crusade Preaching and the Ideal Crusader* (Turnhout, 2018), pp. 32 and 246.

18 See: Markowski, '*Crucesignatus*', pp. 163–4; N. Housley, 'Crusades Against Christians: Their Origins and Early Development, c.1000–1216', in Edbury, *Crusade and Settlement*, pp. 17–36; Mazeika, '"Nowhere was the Fragility of their Sex Apparent"', pp. 229–48.

19 C. Tyerman, 'Were There Any Crusades in the Twelfth Century?', *The English Historical Review*, vol. 110, no. 437 (1995), pp. 553–77, at 567.

20 R. Pernoud, *Femme au temps des Croisades* (Paris, 1990); C.C. Willard, 'Isabel of Portugal and the Fifteenth-Century Burgundian Crusade', in B.N. Sargent-Baur (ed.), *Journeys Toward God: Pilgrimage and Crusade* (Kalamazoo, 1992), pp. 205–14; H.J. Nicholson, 'Women on the Third Crusade', *Journal of Medieval History*, vol. 23, no. 4 (1997), pp. 335–49; G. McLennan, *Women Crusaders: Women and the Holy Land 1095–1195* (Hawker, 1997); Mazeika, '"Nowhere was the Fragility of their Sex Apparent"', pp. 229–48; K. Caspi-Reisfeld, 'Women Warriors During the Crusades, 1095–1254', in Edgington and Lambert, *Gendering the Crusades*, p. 95; B. Hechelhammer, '*Frauen auf dem Kreuzzug*', in H.J. Kotzur, B. Klein and W. Wilhelmy (eds), *Die Kreuzzüge: Kein Krieg ist Heilig* (Mainz am Rhein, 2004), pp. 205–11; Hodgson, *Women, Crusading and the Holy Land*

Introduction

It would also be equally problematic to only discuss individuals who went on the canonical crusades. This phrase is often applied to the large, twelfth- and thirteenth-century papally-sanctioned campaigns that were launched to capture (and subsequently recapture) Jerusalem. In an effort to categorise this period, modern historians numbered these expeditions from First to Ninth. Yet, there were some significant campaigns that were not added to this numbered sequence, and there were many individuals who took crusade vows and went to the Holy Land outside of these large campaigns.[21]

In sum, anyone from any walk of life could have gone on crusade, whatever that meant to them. Where today the term crusader is synonymous with a male combatant doing a pope's bidding in a Mediterranean campaign, to the medieval person, *pilgrim* and *crusader* were not mutually exclusive terms. In Christopher Tyerman's words: "*we* know there were crusaders: *they* did not".[22] Because of these ambiguities, numerous historians have taken a broad-brush approach to the source material, treating references to voyages to the Holy Land as crusade related.[23] In Jochen Schenk's study of the Templars in France, for example, he often trod lightly when remarking on people's preparations to go East, describing them as "crusade or pilgrimage arrangements", admitting that there was no salient difference in the steps they took.[24]

In keeping with this current trend, I will discuss instances where laywomen supported anyone going to the Holy Land as a part of crusade culture. Discussion will also be limited to laywomen's patronage or commemoration of crusaders and

---

in Historical Narrative; S.G. Heller, 'Surprisingly Historical Women in the Old French Crusade Cycle', in S.S. Poor and J.K. Schulman (eds), *Women and Medieval Epic: Gender, Genre, and the Limits of Epic Masculinity* (Basingstoke, 2007), pp. 41–66; E.C. Díaz, 'Maria Balteira, a Woman Crusader to Outremer', in C.A. González-Pas (ed.), *Women and Pilgrimage in Medieval Galicia* (Farnham, 2015), pp. 67–80; N. Christie, 'Fighting Women in the Crusading Period through Muslim Eyes', in Hodgson, Lewis and Mesley, *Crusading and Masculinities*, pp. 183–95; S. Harwood, *Medieval Women and War: Female Roles in the Old French Tradition* (London, 2020), p. 77; Nicholson, *Women and the Crusades*. See also: M.R. Evans, 'Commutation of Crusade Vows, Some Examples for the English Midlands', in Murray, *From Clermont to Jerusalem*, pp. 219–28.

[21] Tyerman, 'Were There Any Crusades in the Twelfth Century?', p. 559; B.W. Reynolds, 'The Prehistory of the Crusades: Toward a Developmental Taxonomy', *History Compass*, vol. 6, no. 3 (2008), pp. 884–97.

[22] Tyerman, 'Were There Any Crusades in the Twelfth Century?', p. 555.

[23] The following studies make use of examples where the individuals were simply described as pilgrims or as travellers to Jerusalem/the Holy Land; Tyerman, *England and the Crusades*, pp. 187–228; Lower, *The Barons' Crusade*, p. 143. See also: J.A. Brundage, '"Cruce Signari": The Rite for Taking the Cross in England', *Traditio*, vol. 22 (1960), pp. 289–310, at 291; G. Constable, *Crusaders and Crusading in the Twelfth Century* (Farnham, 2008), p. 77; Tyerman, 'Were There Any Crusades in the Twelfth Century?', p. 567; D. Webb, *Medieval European Pilgrimage, c.700–1500* (Basingstoke, 2002), pp. 19–20 and 22–3.

[24] Schenk, *Templar Families*, p. 218.

the Military Orders, as opposed to forms of support that were forced on criminals as penance, or crusade taxes, such as the Saladin Tithe or the levies imposed on Jewish communities.[25] As I say, this study focuses on those who supported individuals travelling from England to the Holy Land. This encompasses crusades aimed at the Levant and North Africa, all of which were conceived as strategic attempts to wrest control of Jerusalem away from Islam. This is a reflection of the English evidence, which shows that participants in crusade from this kingdom during the High Middle Ages almost exclusively favoured the Jerusalem-crusade.[26] There will, nevertheless, be some limited discussion of political conflicts within England, such as the First and Second Barons' Wars, which harnessed the rhetoric of crusade and may have galvanised some supporters because of this.

The time period, c.1150–1300, also requires some explanation. Landholders in England certainly joined crusades from their outset in the 1090s.[27] However, the majority of surviving evidence of crusade preparations in England dates from around the time of the Second Crusade (1147–50), in which a significant Anglo-Flemish fleet sacked Lisbon in 1147.[28] Likewise, a consistent stream of crusaders from England headed east following the fall of Christian Jerusalem in 1187.[29] Although there was continued enthusiasm for holy war into the fourteenth century and beyond – with much English participation in Holy Land crusades in the 1360s, and the Crusade of Nicopolis in 1396 – landholders in the Kingdom of England participated less frequently in expeditions to the Near East after the fall of the last Latin Christian outpost on the mainland of the Levant, Acre, in 1291.[30]

---

[25] See: Tyerman, *England and the Crusades*, pp. 191–3; C. Tyerman, *How to Plan a Crusade: Reason and Religious War in the High Middle Ages* (London, 2015), pp. 218–23. For a discussion of papal funding and crusade taxation, see: W.E. Lunt, *Financial Relations of the Papacy with England to 1327* (Cambridge, 1939), see particularly pp. 446–8; D. Edwards, *Finance and the Crusades: England, c.1213–1337* (Abingdon, 2022), pp. 34–56.

[26] Lower, *The Barons' Crusade*, p. 130; C. Tyerman, 'Some English Evidence of Attitudes to Crusading in the Thirteenth Century', in P.R. Coss and S.D. Lloyd (eds), *Thirteenth Century England I: Proceedings of the Newcastle-upon-Tyne Conference 1985* (Woodbridge, 1986), pp. 168–74, at 170–1; K. Hurlock, *Britain, Ireland and the Crusades, c. 1000–1300* (Basingstoke, 2013), p. 93.

[27] There was significant Anglo-Norman participation in the First Crusade under the leadership of Robert Curthose, see: W.M. Aird, *Robert Curthose, Duke of Normandy, c.1050–1134* (Woodbridge, 2008), pp. 153–90; N. Hooper, 'Edgar the Aetheling: Anglo-Saxon Prince, Rebel and Crusader', *Anglo-Saxon England*, vol. 14 (1985), pp. 197–214.

[28] J. Phillips, *The Second Crusade: Extending the Frontiers of Christendom* (London and New Haven, 2007), pp. 136–67.

[29] S. Lloyd, *English Society and the Crusade, 1216–1307* (Oxford, 1988), pp. 84–6; Hurlock, *Britain, Ireland and the Crusades*, pp. 89–90.

[30] Lloyd, *English Society and the Crusade*, pp. 84–6; A. Luttrell, 'English Levantine Crusaders, 1363–1367', *Renaissance Studies*, vol. 2, no. 1 (1988), pp. 143–53, at 144;

Introduction

During this period, people from all social strata undoubtably took part in crusade just as they took part in supporting the effort; however, the evidence that has survived does not reflect such parity.[31] This study predominantly considers the elite in England's society – encompassing the nobles and knightly classes at one end and the upwardly mobile gentry at the other – as opposed to the royalty or commoners.[32] The elite did not necessarily devote the most wealth to crusade or produce the most crusaders, but their affluence and numbers combined with their litigiousness and intention to preserve titles to lands have meant that the evidence of their crusade preparations is vastly more plentiful than that of any other group.[33] In short, this book investigates the activity of women of a socio-economic class who had the assets to support or commemorate crusade and leave written records of their activity.

I should be clear, however, that this is an investigation into one avenue of women's involvement in crusade, and by no means the only one open to them. Nor was the support of crusade within western Europe necessarily dominated by women; many people involved themselves in the ubiquitous alms-giving or prayers for the Holy Land. However, scrutinising women's support for crusade allows for a detailed exploration of medieval concepts of various idealised, gendered models and the contradictions therein. This helps to colour in our understanding of a grey area in crusading history, giving us a better view of what holy war was during the Middle Ages.

T. Guard, *Chivalry, Kingship and Crusade: The English Experience in the Fourteenth Century* (Woodbridge, 2013), pp. 21–50.

[31] See: Housley, *Contesting the Crusades*, pp. 8–9; G. Dickson, *The Children's Crusade: Medieval History, Modern Mythistory* (Basingstoke, 2008), p. 16.

[32] Similar terminology was employed in the following: Wilkinson, *Women in Thirteenth-Century Lincolnshire*; H.J. Tanner (ed.), *Medieval Elite Women and the Exercise of Power, 1100–1400: Moving Beyond the Exceptionalist Debate* (New York, 2019). See also: D. Crouch, *The English Aristocracy 1070–1272, a Social Transformation* (New Haven, 2011), pp. 37–9. Cf. discussions of "gentry" in medieval England; P.R. Coss, *The Origins of the English Gentry* (Cambridge, 2003), pp. 1–19.

[33] P. Coss, *The Foundations of Gentry Life: The Multons of Frampton and their World 1270–1370* (Oxford, 2010), pp. 185–6. See also: Helen Nicholson's discussion of the visibility of wealthy women within source material on crusading: Nicholson, 'Women's Involvement in the Crusades', p. 62. Similar criteria have been applied in the following studies: P. Ricketts, *High-Ranking Widows in Medieval Iceland and Yorkshire: Property, Power, Marriage and Identity in the Twelfth and Thirteenth Centuries* (Leiden, 2010); L.E. Mitchell, *Portraits of Medieval Women: Family, Marriage, and Politics in England 1225–1350* (New York, 2003).

Laywomen and the Crusade in England, 1150–1300

Historians and the Supporters of Crusade

The subject of laywomen's support for crusade is not a completely unchartered area of historic research, but usually it forms part of a wider milieu of studies on the preparations, gender roles and, more recently, the ideals within the culture of medieval crusade. Modern commentators have occasionally talked about a crusading "home front". While fleshing out this topic, historians have often focused on the social/fiscal effects of crusade upon the populace in Europe, the papal directives aimed at those same people, the geopolitics surrounding crusade support, and the legal protections for crusaders' families and property. Christopher Tyerman, Constance Rousseau, Joanna Drell and Danielle Park have all been highly influential in studying these aspects of wider crusading culture.[34] As Tyerman put it, the experiences of those who went on crusade "cannot be separated from the domestic experience of western Europe".[35] Certainly, by the thirteenth century, the crusading war effort was perceived as a struggle in which all Latin Christendom should take part.[36]

Jonathan Riley-Smith's work has perhaps been the most influential on current scholarship respecting women's support for the crusades. He investigated women's efforts in recruitment in early twelfth-century France.[37] Using case studies from the

---

[34] Tyerman, *England and the Crusades*, pp. 187–228; Rousseau, 'Home Front and Battlefield', pp. 31–44; J. Drell, 'Norman Italy and the Crusades, Thoughts on the "Homefront"', in K. Hurlock and P. Oldfield (eds), *Crusading and Pilgrimage in the Norman World* (Woodbridge, 2015), pp. 51–63; D.E.A. Park, *Papal Protection and the Crusader: Flanders, Champagne, and the Kingdom of France, 1095–1222* (Woodbridge, 2018), p. 47. However, Park has pointed out the anachronistic problems with the term "home front". See also: J.T. Appleby, *England Without Richard 1189–1199* (London, 1965); Nicholson, 'The Home Front', in *Women and the Crusades*, pp. 97–128. More generally, see: S. Shahar, *The Fourth Estate: A History of Women in the Middle Ages, Revised Edition*, C. Galai (ed. and trans.) (London, 2003), p. 127; C. Allmand, 'War and the Non-Combatant in the Middle Ages', in M. Keen (ed.), *Medieval Warfare: A History*, 2nd edn (Oxford, 2010), pp. 253–72, at 254. Susanna Throop describes women's non-violent support as an aspect of crusade, see: S.A. Throop, *Crusading as an Act of Vengeance, 1095–1216* (Farnham, 2011), pp. 39–40.

[35] Tyerman, *England and the Crusades*, p. 188.

[36] M. Lower, *The Barons' Crusade, A Call to Arms and its Consequences* (Philadelphia, 2005), pp. 13–36; J. Bird, E. Peters and J.M. Powell (eds and trans.), *Crusade and Christendom: Annotated Documents in Translation from Innocent III to the Fall of Acre, 1187–1291* (Philadelphia, 2013), pp. 1–23; C. Libertini, 'Practical Crusading: The Transformation of Crusading Practice 1095–1221', in M. Balard (ed.), *Autour de le Première Croisade. Actes du Colloque de le Society for the Study of the Crusades and the Latin East* (Paris, 1996), pp. 281–91, at 290–1.

[37] J. Riley-Smith, 'Family Traditions and Participation in the Second Crusade', in M. Gervers (ed.), *The Second Crusade and the Cistercians* (New York, 1992), pp. 101–8; J. Riley-Smith, *The First Crusaders, 1095–1131* (Cambridge, 1997).

Introduction

Monthléry, Courtenay and le Puiset families in particular, Riley-Smith suggested that women with a history of crusading in their natal families encouraged that same enthusiasm in their husbands and/or children.[38] Although others had noted that some royal and knightly dynasties had a tradition of crusading, Riley-Smith championed the view that crusading was a family enterprise: a joint effort between those who actually went and those who encouraged crusade.[39] This view has been routinely upheld by many historians.[40]

While considering women's involvement in these family enterprises, scholars have typically taken a top-down approach, focusing on the messaging of the Latin papacy. Rousseau made the astute observation that Pope Innocent III (r.1198–1216) had made concentrated attempts to incorporate women into papal crusade policy, spiritually incentivising their engagement with crusade.[41] She considered that this may have ushered in a new era for women's participation in crusade. However, the wider effects of Innocent's papacy on laywomen's interest in crusade have never been fully investigated. The significance and systemisation of similar papal directives have, however, been further explored by Michael Lower. He has shown that contemporaries' belief that crusade formed a universal Christian duty only heightened as the thirteenth century wore on, especially under Pope Gregory IX (r.1227–41).[42] These studies have certainly helped develop modern understanding that support for holy war formed a sphere of crusade.

Perhaps the most productive scholarship regarding crusade support in the West, and women's involvement, has focused on the activities of the Military Orders. Schenk's extensive study of the Templars establishments in France links the laity's patronage of the order, including that of women, with general enthusiasm for

---

[38] Riley-Smith, 'Family Traditions', p. 104; Riley-Smith, *The First Crusaders*, pp. 93–9.

[39] For earlier examinations of family crusading tradition and women's involvement, see: Lloyd, *English Society and the Crusade*, pp. 108–9; E. Mason, 'Fact and Fiction in the English Crusading Tradition: The Earls of Warwick in the Twelfth Century', *Journal of Medieval History*, vol. 14, no. 2 (1988), pp. 81–95, at 82–3. James Brundage had also investigated the canonical laws that prohibited husbands leaving for crusade without their wives' permission: J.A. Brundage, 'The Crusader's Wife: A Canonistic Quandary', *Studia Gratiana*, vol. 12 (1967), pp. 425–41; J.A. Brundage, 'The Crusader's Wife Revisited', *Studia Gratiana*, vol. 14 (1967), pp. 243–51.

[40] N.L. Paul, *To Follow in Their Footsteps: The Crusades and Family Memory in the High Middle Ages* (Ithaca, 2012), pp. 55–89; N.L. Paul and J.G. Schenk, 'Family Memory and the Crusades', in M. Cassidy-Welch (ed.), *Remembering the Crusades and Crusading* (London, 2017), pp. 173–86; S.J. Allen, *An Introduction to the Crusades* (Toronto, 2017), p. 33; Park, *Papal Protection and the Crusader*, p. 1; C. Tyerman, *The World of the Crusades* (New Haven, 2019), pp. 25–6.

[41] Rousseau, 'Home Front and Battlefield', pp. 31–44. See also: T.W. Smith, 'How to Craft a Crusade Call: Pope Innocent III and *Quia Maior* (1213)', *Historical Research*, vol. 92, no. 255 (2019), pp. 2–23 at 20–1.

[42] Lower, *The Barons' Crusade*, pp. 13–36.

crusade.[43] Jürgen Sarnowsky and Myra Bom have made similar observations when discussing the women who joined these orders as *sorores* (sisters), helping in the running of the orders' houses in the West and offering prayer for the success of crusade.[44] The spiritual support that women offered through prayer and liturgical procession, more widely, has been scrutinised by Christoph Maier, Iris Shagrir and Cecilia Gaposchkin; while Anne Lester has further highlighted women's interests in commemoration of crusade.[45] Many of these roles – fiscal and spiritual – have been referred to as forms of "indirect" or "passive" crusading, perhaps part of the wider culture, but divergent from the act of armed pilgrimage itself.[46] However, contemporary perceptions of these forms of support have not been explored as thoroughly.

Historians have been interested in noblewomen's lives in the absences of their crusading kinsmen, particularly respecting their capacity as regents or custodians

---

[43] J. Schenk, *Templar Families: Landowning Families and the Order of the Temple in France, c. 1120–1307* (Cambridge, 2012), pp. 203–49. This builds on Malcolm Barber's work on the Templars' support for crusaders, see: M. Barber, 'Supplying the Crusader States: The Role of the Templars', in B.Z. Kedar (ed.), *The Horns of Hattīn* (Jerusalem, 1992), pp. 314–26.

[44] J. Sarnowsky, 'Gender-Aspekte in der Geschichte der geistlichen Ritterorden', in R. Hering (ed.), *Lebendige Sozialgeschichte, Gedenkschrift für Peter Borowsky* (Wiesbaden, 2003), pp. 168–88; M.M. Bom, *Women in the Military Orders of the Crusades* (New York, 2012). See also: H.J. Nicholson, 'Relations between Houses of the Order of the Temple in Britain and their Local Communities, as Indicated during the Trial of the Templars, 1307–12', in N. Housley (ed.), *Knighthoods of Christ, Essays on the History of the Crusades and the Knights Templar, Presented to Malcolm Barber* (Aldershot, 2007), pp. 195–207; A. Luttrell and H.J. Nicholson (eds), *Hospitaller Women in the Middle Ages* (Aldershot, 2006).

[45] C.T. Maier, 'Mass, the Eucharist and the Cross: Innocent III and the Relocation of the Crusade', in J.C. Moore (ed.), *Pope Innocent III and His World* (Aldershot, 1999), pp. 351–60; C.T. Maier, 'Crisis, Liturgy and Crusade in the Twelfth and Thirteenth Centuries', *Journal of Ecclesiastical History*, vol. 48, no. 4 (1997), pp. 628–67; I. Shagrir and C. Gaposchkin, 'Liturgy and Devotion in the Crusader States: Introduction', *Journal of Medieval History*, vol. 43, no. 4 (2017), pp. 359–66; A.E. Lester, 'A Shared Imitation: Cistercian Convents and Crusader Families in Thirteenth-Century Champagne', *Journal of Medieval History*, vol. 35, no. 4 (2009), pp. 353–70; A.E. Lester, 'What Remains: Women, Relics, and Remembrance in the Aftermath of the Fourth Crusade', *Journal of Medieval History*, vol. 40, no. 3 (2014), pp. 311–28. See also: I. Shagrir, 'The "Holy Women" in the Liturgy and Art of the Church of the Holy Sepulchre in Twelfth-Century Jerusalem', in E. Lapina and N. Morton (eds), *The Uses of the Bible in Crusader Sources* (Leiden, 2017), pp. 455–75; Nicholson, *Women and the Crusades*, pp. 121–8.

[46] J. Riley-Smith, 'Frauen auf Kreuzzügen, 1096–1291, by Sabine Geldsetzer', *The English Historical Review*, vol. 119, no. 484 (2004), pp. 1386–7; D. Marcombe, *Leper Knights: The Order of St Lazarus of Jerusalem in England, 1150–1544* (Woodbridge, 2003), p. 47. See also: Maier, 'The Roles of Women in the Crusade Movement', p. 81.

Introduction

of property.⁴⁷ Indeed, such studies tackle classic quandaries regarding feminine gender roles within the frame of crusade.⁴⁸ Historians have shown that there can be no doubt that many women were able to take control of crusaders' property while the latter were abroad, but that it would be wrong to assume that this was a novel situation and that women did not routinely govern family lands. Likewise, we cannot view women's involvement as a (direct or indirect) consequence of their male family members' crusading.⁴⁹ We can rarely be sure if a husband set off on holy war despite their wife's objections, or whether a wife pressured their husband to go on holy war in the first place, or neither.

These are interesting points to consider, because numerous studies have been coloured by the discussions of the medieval women who suffered the fallout of crusade preparations. Tyerman has used a close examination of judicial records and charters to draw attention to the effects of crusade upon women in England, something that has been discussed more recently by Kathryn Hurlock.⁵⁰ These studies highlight numerous fascinating and informative legal cases that arose from the disappearance, deaths or sudden return of long-lost crusaders – many of which will be revisited in this book – and the confusion this brought to family at home. Yet, how representative are these cases of the typical experience of families who were involved in crusade?⁵¹ This is something that this book will attempt to approach.

Crusade preparations more generally have seen a flurry of publications over the past few decades.⁵² Nevertheless, scholarship has tended to focus on crusaders'

---

[47] P.A. Adair, '"Ego et mea uxor…": Countess Clemence and her Role in the Comital Family and in Flanders (1092–1133)' (Unpublished PhD Thesis, University of California, 1993); T. de Hemptinne, 'Les épouses de croisés et pèlerins flamands aux XIe et XIIe siècles: l'exemple des comtesses de Flandre Clémence et Sibylle', in Balard, *Autour de la Première Croisade*, pp. 83–95; E.A. Haluska-Rausch, 'Family, Property, and Power: Women in Medieval Montpellier, 985–1213' (Unpublished PhD Thesis, Harvard University, 1998); C. Dernbecher, 'Die zuhausebleibenden Frauen der Kreuzfahrer', in *Deus et virum suum diligens. Zur rolle und Bedeutung der Frau im Umfeld der Kreuzzüge* (St Ingbert, 2003), pp. 27–52; LoPrete, *Adela of Blois*; Park, *Papal Protection and the Crusader*.

[48] D. Gerish, 'Gender Theory', in H.J. Nicholson (ed.), *Palgrave Advances in the Crusades* (Basingstoke, 2005), pp. 130–47, at 134–5.

[49] Hodgson, *Women, Crusading and the Holy Land in Historical Narrative*, p. 5.

[50] Tyerman, *England and the Crusades*, pp. 187–228; Hurlock, *Britain, Ireland and the Crusades*, pp. 118–9. See also: B. Siedschlag, *English Participation in the Crusades, 1150–1220* (Privately Published, 1939).

[51] Riley-Smith, *The First Crusaders*, p. 98.

[52] J.M. Powell, *Anatomy of a Crusade, 1213–1221* (Philadelphia, 1986); A.V. Murray, 'Finance and Logistics of the Crusade of Frederick Barbarossa', in I. Shagrir, R. Ellenblum and J. Riley-Smith (eds), *In Laudem Hierosolymitani, Studies in Crusades and Medieval Culture in Honour of Benjamin Z. Kedar* (Aldershot, 2007), pp. 357–68; A.V. Murray, 'Roads, Bridges and Shipping in the Passage of Crusade Armies by

preparations, rather than the motivations of the creditors and supporters. Likewise, scholars have been very mindful of the ways in which medieval people formed their identity around crusade, focusing on martial, dynastic, ecclesiastic, regional and gendered themes.[53] Indeed, it is clear that crusade offered opportunities for male contemporaries to find identity by striving for a knightly ideal.[54] Yet, we must consider that other spheres of crusade, in turn, allowed for other models, other ways of connecting with holy war. As Christoph Maier notes, although aspects of women's contribution to the crusade movement within western Europe have been studied, there has been "no systematic research" into the topic.[55]

Overland Routes to the Bosporus 1096–1190', in K. Holzner-Tobisch, T. Kühtreiber and G. Blaschitz (eds), *Die Vielschichtigkeit der Straße: Kontinuität und Wandel in Mittelalter und Früher Neuzeit* (Vienna, 2012), pp. 183–207; A.V. Murray, 'The Middle Ground: The Passage of Crusade Armies to the Holy Land by Land and Sea, 1096–1204', in G. Theotokis and A. Yildiz (eds), *A Military History of the Mediterranean Sea: Aspects of War, Diplomacy and Military Elites* (Leiden, 2018), pp. 185–201; D. Power, 'The Preparations of Count John I of Sées for the Third Crusade', in S. John and N. Morton (eds), *Crusading and Warfare in the Middle Ages, Realities and Representations: Essays in Honour of John France* (Farnham, 2014), pp. 143–66; Drell, 'Norman Italy and the Crusades', pp. 51–2; Tyerman, *How to Plan a Crusade*; Lower, *The Barons' Crusade*, pp. 140–8; Lloyd, *English Society and the Crusade*, pp. 154–97; Edwards, *Finance and the Crusades*.

53 Tamminen, *Crusade Preaching and the Ideal Crusader*; N.L. Paul, 'Writing the Knight, Staging the Crusade: Manasses of Hierges and the Monks of Brogne', in D. Crouch and J. Deploige (eds), *Knighthood and Society in the High Middle Ages* (Leuven, 2020), pp. 167–92; Paul, *To Follow in Their Footsteps*, pp. 165–70; Paul and Schenk, 'Family Memory and the Crusades', pp. 173–86; S. Vander Elst, *The Knight, the Cross, and the Song: Crusade Propaganda and Chivalric Literature, 1100–1400* (Philadelphia, 2017), pp. 75–9; M. Cassidy-Welch, *War and Memory at the Time of the Fifth Crusade* (Philadelphia, 2019).

54 Hodgson, Lewis and Mesley, *Crusading and Masculinities*; L. Ashe, 'The Ideal of Knighthood in English and French Writing, 1100–1230: Crusade, Piety, Chivalry and Patriotism', in M. Bull and D. Kempf (eds), *Writing the Early Crusades: Text, Transmission and Memory* (Woodbridge, 2014), pp. 155–68; J.D. Hosler, 'Knightly Ideals at the Siege of Acre, 1189–1191', in Crouch and Deploige, *Knighthood and Society in the High Middle Ages*, pp. 145–66; I. Baumgärtner and M. Panse, 'Kreuzzüge aus der Perspektive der Genderforschung. Zielsetzung und Forschungsansätze', *Das Mittelalter*, vol. 21, no. 1 (2016), pp. 1–18; R.W. Kaeuper, 'Exempla, Crusade, and Chivalry', in J.D. Hosler and S. Isaac (eds), *Military Cultures and Martial Enterprises in the Middle Ages: Essays in Honour of Richard P. Abels* (Woodbridge, 2020), pp. 211–22.

55 Maier, 'The Roles of Women in the Crusade Movement', pp. 74–5. See also: Hodgson, *Women, Crusading and the Holy Land in Historical Narrative*, p. 5, n. 13. Three exceptions may be seen in James Powell and Park's work, see: J.M. Powell, 'The Role of Women in the Fifth Crusade', in Kedar, *The Horns of Hattīn*, pp. 294–313; D.E.A. Park, 'The Power of Crusaders' Wives in Narrative and Diplomatic Sources,

Introduction

This book is structured around the organisational stages of crusades, divided into three parts, broadly centred on propaganda, support and memory. Part I will explore the presence of crusade within everyday culture in England, the papacy's policy regarding supporters and preachers' tactics within England. Part II considers the 'how' and 'why' of laywomen's support. Finally, Part III focuses on the memory of crusade support. This will involve an in-depth discussion of women's commemoration of crusade, cementing their links to the movement, as well as dynastic and regional memories of women who patronised holy war.

Part I will provide an overview of the place of crusade within English lay culture, synthesising work on poetry, song and the place of crusade within church service, art and architecture. By looking at these media, we may consider how the culture in England fostered a sense of *Christianitas*, or Christian community and duty, toward crusade.[56] Jessalynn Bird and Elizabeth Lapina have asked questions respecting the accessibility of crusade-themed art and the breadth of the medieval audience who viewed it.[57] We can rarely be sure of the precise intention behind those who commissioned crusade-themed media; however, as Bird has pointed out, very little research has been devoted to the effects of such media upon those discouraged from or unable to join crusading expeditions.[58]

Papal decretals – letters drawn up under the direction of medieval popes and sent to recipients from the laity or clergy, which informed upon, and augmented, canon law – will also be used within this exploration of crusade and *Christianitas*. These sources are predominantly taken from the volumes of papal registers, mostly edited in Paris in the late nineteenth and early twentieth centuries.[59] Crusade preaching

---

c.1096–1149', *The Reading Medievalist*, vol. 1, no. 2 (2014), pp. 18–31; Nicholson, *Women and the Crusades*, pp. 97–128.

[56] Jessalynn Bird has highlighted that crusade art, as a form of propaganda, was on display to all levels of society, see: J.S. Bird, 'Preaching and Crusading Memory', in Cassidy-Welch, *Remembering the Crusades and Crusading*, pp. 13–33, at 20–1. Arnoud-Jan Bijsterveld has been unequivocal on the need to draw from a variety of sources to nuance a study of legal and charter material, see: A.J. Bijsterveld, *Do ut Des: Gift Giving, Memoria, and Conflict Management in the Medieval Low Countries* (Hilversum, 2007), p. 61.

[57] Bird, 'Preaching and Crusading Memory', p. 20; E. Lapina, 'Crusades, Memory and Visual Culture: Representations of the Miracle of Intervention of Saints in Battle', in Cassidy-Welch, *Remembering the Crusades and Crusading*, pp. 49–72. See also: L.J. Whatley, 'Localizing the Holy Land: Visual Culture of Crusade in England, Circa 1140–1307' (Unpublished PhD Thesis, University of Illinois at Urbana-Champaign, 2010); J. Folda, *Crusader Art in the Holy Land, From the Third Crusade to the Fall of Acre, 1187–1291* (Cambridge, 2005).

[58] R. Rosewell, *Medieval Wall Paintings in English and Welsh Churches* (Woodbridge, 2008), p. 179; Bird, 'Preaching and Crusading Memory', p. 20.

[59] See, for example: E. Berger (ed.), *Les Registres D'Innocent IV*, 4 vols (Paris, 1881–1921). The following have similarly relied on this evidence for gauging papal crusading

sermons, also, have been particularly well-researched, and the twenty-two known thirteenth-century sermons, expressly for preaching crusade to the Holy Land, have been edited and are easily available.[60] All of these sermons are, however, model texts, altered since they were first delivered to thirteenth-century audiences.[61] The intricacies of these sources will be discussed in due course.

The vast majority of this book's discussion focuses on cartularies. Medieval cartularies are made up of copies of charters, which take the form of gages, sales, pledges, donations (particularly to religious houses), and confirmations of gifts. These various deeds provide information on the transfer of rights, money and land, while occasionally detailing reasons for doing so. Writers transcribed the documents (and perhaps oral agreements) which pertained to particular religious or secular institutions, usually quite selectively, for posterity and later consultation.[62] Many of these transcriptions were made many years after the original documents were drafted. This was not always a seamless process. In some cases, where the originals survive, the transcriptions may be seen to contain errors, later alterations or even complete fabrications to bolster fraudulent claims.[63] Historians long thought that cartularies were used either for record-keeping or to prove ownership of property. However, they are now understood to have been an important means of creating and augmenting memory by the institutions that commissioned them.[64]

---

policy: M. Purcell, *Papal Crusading Policy, 1244–1291* (Leiden, 1975); A.L. Bysted, *The Crusade Indulgence: Spiritual Rewards and the Theology of the Crusades, c. 1095–1216* (Leiden, 2015); Parker, '*Papa et pecunia*', pp. 1–23. See also: K.M. Setton, *The Papacy and the Levant: 1204–1571*, 4 vols (Philadelphia, 1976–84).

[60] C.T. Maier, *Preaching the Crusades: Mendicant Friars and the Cross in the thirteenth Century* (Cambridge, 1994), app. 2, p. 171; Tamminen, *Crusade Preaching and the Ideal Crusader*, p. 42. There are as many as thirty-six surviving sermons that are considered to have broadly conveyed crusading propaganda, however: Maier, 'Propaganda and Masculinity', p. 22. For more on the definition of crusade sermons, see: Tamminen, *Crusade Preaching and the Ideal Crusader*, pp. 24–35.

[61] M. Tamminen, 'Crusading in the Margins? Women and Children in the Crusade Model Sermons of the Thirteenth Century', in S. Katajala-Peltomaa and V. Vuolanto (eds), *Religious Participation in Ancient and Medieval Societies: Rituals, Interaction and Identity* (Rome, 2013), pp. 145–58, at 146.

[62] J. Tucker, *Reading and Shaping Medieval Cartularies: Multi-Scribe Manuscripts and their Patterns of Growth* (Woodbridge, 2020); O. Guyotjeannin, J. Pycke and B.N. Tock, *Diplomatique médiévale* (Turnhout, 1993), p. 277; E. Jamroziak, *Rievaulx Abbey and its Social Context, 1132–1300: Memory, Locality, and Networks* (Turnhout, 2005), pp. 19–21.

[63] P.J. Geary, *Phantoms of Remembrance: Memory and Oblivion at the End of the First Millennium* (Princeton, 1994), pp. 81–114; C.B. Bouchard, *Rewriting Saints and Ancestors: Memory and Forgetting in France, 500–1200* (Philadelphia, 2015), pp. 63–86.

[64] C.B. Bouchard, 'Monastic Cartularies: Organizing Eternity', in A.J. Kosto and A. Winroth (eds), *Charters, Cartularies, and Archives: The Preservation and Transmission*

Introduction

The English cartularies that survive are only a small proportion of the number originally drafted: the majority were lost or, as in the Reformation of the sixteenth century, destroyed along with the monasteries that often housed them.[65] Therefore, the charters that pertain to crusade preparations are only a snapshot of the original abundance of records of preparations and support.[66] The value of these records in the study of crusade organisation is immeasurable. Analysis of their use of language and symbolism has uncovered a tremendous amount of information on recruitment, motivations, funding and family networks, as well as the memorialisation of the movement.[67]

From the beginning of the crusade movement, western Europeans took pride in peers and forebears who had been to holy war. There is, then, a real possibility that some charters relating to crusade were forged by families claiming chivalric pedigree. This was done from the Middle Ages into the modern day. For instance, many loose charters from France that mention crusade were in fact commissioned in the 1830s for the French elite, so that their families could be commemorated in the rooms of the palace of Versailles known as the *Salles des Croisades*.[68] The practice was, seemingly, less common in England.[69] Nevertheless, any study

---

    of Documents in the Medieval West (Toronto, 2002), pp. 22–32.

[65] G.R.C. Davis, *Medieval Cartularies of Great Britain and Ireland* (London, 2010), p. xvii; M.T. Clanchy, *From Memory to Written Record: England 1066 – 1307*, 2nd edn (Oxford, 1993), pp. 45 and 48.

[66] M. Bull, *Knightly Piety and the Lay Response to the First Crusade: The Limousin and Gascony, c. 970–1130* (Oxford, 1993), pp. 252–6; Tyerman, *England and the Crusades*, p. 189.

[67] G. Constable, 'The Second Crusade as Seen by Contemporaries', *Traditio*, vol. 9 (1953), pp. 213–79, at 241–3; G. Constable, 'The Financing of the Crusade in the Twelfth Century', in B.Z. Kedar, H.E. Mayer and R.C. Smail (eds), *Outremer: Studies in the History of the Crusading Kingdom of Jerusalem* (Jerusalem, 1982), pp. 64–88; Bull, *Knightly Piety*, pp. 250–81; J. Riley-Smith, 'The Idea of Crusading in the Charters of Early Crusaders, 1095–1102', in A. Vauchez (ed.), *Le Concile de Clermont de 1095 et l'appel à la Croisade* (Rome, 1997), pp. 155–66; Riley-Smith, *The First Crusaders*; C.K. Slack and H.B. Feiss (eds and trans.), *Crusade Charters 1138–1270* (Tempe, 2001); Constable, *Crusaders and Crusading*, pp. 73–89; D. Power, 'Who Went on the Albigensian Crusade?', *English Historical Review*, vol. 128, no. 534 (2013), pp. 1049–85; Power, 'The Preparations of Count John I of Sées for the Third Crusade', p. 143; S. Bennett, *Elite Participation in the Third Crusade* (Woodbridge, 2021), pp. 9–12. Cf C. Smith, *Crusading in the Age of Joinville* (Aldershot, 2006), p. 45.

[68] Constable, *Crusaders and Crusading*, p. 73; D. Abulafia, 'Invented Italians in the Courtois Forgeries', in Edbury, *Crusade and Settlement*, pp. 135–47; R.H. Bautier, 'La collection de chartes de croisades dite "Collection Courtois"', *Comptes rendus des séances de l'Académie des Inscriptions et Belles-Lettres*, vol. 100, no. 3 (1956), pp. 382–6.

[69] Some early modern English families fabricated evidence, or fantasised, that their ancestors had been crusaders, and some of these myths were taken at face value by

must contextualise charter material and proceed with caution given the possibility of forgery. By focusing on England, however, this study will make use of the royal chancery records for context. These include letters authenticated with the royal seal, which expressed the sovereign's pronouncements, such as those for public knowledge (the Patent Rolls) or those instructing private individuals (the Close Rolls), as well as charters and writs. The thirteenth-century English royal chancery records are the most extensive collection of European royal accounts from the Central Middle Ages.[70] These sources have proven vital in past studies that examined elite medieval women's lives and financial activities in England, and they will serve the same function in this study.[71]

Court rolls also form a core source material for this book. Various English royal records of the courts *coram rege* survive in abundance from the period; plea rolls, Curia Regis Rolls and the rolls of various itinerant *eyre* courts are particularly useful.[72] This book does not, however, make significant use of manorial court records, as none survive that can be dated before c.1220, and these courts generally only concerned disputes between lesser free and unfree tenants, whose crusade preparations typically left no written record.[73] Despite their official nature, it is crucial to appreciate that medieval court records do not present irrefutable facts. As Caroline Dunn reminds us, these documents are the product of male scribes' interpretations of proceedings, (generally) translated into Latin from testimony that was heard in the vernacular and used formulaic phrasings and legal jargon that probably differed from plaintiffs' and defendants' actual statements.[74] The insight

---

antiquarians, see: E. Siberry, *Tales of the Crusaders: Remembering the Crusades in Britain* (London, 2021), pp. 61–2. See also: R.F. Berkhofer III, *Forgeries and Historical Writing in England, France, and Flanders, 900–1200* (Woodbridge, 2022).

[70] D. Carpenter, 'The English Royal Chancery in the Thirteenth Century', in A. Jobson (ed.), *English Government in the Thirteenth Century* (Woodbridge, 2004), pp. 49–69.

[71] For more on the use of these sources in studies of women in medieval England, see: S.S. Walker, 'Litigation as Personal Quest: Suing for Dower in the Royal Courts, circa 1272–1350', in S.S. Walker (ed.), *Wife and Widow in Medieval England* (Ann Arbor, 1993), pp. 81–108; Mitchell, *Portraits of Medieval Women*, p. 6; L.J. Wilkinson, *Women in Thirteenth-Century Lincolnshire* (Woodbridge, 2007), pp. 10–1; Ricketts, *High-Ranking Widows in Medieval Iceland and Yorkshire*, pp. 43–8.

[72] For more on the development of these records in the late twelfth century, see: J. Hudson, *The Oxford History of Laws in England: Volume II, 871–1216* (Oxford, 2012), pp. 537–46.

[73] Z. Razi and R.M. Smith, 'The Origins of the English Manorial Court as a Written Record: A Puzzle', in Z. Razi and R.M. Smith (eds), *Medieval Society and the Manor Court* (Oxford, 1996), pp. 36–68, at 39–40; Tyerman, *England and the Crusades*, pp. 167–8.

[74] C. Dunn, *Stolen Women in Medieval England: Rape, Abduction, and Adultery, 1100–1500* (Cambridge, 2013), pp. 5–6. See also: G. Seabourne, *Women in the Medieval Common Law c.1200–1500* (London, 2021), pp. 85–8.

Introduction

these documents offer regarding crusade typically revolves around disputes that arose following the deaths or disappearances of crusaders. These records then tend to highlight the multifarious preparations that were made before departure and, crucially here, the supporters involved.

From this assortment of sources, we will gain something of an insight into the motivations, actions and perceptions of the laywomen living in medieval England who supported crusade. In essence, this study will look beyond the battlefield, to unpack the ways in which we can see medieval laywomen identifying with crusade and connecting with the movement in their daily lives. Exploring what crusade meant to these people will help fill in our wider picture of the crusading culture that pervaded Latin Christendom in the twelfth and thirteenth centuries. It may seem incongruous to look at crusading by scrutinising those who 'stayed behind', but as we shall see, this offers vivid opportunities to understand the mindset that lay behind one of the most devastating movements of the Middle Ages.

PART I

Propaganda

1

Crusade and Culture in England

…deeds of the soldiers of Christ are painted in the church, and recalled in the Scriptures, and recited by preachers, to inspire the faithful.

(Humbert of Romans, *De Predicatione Crucis*, c.1266–8)[1]

The First Crusade had been a resounding success (or perhaps more of a perverse fluke) for the Christian armies that travelled East and eventually took control of Jerusalem. This was of monumental eschatological significance for Latin Christendom, as much as it was a catastrophe for Islam. The crusaders had captured the holiest site in the medieval Christian mind. The taking of Jerusalem, and the subsequent crusades and pilgrimages to the Holy Land that it inspired, created a looping effect of crusading-feedback. There was an explosion of stories, songs, literature and art, all across western Europe, celebrating the victory and propelling the ideals of crusade.[2] By the 1200s, living in England meant being near constantly reminded of holy war propaganda. For contemporaries, this involved a heady mix of self-congratulation on Christian victories and, simultaneously, an anxiety over perceived threats to Christendom, resulting in a supposed need to take up the crusading mantle. It is important that we consider how this worldview took shape and influenced people in England who, paradoxically, had no intention of ever actually travelling to a theatre of crusading warfare. In this chapter, we will see how crusading culture manifested itself within daily life in England.

---

[1] Humbert of Romans, *De Predicatione Crucis*, V. Portnykh and C. Vande Veire (eds) (Turnhout, 2018), cpt. 16, p. 58, "Simili modo eadem de causa in ecclesia et gesta militum Christi depinguntur et rediguntur in scripturis et a predicatoribus recitantur ad animandum fideles".

[2] Vander Elst, *The Knight, the Cross, and the Song*, p. 107; A.V. Murray, 'Friedrich von Hausen on the Third Crusade and the Performance of Middle High German Crusading Songs', in S. John and N. Morton (eds), *Crusading and Warfare in the Middle Ages, Realities and Representations, Essays in Honour of John France* (Farnham, 2014), pp. 119–28, at 119; C. Dijkstra, 'Troubadours, Trouvères and Crusade Lyrics', in A.H. Touber (ed.), *Le Rayonnement des troubadours: actes du colloque de l'AIEO, Association Internationale d'Etudes Occitanes, Amsterdam, 16–18 Octobre 1995* (Amsterdam, 1998), pp. 173–84, at 174.

Conversation and Pageantry

At its most basic, many people living in England would have learned about crusade, pilgrimage, holy war and the world outside of Christendom through conversation. These were lively topics and there would have been many informed people who could speak to their experiences as well as the cultures, features and climate of the Holy Land. In an age where overseas travel was that much more dangerous and difficult, we can well imagine that people who had been on crusade would remain a font of interesting stories to their peers and community.

There are scant references to the details of the discussions that people would have had about the crusading world, particularly amongst lay people, but we can be sure they regularly took place. John of Forde's *Life* of the Somerset anchorite Wulfric of Haselbury (d.1154) has an intriguing passage. John describes a wealthy layman, Alfred of Lincoln, who came to speak to Wulfric. During the conversation, the two men remarked on the coming Second Crusade (1147–50) and the atmosphere around the expedition: "at the time when the man of God and his visitor were conversing about these matters, the enterprise was still in preparation, and armed and unarmed were alike boasting".[3] Perhaps the memory of that excitement was still strong when John was writing in the early 1180s. He hoped to impress upon his readers that, despite the jovial atmosphere in the 1140s, Wulfric 'miraculously' predicted that the Second Crusade would be a failure.

There is no doubt that women habitually took an active part in these sorts of conversations, hearing exciting stories and advising those considering the journey. Until Pope Innocent III issued the letter *Ex multa*, in 1201, the papacy demanded that anyone who wished to take vows to become a crusader had to first obtain permission from their spouse.[4] Clearly, there was an assumption of frequent dialogues between husband and wife over crusade. However, holy war was certainly a feature in more casual conversation and storytelling between men and women. Jean de Joinville, a nobleman from the Champagne region of France, wrote about his experiences on the Seventh Crusade, and described a tumultuous moment in the fighting at the Battle of al Mansurah (1250) in Egypt. Jean's friend John II de Nesle took a moment during the intense combat to turn and comment: "by God's coif" – this was the oath he most often swore – "we'll talk of this one day again, you and I, in the ladies' chamber".[5]

---

3   John of Forde, *The Life of Wulfric of Haselbury, Anchorite*, P. Matarasso (ed. and trans.) (Trappist, 2011), bk. 3, p. 196, cpt. 28.
4   C.R. Cheney and M.G. Cheney (eds), *The Letters of Pope Innocent III (1198–1216) Concerning England and Wales* (Oxford, 1967), pp. 57–8, no. 350. For context, see: Brundage, 'The Crusader's Wife', pp. 434–5.
5   Jean de Joinville, 'The Life of Saint Louis', in C. Smith (ed. and trans.), *Joinville and Villehardouin: Chronicles of the Crusades* (London, 2008), pp. 147–336, at 206, § 242. For original Old French, see: J. Monfrin (ed.), *Vie de Saint Louis* (Paris, 2010), p. 120, § 242, "par la quoife Dieu! (ainsi comme il juroit) encore en parlerons nous entre vous

Crusade and Culture in England

Crusading did not necessarily provide a one-way road of Christian pilgrims travelling from England to and from the Mediterranean. On the contrary, it was an opportunity for Muslim, Jewish and Eastern Christian communities to come West, bringing stories and new perspectives with them. Ironically, holy wars were often a time of meaningful cultural exchange as well as confrontation. This meant that medieval Christendom was far more diverse during this era than many people today might imagine, and this must have shaped contemporaries' understanding of, and interest in, the world beyond Latin Europe. The twelfth-century Arab writer, Usāma ibn Munqidh (d.1188), amused his Muslim readers with an anecdote about a crusader who offered to take Usāma's fourteen-year-old son back to Europe to be trained as a knight.[6] Although an unappealing offer for Usāma, the story is not too outlandish. When King Louis IX of France (r.1226–70) embarked on the Seventh Crusade (1247–54), he did so with the express intention of converting Muslims to Christianity. Dozens of converts later accompanied the crusaders back to Europe and settled across France, many of them taking up jobs in royal administration.[7]

There are similar examples of people from around the Mediterranean coming to England. King Richard I retained a troop of mercenaries (at least while in his French holdings) described in the Pipe Rolls as "Saracens" – a pejorative catch-all term that referred generally to Muslims and sometimes other non-Christians.[8] Chancery records from the 1160s reveal one man named Muhammad living in Wiltshire who had been involved in an illegal duel.[9] Likewise, in the 1250s, King Henry III sent a couple of robes to a man identified as Muhammad Saracen.[10] These people may well have been Muslims or Christian converts, but we do not know much more of their personal stories. In a clearer instance of emigration to the British Isles, in 1319, the crusader Roger of Stanegrave returned to England after 34 years in captivity in Egypt. He was joined by his rescuer, a Jewish man

---

et moy de ceste journee es chambres des dames". For context, see: Paul, *To Follow in Their Footsteps*, p. 69.

[6] Usāma ibn Munqidh, *An Arab-Syrian Gentleman and Warrior in the Period of the Crusades: Memoirs of Usama ibn-Munqidh*, P.K. Hitti (ed. and trans.), 2nd edn (Princeton, 1987), p. 161.

[7] W.C. Jordan, *The Apple of His Eye: Converts from Islam in the Reign of Louis IX* (Princeton, 2019). See also: B.A. Catlos, *Muslims of Medieval Latin Christendom, c.1050–1614* (Boulder, 2014).

[8] Jordan, *The Apple of His Eye*, pp. 43–4; J. Gillingham, *Richard I* (New Haven and London, 2002), p. 295; F.M. Powicke, 'The Saracen Mercenaries of Richard I', *Scottish Historical Review*, vol. 8, no. 9 (1910), pp. 104–5.

[9] J.S. Moore, 'Who was "Mahumet"? Arabs in Angevin England', *Prosopon*, vol. 11 (2000), pp. 1–7.

[10] *CCR, 1253–54*, p. 211. See also the discussion in: M. Ray, 'A Black Slave on the Run in Thirteenth-Century England', *Nottingham Medieval Studies*, vol. 51 (2007), pp. 111–20.

named Isaac, who settled in the kingdom.[11] Unfortunately, we cannot now know what any of these people thought of crusade. Nevertheless, they must have been able to shape others' understanding of the Holy Land.

If not heard directly through word of mouth, many people in England would have learned of crusading-events from letters sent by their kin. There is extensive evidence that communication flowed back and forth between the East and West in this period, even during campaigns.[12] The noblewoman, Hawisa de Nevill, for example, whom we met at the beginning of this book, was in close correspondence with her son while he was on crusade in the 1260s. The surviving letter that she addressed to him while he was in Acre confirms as much. Hawisa began her message saying she was: "much rejoiced with the news that William FitzSimon brought me of your health".[13] However, the speed at which people could get a message to each other could be unpredictable. Hawisa lamented not knowing of a reliable stream of people going to the Holy Land that she could call upon to quickly send word to Hugh: "for never can I find a man who should go to that part that I should send you letters".[14]

More formal storytelling and renditions of crusade took place within homes, and noblewomen were undoubtedly key audiences for these dramatic retellings. Nicholas Paul argues that we cannot downplay the influence that noblewomen had in the transmission of songs and dynastic stories, many of which revolved around holy war.[15] There must have been a myriad of ways in which families and communities taught the next generation about crusading forebears, surely conditioning their outlook in life. For instance, the Scottish Arthurian epic *Roman de Fergus* – a late twelfth- or early thirteenth-century story – placed great importance on women inspiring chivalric ideals. The title character, Fergus, begs his father to give him weapons and armour, and make him a knight. Fergus's father is infuriated by his son's impudence, but the miserly man is soon reprimanded by his wife:

---

[11] R. MacLellan, 'An Egyptian Jew in King Edward's Court: Jewish Conversion, Edward II, and Roger de Stanegrave', *Crusades*, vol. 19 (2020), pp. 143–53.

[12] Lloyd, *English Society and the Crusade*, App. 1, pp. 248–52; M. Barber and K. Bate (eds and trans.), *Letters from the East: Crusaders, Pilgrims and Settlers in the 12th-13th Centuries* (Farnham, 2013); T.W. Smith, *Rewriting the First Crusade: Epistolary Culture in the Middle Ages* (Woodbridge, 2024), pp. 57–8. My sincere thanks to Thomas Smith for allowing me to read his book ahead of its publication.

[13] Giuseppi, 'XIX – On the Testament of Sir Hugh de Nevill', p. 360, for Old French, see p. 358, "…e mut sui reioie de noueles ke Will le fiz Simun me porta de uostre sainte…".

[14] Giuseppi, 'XIX – On the Testament of Sir Hugh de Nevill', p. 360, for Old French, see p. 358, "Ker vnkes ne poai espier hōme ke cele part alast. ke io ne uus enueiasse lettres".

[15] Paul, *To Follow in Their Footsteps*, p. 69; Nicholson, *Women and the Crusades*, p. 31.

And regarding this young man, let me tell you that you should not be surprised if he is set on a life of prowess, for he has many fine knights in his family on my side! So it is my belief he is taking after them. And if you want my advice, you will not make any difficulty about him setting off.[16]

Leaving behind the letters or the private audience in the ladies' chambers, and entering a hall or communal space, one might be met with songs or poetry that centred on crusade. I say 'might', as there are no descriptions of the performance of crusade songs, so it is hard to be precise about the setting or occasions in which they featured in laypeople's lives.[17] Indeed, the content and emotion behind crusade songs varied greatly. They can be defined broadly as songs that owe their existence to the wider context of crusade and have to be understood through that prism.[18] Some surviving examples wholly revolve around crusade, while many others mention aspects of holy war in passing. This form of art did not necessarily retell individuals' true experiences or particular events, but they reflected the concerns of these aristocratic poets and their wider society.[19] Crusading, as a topic, could be reinvented and given new meanings by each generation, making these songs an enduring aspect of medieval entertainment.[20] Unfortunately, only a small minority of surviving twelfth- and thirteenth-century crusade songs were produced (or definitely circulated) in England.[21] However, they would have formed

---

[16] Guillaume le Clerc, *Fergus of Galloway: Knight of King Arthur*, D.D.R. Owen (ed. and trans.) (Edinburgh, 2018), p. 8. For the original Old French, see: Guillaume le Clerc, *The Romance of Fergus*, W. Frescoln (ed.) (Philadelphia, 1983), p. 46, ll. 495–502, "Et si vos di de cest vallet, se de prouēce s'entremet, nes vos en devés mervillier, car il a maint bon chevalier en son lingnage de par moi. Si i retrait, si com je croi, et se men consel volés croire, ja ne destorberés son o[i]rre."

[17] Murray, 'Friedrich von Hausen on the Third Crusade and the Performance of Middle High German Crusading Songs', p. 119.

[18] Dijkstra, 'Troubadours, Trouvères and Crusade Lyrics', p. 174; M. Galvez, *The Subject of Crusade: Lyric, Romance and Materials, 1150–1500* (Chicago, 2020), pp. 153–206.

[19] L. Paterson, *Singing the Crusades: French and Occitan Lyric Responses to the Crusading Movements, 1137–1336* (Cambridge, 2018), pp. 14–5; Paul, *To Follow in Their Footsteps*, pp. 131–3.

[20] Dijkstra, 'Troubadours, Trouvères and Crusade Lyrics', p. 174; Paul, *To Follow in Their Footsteps*, pp. 131–3; Paterson, *Singing the Crusades*, pp. 14–5; Galvez, *The Subject of Crusade*, pp. 153–206; L. Manion, 'The Crusading Romance in Britain: Religious Violence and the Transformation of Popular Chivalric Narratives', in R.L. Krueger (ed.), *A New Cambridge Companion to Medieval Romance* (Cambridge, 2023), pp. 101–18.

[21] A. Radaelli, '"*Voil ma chançun a la gent fere oïr*", An Anglo-Norman Crusade Appeal (London, BL Harley 1717, fol. 251ᵛ)', in S.T. Parsons and L.M. Paterson (eds), *Literature of the Crusades* (Woodbridge, 2018), pp. 109–33, at 110; J. Haines, 'The Songbook for William of Villehardouin, Prince of the Morea (Paris, Bibliothèque nationale de France, fonds français 844): A Crucial Case in the History of Vernacular Song Collections',

an aspect of crusading culture within the kingdom during this period, known to returned crusaders and their families.

Not all laypeople were enamoured by crusade, and there is plenty of surviving evidence of the laity's criticisms of the enterprise within crusade songs specifically.[22] In 1187, Salāh al-Dīn (r.1174–93) – or Saladin as he is known in the West – captured Christian-held Jerusalem. The event shook the Latin world to its core and caused many poets and song-writers to question the direction of holy war. For instance, Occitan crusade songs composed at this time exhibited noticeable "ideological critique" of the very point and value of crusading.[23] That uncertainty was felt throughout Christendom. A contemporary canon of Lincoln Cathedral, Ralph Niger, was one voice in England who similarly noted genuine concerns about the worth of crusade at that time.[24]

Indeed, female characters appear quite frequently in songs bidding farewell to distraught loved ones or wishing they had never gone at all. It is important to appreciate that these scenes usually served to glorify men's sacrifice in going on crusade, but they often present crusade in a negative light.[25] Crusading was habitually associated with the emotional pain of separation from spouses and family for months, if not years, and this would have been a core aspect to the conversation within society.[26] A good example of this from England can be seen in the song *Sire Gauter, dire vos voil*. It survives in manuscripts from the early fourteenth century but was probably composed by Henry de Lacy earl of Lincoln (d.1311), around the time of Lord Edward's Crusade (1270–2). Henry voices his concerns about leaving his lover in a (perhaps imagined) discussion with his friend Walter of Bibbesworth:

---

in S.E.J. Gerstel (ed.), *Viewing the Morea: Land and People in the Late Medieval Peloponnese* (Washington DC, 2013), pp. 57–109, at 63–8.

22 E. Siberry, *Criticism of Crusading 1095–1274* (Oxford, 1985).

23 J. Curbet, 'Two-Faced Eloquence. A Brief Note Towards Re-Evaluating the Troubadour Crusade Corpus, 1187–1200', *Medievalia*, vol. 16 (2013), pp. 47–53, at 52.

24 J.D. Cotts, 'The Exegesis of Violence in the Crusade Writings of Ralph Niger and Peter of Blois', in Lapina and Morton, *The Uses of the Bible in Crusader Sources*, pp. 273–95.

25 W.E. Jackson, 'Poet, Woman, and Crusade in Songs of Marcabru, Guiot de Dijon, and Albrecht von Johansdorf', *Mediaevalia*, vol. 22, no. 2 (1999), pp. 265–89; W.E. Jackson, *Ardent Complaints and Equivocal Piety: The Portrayal of the Crusader in Medieval German Poetry* (Lanham, 2003), p. 88; L. Barbieri, 'Crusade Songs and the Old French Literary Canon', in S.T. Parsons and L.M. Paterson (eds), *Literature of the Crusades* (Woodbridge, 2018), pp. 75–95.

26 S.J. Spencer, *Emotions in a Crusading Context, 1095–1291* (Oxford, 2019), pp. 160–4. See also: K. Day, 'Sorrow, Masculinity and Papal Authority in the Writing of Pope Innocent III (1198–1216) and his *curia*', *Journal of Medieval History*, vol. 49, no. 2 (2023), pp. 201–26.

> Sir Walter, I wish to tell you
> of a difficulty of mine which is causing me much grief,
> and do advise me how to choose.
> I continue to love, as ever,
> the lady of the lovely face and laughing eyes
> from whom I seek never to part.
> But now I have taken the cross to serve God,
> and if I go overseas, I lose her favour
> for good for abandoning her;
> and if I stay behind, I am well aware
> that apart from her everyone must find me odious,
> since I am stripping myself of all honour.[27]

This is a valuable insight into the medieval perception that crusade was a constant looming expectation.

Preparations ahead of expeditions themselves often featured some theatrics that celebrated the venture and broadcast the Christian community's shared responsibility towards holy war. When nobles took vows to go on crusade, or when they departed, the scene and ceremony of these events could include an element of pageantry. Modern historians have even described these displays as "crusade jamborees".[28] Matthew Paris (d.1259), the famous monk and chronicler at St Albans Abbey (Hertfordshire), for example, described the well-orchestrated day Theodoric, the prior of the Knights Hospitallers at Clerkenwell (London), and several of his brethren rode out for the Holy Land in 1237. Matthew claimed that the knights paraded across a bridge over the Thames in their full regalia, with arms and banners, while crowds of people gathered to watch and offer prayers.[29]

---

[27] 'Henry de Lacy/Walter de Bibbesworth, *Sire Gauter, dire vos voil* (RS 1780a)', https://warwick.ac.uk/fac/arts/modernlanguages/research/french/crusades/texts/of/rs1780a/#page1 Published Online 27 Apr 2018 (accessed 20 Feb 2024). For original Old French, see: S. Thiolier-Méjean, 'Croisade et registre courtois chez les troubadours', in J.M. d'Heur and N. Cherubini (eds) *Études de philologie romane et d'histoire littéraire offertes à Jules Horrent à l'occasion de son soixantième anniversaire* (Liege, 1980), pp. 295–307, at 305, "Sire Gauter, dire vus voil; Un mien bosoing dont trop m'endoil, Et si me loez a choisir, Jeo aim oncore, cum faire soil, Cele au cler vys, au ryaunt oil; Dont ja ne mi quer departir. Ore sui croisee pur Deu servir. Et si utre mer vois pur lui guerpir, Sanz recoverir perc son akoil; Et si demur, bien pus sentir; Ffors lui me deyvent tuz haïr, Car de tuz honurs mi despoil".

[28] Tyerman, *How to Plan a Crusade*, p. 65.

[29] *Chronica Majora*, vol. 3, p. 406.

Art, Architecture and Display

Aside from the literary and theatrical side of crusading culture, the medieval English landscape held a huge variety of art and architecture designed to remind the viewer of the necessity of holy war. This included wall paintings and sculpture that adorned churches and noble spaces, and architectural forms based on holy sites in the East, as well as illuminations in manuscripts, to name but a few. As Jessalynn Bird and Laura Whatley have pointed out, we should be conscious of the fact (and consider the implications) that many people who were discouraged from joining crusades or were disinclined or unable to physically take part were, nonetheless, routinely exposed to a range of crusade-themed art.[30] Bird has even pointed out that crusade preaching, art and architecture "intersected": the visual culture of crusade was all around and easily referred to by recruiters.[31]

Contemporaries alluded to holy war through a surprising array of topics. Much like crusade songs, relatively little pro-crusade art (as it may be termed) strictly depicted historical figures or real events of crusade history. Instead, it generally took the form of allegory or representations of popular romances and fanciful stories. The famous c.1250 Chertsey Tiles are a good example. They were made for a royal palace floor and depict scenes from a now-lost crusading epic that celebrated a fictitious duel between Richard the Lionheart and Saladin.[32] Despite leading opposing armies during the Third Crusade (1189–92), these two men never actually met; but that did not slow medieval fantasies. Amanda Luyster argues forcefully that these tiles were commissioned by Eleanor of Provence (d.1291), queen of England and wife of Henry III. Surviving records indicate that Eleanor had a room within Westminster Palace adorned with imagery of crusades – especially the "deeds of Antioch and the king and others" – at the time the tiles were being produced.[33] The mention of Antioch referred to the First Crusade's cataclysmic siege of the city from 1097–8. But, more than that, this siege had given rise to a phalanx of stories and literature in the decades that followed, such as the *Chanson d'Antioche*. These retellings blended various elements of crusading history and characters. The appearance of King Richard and Saladin (two leaders who flourished nearly a century after the Siege of

---

[30] Bird, 'Preaching and Crusading Memory', p. 20; L.J. Whatley, 'Localizing the Holy Land: Visual Culture of Crusade in England, Circa 1140–1307' (Unpublished PhD Thesis, University of Illinois at Urbana-Champaign, 2010).
[31] Bird, 'Preaching and Crusading Memory', p. 20.
[32] A. Luyster, 'Fragmented Tile, Fragmented Text: Richard the Lionheart on Crusade and the Lost Latin Texts of the Chertsey Combat Tiles (c.1250)', *Digital Philology*, vol. 11, no. 1 (2022), pp. 86–120. My thanks to Amanda Luyster for sharing her thoughts on this with me.
[33] As quoted in: A. Luyster, *The Chertsey Tiles, the Crusades, and Global Textile Motifs* (Cambridge, 2023), p. 63, see also 64–8.

Antioch) in the decor of the so-called Antioch Chamber would not be out of step with the medieval love for layering imagery.

This crusade-themed room in Westminster was considered so impactful that it inspired other Antioch Chambers (or was just the first in a series) quickly commissioned for the royal houses at Clarendon, Winchester and the Tower of London. The nobility who moved in royal circles were more than likely to come across these spaces. The imagery and crusading celebrations in the Chertsey Tiles feature elsewhere, too. The English and Welsh abbeys of Neath, Tintern, Glastonbury and Cleeve all contained floor tiles that depicted this same legendary duel between warriors of the Third Crusade.[34] Elite visitors who had a knowledge of famous romances, like *Pas Saladin* or *Richard Coer de Lyon*, would have easily spotted the significance of these schema and the ideals they displayed.

Artistic allegories were not solely focused on secular literature; they also often featured scenes from the Bible. Numerous biblical events were depicted and viewed as part of a "shared visual language" with crusade.[35] Imagery of Old Testament warfare was a major focus, notably the revolt of the Maccabees. The latter's struggle, as God's Chosen People, against the Seleucid Empire was used in metaphors for the then-contemporary battle for the Holy Land.[36] An interesting example of this within medieval English art could once be seen in the wall paintings of rooms of state in Old Westminster Palace. These images were completed in two phases: sometime soon after the palace fire of 1263 and then at some point between 1292 and 1297.[37] The schema of the Painted Chamber, as it became known, was uncovered in 1800 beneath a coat of whitewash. They are known today from a series of sketches that were made prior to the Painted Chamber's destruction in a fire in 1834. It is clear that, amongst other subjects,

---

[34] Hurlock, *Britain, Ireland and the Crusades*, p. 121; R.S. Loomis, 'Richard Cœur de Lion and the *Pas Saladin* in Medieval Art', *PMLA*, vol. 30, no. 3 (1915), pp. 509–28.

[35] M.M. Reeve, 'The Painted Chamber at Westminster, Edward I, and the Crusade', *Viator*, vol. 37 (2006), pp. 189–221, at 198. This idea was pioneered by Adolf Katzenellenbogen's discussion, see: A. Katzenellenbogen, 'The Central Tympanum at Vézelay: Its Encyclopaedic Meaning and its Relation to the First Crusade', *The Art Bulletin*, vol. 26, no. 3 (1944), pp. 141–51, at 149. See also the comparison made by Anne Derbes between depictions of Moses in the Cathedral of Le Puy and bishop Adhémar le Puy, a leader of the First Crusade: A. Derbes, 'A Crusading Fresco Cycle at the Cathedral of Le Puy', *The Art Bulletin*, vol. 73, no. 4 (1991), pp 561–76, at 572–3.

[36] See: Maier, *Crusade Propaganda and Ideology*, pp. 55–6; J. Yolles, 'The Maccabees in the Lord's Temple: Biblical Imagery and Latin Poetry in Frankish Jerusalem', in Lapina and Morton, *The Uses of the Bible in Crusader Sources*, pp. 421–39; N. Morton, 'The Defence of the Holy Land and the Memory of the Maccabees', *Journal of Medieval History*, vol. 36 (2010), pp. 275–93; R.L. McGrath, 'The Visual Tradition', in 'The Romance of the Maccabees in Mediaeval Art and Literature' (Unpublished PhD Thesis, University of Princeton, 1963), pp. 84–130.

[37] Reeve, 'The Painted Chamber at Westminster', p. 191.

the depictions used contemporary medieval dress, armour and weaponry in their portrayal of biblical warfare – portraying events of the Bible as crusade.[38]

More generally, it has been argued that Western artistic depictions of mythical human races – such as *Monopods* (humans with one oversized foot) and *Synocephali* (dog-headed people) – entreated the medieval viewer to think of anyone they considered 'other' who they would encounter in the East on crusade.[39] By the fourteenth century, vernacular literature and song frequently featured tropes such as a "noble Saracen knight" or a Muslim princess who converted to Christianity.[40] These characters were typically included to explore (in what would now be viewed as deeply xenophobic and self-gratifying terms) English identity. Depictions of Jerusalem itself, or of the Romans' sack of the city in AD 70, could also act as metaphors for the events of 1099 during the First Crusade.[41] To borrow Dorothy Glass's expression, all of these media "blurred the boundaries" in the medieval mind between contemporary events, ancient history and biblical precedent.[42]

One of the few scenes of crusading history that was popular amongst medieval artists was a supposed miraculous intervention that took place during the Battle of Antioch in 1098.[43] Chroniclers such as the anonymous writer of the *Gesta Francorum* reported that while the desperate army of the First Crusade fought the forces of Kerbogha outside the city walls of Antioch, a heavenly host of knights clad in white came to the crusaders' rescue. This divine host was led by St George, St Demetrius and St Mercurius.[44] There are eleven extant depictions of this scene within Western art, which date between the twelfth and fourteenth

---

[38] Reeve, 'The Painted Chamber at Westminster', pp. 205 and 208.
[39] D.H. Strickland, *Saracens, Demons, & Jews: Making Monsters in Medieval Art* (Princeton, 2003), p. 159.
[40] S.B. Calkin, *Saracens and the Making of English Identity: The Auchinleck Manuscript* (New York and London, 2005); A.S. Ambrisco, 'Cannibalism and Cultural Encounters in *Richard Coeur de Lion*', *Journal of Medieval and Early Modern Studies*, vol. 29, no. 3 (1999), pp. 499–528. See also: L. Ramsey, 'Orientalism and the "Saracen"', in A. Bale (ed.), *The Cambridge Companion to the Literature of the Crusades* (Cambridge, 2019), pp.136–45.
[41] A. Heyman, 'The Representation of the Holy Sepulchre in Auvergnat Romanesque Sculpture: a Reflection of Crusader Patrons?', in Balard, *Autour de la Première Croisade*, pp. 632–42; L. Seidel, 'Images of the Crusades in Western Art: Models and Metaphors', in V.P. Goss and C.V. Bernstein (eds), *The Meeting of Two Worlds: Cultural Exchange between East and West during the Period of the Crusades* (Kalamazoo, 1986), pp. 377–91, at 386.
[42] D.F. Glass, *Portals, Pilgrimage, and Crusade in Western Tuscany* (New Jersey, 1997), p. 59.
[43] Lapina, 'Crusades, Memory and Visual Culture', p. 51.
[44] E. Lapina, *Warfare and the Miraculous in the chronicles of the First Crusade* (Philadelphia, 2015), pp. 37–53; B.C. Spacey, *The Miraculous and the Writing of Crusade Narrative* (Woodbridge, 2020), pp. 34–6.

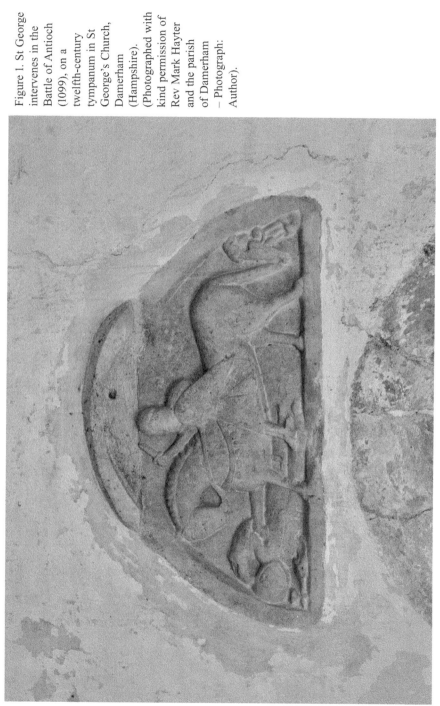

Figure 1. St George intervenes in the Battle of Antioch (1099), on a twelfth-century tympanum in St George's Church, Damerham (Hampshire). (Photographed with kind permission of Rev Mark Hayter and the parish of Damerham – Photograph: Author).

Figure 2. Twelfth-century wall paintings on the north wall of St Botolph's Church, Hardham (Sussex), featuring the life of St George. In the bottom-left panel, the saint intervenes in the Battle of Antioch (1099). (Photographed with kind permission of the Parish of Bury, Coldwaltham, Hardham and Houghton – Photograph: Author).

centuries. Three of those examples, all of which are twelfth century, survive in parish churches in southern England: a wall painting in St Botolph's Church in Hardham (West Sussex, Figure 2) and two stone relief tympana (lintels) in St George's Church in Fordington (Dorset) and Damerham Church (Hampshire, Figure 1).[45] These depictions are located within a hundred miles of each other, and so it has been suggested that such depictions enjoyed especial popularity in southern England.[46] That said, much medieval religious art did not survive the Reformation in England, and so we have to be circumspect when thinking about the popularity of particular artistic schemes.[47]

In the past, it has generally been assumed that knightly men were the typical audience for crusade art.[48] This was certainly implied by the Dominican friar Humbert of Romans. He wrote in his c.1266–8 work *De Predicatione Crucis* that preachers could encourage men to join crusades by drawing attention to the: "palaces of the nobility, where many nobles tend to convene, where there are paintings on the walls of the brave deeds of ancient warriors", or churches where similarly, "the deeds of the knights of Christ are painted".[49] Humbert's advice for fellow preachers is a valuable reminder of how ubiquitous this artistry was. However, we cannot forget that while a wide section of communities would have visited noble residences, parish churches were accessible to everyone in society.[50] The art that Humbert alluded to would have regularly been viewed by far more people than just knights.

The thirteenth-century wall paintings in Claverley Church (Shropshire) (Figures 3 and 4) are an interesting example to consider. This was a parish church frequented

---

[45] Lapina, 'Crusades, Memory and Visual Culture', pp. 53–5. See also figs. 4.1, 4.2, and 4.3. on pp. 53–5.
[46] Lapina, 'Crusades, Memory and Visual Culture', pp. 62–3.
[47] The lost "crusading window" of the Abbey of Saint-Denis is a prime example of famed crusade artistry that has been destroyed, see: E.A.R. Brown and M.W. Cothren, 'The Twelfth-Century Crusading Window of the abbey of Saint-Denis: *Praeteritorum Enim Recordatio Futurorum est Exhibitio*', *Journal of the Warburg and Courtauld Institutes*, vol. 49 (1986), pp. 1–40.
[48] A. Derbes, 'Crusading Ideology and the Frescoes of S. Maria in Cosmedin', *The Art Bulletin*, vol. 77, no. 3 (1995), pp. 460–78, at 460–1. See also: D.H. Weiss, *Art and Crusade in the Age of Saint Louis* (Cambridge, 1998), p. 213.
[49] Humbert of Romans, *De Predicatione Crucis*, cpt. 16, p. 58, "propter quod in palatiis nobilium, ubi solent multi nobiles conuenire, depinguntur in parietibus gesta fortia antiquorum bellatorum... Simili modo eadem de causa in ecclesia et gesta militum Christi depingutur". For more on the context, see: P.J. Cole, 'Humbert of Romans and the Crusade', in M. Bull and N. Housley (eds), *The Experience of Crusading: Volume 1, Western Approaches* (Cambridge, 2003), pp. 157–74.
[50] See especially: Katherine Weikert's discussion of 'private' built space: K. Weikert, *Authority, Gender and Space in the Anglo-Norman World, 900–1200* (Woodbridge, 2020), p. 54.

by the laity, who would have easily seen the art that decorates the nave. This space contains a large frieze showing mounted knights fighting in single combat. The church's paintings have been interpreted in a variety of ways. It was thought that they represented the *psychomachia*, an allegorical battle between virtues and vices.[51] However, Christopher Barrett argues that the figures are not differentiated in any specific way to show which vice or virtue they are. Instead, he argues, they are depictions of the victories of Christian warriors (similar to Humbert's description), including a scene of Roland blowing his famous horn during a struggle with Muslim adversaries, from the medieval epic *Song of Roland*. This may be, as Barrett put it, an aid to "inspire action" to crusade.[52]

The appearance of these artistic celebrations in a communal space raises thought-provoking questions. If images of Christian warriors engaged in crusade were meant to prompt knights to go to the Holy Land, what were they meant to entreat other people to do? Situating crusade-themed art in a parish church, for instance, one of the most fundamental structures for a medieval community, shows an attempt to consistently invoke crusade in the minds of all the laity, rather than a select few.[53]

We cannot imagine that laywomen disregarded such chivalric imagery. Women featured prominently in chivalric romance, observing and often directing knights to perform feats of combat and honour. This was not limited to literature; it was a feature of medieval elite society and pageantry, particularly at tournaments.[54] Indeed, some noblewomen's personal rooms were described in the sources as containing decor and art that centred on chivalric values.[55] It is not always clear how women were expected to react or interact with imagery of legendary or biblical warfare. It is clear, however, that the Maccabees revolt was used to allegorise the spiritual struggle against evil as much as the physical. An individual could fight "a Maccabean campaign through prayer".[56] It must be said, then, that

---

[51] J.S. Norman, *Metamorphoses of an Allegory: The Iconography of the Psychomachia in Medieval Art* (New York, 1988), p. 54; E.W. Tristram and W.G. Constable, *English Medieval Wall Painting: The Twelfth Century* (Oxford, 1944), pp. 48–9.

[52] C. Barret, 'Roland and Crusade Imagery in an English Royal chapel: Early Thirteenth-Century Wall Paintings in Claverley Church, Shropshire', *The Antiquaries Journal*, vol. 92 (2012), pp. 129–68.

[53] K.L. French, *The People of the Parish: Community Life in a Late Medieval English Diocese* (Philadelphia, 2001), p. 22.

[54] E. L'Estrange, 'Gazing at Gawain: Considering Tournaments, Courtly Love, and the Lady Who Looks', *Medieval Feminist Forum*, vol. 44, no. 2 (2008), pp. 74–96.

[55] See the following for a discussion of Baudri of Bourgueil's poem concerning Adela of Blois' room, and the idealised notions contained in it: Weikert, *Authority, Gender and Space in the Anglo-Norman World*, pp. 164–9.

[56] Morton, 'The Defence of the Holy Land and the Memory of the Maccabees', p. 279; K.A. Smith, *War and the Making of Medieval Monastic Culture* (Woodbridge, 2011), pp. 71–111, especially at 104; E. Lapina, 'The Mural Paintings of Berzé-la-Ville in the

Figure 3. Thirteenth-century frieze of knights in combat, north wall of the nave of St Mary's Church, Claverley (Shropshire). (Photographed with kind permission of Rev Gary Ward and the parish of Claverley – Photograph: Author).

Figure 4. Detail of Knights in the Claverley Frieze. (Photographed with kind permission of Rev Gary Ward and the parish of Claverley – Photograph: Author).

imagery related to these Old Testament battles could have acted as a metaphor for a variety of responses to holy war. Crusade art ultimately allegorised then-contemporary Christians as the Chosen People and reminded them of their responsibility to conquer in God's name.[57] In other words, this imagery promoted a sense of *Christianitas*, or shared Christian obligation, to support crusade and encourage those considered capable of waging war.[58]

There were even more imposing reminders of crusade within England's landscape. During the High Middle Ages, numerous churches were constructed with rounded naves. These architectural forms were modelled on the Byzantine *anastasis* of Holy Sepulchre Church in Jerusalem, the most sacred site to medieval Christians.[59] The distinctiveness of these recreations would have made them easily identifiable in the landscape. There are a remarkable number of these structures in England (see Figure 5).[60] The Military Orders, such as the Knights Templar and Hospitaller, as well as returned pilgrims and crusaders predominantly erected these round churches.[61] Some examples in western Europe may predate the First Crusade, but the vast majority were built after the crusaders captured Jerusalem in 1099.[62] In England, round churches were exclusively constructed while Christians were in control of Jerusalem (1099–1187 and 1229–44), highlighting

---

Context of the First Crusade and the *Reconquista*', *Journal of Medieval History*, vol. 31, no. 4 (2005), pp. 309–26, at 318 and 321–2.

[57] D.H. Weiss, 'Biblical History and Medieval Historiography: Rationalizing Strategies in Crusader Art', *MLN*, vol. 108, no. 4 (1993), pp. 710–37, at 732–3.

[58] Bird, 'Preaching and Crusading Memory', pp. 20–1

[59] É. Lambert, *L'Architecture des Templiers* (Paris, 1978), pp. 61–91; B. Sloane and G. Malcolm, *Excavations at the Priory of the Order of the Hospital of St John of Jerusalem, Clerkenwell, London* (London, 2004), p. 4; P. Ritoók, 'The Architecture of the Knights Templars in England', in M. Barber (ed.), *The Military Orders: Fighting for the Faith and Caring for the Sick* (Aldershot, 1994), pp. 167–78, at 170; H.J. Nicholson, 'At the Heart of Medieval London: The New Temple in the Middle Ages', in R. Griffith-Jones and D. Park (eds), *The Temple Church in London: History, Architecture, Art* (Woodbridge, 2010), pp. 1–18, at 2.

[60] For a comprehensive list, see Appendix 2. See also: Lambert, *L'Architecture des Templiers*, p. 76; RCHM, *An Inventory of the Historical Monuments in the County of Northampton, Vol. 5, Archaeological Sites and churches in Northampton* (London, 1985), p. 61.

[61] S. Bradley and N. Pevsner, *London: The City Churches* (New York, 2002), pp. 133–4; Whatley, 'Localizing the Holy Land', p. 20.

[62] G. Coppack, 'The Round Chapel of St. Mary Magdalene', in R. Shoesmith and A. Johnson (eds), *Ludlow Castle: Its History & Buildings* (Logaston, 2000), pp. 145–54, at 149–50; G. Bresc-Bautier, 'Les imitations du Saint-Sépulcre de Jérusalem (IXe-XVe siècles): Archéologie d'une dévotion', *Revue d'histoire la spiritualité*, vol. 50, no. 1 (1974), pp. 319–42, at 322–3; M. Gervers, 'Rotundae Anglicanae', in *Actes du XXII congrès International d'Histoire de l'Art, Budapest 1969: Évolution génerale et développements régionaux en histoire de l'art* (Budapest, 1972), pp. 359–76, at 360–2.

Laywomen and the Crusade in England, 1150–1300

their association with crusade and the violent capture of the city.[63] We cannot assume a collective intention behind the foundation of these churches. However, these *rotundae anglicanae*, as they are sometimes called, show remarkably little architectural variation, indicating that there was some shared ethos.[64]

Women (and men) may have visited round churches as a form of proxy pilgrimage to ponder the earthly and celestial Jerusalem.[65] Helen Nicholson argues convincingly that non-members of the Templars or Hospitallers would have visited these orders' round churches and chapels to pray, view relics and attend funerals or initiation ceremonies.[66] Although these orders were, to a certain extent, expected to avoid interacting with women, they did consort with female family members. There are, frustratingly, no records of these visitors' opinions regarding round churches. However, considering that the round church at Northampton was visited by both Richard earl of Cornwall in 1239 and Prince Edward in 1270 before they departed on crusade, it may be conjectured that holy war would not have been far from people's minds when entering.

There were probably many other recreations of the Holy Land in the English landscape that contemporaries were familiar with, but that are less obvious to the modern observer. In the 1960s, a Holy Sepulchre Chapel was discovered within Winchester Cathedral. It is a small, unobtrusive niche, intricately covered in wall paintings. The feature has been dated on stylistic grounds to around the 1180s. It is an imitation of the Holy Sepulchre in "form, function, and painted scheme", rather than an architectural recreation like a round church.[67] This chapel, and others like

---

[63] C.E. Hundley, 'The English Round Church Movement', in R. Griffith-Jones and E. Fernie (eds), *Tomb and Temple: Re-Imagining the Sacred Buildings of Jerusalem* (Woodbridge, 2018), pp. 352–75, at 353; M. Gervers, 'The Use and Meaning of the Twelfth- and Thirteenth-Century Round Churches of England', in Griffith-Jones and Fernie, *Tomb and Temple*, pp. 376–86, at 378.

[64] Whatley, 'Localizing the Holy Land', p. 54; Hundley, 'The English Round Church Movement', pp. 357–8.

[65] R.G. Ousterhout, 'The Church of Santo Stefano: A "Jerusalem" in Bologna', *Gesta*, vol. 20, no. 2 (1981), pp. 311–21, at 311; S.M. Yeager, *Jerusalem in Medieval Narrative* (Cambridge, 2008), p. 138; Bresc-Bautier, 'Les imitations du Saint-Sépulcre de Jérusalem', pp. 327–8; L. Slater, 'Finding Jerusalem in Medieval Pontefract', *Northern History*, vol. 51, no. 2 (2014), pp. 211–20, at 214–5.

[66] Nicholson, 'At the Heart of Medieval London', pp. 11–12. See also: H.J. Nicholson, 'How Secret was the Templar Admission Ceremony? Evidence from the Proceedings in Britain and Ireland', in S. Sammarco (ed.), *Commilitones Christi: Miscellanea di studi per il Centro Italiano di Documentazione sull'Ordine del Tempio, MMXI-MMXVI* (Rome, 2016), pp. 85–98; H.J. Nicholson, 'The Military Religious Orders in the Towns of the British Isles', in D. Carraz (ed.), *Les Orderes Militaires dans la Ville Médiévale (1100–1350)* (Clermont-Ferrand, 2013), pp. 113–26, at 125.

[67] Whatley, 'Localizing the Holy Land', p. 121; P. Sheingorn, *The Easter Sepulchre in England* (Kalamazoo, 1987), pp. 6–9.

Figure 5. The twelfth-century Church of the Holy Sepulchre, Cambridge, a well preserved example of a 'round church'. (Reproduced by kind permission of Round Church Cambridge. © Christian Heritage Cambridge).

it, would have been used for liturgical services on Good Friday and Easter Sunday – dates that have been identified as key times for crusade preaching.[68] David Park has postulated that, given the timing of the chapel's construction (around the time the Christian Kingdom of Jerusalem fell to Saladin), its foundation could be linked to preparations and celebrations of the impending Third Crusade.[69] Secular rulers like Henry III and his son Edward I both redecorated important rooms of state with crusade imagery when they assumed the cross; ecclesiastics may have felt the same impulse.[70]

That same urge to commemorate crusade with physical monuments in England was felt by nobles, too. While on campaign during the Fifth Crusade (1217–21), John de Lacy the constable of Chester made sizeable grants to All Saints Church in Pontefract (Yorkshire). He asked for the burial ground to be expanded and the erection of a charnel house with a chapel dedicated to the Holy Sepulchre and Holy Cross.[71] John was especially conscious of his impending mortality at the time, and so he directed his heirs to arrange this Jerusalem-themed dedication. John lived, however, so it is hard to say whether his family actually committed to building the memorial. Either way, his intentions were clear.

Much smaller, mobile commemorations also circulated. The High Middle Ages saw an explosion in the number of people using seal matrices to affirm their agreement or 'signature' on letters, legal pronouncements and charters. Some of the designs of these seals referenced the owners' interest in crusading culture, featuring images of palm fronds, holy sites in the Jerusalem or, in Hugh de Neville's (d.1234) case, his violent encounter with an Asiatic lion during the Third Crusade.[72] Likewise,

---

[68] D. Park, 'The Wall Paintings of the Holy Sepulchre Chapel', in T.A. Heslop and V.A. Sekules (eds), *Medieval Art and Architecture at Winchester Cathedral* (Leeds, 1983), pp. 38–62, at 50; J. Bird, '"Far be it from me to Glory Save in the Cross of our Lord Jesus Christ" (Galatians 6:14): Crusade Preaching and Sermons for Good Friday and Holy Week', in M.E. Parker, B. Halliburton and A. Romine (eds), *Crusading in Art, Thought and Will* (Leiden, 2018), pp. 129–65, at 129–30.

[69] Park, 'The Wall Paintings of the Holy Sepulchre Chapel', p. 51. For a comprehensive list of medieval and renaissance Easter Sepulchre chapels in England, see: Sheingorn, *The Easter Sepulchre in England*, pp. 77–368.

[70] Reeve, 'The Painted Chamber at Westminster', p. 211; L.J. Whatley, 'Romance, Crusade, and the Orient in King Henry III of England's Royal Chambers', *Viator*, vol. 44, no. 2 (2013), pp. 175–98. Paul Binski, however, places far less emphasis on these kings' status as *crucesignati* when considering these commissions: P. Binski, *The Painted Chamber at Westminster* (London, 1986), pp. 111–2.

[71] R. Holmes (ed.), *The Chartulary of St. John of Pontefract*, 2 vols (Leeds, 1899–1902), at vol. 1, pp. 36–7, no. 21; Slater, 'Finding Jerusalem in Medieval Pontefract', pp. 212–15; Lloyd, *English Society and the Crusade*, pp. 161–2.

[72] G.M. Reynolds, 'Battling the Lion: Visual Commemorations of Crusade in Twelfth- and Thirteenth-Century Seals from the British Isles', *The Antiquaries Journal*, vol. 103 (2023), pp. 240–62.

relics, valuable silks and souvenirs of battle were all brought back from the Levant in huge quantities and became symbols of victory and divine providence.[73] King Alexander I of Scotland (r.1107–24), though not a crusader himself, bestowed an array of tokens on the Church of St Andrews (Fife) that he probably received from a returning Anglo-Norman crusader. They included an Arabian horse with its bridle, saddle, shield, silver lance and a precious cloth, as well as an assortment of Turkish weapons. These were duly displayed in the church in remembrance.[74] The twelfth-century writer of the *Foundation of Walden Monastery* comes across rather smugly when he recalled William de Mandeville III earl of Essex (d.1189) returning from crusade in 1170s:

> ...to all the churches in his fee he sent silken cloths for them to make chasubles or to adorn their altars, and to us one piece of cloth of marvellous workmanship which was better than the others. Before he set out on his pilgrimage he had already presented us with a fine chasuble, many silken cloths, and some hangings to adorn the church.[75]

William was very deliberately scattering tangible mementos of crusade (and his own achievements) across Essex. Similarly, when William II Longespée returned from the Barons' Crusade in 1242, he brought back an expensive red cloth decorated with yellow parrots and trees, which he gave to St Paul's Cathedral.[76] To men and women living in medieval England, these souvenirs could act as a touchstone with crusading culture, sometimes quite literally. One thirteenth-century Anglo-Norman noblewoman living in Glamorgan, Mabelle of Bonville, used a seal matrix for validating documents that incorporated an intaglio gem

---

[73] C. Morris, 'Picturing the Crusades: The Uses of Visual Propaganda, c. 1095–1250', in J. France and W.G. Zajac (eds), *The Crusades and Their Sources, Essays Presented to Bernard Hamilton* (Aldershot, 1998) (reprinted: Abingdon, 2016), pp. 195–215, at 207; N. Housley, *Fighting for the Cross: Crusading to the Holy Land* (New Haven, 2008), pp. 273–4.

[74] M.A. Bibby, 'Alexander's Arabian: Noble Steed or Fantastic Beast?', in M.A. Bibby and B.G. Scott (eds), *The Materiality of the Horse* (Budapest, 2020), pp. 175–202, at 179; Paul, *To Follow in Their Footsteps*.

[75] D. Greenway and L. Watkiss (eds and trans.), *The Book of the Foundation of Walden Monastery* (Oxford, 1999), bk ii, cap. 5, p. 59. For Latin, see p. 58, "ad omnes in feodo suo ecclesias pannos sericos ad casulas faciendas uel altaria honoranda, nobis uero mirandi operis unum ceteris meliorem transmisit. Casulam insuper bonam, pannos etiam sericos plures cum tapetis, ante peregrinationis sue tempus in decorem ecclesie nobie donauit".

[76] W. Sparrow Simpson, 'Two Inventories of the Cathedral Church of St. Paul, London, dated respectively 1245 and 1402', *Archaeologia*, vol. 1, no. 2 (1887), pp. 439–524, at 451 and 494.

inscribed with lines of Arabic.[77] Perhaps this precious stone had been taken as booty or bought as a souvenir.

Many of these items had deep religious significance that attracted attention. For instance, supposed pieces of the True Cross on which Christ was crucified were brought to England by crusaders and gifted to religious houses, turning the sites into places of pilgrimage. Norton Priory (Cheshire) received a piece from Geoffrey of Dutton when he came home from the Fifth Crusade in the 1220s.[78] Likewise, Bromholm Priory (Norfolk) received a piece in 1205 from a priest returning from the Fourth Crusade's sack of Constantinople.[79] Bromholm, in particular, became deeply renowned for this relic. Geoffrey Chaucer even had the character of Symkyn's Wife in his *Canterbury Tales* call out for divine assistance with: "Help, holy cros of Bromehom! [*sic*]".[80]

Laywomen living in medieval England inhabited a landscape that was brimming with reminders of crusade. It was an integral facet of contemporary culture, and the artistic responses that it inspired would have agitated a reaction. Although we seldom get glimpses of women's genuine opinions on the crusade-themed poetry, art or objects in their world, their daily lives were profoundly linked with the culture of holy war. It is hard to speculate on how these media impacted on their outlook on crusade and their place in it. Nevertheless, laywomen would have been mindful of a spiritual and material bridge between themselves and the events in the Holy Land and beyond.

---

[77] P.R. Schofield, E.A. News, S.M. Johns and J.A. McEwan (eds), *Seals and Society: Medieval Wales, the Welsh Marches and their English Border Region* (Cardiff, 2016), p. 134, no. 47.

[78] K. Hurlock, 'A Transformed Life? Geoffrey of Dutton, the Fifth Crusade, and the Holy Cross of Norton', *Northern History*, vol. 54, no. 1 (2017), pp. 15–27, at 18–20.

[79] Hurlock, *Britain, Ireland and the Crusades*, p. 123.

[80] Geoffrey Chaucer, *The Canterbury Tales*, J. Mann (ed.) (London, 2005), p. 157.

2

The Papacy and Incentives to Support

But, to those who do not make the journey in person, but send suitable men at their expense according to their ability and income, and to those also who even at the expense of another, make the journey personally, we grant the full pardon of their sins.

(Pope Innocent III in his crusade encyclical *Quia maior*, in 1213)[1]

When Pope Urban II (r.1085–99) stood at the Council of Clermont in 1095, he set the First Crusade in motion. He framed this new enterprise as a means for the laity to gain plenary indulgences.[2] Exactly what that meant to the people who were there, or those who subsequently heard the news, appears to have been surprisingly varied. There certainly was no consensus on what the crusade's spiritual reward was, or under what exact circumstances one could win it. Over the course of the twelfth and thirteenth centuries contemporaries developed diverse understandings. It was generally believed, however, that an indulgence for crusading could involve the remittance of temporal punishment. That is to say: a person could shorten the amount of time they would inevitably have to spend in Purgatory before arriving at heaven. Alternatively, some people believed that, depending on a person's degree of participation in crusade, they could be absolved of their sins entirely – a 'clean slate' so to speak.[3] As an alternative to entering a monastery, crusade offered laypeople an opportunity to temporarily become penitents as *milites Christi* – "soldiers of

---

[1] Bird, Peters and Powell, *Crusade and Christendom*, p. 109. For original Latin, see: *Patrologiae Latinae cursus completus*, 222 vols, J.P. Migne (ed.) (Paris, 1844–1903), vol. 216, p. 818, "Eis autem qui non in personis propriis illuc accesserint, sed in suis duntaxat expensis juxta facultatem et qualitatem suam viros idoneos destinarint, et illis similiter qui licet in alienis expensis, in propriis tamen personis accesserint, plenam suorum concedimus veniam peccatorum.".
[2] J.A. Brundage, *Medieval Canon Law and the Crusader* (Madison, 1969), pp. 31–3; J. Riley-Smith, *The First Crusade and the Idea of Crusading* (London, 1993) (reprinted: London, 2003), pp. 27–8.
[3] Bysted, *The Crusade Indulgence*, pp. 10–15.

Christ" – before returning to their secular lives, spiritually cleansed.[4] This bargain was overwhelmingly appealing for thousands of medieval people.

Although crusading was often described as an ideally masculine endeavour, a particular pursuit of the male knightly classes, crusade indulgences were not limited to men and certainly not just warriors.[5] Anyone who wished to take crusading vows and travel to the Holy Land, or other theatres, could qualify for an indulgence, and many women took this opportunity.[6] During the twelfth century, however, in an effort to recruit greater numbers of capable male warriors, women were increasingly discouraged from joining expeditions to the Holy Land.[7] Many women remained enthusiastic in spite of this, and so medieval popes increasingly tried to direct women's enthusiasm toward efforts that the papacy felt was more suitable than travel to the East. The spiritual rewards of crusade were used to incentivise women's fiscal and spiritual aid for crusade. These papal directives were not, it must be said, the Machiavellian schemes of individual popes, but rather were a product of a wider community of churchmen, the papal court and broader secular societal pressures and gendered perspectives.

Laypeople had innumerable motivations for participating in holy war, but the general appeal is currently thought to have lain in the spiritual benefits of indulgences.[8] This chapter will consider the messages and directives that the papacy angled toward women in England, and how these reflected women's attitudes toward supporting crusade as opposed to embarking on it.

Incentives to Remain

When the murmurings of the First Crusade began, people were quick to develop ideas about who exactly should go. At a local level, some volunteers would have been turned away from crusade recruiters or advised to support the movement in other ways. Most of this was probably done in an arbitrary or *ad hoc* manner, and had more to do with individual recruiters or clergymen's prejudices and beliefs than any overarching crusade policy. For example, we know that many women joined the First Crusade, marched with these armies and settled in the Near East. Nevertheless,

---

[4] On crusade as penance, see: P.J. Cole, *The Preaching of the Crusades to the Holy Land, 1095–1270* (Cambridge, 1991), pp. 142–76.

[5] Bull, *Knightly Piety*, pp. 166–7; Maier, 'Propaganda and Masculinity', pp. 23–6.

[6] See: Hodgson, *Women, Crusading and the Holy Land in Historical Narrative*; Nicholson, *Women and the Crusades*.

[7] Kedar, 'The Passenger List of a Crusader Ship', p. 279; Evans, 'Commutation of Crusade Vows', pp. 219–28; Bysted, *The Crusade Indulgence*, p. 161; Nicholson, 'Women's Involvement in the Crusades', p. 55.

[8] Bull, *Knightly Piety*, p. 282; Riley-Smith, *The First Crusaders*, p. 21; Housley, *Contesting the Crusades*, p. 79; N. Morton, *Encountering Islam on the First Crusade* (Cambridge, 2016), pp. 94–6.

The Papacy and Incentives to Support

in 1098, when one French noblewoman named Emerias de Alteias took a crusade vow and asked her bishop for his blessing, he instead convinced Emerias to stay behind and commute her vow by founding a hospice.[9] Similar attitudes surfaced during campaigns themselves. A couple generations later, in the 1140s, the Anglo-Flemish leaders of a fleet of crusades laid down a series of rules for the army and sailors to abide by. The writer of the book *De Expugnatione Lyxbonensi* claimed that one of the rules was: "women should not go out in public".[10] This statement is the last reference to women on this campaign in the whole text. Over the course of the twelfth century, the papacy would develop a more formalised sense of who should not go on crusade, and what they should do instead.

Our earliest reference to crusade indulgences being offered not to warriors but to people supporting crusade is in a letter written by Pope Adrian IV (r.1154–9). Adrian – born Nicholas Breakspear, in Hertfordshire – sent a letter in 1157 to Samson of Mauvoisin archbishop of Reims. He urged Samson to encourage more combatants to go to the aid of the Holy Land. Adrian was aware, though, that many people in Christendom were sympathetic to the idea of crusade but unlikely or unable to physically take part. Therefore, Adrian further proposed that anyone who was unable to go could give horses, arms and other necessaries, "for the salvation of their souls and the remission of sin which they are eager to address".[11] Adrian's request for arms and equipment appears to have been aimed at civic authorities who would have had stores of armaments, or at nobles who might have been capable of disposing of some. There is nothing in his language to suggest that women with access to such wealth would have been excluded from this promise. That said, it does not appear that Adrian pressed the offer he suggested.[12] His letter nevertheless represents a milestone in papal thinking on crusade. It demonstrates an awareness of the wide appeal that crusade held for laypeople and, perhaps, that those who were already supporting crusade believed that their actions formed an aspect of holy war.

Adrian's successors in office did not issue similar offers to the wider laity for another thirty years; the next indication of similar actions taking place appeared during Urban III's papacy (r.1185–7). In the years before his pontificate, the

---

[9] Riley-Smith, *The First Crusaders*, p. 108.

[10] C.W. David (ed. and trans.), *The Conquest of Lisbon: De Expugnatione Lyxbonensi*, foreword and bibliography by J. Phillips (New York, 2001), p. 57. For Latin, see p. 56, "Ne item mulieres in publico prodirent".

[11] M.J.J. Brial (ed.), *Recueil des Historiens des Gaules et de la France* (Paris, 1808), vol. 15, p. 682, "pro animarum suarum salute et peccatorum remedio illuc studeant destinare". I was made aware of this source through: C. Tyerman, *The Invention of the Crusades* (Basingstoke, 1998), pp. 14–5.

[12] Tyerman, 'Were There Any Crusades in the Twelfth Century?', p. 561. For more on Adrian IV's wider interest in crusade, see: D.J. Smith, 'The Abbot-Crusader: Nicholas Breakspear in Catalonia', in B. Bolton and A.J. Duggan (eds), *Adrian IV The English Pope (1154–1159)* (Aldershot, 2003), pp. 29–39.

Military Orders had suffered several setbacks in the East. One of their most notably losses occurred when Saladin besieged the Templars' unfinished fortress at Jacob's Ford in 1179, massacring the defenders.[13] Much like Adrian IV, Urban III felt he could drum up support from the laity to keep these orders afloat. He tried to galvanise laypeople in England by asking local clergy to encourage them to help the Knights Templar: "induce the rulers and barons and other faithful and enjoin them for remission of their sins ... in mercifully helping the brethren of the Temple with horses and arms".[14] Urban III's language was similar Adrian IV's. Urban was equally vague on how this process would work, who would administer these indulgences and how these items would be collected – this was all academic. Whatever he planned, it was too little too late, on a monumental scale.

In 1187, Christendom was rocked by events in the Holy Land. Saladin shattered the armies of the Latin Kingdom of Jerusalem at the Battle of Hattin, capturing King Guy de Lusignan (d.1194) and the Relics of the True Cross that were carried into battle. Saladin pressed on, retaking much of the Crusader States's territory.[15] Supposedly, the shock of hearing this news caused Urban III to literally drop dead. He was succeeded by Gregory VIII (r. Oct–Dec 1187), whose papacy was a baptism of fire that only got hotter. News soon arrived that Saladin had kept up his momentum and retaken the city of Jerusalem. Encapsulating the gravity of these events to Latin contemporaries is nearly impossible. Walter Bower – a fifteenth-century chronicler and abbot of Inchcolm Abbey (Scotland) – believed that Jerusalem's fall was so monumental that it caused a subtle bodily disfigurement amongst generations of Christians. He used an array of older source material for his chronicle, which may have informed his claim that:

> Children born after 1187, the year in which the cross of the Lord was captured, have no more than twenty-two or twenty-three teeth, whereas those born before that date usually have thirty or thirty-one.[16]

---

[13] P.D. Mitchell, Y. Nagar and R. Ellenblum, 'Weapon Injuries in the 12th Century Crusader Garrison of Vadum Iacob Castle, Galilee', *International Journal of Osteoarchaeology*, vol. 16 (2006), pp. 145–55.

[14] Gerald of Wales copied the letter, see: Gerald of Wales, *Instruction for a Ruler, De Principis Instructione*, R. Bartlett (ed. and trans.) (Oxford, 2018), p. 523. For Latin see p. 522, "mandamus atque precipimus, quatinus principes et barones et fideles alios crebris monitis et exhortacionibus inducatis et iniungatis | eis in remissionem peccatorum, ut Christianitati iam dicte terre pro Deo et salute sua potenti manu succurrant, et fratribus milicie Templi in equis et armis, quibus terram illam melius defendere ualent, non differant misericorditer subuenire".

[15] J. Phillips, *The Life and Legend of the Sultan Saladin* (London, 2019), pp. 172–205.

[16] Walter Bower, *Scotichronicon*, 9 vols, D. Watt, *et al* (eds and trans.) (Aberdeen, 1993–8), at vol. 4, bk. viii, p. 377. For original Latin, see p. 376, "Ab ipso autem anno domini mclxxxvii quo crux Domini capta est infantes qui postea nati sunt non nisi xxii vel xxiii dentes habent, cum antea xxx vel xxxi habere solent".

The Papacy and Incentives to Support

Suffice it to say that Saladin's capture of Jerusalem acted as an overnight catalyst for debates over the direction and necessity of the crusade movement. Gregory VIII reacted by issuing the papal bull *Audita Tremendi* in October of that same year. This declaration called on secular leaders to assemble (what would later be known as) the Third Crusade. Gregory indicated that all Christendom was responsible for the success of this crusade, not simply the men-at-arms who would embark. The bull stipulated that for the following five years, every Friday during Advent, all Christians were to fast and perform intercessory and penitential psalms and prayers for the recovery of the Holy Land.[17] The version of *Audita Tremendi* that was sent to Germany was very clear on this stance: "it is therefore, incumbent upon all of us to choose to amend our sins by voluntary chastisement and to turn to the Lord our God with penance and works of piety".[18]

By leading spiritually pure lives and avoiding sin, every Christian was entreating God's favour on Christendom's endeavours. To put it another way: the propaganda claimed that if Christians confessed their sins, they would ensure the crusade was brought to a swift victory. There is very little in the surviving records of Gregory VIII's pontificate that indicates that he offered indulgences to the laity for financially sponsoring crusade. This is somewhat unsurprising given how brief his time in office was. However, his successor, Clement III (r.1187–91) claimed he acted in keeping with Gregory's practices. Clement sent a letter in February 1188 to the archbishop of Canterbury that clearly suggested this:

> You should also induce your subordinates effectually to do this, so that, since you and they will have been 'partakers in the suffering', you ought to be, as the Apostle says, partakers also of that 'consolation' and remission that was granted formerly by our predecessor of good memory, Pope Gregory, and afterwards by us, generally to those who set out there [to the Holy Land] or send appropriate help.[19]

---

[17] Rousseau, 'Home Front and Battlefield', p. 35.

[18] L. Riley-Smith and J. Riley-Smith (eds and trans.), *The Crusades: Idea and Reality, 1095–1274* (London, 1981), p. 66, no. 8. For Latin, see: A. Chroust (ed.), *Monumenta Germaniae Historica, Scriptores rerum Germanicarum, Nova Series* (Berlin, 1928), vol. 5, pp. 8–9, "Unde hoc universis et cogitandum et eligendum imminet, ut peccata nostra castigatione voluntaria emendemus et per penitentiam et opera pietatis convertamur ad dominum deum nostrum".

[19] Gerald of Wales, *Instruction for a Ruler*, p. 583. For Latin, see p. 582, "Subiectos quoque uestros efficaciter inducatis ad hoc ipsum agendum, ut, cum uos et illi 'socii fueritis passionis', debeatis esse, quemadmodum dixit apostolus, et participes 'consolacionis' ac remissionis illius que proficiscentibus illuc uel congrua suffragia transmittentibus prius a predecessore nostro bone memorie Gregorio papa et postmodum a nobis generaliter est indulta".

The historian Ane Bysted argues that a trace of Gregory's rhetoric concerning indulgences for financial support may be seen in his decree, *Compilatio secundae*, which vaguely promised privileges for those who aided crusade.[20]

The letter that Pope Clement III sent to the archbishop of Canterbury outlined his plan to offer indulgences to those who supported the impending Third Crusade.[21] Clement also urged the archbishop to lead this drive, asking him to personally send men and equipment, so that others would be inspired by his example.[22] On 27 May, Clement further specified that everyone who sent aid would gain a remission of sin.[23] Like his predecessors, he again did not explain who would confirm the indulgence or how the donations would be collected. Still, Clement kept his language around indulgences quite open-ended, allowing for any of the faithful to capitalise on this offer.

There was a clear feeling by the 1180s that many Latin Christians wanted to connect with crusade and reap the spiritual benefits of the movement. Despite this, the papacy appears to have been unsure of exactly how to engage with this mood. There was an anxiety that they might inadvertently prompt mass 'popular crusades'. This had famously happened during the First Crusade. This expedition was made up of numerous contingents that travelled independently. The contingent led by the charismatic preacher Peter the Hermit – the Peasants' Crusade – proved difficult to check. Peter's army strained diplomatic relations with Byzantine allies, most of the participants accomplished little and nearly all of them perished in ambushes in Anatolia. There were various popular crusading surges that followed later in the period. The uncontrolled armies of the so-called Children's Crusade in 1212, for example, wreaked havoc while roaming French- and German-speaking parts of Europe.[24] For the Latin Church, the problem lay in how they could harness popular feeling, without whipping up a storm that did more harm in Europe than in the Holy Land.

Innocent III and his Legacy

It was not until the pontificate of Pope Innocent III (r.1198–1216) that women were targeted explicitly in offers of indulgences for crusade support. This has been seen as a watershed moment in crusade history, in which Latin Christian women's aspirations catalysed papal policies.[25] In 1213, Innocent III issued the

---

[20] Bysted, *The Crusade Indulgence*, p. 160.
[21] Bysted, *The Crusade Indulgence*, p. 160.
[22] Gerald of Wales, *Instruction for a Ruler*, pp. 582–3.
[23] P. Jaffé (ed.), *Regesta Pontificum Romanorum, ab Condita Ecclesiae ad annum post Christum Natum MCXCVIII*, 2 vols, 2nd edn (Lipsiae, 1885–8), at vol. 2, p. 546, no. 16252.
[24] See: Dickson, *The Children's Crusade*.
[25] Rousseau, 'Home Front and Battlefield', pp. 39–40. See also: Bysted, *The Crusade Indulgence*, p. 162; Parker, 'Papa et Pecunia', p. 7. For more on Innocent and his

The Papacy and Incentives to Support

crusading encyclical *Quia maior*. The document called for the Fifth Crusade (1217–21). Innocent III did not live to see this campaign unfold, but his actions ahead of it shaped crusading culture for the following century. He stipulated that he would offer a full remittance of sin for anyone (without specifying their gender) who was unable to go in person, but who instead covered the total costs of a man's crusade.[26]

The language he used was crucial, as it cemented the notion that it was a masculine endeavour to go on crusade, while maintaining that supporting could be more gender inclusive. Furthermore, Innocent III promised that if a person made donations towards an man's crusade costs, they would receive a partial remittance of sin in proportion to their gift.[27] This bargain was dependent upon the donor's sense of devotion. Innocent III's phrasing may be interpreted as encouraging those who could not, or would not, travel to the East to identify with crusade and believe in the piousness and usefulness of their aid.

Women, specifically, were also invited to participate in penitential liturgical processions for crusade. These were to be held every month, involving a "separate general procession of men, and, where possible, separate for women".[28] Innocent III went a step further, demanding that every church in Christendom be outfitted with a chest, for clergy and laity, "men and women", to place monetary donations toward the costs of the crusade.[29] This order was particularly enduring and bishops in England – such as Walter Giffard archbishop of York (r.1266–79) – would routinely call for these sorts of chests to be produced and placed in churches within their bishoprics.[30] Nearly a hundred years after Innocent III made that stipulation, it continued to inform papal approaches to crusade funding. In 1308, Pope Clement V (r.1305–14) was adamant in calling for chests to again be placed in all of Christendom's churches to gather donations for a renewed crusade.[31] Given the repeated need to commission new crusade chests, it is likely that clerics or congregations repurposed them in the periods between large campaigns. There was obviously a significant number of these objects circulating. The fabric of the medieval parish church was thus restructured to ensure those at home would participate in holy war.

---

ideas around masculinity, particularly in the context of crusade, see: Day, 'Sorrow, Masculinity and Papal Authority', pp. 201–26.

[26] Bird, Peters and Powell, *Crusade and Christendom*, p. 109.
[27] Bird, Peters and Powell, *Crusade and Christendom*, p. 109.
[28] Bird, Peters and Powell, *Crusade and Christendom*, p. 111. For original Latin, see: *Patrologiae Latinae cursus completus*, vol. 216, p. 820, "seorsum virorum, ac seorsum, ubi fieri poterit, mulierum".
[29] Bird, Peters and Powell, *Crusade and Christendom*, p. 112. For original Latin, see: *Patrologiae Latinae cursus completus*, vol. 216, p. 821, "viri et mulieres".
[30] W. Brown (ed.), *The Register of Walter Giffard, Lord Archbishop of York, 1266–1279* (Durham, 1904), p. 277, no. 857.
[31] S. Menache, *Clement V* (Cambridge, 1998) (reprinted: 2002), p. 109.

Rather than ostracise women from the crusade movement or circumvent the topic, Innocent III defined and incentivised a feminine support role. He firmly believed in the importance of Christendom's total involvement in holy war. In 1212, he had personally organised liturgical processions in Rome to entreat divine favour for crusade, and he demanded laywomen's participation.[32] These mass processions were planned to (in theory) coincide with King Alfonso VIII of Castile's (r.1158–1214) battle with the army of the Almohad Caliphate at Las Navas de Tolosa. The formal inclusion of women in the processions became something of a model. For the pope, this structure allowed Latin women to perform an act of crusade that mirrored the combat taking place abroad.[33]

We can be certain this kind of rhetoric reached England directly and early on in Innocent III's pontificate. The chronicler Roger of Howden (d.1202) transcribed a letter dated 13 August 1198, which Innocent III had sent to the diocese of York. In this letter, the pope outlined his stance: he would grant remission of sins to anyone funding crusaders, proportional to the donors' generosity.[34] Such attitudes toward crusade funding may have been quickly disseminated. Preachers like Fulk of Neuilly and Eustace of Fly came from France to tour England in 1198 and, according to Roger of Howden, they railed against the sin of usury – a fairly nebulous concept that is difficult to define, but generally centred on medieval prohibitions against Christians charging interest on loans.[35] Attention to this topic suggests that, in line with Innocent III's letter, Eustace and his colleagues were interested in ensuring that crusade was not funded sinfully. It is plausible, then, that they were preaching to groups of potential crusade supporters. However, nothing certain is known of the content of their preaching, other than it was not especially impactful.[36] Despite these preachers' shortcomings, Innocent III's concepts of ideal crusading gender roles continued to be spread in England. Another chronicler, Roger of Wendover (d.1236), transcribed a letter that the pope sent to all the clergy in England in 1215. In it, Innocent III emphasised that clerics should impress upon the laity that only male warriors ought to go abroad to the Holy Land: a reminder that would not have been necessary unless considerable numbers of women were joining expeditions at the time.[37]

---

[32] Maier, 'Mass, the Eucharist and the Cross', p, 353.
[33] Lester, 'A Shared Imitation', p. 356. See also: M.C. Gaposchkin, 'The Pre-Battle Processions of the First Crusade and the Creation of Militant Christian *Communitas*', *Material Religion*, vol. 14, no. 4 (2018), pp. 454–68.
[34] Roger of Howden, *Chronica Magistri Rogeri de Houedene*, 4 vols, W. Stubbs (ed.) (London, 1868–71), at vol. 4, p. 74. On Roger of Howden, see: M. Staunton, *The Historians of Angevin England* (Oxford, 2017), pp. 51–66.
[35] Roger of Howden, *Chronica Magistri Rogeri de Houedene*, vol. 4, p. 76.
[36] Cole, *The Preaching of the Crusades to the Holy Land*, p. 88.
[37] Roger of Wendover, *Rogeri de Wendover liber qui dicitur Flores Historiarum ab anno domini MCLIV annoque Henrici Anglorum Regis Secundi Primo*, 3 vols, H.G. Hewlett (ed.) (London, 1886–9), at vol. 2, pp. 156–7.

The Papacy and Incentives to Support

Despite Innocent III's attempt to galvanise women's support, some of his directives betray a fear that laywomen might hamper his crusading vision. In medieval Europe, there was a persistent perception, or perhaps better described as an anxiety, that women would inhibit crusade. This ultimately stemmed from concerns that the obligations of marriage vows superseded crusade vows. Although criminals were sometimes sent on crusade and many commoners would have been obliged to follow their crusading lord, in theory, people were only supposed to take crusade vows voluntarily. Canon lawyers considered that if a married individual took a crusade vow without their spouse's blessing, this might, inadvertently or otherwise, contravene their sacred marriage vows that forbade a spouse from abandoning their partner. In effect, they feared that some crusaders were acting sinfully and illegally (as well as immorally). To alleviate this confusion, canon law made the provision that a married person had to have their spouse's express permission before embarking on holy war.[38] This had a knock-on effect: when crusades were mustering, the clerical leadership of these expeditions were often uneasy, contemplating the possibility that wives might deny their husbands leave to go and therefore deplete the number of recruits.

Pope Innocent III took drastic action to avoid this potential hinderance. In 1201, he sanctioned a decretal – *Ex multa* – which nullified the need for crusaders to get spousal consent for their pilgrimage. In the version of this letter that was sent to the archbishop of Canterbury, it simply said that husbands no longer needed their wives' consent to go on crusade.[39] The significance of this decretal should not be understated. It undermined a woman's right to seek justice in an ecclesiastical court if her husband deserted her. The decretal remained in force throughout the thirteenth century, though some canon lawyers still considered that it conflicted with the oaths of loyalty and cohabitation that were made during marriage ceremonies.[40] Despite *Ex multa*, those who preached holy war remained cautious that spouses might dissuade would-be crusaders. The French theologian and chronicler Jacques de Vitry, writing between 1225 and 1240, pointedly noted that during his own preaching ahead of the Fifth Crusade (1217–21), one wife locked her husband in their home so that he could not hear the sermon.[41]

Innocent III's approach to furthering crusade was certainly shrewd; he strove to reward those who supported the endeavour, and he mitigated the power of those

---

[38] Brundage, 'The Crusader's Wife', pp. 430–3; Park, *Papal Protection and the Crusader*, p. 39.
[39] Cheney and Cheney, *The Letters of Pope Innocent III*, pp. 57–8, no. 350. For context, see: Brundage, 'The Crusader's Wife', pp. 434–5.
[40] Brundage, 'The Crusader's Wife', pp. 437–9.
[41] James of Vitry, 'Sermo II', in Maier, *Crusade Propaganda and Ideology*, pp. 100–27, at 121, cpt 37. For the dating of his writing see p. 9. The woman was unsuccessful in her attempt, and the man was able to escape and take his vow. Jacques used this story to show the merits of crusade, and the futility of opposing it.

who might object to it. His successor, Pope Honorius III (r.1216–27), was eager to maintain the momentum by explicitly affirming the papacy's stance on crusade support.[42] In 1217, Honorius III sent a letter to the archbishop of Tyre, in which he stated that members of the clergy and laywomen, particularly wealthy ones, should avoid active service in the Holy Land and should instead strive to gain the spiritual rewards of crusade by sponsoring warriors.[43] Pierre-Vincent Claverie has stressed that these stipulations on indulgences concretely guaranteed supporters the same spiritual reward as warriors.[44] Similar directives were sent to England throughout the thirteenth century. They typically offered indulgences to those who contributed toward crusade collections or financially supported individual crusaders, and the language did not vary dramatically from that of *Quia maior*.[45]

A new shift in papal attempts to rally support for crusade began under Pope Gregory IX (r.1227–41). What had at first been an invitation to take part soon became an expectation. Gregory IX was not only adamant that all Christians could take part in crusade, in one form or another, but that they all had a responsibility to do so. In 1234, he drafted a renewed call for crusade in the encyclical, *Rachel suum videns*.[46] Penny Cole has pointed out that the chronicler Roger of Wendover had access to a version of this encyclical (presumably the one that circulated England), which not only promised indulgences to people who offered money toward crusade but also those who gave "advice or timely aid" (*consilium vel auxilium opportunum*) to crusaders.[47] In other words, pressuring people to go on crusade became an identifiable (and an incentivised) form of support for holy war.

Gregory IX's pontificate also saw the first significant implementation of a unique money-making exercise: crusade-vow redemptions. This involved an individual initially taking a legally (and spiritually) binding vow to go on crusade, only to, sometimes immediately, pay a fee proportionate to their wealth and standing in lieu of actually going on crusade, thus commuting their vow.[48] Papal

---

[42] Park, *Papal Protection and the Crusader*, p. 102. See also: T.W. Smith, *Curia and Crusade: Pope Honorius III and the Recovery of the Holy Land: 1216–1227* (Turnhout, 2017), pp. 297–342; J. Vandeburie, 'The Preacher and the Pope: Jacques de Vitry and Honorius III at the Time of the Fifth Crusade (1216–27)', in J.L. Bird (ed.), *Papacy, Crusade, and Christian-Muslim Relations* (Amsterdam, 2018), pp. 131–54.

[43] P. Pressutti (ed.), *Regesta Honorii Papae III*, 2 vols (Rome, 1888–95), at vol. 1, p. 93, n. 529.

[44] P.V. Claverie, *Honorius III et l'Orient (1216–1227)* (Leiden, 2013), p. 40. Cf: Park, *Papal Protection and the Crusader*, p. 99.

[45] E.g., Innocent IV's letters to the Bishop of Worcester ahead of the Seventh Crusade: Berger, *Les Registres D'Innocent IV*, vol. 1, p. 444, no. 2939.

[46] Bird, Peters and Powell, *Crusade and Christendom*, pp. 269–70, no. 30.

[47] Translation and analysis by: Cole, *The Preaching of the Crusades to the Holy Land*, p. 160. For original Latin, see: Roger of Wendover, *Flores Historiarum*, vol. 3, p. 106.

[48] I.L. Bass, 'The Crozier and the Cross: Crusading and the English Episcopate, c.1170–1313' (Unpublished PhD Thesis, Manchester Metropolitan University, 2019), pp. 118–25;

coffers could be filled and used for warriors destined for the Holy Land, while the vow redeemers enjoyed the spiritual rewards of crusade without departing. The laypeople who participated would have received an indulgence that was, again, in theory, equal to that which could be earned by going on crusade.

The concept of crusade-vow redemption already existed well before Gregory IX's time in office, but he is thought to have been the first to systematically promote it across Christendom, doing so ahead of the Barons' Crusade (1234–41). The practice of redeeming vows would become one of the defining features of thirteenth-century crusade preparations.[49] I would argue that by briefly becoming *crucesignati*, medieval individuals may have felt more connected with the movement than if they had simply donated cash. Perhaps this was the critical aspect behind the implementation of this funding tool. All members of society took part in vow redemption, but it was typically aimed at those considered unsuited for battle, as well as the wealthy whose proportionate donation would be that much greater.[50]

Reflections of Reality?

The policies that the papacy had developed around crusade support were not wholly novel ideas. There was no point in offering incentives that did not resonate with the laity's concerns. Therefore, it has been suggested that these papal strategies capitalised on existing known desires amongst women and other groups who were marginalised by the rhetoric that championed martial crusading.[51] By interrogating the papal mandates sent to England, specifically, it may be possible to gain some idea of women's aspirations to support crusade within this kingdom.

One of Pope Innocent IV's (r.1242–54) decretals offers a tremendous insight on this theme. Not long after the crusading forces of King Louis IX of France were crushed at the Battle of al Mansurah (1250), Innocent IV began considering relief efforts to send more forces to the Holy Land. On 3 September 1252, the pope sent a letter to the archbishops of Canterbury and York giving "authorisation to grant the wives of crusaders the same pardon for sins as their husbands".[52] Innocent IV intimated that women's sins could be cleansed simply if their husbands went on crusade. This is not a general decretal but rather appears quite isolated. It only applied to the Kingdom of England or lands subject to Henry III, seemingly without any other related letters being sent to other kingdoms or principalities at this time. No other letters within Innocent's registers refer to wives receiving

---

Tamminen, *Crusade Preaching and the Ideal Crusader*, p. 227.
[49] Lower, *The Barons' Crusade*, pp. 13–7; Maier, *Preaching the Crusades*, pp. 135–40.
[50] Maier, *Preaching the Crusades*, p. 135.
[51] Rousseau, 'Home Front and Battlefield', p. 39.
[52] Berger, *Les Registres D'Innocent IV*, vol. 3, p. 111, no. 5980, "Licentia concedendi uxoribus crucesignatorum quod eamdem, quam viri sui, peccatorum veniam habeant".

Laywomen and the Crusade in England, 1150–1300

indulgences on behalf of their husbands' crusades. Nevertheless, the ideas coming through this letter are extremely valuable for our understanding of the thinking at the time.

Interpreting the implications of this letter is complex, but presents some interesting possibilities. It may be that the letter was both an attempt to dissuade women in England from joining expeditions, while also incentivising them to support crusade.[53] This perhaps betrays something of a common clerical anxiety that women would dissuade their husbands from going on crusade, and hinder the movement, as we have seen. However, there seems to be more to this letter. The text presumed that an English crusade was imminent. The entirety of the text has not survived, but in one incomplete sentence it states, "the illustrious King of England departs in aid of the Holy Land".[54] This is a reference to the vow that King Henry III had made to go on crusade in 1250, his second of three vows. He would never actually depart – a source of deep contention between him and the papacy.[55] Only a day before sending the letter, Innocent had ordered the archbishops of Canterbury and York, and the bishops of Hereford, Ely and Durham, to gather the money that they had collected for the recovery of the Holy Land and hand it over to King Henry, for his "journey overseas".[56] Innocent hoped that Henry would go on crusade, and so he wanted to create a situation that ensured Henry do so. By offering women indulgences if their husbands went on crusade and simultaneously placing the revenue of crusade taxes in Henry's hand, Innocent hoped to create an influx of crusade recruits and pressurise Henry III to lead them.

It is plausible that Innocent IV's letter refined and ratified ideas about the links between a crusader and their kinfolk that were already circulating in England and perhaps further afield. Individuals were already making use of crusade proxies by this time. This usually involved a person taking a crusade vow and then – either because they became sick, there was a threat of war or they simply did not want to make the journey to the Holy Land – they covered the costs of a proxy to go on crusade/pilgrimage in their stead. Both the proxy and the sponsor were thought to gain the spiritual reward of crusade through these arrangements: one was risking their physical safety, the other their financial security.[57] It is not

---

[53] See also: E. Siberry, *Criticism of Crusading 1095–1274* (Oxford, 1985), p. 46.

[54] Berger, *Les Registres D'Innocent IV*, vol. 3, p. 111, no. 5980, "[…] illustris regis Anglie proficiscentium in subsidium Terre Sancte".

[55] Lloyd, *English Society and the Crusade*, pp. 58 and 208–18. See also: Purcell, *Papal Crusading Policy*, p. 81.

[56] A. Potthast (ed.), *Regesta Pontificum Romanorum, inde ab a post Christum Natum MCXCVIII ad a. MCCCIV*, 2 vols (Berlin, 1873–5), at vol. 2, p. 1212, no. 14704, "trans marinum".

[57] C. Tyerman, *God's War: A New History of the Crusades* (Cambridge, 2006), pp. 613–4. See also Kathryn Hurlock's discussion of individuals performing the vows

impossible that some people simply affirmed that they were going on crusade on behalf of a family member, hoping to spread the divine rewards. Innocent IV's decree indicates that the ideas around proxy pilgrimage may have been taken a step further by some people in England. By the mid-thirteenth century, simply being related to a crusader was considered to be highly prestigious and gave people more social standing.[58] Perhaps there was also, to some extent, a belief that by going on a crusade, a person could not only bring good repute to their family but also gain God's favour.

There are some wider indications that women in England were receptive to the papacy's offers of indulgences for those who pressed, prayed or paid for crusade. Matthew Paris reported that Ela of Salisbury (d.1261), abbess of Lacock (Wiltshire), had dreams of her son, William II Longespée, while William was on the Seventh Crusade. Ela supposedly dreamt that her son was killed at the Battle of al Mansurah; months later she was told that her son had been a casualty and that his death occurred on the exact day of her dream. Rather than becoming distressed, Ela rejoiced and believed that her son's death was martyrdom, and that she too "would be moved more quickly to the heights of the heavenly Kingdom".[59] We cannot be sure that Ela had these apparently prophetic dreams or that she thought her son's crusade would bring her salvation. Irrespective of the reality, Matthew Paris portrayed this as a model way for noblewomen in thirteenth-century England to react to such news.

Similar concepts may have had limited currency in German-speaking parts of Europe at an earlier period.[60] Hartmann von Aue, probably a crusader himself, composed a poem c.1188 in which he remarked:

> If a woman sends off her beloved
> On a crusade with the right intention,
> She receives half the reward for it
> If she so conducts herself at home
> That she deserves to have chaste words spoken of her.
> Let her pray for them both here
> As he goes off to fight for them both there.[61]

---

of *crucesignati* who died intestate: Hurlock, 'A Transformed Life?', p. 16; Hurlock, *Britain, Ireland and the Crusades*, p. 88.
58 Paul and Schenk, 'Family Memory and the Crusades', pp. 178–9.
59 *Chronica Majora*, vol. 5, p. 173, "Spero utique, quod ipsius patrocinio citius ad culmen caelestis patriae promovebor". For analysis of this source and scene, see: G.M. Reynolds, 'A Paragon of Support? Ela of Salisbury, Martyrdom, and the Ideals of Sponsoring Crusade', *Crusades*, vol. 20 (2021), pp. 247–66.
60 Jackson, *Ardent Complaints and Equivocal Piety*, pp. 70–2.
61 Hartmann von Aue, 'If a woman sends off her beloved', in F. Tobin, K. Vivian and R.H. Lawson (eds and trans.), *Arthurian Romances, Tales, and Lyric Poetry: The Complete Works of Hartmann von Aue* (University Park, 2001), p. 38, no. 6. For original German,

Laywomen and the Crusade in England, 1150–1300

Hartmann's 'praying wife' and 'crusading husband' characters equally support each other's spiritual health, so long as they operate within those respective spheres.[62] It seems that he was trying to describe a symbiotic relationship between two differing ideal roles. Perhaps the actions of the wife character may be interpreted, not as magnifying the spiritual impact of her husband's crusade, but, in a sense, validating crusade as a joint enterprise. Hartmann's ideas are a fascinating hint at the nuanced perceptions of crusading culture that existed, but his is quite an isolated reference to such beliefs.

The papacy's offer of indulgences to laypeople who supported crusade, then, developed slowly over the second half of the twelfth century and into the opening decades of the thirteenth century. Theoretically, women could have gained indulgences for funding crusaders perhaps as early as the 1150s, but their support was not explicitly sought by the papacy until the early 1200s. Two points must be stressed, however, at this juncture. First, women were not alone in being incentivised to support crusade as an alternative to going into battle. Clergy, children, and laymen who were unable or prevented from participating in holy warfare were also encouraged to engage in these supportive activities. Second, it cannot be overlooked that many women continuously travelled to the Levant to physically participate in holy war and visit pilgrimage sites, and such individuals were praised by contemporaries for their daring.[63] Despite the papacy's attempt to portray support from the West as an ideal feminine role within crusade, there is likely to have been a broader spectrum of feminine ideals circulating amongst the laity that are hard to gauge from the surviving evidence.[64] Nevertheless, sponsoring or praying for crusade became an established means for all Latin Christians to meaningfully, tangibly and spiritually link themselves with crusade.

---

see: Hartmann von Aue, 'Swelch vrowe sendet lieben man…', in Ulrich Müller (ed.), *Kreuzzugsdichtung* (Tübingen, 1969), no. 37, p. 57, "Swelche vrowe sendet lieben man; mit rehtem muote ûf dise vart, diu koufet halben lôn dar an, ob sî sich heime alsô bewart; daz sî verdienet kiuschiu wort. sî bete für sî beidiu hie, sô vert er für sî beidiu dort".

[62] Cf: Paul, *To Follow in Their Footsteps*, p. 3. See also: W.E. Jackson, 'Poet, Woman, and Crusade in Songs of Marcabru, Guiot de Dijon, and Albrecht von Johansdorf', *Mediaevalia*, vol. 22, no. 2 (1999), pp. 265–89, at 267 and 284, n. 17.

[63] See: Hodgson, *Women, Crusading and the Holy Land in Historical Narrative*; Nicholson, *Women and the Crusades*.

[64] See, for instance, the number of women travelling to the Levant on the ship St Victor in 1250: Kedar, 'The Passenger List of a Crusader Ship, 1250', pp. 267–79.

3

Preaching Patronage

> If, therefore, you are not suitable to accept the cross, to go to the Holy Land, then take the cross and give the cross back, that is, [by giving] money for the sign of the cross, according to your means, thereby gaining the merits of the cross.
>
> (John Russel, English Franciscan friar, c.1291)[1]

Much of the rhetoric explored so far conveyed the papacy's ideas on crusade, but that information reached the laity by a variety of channels. These directives were read out, repackaged or interpreted by a myriad of others who transmitted the message to laypeople. It is important now to consider the language and techniques of those who communicated these ideals specifically to people in England: this task mainly fell to crusade preachers. These spokespersons of the *negotium crucis* – "business of the cross" – often engaged women throughout the period under discussion: speaking directly to them, using individuals as exemplars and others as cautionary tales. Preachers were eager to promote the concept that it was women's duty, not to bemoan husbands or family members' choice to go on crusade, but to pressure them into going. Preachers were the first official point of contact for anyone wishing to join or support holy war during the Middle Ages. Their experiences, opinions and sermons tell us much about the society that they walked amongst.

Preachers, Audiences and Sources

Preaching was necessary ahead of any crusading expedition to raise funds, gather recruits and broadcast the aims of a campaign. How this worked in practice could vary depending on the kingdom; there was a distinct regionality to the culture of crusade and its formation across the Latin West. The organisation of crusade preaching in twelfth-century England was closely regulated or at least scrutinised,

---

[1] B. Smalley, 'John Russel O.F.M.', *Recherches de théologie ancienne et médiévale*, vol. 23 (1956), pp. 277–320, at 280, "si ergo non vales accipere crucem, ut terram sanctam adeas, accipe crucem et da crucem, id est pecuniam cruce signatam, secundum tuam facultatem, ut meritum cruces obtineas".

by the Crown and episcopacy.[2] When the papacy called for renewed efforts in crusading, it was largely down to these local powers in England to spread the word. This framework was typified in the 1188 tour of Baldwin of Forde (d.1190), archbishop of Canterbury. Although it was Pope Gregory VIII who called for the Third Crusade and requested preaching drives at this time – and this was an international expedition in many senses – in England, it was a royal council at Geddington (Northamptonshire) that organised and designed the preaching mission that Baldwin would lead.[3]

From the 1230s onwards, the papacy tended to appoint legates to oversee regions where preaching would take place. The legates would, in turn, employ deputies amongst the English clergy. These clerics would then tour the country and give sermons on the necessity of crusade, while advising laypeople on how they could help the movement.[4] Groups of preachers would coordinate their engagements by messaging ahead to local clergy or parish priests, instructing them to muster as many laypeople as possible on the appropriate day to hear the sermons.[5]

There is no reason to believe that these local clerics only rounded up knightly men. Audiences appear to have contained people from all ranks of society, many of whom may have heard sermons in smaller *ad hoc* events on a semi-regular basis.[6] Crusade preaching events were frequently staged to coincide with religious feast days or celebrations and were often hosted in parish churches, in order to engage with as many of the laity as possible.[7] Pope Innocent III sent one letter to his legate, Robert Courçon, in which he maintained that any person, including women, would receive a partial remission of their sins if they so much as came to hear sermons that centred on the restoration of the Latin East.[8] In 1263, Pope Urban IV (r.1261–4) instigated a crusade preaching tour in England and, in very inclusive terms, offered a hundred days plenary indulgence to any penitents who attended the accompanying processions and sermons.[9] In 1291, John le Romeyn,

---

[2] C.T. Maier, *Crusade Propaganda and Ideology, Model Sermons for the Preaching of the Cross* (Cambridge, 2000), pp. 5–8; Maier, *Preaching the Crusades*.

[3] Tyerman, *England and the Crusades*, p. 161; Hurlock, *Britain, Ireland and the Crusades*, pp. 30–7; Bennett, *Elite Participation in the Third Crusade*, pp. 53–63.

[4] Tyerman, *England and the Crusades*, pp. 162–3.

[5] Lloyd, *English Society and the Crusade*, pp. 46–7.

[6] Hurlock, *Britain, Ireland and the Crusades*, p. 38.

[7] Bird, 'Preaching and Crusading Memory', pp. 20–1; P.W. Edbury, 'Preaching the Crusade in Wales', in A. Haverkamp and H. Vollrath (eds), *England and Germany in the High Middle Ages* (Oxford, 1996), pp. 221–33, at 224; M.C. Gaposchkin, 'The Liturgical Memory of July 15, 1099: Between History, Memory and Eschatology' in Cassidy-Welch, *Remembering the Crusades and Crusading*, pp. 34–48.

[8] Rousseau, 'Home Front and Battlefield', p. 37.

[9] W.H. Bliss (ed.), *Calendar of Papal Registers Relating to Great Britain and Ireland: Vol 1, 1198–1304* (London, 1893), p. 394.

archbishop of York (r.1286–96) asked preachers to deliver crusade sermons simultaneously at Howden, Selby and Pocklington (Yorkshire), so as to catch crowds of listeners.[10] This approach was designed to reach as many people as possible, but it may also hint at an anxiety that parishioners would try and evade the preachers. These churchmen were intent on broadcasting the necessity of crusade to the community *en masse*, hoping that this would put pressure on the more desirable recruits – knightly men – to sign up. Preachers were highly tactical in this pursuit.

The business of the cross became more centralised during the thirteenth century with the formation of two mendicant orders: the Franciscans (often referred to as the Friars Minor or Greyfriars, in reference to their grey habit) and the Dominicans (Friars Preachers or sometimes called Blackfriars, likewise because of their dark clothing). These religious orders produced itinerant friars, who preached in variety of areas, and others who were sent by their superiors to specific locations, amongst other things, to encourage crusade. Members of the mendicants, similarly to the Military Orders, were not rigidly fixed to one location, spending their lives in a monastery; they were, instead, a mobile logistical arm in the spread of crusade propaganda.[11] For the remainder of the 1200s, these orders were the primary source of professional preachers, funded by the papacy and ready to deliver sermons at any time.[12] There were, however, some complicated paradoxes in their actions. When these orders were initially founded, they envisioned that their members would live a life of poverty and asceticism. This ideal did not entirely align with their subsequent role in handling vast amounts of money used for crusade. Writers like Matthew Paris thought of them as arrogant and hypocritical. He commented, with no small degree of distaste, on these preachers' clear successes in England during crusade-drives in the 1230s:

> [The Friars] Preachers and Minors – who have chosen humility and voluntary poverty – take care to be received in monasteries and towns in solemn procession, with banners, lit candles, and clothed in festive vestments: and they confer many days pardon on those who listen to them – those they sign with the cross today [i.e. make crusaders], they absolve of their vows tomorrow in return for a gift of money.[13]

---

[10] J. Raine (ed.), *Historical Papers and Letters from the Northern Registers* (London, 1873), pp. 93–6, at 93.

[11] J. Sarnowsky, 'Regional Problems in the History of the Mendicant and Military Orders', in J. Sarnowsky (ed.), *Mendicants, Military Orders, and Regionalism in Medieval Europe* (Aldershot, 1999), pp. 1–15, at 2–3; C.H. Lawrence, *The Friars: The Impact of the Early Mendicant Movement on Western Society*, 2nd edn (London and New York, 2013), pp. 185–8.

[12] Maier, *Preaching the Crusades*, pp. 111–22. For more on the training of preachers, see: Cole, *The Preaching of the Crusades to the Holy Land*, pp. 112–7.

[13] *Chronica Majora*, vol. 3, p. 287, "Praedicatores et Minores, qui spontaneam paupertatem cum humilitate elegerunt, ut recipi curarent in coenobiis et civitatibus in processione

Laywomen and the Crusade in England, 1150–1300

Although we have a reasonably clear picture of the mechanics behind crusade preaching, there are some crucial caveats to our sources for the sermons that were delivered in England. There is very little known of the content of crusade sermons that were preached in this kingdom before the 1150s or so; there are more prevalent examples from the end of the twelfth century, such as those by Peter of Blois.[14] The picture becomes much clearer in the 1200s. There are twenty-two known thirteenth-century sermons from Latin Christendom that were written expressly for preaching crusade to the Holy Land, yet only two are from England.[15] These texts have to be read critically, as they are all model sermons. That is to say, they were drafted to teach other preachers how to structure their material. Some surviving texts are likely to have been based on sermons that were used at events, but when the sermons were committed to writing they were reworked, altering the language, phrasing and stresses that were originally employed.[16] This restructuring of the original language of crusade preaching obscures our view of who the ideal audiences were at the time of the events, or how the material was adapted to suit particular occasions.[17]

It has been suggested that the papal crusade encyclicals, like those explored in Chapter 2, were typically read aloud or modified by preachers. This may account for the lack of surviving sermons.[18] If this were the case, then laywomen would likely have heard the papacy's expectations of them in language similar or identical to the phrasings discussed within *Quia maior*. Still, many individuals raised money themselves and went on crusade of their own accord in smaller, private expeditions (as they are sometimes called) outside of the larger canonical crusades that the papacy called for. Local clergy, as well as good public speakers from the laity, may have spread news of these comparatively smaller ventures, preaching through a particular locale. Given the relatively lax centralised control over who could preach crusade, we know very little of the publicising methods (if there was much at all) of these sorts of grass-roots movements.[19] It is also interesting to note that there is remarkably little surviving evidence that sermons were conducted in

---

sollempni, in vexillis, cereis accensis, et in dispositione vestimentis festivis indutorum; et concessa est eis veniam multorum dierum suis conferre auditoribus, signatosque hodie cras data pecunia a crucis voto absolverunt".

[14] See: A. Marx, 'The *Passio Raginaldi* of Peter of Blois: Martyrdom and Eschatology in the Preaching of the Third Crusade', *Viator*, vol. 50, no. 3 (2019), pp. 197–232.

[15] Maier, *Preaching the Crusades*, app. 2, p. 171; Tamminen, *Crusade Preaching and the Ideal Crusader*, p. 42. There are as many as thirty-six surviving sermons that are considered to have broadly conveyed crusading propaganda, see: Maier, 'Propaganda and Masculinity', p. 22; Tamminen, *Crusade Preaching and the Ideal Crusader*, pp. 24–35.

[16] Tamminen, 'Crusading in the Margins?', p. 146.

[17] Maier, 'Propaganda and Masculinity', pp. 22–3.

[18] Bird, 'Preaching and Crusading Memory', p. 18.

[19] See: Tyerman, *How to Plan a Crusade*, pp. 66–9.

English – the language the majority of commoners would have spoken, unlike the elite who spoke French.[20] In all likelihood, speakers may well have translated all or some of their sermons for wider listeners, or perhaps local interpreters did so. Unfortunately, we can only speculate on what that scene looked like.

Of those preachers' sermons that do survive, there are no examples that imply that women were the primary audience. Writers did refer to women in many of these texts, but, more often than not, they use highly disparaging terms.[21] Preachers were aware that crusading involved separation from family, with little certainty of return. Rather than shy away from this emotional reality, they frequently used women as allegories of the comforts of home, which crusaders would have to forgo if they were to act as ideal penitents. The intention was to shame those who would not sign up by mocking their inability to bear the earthly sacrifice. In doing this, preachers regularly characterised women as inhibitors of crusade, a hurdle that recruits would have to bypass if they were to become *milites Christi*.[22] Over the past few decades, scholars have done much to further our understanding of why contemporaries felt the need to portray women like this.[23] It is an important point to consider, as numerous contemporary chroniclers and preachers noted the many crusade-positive women that they engaged with. It is crucial that we analyse the messages that were transmitted to women during crusade preaching, the advice given to them over supporting the movement and women's reactions to the propaganda that they were exposed to.

Gerald of Wales

The most extensive and detailed description of crusade preaching in the British Isles is Gerald of Wales's (d.c.1223) *Itinerarium Kambriae*.[24] Gerald's text narrates Baldwin of Forde's 1188 tour through Wales and the Welsh Marches (the fluctuating border territories with England) to find recruits for the Third Crusade. Over the course of eight weeks, the archbishop and his accompanying preachers mostly toured urban centres, aiming to engage with as many people as possible. If we are

---

[20] Tyerman, *England and the Crusades*, p. 161. Cf: Tamminen, *Crusade Preaching and the Ideal Crusader*, pp. 72–3, n. 105.

[21] Maier, 'Propaganda and Masculinity', p. 28; Tamminen, *Crusade Preaching and the Ideal Crusader*, p. 262; Tamminen, 'Crusading in the Margins?', pp. 145–58.

[22] Hodgson, *Women, Crusading and the Holy Land in Historical Narrative*, pp. 44–52; Tamminen, *Crusade Preaching and the Ideal Crusader*, p. 206.

[23] Lambert, 'Crusading or Spinning', pp. 8–9; Riley-Smith, 'Family Traditions', p. 101; Riley-Smith, *The First Crusaders*, p. 93. See also: K.L. French, 'Medieval Women's history: Sources and issues', in J.T. Rosenthal (ed.), *Understanding Medieval Primary Sources: Using Historical Sources to Discover Medieval Europe* (London, 2012), pp. 196–209, at 196.

[24] For a study of Gerald's tour and its context, see: K. Hurlock, *Wales and the Crusades c.1095–1291* (Cardiff, 2011), pp. 58–91.

to believe the text's claim, they signed 3,000 people with the cross. The trip was a well-choreographed propaganda campaign. It even included a staged spectacle where Baldwin himself took a crusade vow at an event in Bangor Cathedral – whipping up enthusiasm.[25] Gerald, the *Itinerarium*'s author, was a royal clerk and archdeacon of Brecon at the time, and he accompanied the mission as one of its preachers.[26] He completed his account of the trip roughly four years later, giving us a unique (if suspiciously self-congratulatory) insight into the preaching tactics of the period.[27]

Gerald's text is incredibly useful for our understanding of the culture of crusade preaching that took place in Wales and helps give an idea of how this would have worked in England. As Peter Edbury notes, there were no recruitment drives in England in the 1180s that matched the scale of Baldwin's 1188 Welsh tour, probably because the political elite wanted to avoid gathering masses of non-combatants in their army.[28] Nevertheless, Gerald was unambiguous that the objective of the preaching in Wales was part of a broader scheme to recruit "good men" (*probos viros*) from across England and Wales.[29] Aside from issues in translating the sermons for the Welsh, Flemish or Anglo-Norman laity that they encountered, there is little reason to think that the preachers on the Welsh tour engaged women differently than they would have in England.[30] Indeed, Gerald and his companions certainly preached to crowds of English and Welsh laity simultaneously in the Welsh Marches.[31]

The *Itinerarium Kambriae* contains many descriptions of preachers' interactions with, and opinions of, women. Gerald and his colleagues' attitudes came into being at a pivotal moment, when the papacy was beginning to incorporate women into crusading policy. In the lead up to the Third Crusade, as Gerald was preaching in Wales, the laity's supportive actions were on the cusp of not only being praised but actively incentivised. Despite this shift, Gerald portrayed crusade as a pious masculine pursuit in which laywomen were just one of the

---

[25] Hurlock, *Wales and the Crusades*, pp. 67–8.
[26] R. Bartlett, *Gerald of Wales, A Voice of the Middle Ages* (Stroud, 2006), pp. 68–73.
[27] Hurlock, *Wales and the Crusades*, p. 58.
[28] Edbury, 'Preaching the Crusade in Wales', pp. 230–1; Hurlock, *Britain, Ireland and the Crusades*, p. 37.
[29] 'De Rebus a se Gestis', in Gerald of Wales, *Giraldi Cambrensis Opera*, 8 vols, J.S. Brewer, J.G. Dimock and G.F. Warner (eds) (London, 1861–91), vol. 1, pp. 1–122, at 73. For a translation see: H.E. Butler, C.H. Williams and J. Gillingham (eds), *The Autobiography of Gerald of Wales* (Woodbridge, 2005, Originally published 1937), p. 98.
[30] Tyerman notes the contemporary descriptions of the *unica causa* of all crusade preaching that emanated from England, one unified message, see: Tyerman, *England and the Crusades*, p. 153.
[31] Gerald of Wales, 'Itinerarium Kambriae, et Descriptio Kambriae', in *Giraldi Cambrensis Opera*, Brewer, Dimock and Warner, vol. 6, p. 67.

worldly temptations that held men back from taking the cross. His sentiments were largely representative of other twelfth-century writers.[32] Gerald repeatedly highlighted examples of women who hindered the would-be crusaders that his colleagues were attempting to recruit, sometimes quite literally. He claimed that at the sermon at Hay-on-Wye, many men wanted to take the Cross: "we saw them leave their cloaks behind – some with their friends, others with their wives, who had tried to hold them back – and they came quickly running into the castle to the archbishop".[33]

Similarly, the *Itinerarium* explained that Rhys ap Gruffydd (d.1197), the Prince of Deheubarth, was initially interested in taking the cross but soon had a change of heart. In Gerald's view, the prince's wife, Gwenllian, had used her "womanly" charms to dissuade Rhys from taking a crusade vow.[34] Gerald also described an episode where a woman in Cardigan discouraged her husband from taking a vow. She later accidentally smothered her infant in bed while they slept. To Gerald's mind, this was a divine punishment from God, because she had attempted to obstruct crusade.[35]

In keeping with this trend, the *Itinerarium Kambriae* described a moment when an Abergavenny nobleman, Arthenus, was being goaded into signing up to join the crusade. Having heard Archbishop Baldwin's arguments, Arthenus wished to consult with his friends before taking the legally binding crusade vow. Baldwin reminded Arthenus that he should consult his wife as well. Crucially, at this point in time, a married person still had to have the express permission of their spouse before they could go on crusade. Gerald quoted Arthenus's reaction: "we are undertaking man's work; there is no need to seek counsel from a woman".[36] Given the pattern in his stories about women, I am inclined to think that Gerald rather approved of Arthenus's misogynistic reaction; he certainly did not rebuke the outburst.

Gerald's anecdotes seem to be a highly constructed lament at the need for recruits to consult their spouses. He was determined to prove that anyone who deterred a potential crusader would suffer God's ire. The case of Archbishop Baldwin and Arthenus confirms that Gerald's colleagues reminded married people of their responsibilities.[37] Nevertheless, Gerald used, or composed, stories about

---

[32] S. Lambert, 'Crusading or Spinning', in Edgington and Lambert, *Gendering the Crusades*, pp. 1–15, at 7.
[33] Gerald of Wales, 'Itinerarium Kambriae, et Descriptio Kambriae', p. 20, "quosdam vidimus qui relictis vestibus, quibus alii ab amicis, alii ab uxoribus retinebantur, usque in castrum ipsum cursim ad archiepiscopum evaserunt
[34] Gerald of Wales, 'Itinerarium Kambriae, et Descriptio Kambriae', p. 15, "muliebriter".
[35] Gerald of Wales, 'Itinerarium Kambriae, et Descriptio Kambriae', p. 113.
[36] Gerald of Wales, 'Itinerarium Kambriae, et Descriptio Kambriae', p. 49. "Ad aggrediendum", inquit, "opus virile, non est expetendum consilium muliebre".
[37] Edbury, 'Preaching the Crusade in Wales', p. 227.

Laywomen and the Crusade in England, 1150–1300

women who inhibited crusade so that he could demonstrate moralising tales, emphasising the pious, self-sacrificing act of assuming the cross. His portrayal of the wives holding onto their husbands' cloaks quoted above, for example, bears an uncanny resemblance to a scene in the Old Testament where the lustful wife of Potiphar was left holding the cloak of the unswerving, devout Joseph who refused her advances.[38] Despite these prevailing negative attitudes within Gerald's text, there is strong reason to believe that women engaged with preachers (and perhaps with Gerald and his colleagues) more directly and positively than the *Itinerarium Kambriae* would lead us to believe. Given that Gerald and his colleagues had a responsibility to only administer crusade vows to husbands who had consulted with their wives, we might speculate that the preachers also encouraged wives to give their consent. Crusading was one of many pious acts that churchmen hoped laypeople would direct their kin toward.[39]

Gerald did take the time to recall one elderly mother who was especially thankful that her son had taken a crusade vow; she apparently exclaimed: "dearest Lord Jesus Christ, I give you my innermost thanks, for judging my son worthy to be accepted into your service".[40] Other contemporary writers noted the influence that mothers had on their crusading sons.[41] The Norman writer Ambroise composed an account of the Third Crusade around 1195 – he had accompanied King Richard I on the expedition – and described the recruits who joined the army: "many mothers' sons filled the slopes and vineyards".[42] Similarly, around 1220, an anonymous English writer drafted a prose chronicle of the expedition, the *Itinerarium Peregrinorum et Gesta Regis Ricardi*, and commented on the many women who had enabled their relatives: "brides urged their husbands, and mothers incited their sons to go".[43] That said, neither of these texts intimate that preachers influenced these enabling women, nor does Gerald of Wales's account discuss

---

[38] Genesis 39:7–13.

[39] See the following arguments regarding piety within medieval families: S. Farmer, 'Persuasive Voices: Clerical Images of Medieval Wives', *Speculum*, vol. 61, no. 3 (1986), pp. 517–43.

[40] Gerald of Wales, 'Itinerarium Kambriae, et Descriptio Kambriae', p. 113, "Gratias tibi, carissime Domine Christe Jhesu, intimas ago, quod talem mihi filium quem tuo dignareris obsequio parere concessisti".

[41] Hodgson, *Women, Crusading and the Holy Land in Historical Narrative*, pp. 162–3.

[42] Ambroise, *The History of the Holy War, Ambroise's Estoire de la Guerre Sainte*, M. Ailes (ed. and trans.) (Woodbridge, 2003), p. 35; Ambroise, *L'Estoire de la Guerre Sainte: histoire en vers de la troisième croisade (1190–1192)*, G. Paris (ed.) (Paris, 1897), p. 10, ll. 351–2, "E es vignes e es costiz, Ot de meintes meres les fiz".

[43] H.J. Nicholson (ed.), *The Chronicle of the Third Crusade: The Itinerarium Peregrinorum et Gesta Regis Ricardi* (Aldershot, 2001), bk I, cpt. 17, p. 48; W. Stubbs (ed.), *Itinerarium Peregrinorum et Gesta Regis Ricardi* (London, 1864), bk. I, cap. 17, p. 33, "nuptae viros, et matres incitabant filios".

the content of the sermons that he or his colleagues employed. Therefore, we cannot be sure of exact interaction between preachers and their female audience.

That being said, preachers clearly did have close discussions with women over the topic of crusade. The author of the Melrose Chronicle – writing within the Kingdom of Scotland in the later thirteenth century – made some interesting observations. He noted that, as royalty and magnates took the cross in 1188, "innumerable" people "of both sexes" also signed up.[44] It can be difficult to take medieval writers at their word when it comes to numbers. Still, it appears that a considerable, and diverse, group of people approached the clerics to receive their vow. Extant records of named crusaders can confirm this. Preachers kept lists of those they signed with the cross, and women appear in English examples. Two lists concerning the Third Crusade have survived, one from Lincolnshire and the other from Cornwall.[45] These both appear to be accounts of individuals who had taken vows ahead of this campaign but, for whatever reason, had not departed nor commuted their vows. The Cornish list names Hawisa of *Trevisac* and *Uxor* [Wife] *Porttejoie* amongst the people who had taken crusade vows.[46] A third crusader, mononymously named *Pilia*, had a feminine name (given the Latinised ending -*a*), but this was also a local surname and so the individual's sex, or how they identified, is uncertain.[47]

It is unfortunate that more lists of *crucesignati* have not come to light, since at one time, there must have been huge numbers of these records. In 1254, the papal chaplain Bernard de Nimphia and his entourage were apparently carrying lists of every crusader from England who had not fulfilled their vows: impressive book-keeping, if true.[48] There may have been other, less official, lists of crusaders circulating. In 1221, a Warwickshire man fraudulently claimed his uncle had been a crusader, so as to use a legal loophole that would allow him to claim some land, but: "the jurors said that this Gilbert was never a crusader".[49] It is unclear

---

[44] J. Stevenson (ed.), *Chronica de Mailros* (Edinburgh, 1835), p. 96, "populus innumerabilis" and "utriusque sexus".

[45] Lloyd, *English Society and the Crusade*, p. 71. For a transcription of the documents relating to Lincolnshire and Cornwall, see respectively: HMC, *Report on Manuscripts in Various Collections* (London, 1901), vol. 1, pp. 235–236, no. 227; N. Orme and O.J. Padel, 'Cornwall and the Third Crusade', *Journal of the Royal Institution of Cornwall* (2005), pp. 71–7, at 75.

[46] Orme and Padel, 'Cornwall and the third Crusade', p. 72.

[47] Orme and Padel, 'Cornwall and the third Crusade', p. 72. The manuscript gives no further indication of the sex of the individuals named, see: Canterbury, Canterbury Cathedral Archives, DCc/MSSB/A/7. A man identified as "Stephanum Pilia" occurs in assize rolls for Cornwall in 1201, see: D.M. Stenton (ed.), *Pleas Before the King or his Justices 1198–1202*, 4 vols (London, 1953–67), at vol. 2, p. 42, no. 194.

[48] *CPR, 1247–58*, p. 371.

[49] D.M. Stenton (ed.), *Rolls of the Justices in Eyre being the Rolls of Pleas and Assizes for Gloucestershire, Warwickshire and Staffordshire, 1221, 1222* (London, 1940), p.

Laywomen and the Crusade in England, 1150–1300

whether they had a list of locals who had made these sacred contracts or if they relied on locals with long memories, or both.

Leaving aside those who never fulfilled their vows, we can be sure that many women certainly did go on the Third Crusade.[50] The experiences of one Englishwoman who lived around this time, Margaret of Beverley, have survived with astounding clarity. Margaret's story was recorded by her brother, Thomas of Froidmont, after she returned from her travels.[51] According to Thomas's text, Margaret went on crusade to the Holy Land just prior to Saladin's campaign against the Kingdom of Jerusalem. She was in the Holy City during its defence in the siege of 1187, where she used a cooking pot to protect herself (probably a gendered joke on Thomas's part) and was wounded by enemy artillery fire. Later, she was captured and enslaved, and forced to do hard labour until a wealthy man from Tyre ransomed her. She used her time in the Holy Land to tour shrines before eventually returning to Europe via other pilgrimage sites. It was during this final leg of her journey that she found her brother in France and gave an account of her sojourn.[52] It had certainly taken its toll – Thomas tells us his sister was unrecognisable when he first saw her. It is uncertain whether women like Margaret, who took crusade vows in the 1180s, were directly encouraged by preachers to do so. Still, these volunteers must have engaged with priests to take their vows and if Thomas of Froidmont is anything to go by, they were considered highly respectable for doing so. It is, therefore, interesting that Gerald of Wales was reluctant to discuss the matter of women volunteering in *Itinerarium Kambriae*; his silence further emphasised that he saw crusading as a masculine pursuit.

We saw in the previous chapter that the papacy generally encouraged fiscal support for crusade and considered offering indulgences for such activity, as early as the 1150s. Despite this, Gerald of Wales's account intimates that preachers in the British Isles did not impress upon the laity to give money toward the Third Crusade. He described an elderly man named Cador who could not go on the expedition, but instead offered a tenth of his possessions for half an indulgence. When Archbishop Baldwin accepted this transaction, Cador offered another tenth for the other half. Baldwin embraced the man and commended his "devotion" and "logic/cleverness".[53] The language here suggests that these preachers had not expected to be given monetary donations and, presumably, had not been

---

275, no. 614.
[50] Nicholson, 'Women on the Third Crusade', pp. 335–49.
[51] P.G. Schmidt, '"*Peregrinatio Periculosa*". Thomas von Froidmont über die Jerusalemfahrten seiner schwester Margareta', in U.J. Stache, W. Maaz and F. Wagner (eds), *Kontinuität und Wandel: Lateinische Poesie von Naevius bis Baudelaire* (Hildesheim, 1986), pp. 461–85, at 472–85.
[52] Maier, 'The Roles of Women in the Crusade Movement', pp. 64–7.
[53] Gerald of Wales, 'Itinerarium Kambriae, et Descriptio Kambriae', p. 74, "devotam viri subilitatem cum admiratione amplexatus est".

encouraging people to donate cash.[54] The 1188 tour of Wales occurred in the wake of a tax that King Henry II levied on a tenth of the moveable wealth of the clergy and laity – the Saladin Tithe – a precedent in the development of income tax.[55] Individuals were instructed to assess what they were personally liable for. Some specific items were treated as exempt, such as knights' arms or clerics' books and vestments. Anyone caught undervaluing their goods, however, was excommunicated and subjected to an audit.[56] This severe hit on laypeople's finances was deeply unpopular, and may have made preachers less inclined to request funds from the laity. Contributing to an imposed crusade tax, albeit in aid of the Holy Land, was not viewed the same as voluntarily donating cash to crusaders. Peter Edbury has pointed out that Cador's charitable donations show some anticipation of Pope Clement III's offer of indulgences to patrons of crusade in May 1188.[57] The anecdote nicely highlights that it was the laity's desires that inspired the papacy's policies concerning crusade support, not necessarily the other way around.

The picture presented in the *Itinerarium Kambriae* is one of minor, if any, engagement between preachers and women. Whether this portrayal was disingenuous or not on Gerald's part, it seems that women were not generally encouraged to take crusade vows at this time. However, if women influenced their kinsmen to become crusaders, they were lauded. Besides praise, little more was offered to these women, as the papacy's rewards for such behaviour were still sufficiently vague. As the parameters around crusade indulgences for support became increasingly codified, however, preachers' attitudes towards women quickly softened.

Preaching in the Thirteenth Century

Following the circulation of *Quia maior* in 1213, preachers suddenly had an imperative to engage women more readily in their sermons and encourage them to donate cash toward crusade. That said, the impact of this new papal crusading policy probably did not have an overnight effect on preachers' tactics. Jacques de Vitry recalled a time when he was preaching crusade the year following the issuing of *Quia maior*. While travelling on his preaching tour, his horses were requisitioned by some Genoese soldiers. Jacques was infuriated that his work had been disturbed, so he retaliated by preaching the crusade to the men's wives. In his now famous turn of phrase: "many of the wealthy and noblewomen

---

[54] Gerald has been described as treating normal preparations for warfare as a "sign of inadequate faith" in God's ability to confirm victory, see: Bartlett, *Gerald of Wales*, p. 70.
[55] Roger of Howden, *Chronica Magistri Rogeri de Houedene*, vol. 2, p. 335.
[56] Edwards, *Finance and the Crusades*, p. 35.
[57] Edbury, 'Preaching the Crusade in Wales', p. 227.

received the sign of the cross: the burghers took my horses, and so I made their wives crusaders".[58]

These wealthy women would have had to part with sizeable donations to commute these vows, and this may have been the blow Jacques intended toward Genoa's burghers. There is something of a sense in Jacques's anecdote that what he did would not have been expected; perhaps, preaching crusade directly to women was not especially typical at this time.[59] That said, in one of Jacques's sermons, that he probably employed ahead of the Fifth Crusade, around 1213–17, he laboured the spiritual rewards that combative crusaders would receive, and followed with: "the spouses and children are included in these benefits in as much as they contribute to the expenses".[60]

Crusade preachers in England may have used similar sentiments at this time, but our first distinct evidence appears during large-scale preaching tours in 1227. Richard Poore, Bishop of Salisbury (r.1217–28), sent a letter to Peter des Roches, Bishop of Winchester (r.1205–38) ahead of this campaign. The letter emphasised that those who took crusade vows could commute their vow for a cash payment.[61] This message appears to have been broadcast to a wide section of society. Roger of Wendover described the subsequent tour and the efforts of one preacher, a Master Hubert, which resulted in over 40,000 men and women being signed with the cross.[62] Even though the figure that Roger offers must be hyperbole, clearly the stress on vow redemptions was exceptionally popular. More than that though, the message preached during this tour seems to have been aimed at both sexes. Preachers were no longer simply demonising women as the ultimate hinderance to effective crusaders. Instead, they were inciting women to directly patronise crusading missions.

That engagement went both ways. Conversing with the Church's officials in crusade became a potent means for women to display their approval of holy war outwardly. Edmund of Abingdon (d.1240) was selected to be one of the preachers in the English tour in 1227, while he worked as treasurer of Salisbury Cathedral.[63] Given his occupation, he may already have met the charismatic local noblewoman,

---

[58] R.B.C. Huygens (ed.), *Lettres de Jacques de Vitry (1160/1170–1240) évêque de Saint-Jean-d'Acre, Edition Critique* (Leiden, 1960), p. 77, "multitudo autem mulierum divitum et nobilium signum crucis recepit: cives michi equos abstulerunt, et ego uxores eorum crucesignavi".

[59] See also: J.M. Powell, *The Crusades, The Kingdom of Sicily, and The Mediterranean* (Farnham, 2007), p. 107.

[60] James of Vitry, 'Sermo II', p. 113, cpt 19. For Latin see p. 112, "Uxores autem filii participes sunt expensarum ita particeps sunt meritorum".

[61] N. Vincent (ed.), *English Episcopal Acta IX, Winchester 1205–1238* (Oxford, 1994), pp. 37–8, no. 47.

[62] Roger of Wendover, *Flores Historiarum*, vol. 2, p. 323.

[63] C.H. Lawrence (ed.), *The Life of St. Edmund by Matthew Paris* (Stroud, 1996; repr. 1999), pp. 41–2.

Ela of Salisbury. But, in the year that Edmund was becoming a recognisable face in the business of the cross, Ela displayed her association with him and had Edmund witness singularly important charters: gifts to Bradenstoke Priory (a house with strong connections to Ela and her forebears), as well as her re-foundation of a charterhouse in Hinton (both Wiltshire).[64] Their friendship was clearly lasting. Edmund witnessed several more of Ela's charters in the following three years.[65] As we saw earlier, Ela became a crucial supporter of her son's crusading, supposedly even believing she would receive salvation through his death in Egypt. For Ela, celebrating her friendship with a successful crusade preacher was just the start of a fascination with crusade.[66]

The shift in the culture of crusade preaching is again evident in the work of Matthew Paris. He described a subsequent preaching tour, in 1235, that again placed huge emphasis on encouraging vow redemptions.[67] According to Matthew, "men and women" converged on the preachers.[68] The friars' success was so great that – much like the Melrose Chronicler's language – within a year they had bestowed the cross on "innumerable people" in England.[69] Times had clearly changed since Gerald of Wales's day.

The historians Simon Lloyd and Christopher Tyerman both felt that, by the thirteenth century, crusade preaching in England had become distinctly angled towards acquiring crusade redemption monies, perhaps to the detriment of recruiting troops.[70] It is possible that such a climate of crusade preaching contributed to the emergence of feminine crusading ideals that began to centre on sponsorship and patronage of holy war. Although this is an intriguing possibility, it does not mean that preachers necessarily only encouraged women to sponsor crusaders or commute their own vows. For instance, sometime between 1246 and 1248, the French theologian and preacher, Eudes of Châteauroux (d.1273), delivered a sermon defending women's choice to journey to the Holy Land.[71]

---

[64] The Pontigny Writer claimed Ela knew Edmund while her husband was still alive, see: 'Vita Beati Edmundi Cantuariensis Archiepiscopi et Confessoris', in E. Martène and U. Durand (eds), *Thesaurus Novus Anecdotorum*, 5 vols (Paris, 1717), vol. 3, pp. 1775–1826, at 1791. On Ela's grants see: V.C.M. London (ed.), *The Cartulary of Bradenstoke Priory* (Stoke-on-Trent, 1979), pp. 143–4; J. Ward (ed. and trans.), *Women of the English Nobility and Gentry, 1066–1500* (Manchester, 1995), pp. 200–1, no. 145.

[65] *Lacock*, pp. 10–1, no. 4 and pp. 18–9, no. 30.

[66] For more on her associations with Edmund, see: Reynolds, 'A Paragon of Support?', pp. 258–9.

[67] Maier, *Preaching the Crusades*, p. 139.

[68] *Chronica Majora*, vol. 3, p. 312, "viros et mulieres"; H.R. Luard (ed.), *Annales Monastici*, 5 vols (London, 1864–9), at vol. 3, p. 142.

[69] *Chronica Majora*, vol. 3, p. 374, "infinitum populum".

[70] Lloyd, *English Society and the Crusades*, pp. 12, 15–16 and 18–33; Tyerman, *England and the Crusades*, p. 162.

[71] Tamminen, *Crusade Preaching and the Ideal Crusader*, pp. 263–6.

Outside of chroniclers' generalising references to women commuting their crusade vows, we do have some documentary evidence for this practice. The registers of Walter Giffard, Archbishop of York (r.1266–79) are particularly revealing.[72] For the years 1274–5, the register lists hundreds of crusaders (both laity and clergy) and the sums of money they would have to pay, in proportion to their wealth and standing, to be free of their obligation to go on crusade.[73] Amongst the names are three women: Beatrice of Blackburn and the unnamed wives of Radulf Mitton and Hugh of *Sestefeld*. The first two are specifically reported as having taken crusade vows "for devotion".[74] These women were instructed to pay 20*s*, 100*s* and 2*s*, respectively. The proportion of women with unredeemed crusade vows in Walter Giffard's register was very small (just over 1% of the total number). That said, if women predominantly took vows with the intention of paying the appropriate redemption fee immediately, perhaps it is unsurprising that few of them ended up on these lists. Interestingly, the archbishop had urged these people to finally commute their vows, as a group of Franciscans were *en route* to Yorkshire; this possibly suggests that the friars were there to specifically preach vow redemption and collect donations.[75] Walter Giffard's register also notes two other women – Heloise Palmer and her daughter Isabel – who commuted their vow to make a pilgrimage to Santiago de Compostela by donating 2*s* toward the recapture of the Holy Land.[76] Heloise's surname, a byword for a pilgrim, may even indicate a previous pilgrimage or a family tradition of crusade/pilgrimage.

By the late thirteenth century, the notion of women taking crusade vows and/or commuting them had become completely normalised. The registers of Richard of Swinfield (Bishop of Hereford r.1283–1317), Oliver Sutton (Bishop of Lincoln r.1280–99) and those of the dean and chapter of Canterbury Cathedral all contain articles of inquiry into *crucesignati*. These are lists of questions that agents would pose to crusaders who had not departed for the Holy Land to determine whether they had a valid excuse or if they needed to pay a redemption fee. In some cases, the crusader in question may have died, and the agents would have had to quiz the deceased's executors. As Ian Bass has observed, all of these texts specifically include an article asking if any of the crusaders, "whether male or female", died intestate or indebted.[77]

---

[72] For more on the crusaders in this registry and its context, see: Bass, 'The Crozier and the Cross', pp. 125–86; Purcell, *Papal Crusading Policy*, pp. 115–6.

[73] Brown, *The Register of Walter Giffard*, pp. 277–86. See also: Raine, *Historical Papers and Letters from the Northern Registers*, pp. 46–58.

[74] Brown, *The Register of Walter Giffard*, p. 284, "pro devotione".

[75] Brown, *The Register of Walter Giffard*, p. 264.

[76] Brown, *The Register of Walter Giffard*, pp. 281–2.

[77] I.L. Bass, '"*Articuli Inquisicionis de crucesignatis*": Late Thirteenth-Century Inquiry into English Crusaders', *Crusades*, vol. 17 (2018), pp. 171–94, at 183, "aliqui vel alique".

Preaching Patronage

Despite the fact that thirteenth-century preachers were clearly pushing vow redemptions, we have not seen what rhetoric this involved. Only two thirteenth-century English crusade sermons have survived, yet both texts show an awareness of a variety of ways for the laity to connect with holy war. The first, dated c.1244–7, is attributed to Master Roger of Salisbury.[78] His preaching is believed to have been widely respected; some medieval compilations of sermons include Roger's work alongside famed preachers like Odo of Cheriton and John of Abbeville.[79] Mikka Tamminen examined Roger's crusade sermon and surmised that it, atypically, included no discussion of the "soldierly" qualities of the ideal crusader.[80] These martial themes dominate the work of continental preachers like Gilbert of Tournai, Humbert of Romans and Bertrand de la Tour, for example.[81] It is plausible that Roger avoided labouring crusade's combative elements so as not to ostracise women and others who were encouraged to take the same vows and then redeem them.

The second surviving English sermon, dated c.1291, was written by John Russel, a Franciscan friar.[82] This text appears in only one manuscript, which is badly damaged; however, in one legible line, John remarked:

> If, therefore, you are not suitable to accept the cross, to go to the Holy Land, then take the cross and give the cross back, that is, [by giving] money for the sign of the cross, according to your means, thereby gaining the merits of the cross.[83]

John's use of the word *vales*, translated here as "suitable", implies that those not considered ideal warriors should follow this guidance. The chronicler Matthew Paris confirmed that such instantaneous redemptions were prevalent in England and were extolled by preachers in 1240 – though he did think this was an "absurd" practice.[84] Both John Russel and Master Roger seem to have appreciated that people could engage in a broader range of activities besides combat to find connection with crusade. They were certainly not isolated in their thinking. One crusade sermon written by the French preacher Eudes of Châteauroux, sometime

---

[78] For a transcription of his sermon see: Cole, *The Preaching of the Crusades*, App. B, pp. 227–31.

[79] Cole, *The Preaching of the Crusades*, p. 168.

[80] Tamminen, *Crusade Preaching and the Ideal Crusader*, p. 281. Tamminen summarised the medieval ideal crusader as, "penitential, mimetic, pious, and soldierly".

[81] For editions of their sermons, see: Maier, *Crusade Propaganda and Ideology*, pp. 176–249.

[82] For more on John Russel, see: Smalley, 'John Russel', pp. 277–320.

[83] Smalley, 'John Russel', p. 280. See beginning of the chapter for Latin text, p. 53 n.1.

[84] Matthew Paris, *Historia Anglorum and Abbreviatio Chronicorum*, 3 vols, F. Madden (ed.) (London, 1866–9), at vol. 2, p. 431, "Ipsis quoque diebus, quod multum multis absurdum videbatur". See also: Tamminen, *Crusade Preaching and the Ideal Crusader*, p. 274.

before 1261, similarly reminded his listeners that instead of going on crusade, they ought to: "...follow them with your heart, your prayer, and your financial help".[85]

Preachers probably relied on exemplars to help guide listeners toward these broader activities within crusading culture. A glimpse of this tactic is apparent in a thirteenth-century text, the *Brevis Ordinacio de Predicacione Sancte Crucis*. This work was intended as a guide for crusade preachers, and it survives in two manuscripts, each originating in Oxford.[86] It was first composed by an anonymous author sometime between 1209 and 1250, in an Anglo-Norman context.[87] The writer offered a moralising story for preachers to incorporate into their sermons, which focused on two Flemish crusading brothers, called simply Eustace and Geoffrey. This is almost certainly an allusion to the names of two famous brothers and leaders of the First Crusade, Eustace III count of Boulogne and Godfrey of Bouillon.[88] The writer of the *Brevis Ordinacio* stated that, on hearing of Eustace's martyrdom in battle, his mother "praised God that he had had such regard for her that she gave birth to such a son who was pleasing" to the Lord.[89] Much like Gerald of Wales's account of the thankful mother, this scene may have been intended as a feminine model. The text emphasised that women should not only enable their kinsmen in crusade, but outwardly celebrate their achievements in holy war, even if that was martyrdom.

Other than taking crusade vows, offering money or simply celebrating crusade, thirteenth-century propaganda laboured the value of prayer and liturgical procession as a means of actively engaging with the movement. One English ordinance for crusade processions encouraged parish priests to enlist the laity's help, using very gender-neutral terms. This document exists only in an untitled late thirteenth-century copy but was probably originally drafted between 1241 and 1261.[90] It details the responsibility of the clergy and laity to entreat God's favour for a proposed crusade against the Tartars. In this context, that referred to the Mongols

---

[85] Eudes of Châteauroux, 'Sermo III', in Maier, *Crusade Propaganda and Ideology*, pp. 152–9, at 159, "et si non vultis eos sequi corpore, saltem corde et oratione et subsidio debetis eos sequi".

[86] C.T. Maier, '*Brevis Ordinacio de Predicacione Sancte Crucis*: Edition, Translation and Commentary', *Crusades*, vol. 18 (2019), pp. 25–65, at 25–6.

[87] Maier, '*Brevis Ordinacio de Predicacione Sancte Crucis*', pp. 27–30; Tyerman, *England and the Crusades*, pp. 163–5; Tamminen, *Crusade Preaching and the Ideal Crusader*, p. 39.

[88] Maier, '*Brevis Ordinacio de Predicacione Sancte Crucis*', p. 56, n. h; Tamminen, *Crusade Preaching and the Ideal Crusader*, pp. 192–3.

[89] Maier, '*Brevis Ordinacio de Predicacione Sancte Crucis*', p. 57, for Latin see p. 56: "hoc audito a matre ipsorum, ipsa laudauit Deum, quod ipse ita respexerat eam, quod ipsa filium talem peperit, qui ei fuit placabilis".

[90] Bird, Peters and Powell, *Crusade and Christendom*, p. 325; F.M. Powicke and C.R. Cheney (eds), *Councils & Synods with Other Documents Relating to The English Church, Vol. II, A.D. 1205–1313, Part I, 1205–1265* (Oxford, 1964), no. iii, p. 338.

Preaching Patronage

who had built up a presence in the Near East, attacking Muslims and Christians alike.[91] The ordinance envisioned that, in rural areas, processions should be held, whenever the parishioners gathered for Sunday mass or feast days.[92] Much like the preaching tactics that John le Romeyn would advise in Yorkshire in the 1290s, the idea was to embed crusading culture into parishioners' daily lives. The Tartars' supposed crimes were to be read out by parish priests so that: "…stricken with fear, their [the parishioners'] devotion might be aroused".[93]

Priests were expected to fast and give alms to the poor on the days of the processions and to, again leading by example, encourage the laity to do likewise.[94] These ordinances highlight that parish priests should incite a communal sense of responsibility for the success of crusade, regardless of the sex or social status of the parishioner. As per *Quia maior*'s regulations, such spiritual support would have been rewarded with indulgences and priests may have pointed this out. The activities outlined in this ordinance probably became a fairly regular occurrence for people living in England during the 1200s.

Everyday Christian acts, such as confessing sins, were harnessed for the crusade movement. This sort of support for the Holy Land was singled out during the Second Council of Lyon. This was a significant Church synod, convened by Pope Gregory X, in 1274. Humbert of Romans, composed his *Opus Tripartitum* for the event, in which he championed acts of communal humility, such as fasting, almsgiving and processions.[95] The Council of Lyon was held during the aftermath of King Louis IX of France's disastrous second crusade, in which he died of disease at Tunis in 1270. In searching for a reason for the habitual failure of crusade, many contemporaries felt that the general sinfulness of Christendom was bringing God's ire on the movement. The shared responsibility of those who remained in England (regardless of gender) toward crusade would have been consistently invoked during this period of introspection. To some extent, clerics may have used slightly more aggressive tactics in this respect, inculcating in the laity a sense of guilt for these failures, pushing pious behaviour as a means to reverse the shortcomings of Christian campaigns.

---

[91] For more on this era, see: N. Morton, *The Mongol Storm: Making and Breaking Empires in the Medieval Near East* (New York, 2022).

[92] Bird, Peters and Powell, *Crusade and Christendom*, p. 326.

[93] Bird, Peters and Powell, *Crusade and Christendom*, p. 326. For original Latin, see: Powicke and Cheney, *Councils & Synods*, no. iii, p. 340, "ut incusso timore eorum excitetur devotio".

[94] Bird, Peters and Powell, *Crusade and Christendom*, pp. 326–7.

[95] 'Opus Tripartitum', in E. Brown (ed.), *Appendix ad Fasciculus Rerum Expetendarum et Fugiendum* (London, 1690), cpt. 25, p. 204. See also: J.A. Brundage, 'Humbert of Romans and the Legitimacy of Crusader Conquests', in Kedar, *The Horns of Hattīn*, pp. 302–13.

Participation in prayer, procession and liturgy became a cornerstone of crusading identity, and evidently huge swathes of society were invited to participate in this.[96] Whatever assortment of tactics and language preachers employed, by the end of 1200s, the crusade had become firmly entrenched in the layperson's spiritual education. Amnon Linder has drawn particular attention to the Holy Land *Clamores* – a series of supplicatory texts that were inserted into the mass following the events of 1187 – they remained an expected feature of Church services for the following three centuries.[97]

Political or Pseudo-Crusades

In England, Church agents predominantly focused their sermons on crusades aimed at the recovery of the Holy Land. Yet, other conflicts developed within the British Isles and throughout the West that were variously treated as crusades and/or harnessed the rhetoric and culture of holy war. The ideology of crusade began to be applied to secular or politically-motivated warfare, as a justification for conquest or perhaps to assuage the aggressors' sense of remorse. Clerics may have directed women toward supporting some of these ventures, too. Although these political crusades were often fuelled by complicated layers of motivations, they again formed part of the backdrop of crusading culture, and particularly violence, that English contemporaries navigated.

Civil unrest and persecutions occurred during this period, which were fuelled by crusade. This happened most notably against Jewish communities. When the First Crusade was developing, horrendous attacks were inflicted against the Jewish population of Europe, particularly in the Rhineland in the spring of 1096.[98] Antisemitism was rampant across medieval Europe, and many used crusades as the moment to initiate pogroms.[99] England was little different in this respect.

---

[96] Maier, 'Crisis, Liturgy and Crusade', p. 628; M.C. Gaposchkin, *Invisible Weapons: Liturgy and the Making of Crusade Ideology* (Ithaca, 2017), pp. 122–9. See also: C. MacEvit, 'Processing Together, Celebrating Apart: Shared Procession in the Latin East', *Journal of Medieval history*, vol. 43, no. 4 (2017), pp. 455–69, at 456.

[97] A. Linder, *Raising Arms: Liturgy in the Struggle to Liberate Jerusalem in the Late Middle Ages* (Turnhout, 2003), p. 3; R.W. Pfaff, *The Liturgy in Medieval England, A History* (Cambridge, 2009), p. 287.

[98] R. Chazan, *God, Humanity, and History: The Hebrew First Crusade Narratives* (Berkeley, 2000); J. Cohen, *Sanctifying the Name of God: Jewish Martyrs and Jewish Memories of the First Crusade* (Philadelphia, 2004), pp. 1–12; K. McGrath, 'The "Zeal of God": The Representation of Anger in the Latin Crusade Accounts of the 1096 Rhineland Massacres', in K.T. Utterback and M.L. Price (eds), *Jews in Medieval Christendom: Slay Them Not* (Leiden, 2013), pp. 25–44.

[99] C.T. Maier, 'Papal Crusade Propaganda and Attacks Against Jews in France in the 1230s: a Breakdown of Communication?', *Journal of Medieval History*, vol. 49, no. 3 (2023), pp. 339–52.

King Richard I took a crusade vow not long before his coronation in September 1189, and his nobles quickly followed suit. While celebrations were underway for Richard's accession to the throne, the population of London began assaulting the city's Jewish quarter. Over the following months, attacks erupted across England. Hundreds if not thousands of Jewish people were harassed or killed in Lincoln, Norwich, Lynn, Stamford, York, Bury St Edmunds and elsewhere.[100] In York, many of the city's Jewish population took refuge in a tower – thought to be Clifford's Tower – and set the building alight, committing mass suicide rather than be captured by the mob. Some of the attackers were themselves crusaders. These individuals were quick to take advantage of the chaos in York and destroyed the Jewish records of loans in the minster, perhaps indicating that certain clauses in these contracts frustrated their departure for the Holy Land.[101] The ferocity of these events was been brought sharply into focus by the archaeological discovery in 2004 of the remains of as many as seventeen victims who were dumped in a well in Norwich.[102] A wider community than just *crucesignati* – those "signed with the cross" – endorsed and participated in these attacks, highlighting that the violent aspects of crusading culture were acutely felt at home. Antisemitism escalated over the following decades and a slew of laws were enacted that marginalised minority groups. This reached a crescendo in England, when King Edward I issued the Edict of Expulsion in 1290, forcing the Jewish population to leave the Kingdom. Although the culture of crusade was not the sole motivation behind antisemitic sentiments in medieval England, it was a serious contributing factor and many would have observed or leveraged the links.

The Cambro-Norman conquest of Ireland is an early example where the crusading ethos was applied to full-scale warfare in the British Isles. A papal bull, *Laudabiliter*, issued in 1155 or early 1156 offered King Henry II a justification for intervening in Ireland and asserting the Church of Canterbury's status over the Irish Church. The document effectively gave Henry II carte blanche to invade the island.[103] The authenticity of this document has been rigorously questioned, and it is true that Henry certainly did not make incursions into Ireland in the 1150s. Yet, *Laudabiliter* was endorsed by Pope Alexander III in the following decades, as a

---

[100] Hurlock, *Britain, Ireland and the Crusades*, pp. 135–9; S. Watson, 'Introduction: The Moment and Memory of the York Massacre of 1190', in S. R. Jones and S. Watson (eds), *Christians and Jews in Angevin England: The York Massacre of 1190, Narratives and Contexts* (York, 2013), pp. 1–14, at 7; T. Booth, 'The Massacres of the Jews under Richard I (A.D. 1189–1190)', *Religions*, vol. 12 (2021), pp. 1–11.

[101] Tyerman, *England and the Crusades*, p. 204; Watson, 'Introduction', p 7.

[102] S. Brace *et al*, 'Genomes from a Medieval Mass Burial Show Ashkenazi-associated Hereditary Diseases pre-date the 12th century', *Current Biology*, vol. 32 (2022), pp. 1–10.

[103] A.J. Duggan, '*Totius christianitatis caput*. The Pope and the Princes', in Bolton and Duggan, *Adrian IV The English Pope (1154–1159)*, pp. 105–55, at 138–46.

spiritual as well as a political rationalisation for Norman invasion and conquest.[104] The arrivals began in earnest in 1169, with opportunists like Richard "Strongbow" FitzGilbert, and culminated with King Henry's assumption of the Lordship over Ireland in 1171. As Colin Veach argues, although Henry II's empire-building in Ireland developed out of opportune circumstances, these events were rooted in an Anglo-Norman belief in their religious and cultural superiority over the Irish.[105] The conquest employed rhetoric concerning the expansion of Christendom and the 'true' Christian faith, making it "rather like" a crusade.[106] However, there was no accompanying formal preaching of indulgences for fighting or supporting early conflicts like this one.[107]

Matters would become more convoluted in the following century, however. Two major civil wars broke out in England during the 1200s. The First Barons' War (1215–7) pitted King John against many of his magnates after he reneged on the guarantees made in Magna Carta, while the Second Barons' War (1264–7) saw Simon de Montfort (d.1265) lead a rebellion against King Henry III. Both of these wars were treated as pseudo-crusades by contemporaries, in part, because both King John and Henry III were *crucesignati* at the time of the conflicts.[108] It has often been noted that these royalist and rebel armies sewed crosses of differing colours onto their clothing to distinguish friend from foe during battle, harnessing the visual culture and trappings of crusaders.[109] Some clergy offered people who were already *crucesignati* the option of commuting their crusade vows by fighting in these wars.[110] This was not just the hollow promises of partisan clerics. In 1263,

---

[104] R.R. Davies, *Domination and Conquest: The Experience of Ireland, Scotland and Wales, 1100–1300* (Cambridge, 1990), pp. 67–8 and 111; M.B. Callan, *The Templars, the Witch, and the Wild Irish: Vengeance and Heresy in Medieval Ireland* (Dublin, 2015), pp. 38–41.

[105] C. Veach, 'Henry II and the Ideological Foundations of Angevin Rule in Ireland', *Irish Historical Studies*, vol. 42, no. 161 (2018), pp. 1–25; M.B. Callan, 'Conquest as Crusade: Ireland's Invasion and a Colonial Plea to the Papacy', in E. Coleman, P. Duffy and T. O'Keeffe (eds), *Ireland and the Crusades* (Dublin, 2022), pp. 52–69.

[106] J. France, *The Crusades and the Expansion of Catholic Christendom, 1000–1714* (London and New York, 2005), p. 144; M.B Callan, *The Templars, The Witch, and the Wild Irish: Vengeance and Heresy in Medieval Ireland* (Ithaca, 2014).

[107] Hurlock, *Britain, Ireland and the Crusades*, pp. 102–5.

[108] F. Hill, *Excommunication in Thirteenth-Century England: Communities, Politics, and Publicity* (Oxford, 2022), pp. 130–6; S. Lloyd, '"Political Crusades" in England, c.1215–17 and c.1263–5', in Edbury, *Crusade and Settlement*, pp. 113–20; Hurlock, *Britain, Ireland and the Crusades*, pp. 94–102. See also: B. Bandlien, 'Civil War as Holy War? Polyphonic Discourses on Warfare During the Internal Struggles in Norway in the Twelfth Century', in R. Kotecki, C.S. Jensen and S. Bennett (eds), *Christianity and War in Medieval East Central Europe and Scandinavia* (Leeds, 2021), pp. 227–43.

[109] Hurlock, *Britain, Ireland and the Crusades*, p. 96; Lloyd, '"Political Crusades"', p. 116; J.R. Maddicott, *Simon de Montfort* (Cambridge, 1994), p. 271.

[110] Hurlock, *Britain, Ireland and the Crusades*, p. 100.

Preaching Patronage

Pope Urban IV clearly stated that crusaders could consider their vows fulfilled if they joined royalist forces in fighting the Montfortian rebels.[111] However, these forms of commutation were unlikely to have been open to many women.

It is at least plausible that anyone who aided either side during these wars may have interpreted their actions as a form of support for holy war, in a broad sense of the term. However, very little is known of the crusade preaching that concerned these rebellions. Cardinal Ottobueno, a papal legate, was appointed to preach the crusade in England towards the end of the Second Barons' War; he emphasised that Henry III's cause was a form of crusade. Yet, none of his sermons have survived, and so it is impossible to determine how the wider laity and, more importantly here, elite women, were instructed to act.[112] King Henry III himself never used his war against the Montfortians as an excuse to commute the vow he had made to go on crusade in 1250. During the early stages of the war, he even waived a debt of 2000*l* that King Louis IX of France owed him, so long as Louis supported 500 knights in the Holy Land, to partly satisfy Henry's crusade vow.[113] This was hardly the act of a king who felt he was already actively engaging in a holy war. Likewise, the bishops supporting Simon de Montfort's rebellion never gave "wholehearted endorsement" to their campaign constituting a crusade.[114] If women were encouraged to support these movements by preachers, it is unlikely that doing so was considered as beneficial, for their souls or Christendom, as supporting crusade to Jerusalem.

King Edward I's various conflicts in Wales (lasting intermittently from 1276–95) and Scotland (1296–1307) were also occasionally linked to crusade. Various factions justified the need for peace talks, because these wars distracted from Christendom's duty in pursuing crusade in the Holy Land. For example, in 1282, during the conquest of Wales, John Pecham, archbishop of Canterbury (r.1279–92), proposed that the Welsh prince Dafydd ap Gruffydd (d.1283) go on crusade as a means to end the conflict in Gwynedd.[115] However, Pecham's motivation may have been to encourage leaders of Welsh resistance to leave their lands undefended. In Scotland, the fighting may have come closer to being defined as crusade. In 1296 and again in 1306, Scottish clerics preached that to fight against Edward I's

---

[111] M.J. Guiraud (ed.), *Registres d'Urbain IV (1261–1264)* (Paris, 1901), p. 300, no. 596.

[112] Lloyd, '"Political Crusades"', pp. 116–7; S. Lloyd, 'The Lord Edward's Crusade, 1270–2: its setting and significance', in J. Gillingham and J.C. Holt (eds), *War and Government in the Middle Ages* (Woodbridge, 1984), pp. 120–33, at 121–2.

[113] *CPR, 1258–66*, p. 317.

[114] Lloyd, '"Political Crusades"', p. 116; Maddicott, *Simon de Montfort*, p. 233.

[115] Hurlock, *Wales and the Crusades*, p. 178; K. Hurlock, 'Power, Preaching and the Crusades in Pura Wallia c.1180-c.1280', in B. Weiler, J. Burton, P. Schofield and K. Stöber (eds), *Thirteenth Century England XI: Proceedings of the Gregynog Conference 2005* (Woodbridge, 2007), pp. 95–108, at 102–8.

incursions was more justified and meritorious than the crusade in the Holy Land.[116] How successful they were in shifting laypeople's perspectives is debatable. In another famous episode, in 1300, King Edward I and his troops entered Annandale (Dumfries and Galloway) and supposedly marked themselves with the sign of the cross and used crosses as insignia.[117] Despite these tantalising examples, there is little evidence that preachers were similarly encouraging the wider English laity to support the conquest of Scotland to the detriment of the recovery of the Holy Land.

Women in medieval England were routinely exposed to the propaganda of crusade. Imagery and rhetoric that extolled holy war were easy to find, but the messages that they conveyed were mixed. In the twelfth century, while women's support was not readily solicited, it was nevertheless considered a welcome and commendable act. This dynamic changed radically by the 1220s. The measures imposed by the thirteenth-century papacy offered women an array of avenues for involving themselves in crusade. Beyond physically going on campaigns, women were advised that they could attain the spiritual rewards of a combative crusader by remaining in England and dedicating themselves to prayer, monetary contributions and enabling holy war. This not only bestowed recognition on those assisting ideal martial recruits, but also cultivated a distinctive paradigm of feminine crusading ideals. Although many people undoubtedly engaged in all these endeavours from the outset of crusade, the idea that this could become model behaviour was, in large part, the construct of churchmen. Affluent women, in particular, were pushed toward these activities and ideals, and encouraged to identify with them on a routine basis.

---

[116] A. MacQuarrie, *Scotland and the Crusades, 1095–1560* (Edinburgh, 1985), p. 71.
[117] Tyerman, *England and the Crusades*, pp. 330–1.

PART II

Support

4

Encouraging Crusaders

> William [II Longespée] – with the permission and blessing of his mother, the noble and holy abbess of Lacock – led all the crusaders from the kingdom of England.
>
> (Matthew Paris [d.1259], monk at St Albans Abbey)[1]

When academics discuss the recruitment for crusade, this typically refers to the preaching drives and the activities of clerics signing laypeople with the cross and administering their vows. This is a perfectly valid means of defining recruitment, but many parties were at play in the conditioning of crusade culture. Laypeople often consulted with numerous individuals before embarking on a pilgrimage, and were undoubtedly swayed in one direction or another by their peers. Gerald of Wales's description of Arthenus, the Welsh nobleman who hesitated in taking a crusade vow so he could consult with his friends, is a classic example. Indeed, many contemporaries went on crusade outside of the large canonical expeditions, travelling on so-called private or independent crusades. In these instances, the impetus to go on crusade may not have come directly from preachers' sermons but from discussions with other laypeople.[2] This chapter investigates the evidence for laywomen's encouragement of their family and peers to go on crusade.

Recruitment

It is patent that many women pushed friends or kin to go to the Holy Land, even when they were reluctant to go on campaign themselves. Adela of Blois (d.1137) is often held up as the example *par excellence*.[3] Her husband, Stephen of Blois, returned to France having abandoned the First Crusaders to their fate at the Siege of Antioch in 1098. The chronicler Orderic Vitalis colourfully details the way

---

[1] *Chronica Majora*, vol. 5, p. 76, "Willelmus igitur cum licentia et benedictione matris suae nobilis ac sanctae abbatissae de Acoc, dux omnium cruce signatorum de regno Angliae".
[2] On women "initialising" crusades, see: Nicholson, *Women and the Crusades,* pp. 21–52.
[3] Rousseau, 'Home Front and Battlefield', p. 31; Hodgson, *Women, Crusading and the Holy Land in Historical Narrative*, p. 116.

83

Laywomen and the Crusade in England, 1150–1300

Adela repudiated her husband while they slept together.[4] Stephen ultimately relented and returned to the East where he was killed in 1102. Adela probably was not alone in encouraging (or pressuring) her family into crusade.[5] Prior to *Ex multa* in 1201 – when Innocent III allowed individuals to take crusade vows without their spouses' consent – theoretically, every married person wishing to go on crusade had to gain the permission of their husband or wife.[6] Despite Innocent III's ruling, it seems highly unlikely that those who went to the Holy Land in the following decades had no dialogue with their kinsfolk.

Helping in recruitment fitted the model of the crusade supporter. It is clear that preachers extolled women who encouraged their family members to take up crusade vows. One of the texts of the encyclical *Rachel suum videns* sent to England in 1234 even offered indulgences to people who gave encouraging counsel to crusaders. One of the clearest examples of this from France can be seen in Alice de Montmorency countess of Montfort (d.1221). She tirelessly pressured soldiers to fight for her husband Simon de Montfort (d.1218) and her son Amaury (d.1241) during the Albigensian Crusades against the Cathars of southern France (1209–29). She was roundly praised by contemporary writers for her help and guidance in this matter.[7] However, Alice de Montmorency and Adela of Blois's examples are unique, not because their actions were atypical, but because similar references in surviving texts are lacking. The writer of the *Itinerarium Peregrinorum* claimed English wives and mothers urged their menfolk to join the Third Crusade, and in all probability this did happen.[8] Yet, the author did not name any crusaders who had gone at the behest of their wife or mother. Such affirmations, in England, are rare. The paradox is: women were very likely to have been instrumental in recruitment and it was considered an ideal form of support, but there are few references to it. Instead, we see indications of women's encouragement within the surviving sources.

Hints appear around the practice of sending so-called crusade proxies. A person could contract another to go on a crusade on their behalf, either by paying their

---

4 Orderic Vitalis, *The Ecclesiastical History of Orderic Vitalis*, 6 vols, M. Chibnall (ed. and trans.) (Oxford, 1969–80), at vol. 5, pp. 324–5; W.M. Aird, '"Many others, whose names I do not know, fled with them": Norman Courage and Cowardice on the First Crusade', in Hurlock and Oldfield, *Crusading and Pilgrimage in the Norman World*, pp. 13–29, at 26–7; LoPrete, *Adela of Blois*, pp. 111–12.
5 Although they were not related, the famous German abbess and polymath, Hildegard von Bingen, was contacted by Philip I Count of Flanders for advice and blessing of his crusade in the 1170s, see: M.R. Tessera, 'Philip Count of Flanders and Hildegard of Bingen: Crusading Against the Saracens or Crusading Against Deadly Sin?', in Edgington and Lambert, *Gendering the Crusades*, pp. 77–93.
6 Brundage, 'The Crusader's Wife', pp. 434–5.
7 Nicholson, *Women and the Crusades*, pp. 42–4.
8 Nicholson, *The Chronicle of the Third Crusade*, bk. I, cpt. 17, p. 48.

expenses or perhaps simply by asking them to go.[9] William Marshal, later earl of Pembroke (d.1219), is probably the most famous example of a crusade-proxy to come out of England. When Henry the Young King (d.1183) lay dying, he gave his cloak – decorated with the crusader's insignia of a cross – to William, entrusting him with undertaking his vow. Henry's father, King Henry II, even paid some of William's expenses, perhaps as an inducement to keep his word.[10] Some people took crusade vows with the sole intention of sending a proxy. In 1292, an ecclesiastical court in Canterbury heard that one John, the vicar of Potterne, had explicitly told the preacher who administered his crusader's vow that he would take the oath on the condition that he could send one or more proxies in his place.[11]

Landholding women in England probably came to similar compromises with the agents of the Cross and their families. In a testament dated January 1268, William III de Beauchamp, sheriff of Worcester, left 200*m* to his crusader son Walter. William stipulated that this was "in aid of his [Walter's] pilgrimage to the Holy Land for me and his mother".[12] Walter's mother, Isabel de Mauduit, was described as being alive in her husband's testament, but she had died by the time it was being executed.[13] Evidently, she would have been aware that her son was going to go on crusade on her spiritual behalf. Isabel may well have urged this action, perhaps with the knowledge that her own end was drawing near. Similarly, it has been suggested that Otto de Grandson, a Savoyard knight and friend of King Edward I, may have gone on crusade on behalf of Eleanor of Castile, Edward's consort. Otto went to the East in 1290 and Eleanor died only months later; she left two manors to Otto in her will, and a depiction of him kneeling at the Holy Sepulchre was painted on Eleanor's tomb in Westminster Abbey.[14] A third example dates from 1291, when Pope Nicholas IV (r.1288–92) directly asked a Suffolk-based noblewoman named Eva Tibetot to redeem her crusade vow by paying the expenses of a warrior to go to the Holy Land.[15] Whether she did so, however, is unknown.

---

[9] G. Fort, 'Suffering Another's Sin: Proxy Penance in the Thirteenth Century', *Journal of Medieval History*, vol. 44, no. 2 (2018), pp. 202–30.

[10] Tyerman, *England and the Crusades*, pp. 49–50; D. Crouch, *William Marshal*, 3rd edn (Abingdon, 2016), pp. 67–8; Hurlock, *Britain, Ireland and the Crusades*, pp. 69–70.

[11] N. Adams and C. Donahue (eds), *Select Cases from the Ecclesiastical Courts of the Province of Canterbury c.1200–1301* (London, 1981), p. 383.

[12] J.W. Willis Bund (ed.), *Episcopal Registers, Diocese of Worcester, Register of Bishop Godfrey Giffard*, 2 Parts (Oxford, 1898–9), Part 1, pp. 7–9, at 8.

[13] E. Mason (ed.), *The Beauchamp Cartulary Charters 1100–1268* (London, 1980), p. lviii.

[14] G.M. Reynolds, 'Proxy over Pilgrimage: Queen Eleanor of Castile and the Celebration of Crusade upon her Funerary Monument(s)', *Peregrinations*, vol. 8, no. 4 (2023), pp. 117–39; E.R. Clifford., *A Knight of Great Renown: The Life and Times of Othon de Grandson* (Chicago, 1961), p. 126.

[15] E. Langlois (ed.), *Les Registres de Nicholas IV*, 2 vols (Paris, 1886–91), at vol. 1, p. 650, no. 4490.

Scholars have considered the problems and possibilities in identifying women's involvement in recruitment. Riley-Smith famously researched the crusading associations of French noble houses, particularly the Monthléry, Courtenay and le Puiset families. He suggested that women with a history of crusading in their natal family probably encouraged that same enthusiasm in their husbands or children.[16] The importance of family traditions as a motivation for crusaders has since attracted considerable attention and clear patterns have been found in many knightly kin groups.[17] Historians have expanded upon these ideas and found some fascinating inroads for understanding how people passed on these traditions. Medieval romance literature, for example, placed great importance on women as transmitters of dynastic oral history, and so it has been argued that this, too, may have been a reflection of their role in retelling stories of crusade.[18]

As with all things, people love finding patterns, and there are some very convincing signs of crusading traditions within medieval families and networks. But it is always hard to confidently state who within these groups urged on crusading habits: a mother, a father or a retainer with an interest in their patron's genealogy? The sermons that championed crusade habitually played upon knights' sense of family lineage by encouraging them to follow in the footsteps of crusading forebears.[19]

Some individuals within dynastic traditions, however, appear to have had such a personal interest in crusade that we might conjecture that they did indeed champion their family's customs. Emma Mason, for example, has suggested that Margaret de Perche pressured her son, Roger de Beaumont of Warwick (d.1153), to go on crusade. Margaret did indeed have a crusading background in her family – her brother had joined the First Crusade – but, as Mason pointed out, Margaret was also a benefactor of the Templars. This is a clear indication that Margaret had intentions to further the crusade.[20] The best evidence for women's involvement in recruitment is their enablement or sponsorship of crusaders, or demonstrations of an interest in crusading culture.

The twelfth-century noblewomen Gundreda de Gournay is a useful example here. Her father was a famed First Crusader and her brother also journeyed to the East.[21] Gundreda married a Yorkshire nobleman, Nigel d'Aubigny (d.1129),

---

16 Riley-Smith, 'Family Traditions', pp. 101–4; Riley-Smith, *The First Crusaders*, pp. 93–9.
17 Paul, *To Follow in Their Footsteps*; Paul and Schenk, 'Family Memory and the Crusades', pp. 177–82; Bennett, *Elite Participation in the Third Crusade*, pp. 90–120.
18 Paul, *To Follow in Their Footsteps*, p. 69. See also: E. van Houts, *Memory and Gender in Medieval Europe, 900–1200* (Basingstoke, 1999), pp. 65–92; S.G. Bell, 'Medieval Women Book Owners: Arbiters of Lay Piety and Ambassadors of Culture', *Journal of Women in Culture and Society*, vol. 7, no. 4 (1982), pp. 742–68.
19 Paul and Schenk, 'Family Memory and the Crusades', p. 177.
20 Mason, 'Fact and Fiction in the English Crusading Tradition', pp. 82–3.
21 For Gerard de Gournay's participation on the First Crusade, see: Riley-Smith, *The First Crusaders*, App. 1., p. 208; D. Power, *The Norman Frontier in the Twelfth and Early Thirteenth Centuries* (Cambridge, 2004), pp. 356–8.

Encouraging Crusaders

whose family had no connections to crusading.[22] The couple had a son, Roger de Mowbray, who Gundreda supported very closely throughout his life. Their shared interests are indicated, around 1138, when Gundreda and her son jointly gifted a yearly rent of 1*m* to the Knights Hospitaller.[23]

When preparations began in western Europe for the Second Crusade (1147–50), Roger decided to leave Yorkshire to join the expedition.[24] By this point, Gunrdeda had been a widow for nearly twenty years, most of Roger's life. Before going on his crusade, Roger drew up a charter in which he agreed to confirm – that is, legally endorse – whatever gift of land his mother would give to the monks of Garendon Abbey (Leicestershire), in return for their prayers for his soul.[25] Gundreda gave them thirty-two acres and a meadow, asking again for prayers for Roger.[26] Sometime later, she gave four bovates of land to the hospital of St. Leonards in York in return for their prayers for Roger (and her husband), in a charter dated between 1142 and 1154.[27] This probably happened while Roger was still on the crusade. Her choice of religious house to patronise mid-campaign is very telling: St Leonard is the patron saint of horses and women in labour, but also captives and prisoners of war.

Gundreda had kin who were crusaders, she was enthusiastic about the Military Orders, and she helped enable her son's crusade (spiritually at least). Her natal family's interest forms a likely motivation for her own activities and Roger's, while her facilitation of Roger's crusading indicates that she encouraged him. The ambitions of would-be crusaders were often checked by the generosity of their friends and family. Therefore, it is highly plausible that if a family member was fiscally supportive then they were probably also encouraging.

---

[22] E.M.C. van Houts (ed. and trans.), *Gesta Normannorum Ducum of William of Jumièges, Orderic Vitalis, and Robert of Torigni*, 2 vols (Oxford, 1992–5, reprinted: 2003), at vol. 2, bk viii, cpt. 8, p. 215.

[23] D.E. Greenway (ed.), *Charters of the Honour of Mowbray, 1107–1191* (London, 1972), p. 124, no. 170.

[24] John of Hexham confirmed Roger's presence on this crusade and one of Roger's later charters referenced his "first" crusade, probably referring to his journey in the 1140s: John of Hexham, 'Historia Regum', in T. Arnold (ed.), *Symeonis Monachi Opera Omnia*, 2 vols (London, 1882–5), vol. 2, pp. 284–332, at 319; Greenway, *Charters of the Honour of Mowbray*, p. 126, no. 174 and p. xlv; J. Burton (ed.), *The Foundation History of the Abbeys of Byland and Jervaulx* (York, 2006), pp. 39–40.

[25] Greenway, *Charters of the Honour of Mowbray*, p. 116, no. 155; p. 118, no. 160.

[26] Greenway, *Charters of the Honour of Mowbray*, p. 116, no. 156.

[27] Greenway, *Charters of the Honour of Mowbray*, p. 197, no. 300.

Financing Crusade

Standing armies were not a fixture of medieval England, so there was no strict machinery in place to deploy an army without support from soldiers' local communities or extended kin groups. Although many individuals (such as knights) were professional soldiers, so to speak, they generally outfitted themselves with all the necessary equipment, weapons and training, and in any case, war was rarely their sole occupation. Crusaders and pilgrims, likewise, largely had to rely on private funding.[28] By the later twelfth and thirteenth centuries crusade organisation was developing rapidly. Secular rulers extracted cash from Jewish communities and taxed their subjects to supplement crusaders.[29] Likewise, the papacy judiciously collected a fortieth from ecclesiastical revenues throughout Christendom to form subsidies that were allocated to royal or noble crusaders.[30] The collection of this money became such a feature of religious communities' lives that, when the Mamluks captured the last Christian city on the mainland of the Levant, Acre in 1291, the anonymous Dunstable Annalist tells us that one of the main concerns regarded future tax:

> How could the town of Acre itself be retaken? How could it be guarded when recaptured? What should be the subsidies and who should pay them? For how long should those subsidies or contributions continue?[31]

Despite the official funding they might receive, crusading was, by its nature, highly unpredictable and contemporaries had to account for financial setbacks. While deep in enemy territory, prices of foodstuffs could quickly skyrocket, and an army carrying heaps of silver bullion and coinage – in an age where barter was common – could cause severe localised inflation.[32] Therefore, many crusaders gathered as much portable wealth as possible before they departed.

---

[28] Powell, *Anatomy of a Crusade*, p. 89; Constable, 'The Financing of the Crusade in the Twelfth Century', p. 70.

[29] Edwards, *Finance and the Crusades*; Hurlock, *Britain, Ireland and the Crusades*, pp. 44–6.

[30] Lunt, *Financial Relations of the Papacy with England to 1327*, see particularly pp. 446–8.

[31] D. Preest and H.R. Webster (eds and trans.), *The Annals of Dunstable Priory* (Woodbridge, 2018), p. 249. For the original Latin, see: Luard, *Annales Monastici*, vol. 3, p. 366, "qualiter iterum posset civitas ipsa capi? qualiter capta custodiri? quibus et quorum subsidiis, et per quantum tempus illud subsidium seu contributio continuari debuisset?".

[32] A.V. Murray, 'Money and Logistics in the forces of the First Crusade: Coinage, Bullion, Service and Supply, 1096–99', in J.H. Pryor (ed.), *Logistics of Warfare in the Age of the Crusades* (Aldershot, 2006), pp. 229–50, at 230–1; Murray, 'Roads, Bridges and Shipping in the Passage of Crusade Armies', pp. 183–207; Murray, 'The Middle Ground', pp. 190–1; Tyerman, *England and the Crusades*, pp. 188–9.

Encouraging Crusaders

Most, if not all, crusaders sought surplus funds, either through the support of their lord, kin and community, by extorting marginalised groups or by plundering on the march. During the Third Crusade (1189–92), as the German contingent marched across Philomelion in Byzantine territory, individuals were forced to pay as much as 1*m* for a loaf of bread, one hundred times what they had budgeted for one day's expenses.[33] The ramifications of being underfunded could have disastrous geopolitical ripples. The Fourth Crusade (1202–4), in particular, gave many Latin Christians cause to be shocked and ashamed. Far fewer crusaders assembled for this expedition than the leaders had expected, and so the participants could not afford their contract for shipping and transport via their Venetian allies. They redeemed their debts by helping the Venetians sack one of their commercial competitors: the Christian city of Zara (modern-day Zadar, Croatia).[34] Later generations would have been keenly aware of the blunders of these previous expeditions. During preparations in England for the Lord Edward's Crusade (1270–2) – despite the large number of royal and papal subsidies on offer – participants frantically hunted for additional funds. The chancery records show that huge volumes of royal licences were given to crusaders, granting them permission to sell their estates or mortgage property for periods of ten years or more.[35] Any woman wishing to help support a crusader would have understood: the more, the better.

In some rare instances, crusading provided a financial reward for some commoners or serfs. A villein from Nottinghamshire named Hugh Travers was manumitted and given land for acting as his lord's crusade-proxy in the 1190s. Hugh's family prospered from the plot for over a century.[36] In another case, dating sometime before 1201, a Lincolnshire lord named Wido of Creon arranged to set out on crusade. While preparing, he was especially mindful of the loyal services he had received from a woman called Dionisia. Wido drafted a charter that promised that if he did not return in four years, Dionisia's husband, Hubert, was to be manumitted and granted hereditable lands.[37] Similarly, the eighteenth-century antiquarian John Collinson unearthed an interesting deed that he believed to date to 1229. The item stated that a commoner called John Gold was rewarded with an estate in Seaborough (Somerset) for acting as a crusade-proxy for his lord, Ralph de Vaux.[38] This medieval deed has unfortunately disappeared since Collinson saw it. However, there are mid-thirteenth-century charters from Forde

---

[33] Murray, 'Finance and Logistics of the Crusade of Frederick Barbarossa', p. 366.
[34] Powell, *Anatomy of a Crusade*, pp. 90–1; N. Hodgson, 'Honour, Shame and the Fourth Crusade', *Journal of Medieval History*, vol. 39, no. 2 (2018), pp. 220–39.
[35] B. Beebe, 'The English Baronage and the Crusade of 1270', *Bulletin of the Institute of Historical Research*, vol. 48, no. 118 (1975), pp. 127–48, at 131.
[36] F.M. Stenton, 'Early Manumissions at Staunton, Nottinghamshire', *English Historical Review*, vol. 26, no. 101 (1911), pp. 93–7.
[37] *CRR*, vol. 2, pp. 13–4.
[38] J. Collinson, *The History of Somersetshire*, 3 vols (London, 1791), at vol. 2, p. 172.

Abbey's cartulary that note property held by an Ellis Gold in Seaborough, and charter witnesses from the area named Alexander Golde and John Palmer, i.e. Pilgrim. At the risk of too much conjecture, it is not impossible that the latter was John Gold the proxy, who had returned.[39]

These three cases are fascinating instances of social mobility. However, the elite in society seldom gained renown as well as wealth through crusading. Examples occurred amongst those who settled in the East, such as Guy de Lusignan – who was exiled from Poitou for murder, went to the Holy Land, and became king of Jerusalem (r.1186–92) through marriage and political manoeuvring – but they were the exception.[40] The majority of crusaders intended on quickly returning from the Latin East, and this incurred costs. Armed pilgrimage typically constituted a financial loss for the nobility. Therefore, very few people would have supported a crusader as a form of monetary investment.

That said, it is difficult to offer an exact figure that a noble would typically have had to set aside for a crusade. Wealthier individuals often required more retainers who would, in turn, need subsidising, such as squires, farriers, chaplains and so on.[41] On top of this, the elite may also have had more liquid cash to hand, and so attempts to estimate their costs from the written record can easily be skewed.[42] There is no individual crusader whose accounts of financial preparations and support have been preserved entirely.[43] Nevertheless, some approximations have been made in the past, and highlight the substantial toll: an average western European knight in the twelfth century would need anywhere between four and seven times their annual income (as much as 35*m*) to go on crusade.[44]

Some cases give an impression of the numbers concerned in England. An inquest in 1201 determined that one Robert de Marisco had recently set out on crusade after his father furnished him with: 22*m*, 22 besants (a gold-based coinage associated with Byzantium), a gold ring, a hauberk (a long mail shirt), iron spurs, a

---

[39] S. Hobbs (ed.), *The Cartulary of Forde Abbey* (Taunton, 1998), p. 131, nos. 496 and 498.

[40] For more on Guy de Lusignan's rise, see: C. de Vasselot de Régné, 'A Crusader Lineage from Spain to the Throne of Jerusalem: The Lusignans', *Crusades*, vol. 16 (2017), pp. 95–114, at 102–6.

[41] Murray, 'Money and Logistics', p. 230; Tyerman, *How to Plan a Crusade*, p. 186.

[42] J. Riley-Smith, 'Early Crusaders to the East and the Costs of Crusading 1095–1130', in M. Goodich, S. Menanche and S. Schein (eds), *Cross Cultural Convergences in the Crusader Period, Essays Presented to Aryeh Grabois on his Sixty-Fifth Birthday* (New York, 1995), pp. 237–57, at 247.

[43] Tyerman, *England and the Crusades*, p. 189; Lloyd, *English Society and the Crusade*, p. 154.

[44] Riley-Smith, *The First Crusaders*, p. 112; Murray, 'Money and Logistics', pp. 231–2; Murray, 'Finance and Logistics of the Crusade of Frederick Barbarossa', p. 360; Powell, *Anatomy of a Crusade*, p. 99.

horse, a helmet, a sword and a red cloak.[45] This is just what Robert received from his father; his total funds may have been even higher. When setting out on their pilgrimage in 1228 – possibly to join the bishop of Winchester, Peter des Roches, or William Briwere, who were leading companies on the Sixth Crusade (1227–9) – an unspecified number of crusaders (*hominibus cruce signatis*) drowned when the bridge at Ferrybridge (Yorkshire) collapsed under them.[46] 17*l* 18*s* 10*d* was found on the bodies. Without being able to identify the dead and their heirs, the local authorities used the money to rebuild the bridge.[47] In 1270, during preparations for the Lord Edward's Crusade, English noblemen like Robert Tibetot, Payn de Chaworth and Adam de Jesmond were offered contracts to serve for one year in return for a 100*m* each.[48] This figure partly reflects the effects of inflation over the thirteenth century, as well as an expectation that these crusaders would subsidise others in their personal retinues.

Supporters and crusaders alike mortgaged or sold assets such as land, privileges and rents, as well as called in debts, in order to raise money. It could, and often did, take months or even years to raise the necessary capital.[49] This was partly because it was extremely difficult to get credit without surrendering sizeable collateral. Mortgages in this period were frequently usufructory pledges. This usually meant that the creditor did not gain profit through interest on the loan. Instead, the debtor offered some useful collateral – such as farmland or the rent on a property – and the creditor enjoyed the use of, and gained profit through, the collateral over an agreed period of time, and/or until the debtor redeemed their assets by paying the principle. Medieval people often relied on this sort of transaction to get credit, while avoiding accusations of the sin of usury – the practice of charging interest on loans. The Church was extremely concerned that crusaders might engage in usury.

Between 1187 and 1188, the papacy decreed that creditors could not charge interest on loans that they had given to *crucesignati*, nor could a moneylender demand past debts until a crusader's vow had been completed. This may have been an attempt to help crusaders who were already hampered by debts, but it made the process of getting a new bond of credit nearly impossible.[50] To make

---

[45] Stenton, *Pleas Before the King or his Justices 1198–1202*, vol. 2, p. 49, no. 248. For a discussion of the source, see vol. 1, p. 135.

[46] For more on the contingent that Peter des Roches lead on crusade, see: N. Vincent, *Peter des Roches: An Alien in English Politics, 1205–1238* (Cambridge, 1996) (reprinted: 2002) pp. 229–58.

[47] *CCR, 1227–31*, pp. 34–5.

[48] Lloyd, 'The Lord Edward's Crusade', p. 126; London, British Library, Additional Charter 19829; H.G. Richardson and G.O. Sayles, *The Governance of Mediaeval England, from the Conquest to Magna Carta* (Edinburgh, 1963), pp. 464–5.

[49] See: Powell, *Anatomy of a Crusade*, pp. 67–87; C. Tyerman, *Fighting for Christendom: Holy War and the Crusades* (Oxford, 2004), p. 125.

[50] Tyerman, *England and the Crusades*, p. 197.

themselves more appealing to creditors, crusaders could take the drastic action of forfeiting the legal protections and privileges that came with their status as penitents. Otherwise, again, they could offer up land as collateral.

Most of the surviving charters and records that detail individuals' crusade preparations, frustratingly, do not detail the money involved or exchanged. This is almost certainly a reflection of the parties' fears over usury. A representative example of this sort of transaction can be seen in the case of Henry of Goxhill. Before going on crusade in the 1150s, he offered two bovates of land in Goxhill (Lincolnshire) to Robert of Sproatley (Yorkshire). Henry stipulated that Robert would not have to pay any rent on the land for eight years. Furthermore, if Henry did not return from the Holy Land within that time, the land was to be jointly held by the Hospital in Goxhill and the canons of Bridlington (Yorkshire), while Robert paid 2*s* each in rent (assuming he still wanted to use that land).[51] This charter does not state that Robert offered any cash up front, but that seems to be implicit. More than just gaining cash, if Henry's land reverted to his favoured religious house, he would have earned the clerics' prayers for his soul if he died on the expedition.

The evidence indicates that religious houses provided more than just spiritual support, they liberally supplied credit. Before departing England, many crusaders and their supporters gifted land to monastic institutions. This happened so frequently that it could cause complex administrative issues for Church leadership. In 1223, Richard Poore bishop of Salisbury was forced to stipulate that all clerics within his jurisdiction needed his express permission before entering into a contract with a crusader.[52] Evidently, he needed to regulate what properties/responsibilities they were taking on. Although the majority of the grants the Church received appear to have been simple *pro anima* gifts, in which the lay person asked for prayers only, there are numerous cases where clerics stated (or it may be inferred) that they offered cash. This has led some scholars to believe that many exchanges made with the Church during crusade preparations were done for undisclosed payments.[53]

For example, an anonymous monk and chronicler from Walden Priory (Essex) described how in 1176 the monks gave William de Mandeville III earl of Essex 100*m* and allowed him to choose clerks for seven of Walden's churches, if in

---

[51] *EYC*, vol. 3, p. 63, no. 1342.
[52] W.R. Jones and W.D. MacRay (eds), *Charters and Documents Illustrating the History of the Cathedral, City, and Diocese of Salisbury in the Twelfth and Thirteenth Centuries* (London, 1891), p. 151.
[53] Tyerman, *England and the Crusades*, pp. 198–9; Lloyd, *English Society and the Crusade*, p. 159. Cf: C.B. Bouchard, *Holy Entrepreneurs, Cistercians, Knights and Economic Exchange in Twelfth-Century Burgundy* (Ithaca, 1991), pp. 75–9. See also: B.H. Rosenwein, *To Be the Neighbor of Saint Peter: The Social Meaning of Cluny's Property, 909–1049* (Ithaca, 1989), p. 37; S. Sweetinburgh, *The Role of the Hospital in Medieval England: Gift-giving and the Spiritual Economy* (Dublin, 2004), pp. 35–7.

return William confirmed his father's foundation of the priory.[54] William was in such desperate need for the cash, and apparently pressed for time, that the monks were forced to get credit from Jewish lenders, which deeply perturbed the anonymous writer.[55] The following year, William departed on crusade with Philip I Count of Flanders. He had undoubtedly needed the money for his impending departure.[56] Both William's charter and stipulation for the seven churches' clerks survive, yet neither of these documents mentions that William was paid 100*m* or that the transaction took place ahead of his pilgrimage.[57] The crucial details that contemporaries deemed unnecessary to mention (or carefully omitted) from their charters can be astounding.

Enablement

There were no self-made crusaders. Anyone wishing to take part in holy war – travelling from England to the Mediterranean, the Holy Land, North Africa or further – needed help from those around them. There were clearly a number of fund-raising processes that a crusader could engage in, but they nevertheless required support and endorsement from their household, friends or the wider community; someone needed to help enable their crusade.

The term 'enablement' is used here to refer to women's consent to, or insistence upon, the disposal of their property or chattels to fund crusade.[58] Frequently, it appears, women in England did so by consenting to the liquidation of their dower lands (not to be confused with dowry). Dower encapsulated a third of the land that a married couple held (or specified lands agreed upon at marriage), which the wife would receive if widowed. Women's interest and personal ownership of

---

[54] For a discussion of the author of this text see: D. Greenway and L. Watkiss (eds and trans.), *The Book of the Foundation of Walden Monastery* (Oxford, 1999), pp. lx–lxi. For the anonymous writer's discussion of the transaction with Earl William, see: bk. ii, cap. 3, pp. 51–3.

[55] Greenway and Watkiss, *The Book of the Foundation of Walden Monastery*, bk. ii, cap. 3, p. 50.

[56] Greenway and Watkiss, *The Book of the Foundation of Walden Monastery*, bk. ii, cap. 4, p. 53, n. 13.

[57] Greenway and Watkiss, *The Book of the Foundation of Walden Monastery*, pp. 175–7, App. 2, no. 3 and pp. 177–8, App. 2, no. 4.

[58] Numerous historians have noted that women helped fund crusade in these ways, see for example: Tyerman, *England and the Crusades*, pp. 200–9; F.A. Cazel Jr., 'Financing the Crusades', in H.W. Hazard and N.P. Zacour (eds), *A History of the Crusades: Vol. VI, The Impact of the Crusades on Europe* (Madison, 1989), pp. 116–49, at 122; Rousseau, 'Home Front and Battlefield', p. 37. Bysted, *The Crusade Indulgence*, p. 162; Park, *Papal Protection and the Crusader*; Parker, 'Papa et Pecunia', p. 7; Riley-Smith, 'Family Traditions', p. 101; Riley-Smith, *The First Crusaders*, p. 93; Nicholson, *Women and the Crusades*, pp. 97–128.

Laywomen and the Crusade in England, 1150–1300

their dower are frequently reflected in the language of their charters and in their appearance as litigants concerning these lands.[59] That said, it can be difficult to determine the freedom of choice that women had when agreeing to the disposal of dower lands, given the principles of coverture. Under English Common Law, when a couple married, the husband took control of all their moveable property (except paraphernalia, like clothing). A wife's land, however, fell under her husband's guardianship, rather than his outright ownership. The husband could sell the dower, so long as he had his wife's explicit permission.[60] Any transfer of dower without a wife's consent was precarious, and it could theoretically be reclaimed from the buyer when the husband died. However, such situations are not commonly seen in the surviving record. The key point is that dower land fundamentally remained a woman's property, even during marriage.[61]

Riley-Smith considers the use of dower in crusade financing, surmising that men typically sold off their wives' dower so that they would not have to fragment their own ancestral lands. He highlighted the case of Boso of La Chèze, a First Crusader from the Limousin (France), who gifted some of his wife's lands to the Church, rather than using any of his property.[62] More recently, Susan Johns and Danielle Park have shown that we cannot ignore the possibility and likelihood of women's agency in such transactions. The disposal of dower, or the assent to grants, were influential means by which women could display their encouragement of holy war.[63]

---

[59] J.M. Kaye, *Medieval English Conveyances* (Cambridge, 2009), p. 187.

[60] Glanvill, a twelfth-century writer, stated that a man could sell his wife's dower without her consent. However, court records are littered with examples of litigation over dower that was sold without a wife's consent, see: G.D.G. Hall and M.T. Clanchy (eds and trans.), *The Treatise on the Laws and Customs of the Realm of England Commonly Called Glanvill* (Oxford, 1993), bk. 6, p. 60, cap. 3; Seabourne, *Women in the Medieval Common Law*, pp. 34–43; Wilkinson, *Women in Thirteenth-Century Lincolnshire*, p. 77.

[61] F. Pollock and F.W. Maitland, *The History of English Law Before the Time of Edward I*, 2 vols (Cambridge, 1898), at vol. 2, p. 407; R.C. DeAragon, 'Power and Agency in Post-Conquest England: Elite Women and the Transformations of the Twelfth Century', in Tanner, *Medieval Elite Women and the Exercise of Power*, pp. 19–43; J. Biancalana, 'Widows at Common Law: The Development of Common Law Dower', *Irish Jurist*, New Series vol. 23, no. 2 (1988), pp. 255–329, at 269; J. Loengard, 'What is a Nice (Thirteenth-Century) English Woman Doing in the King's Courts?', in L.E. Mitchell, K.L. French and D.L. Biggs (eds), *The Ties that Bind: Essays in Medieval British History in Honor of Barbara Hanawalt* (Oxford, 2011), pp. 57–70, at 59–60; C. Beattie and M.F. Stevens, 'Introduction: Uncovering Married Women', in C. Beattie and M.F. Stevens (eds), *Married Women and the Law in Premodern Northwest Europe* (Woodbridge, 2013), pp. 1–10, at 5.

[62] Riley-Smith, *The First Crusaders*, p. 123.

[63] Johns, *Noblewomen*, p. 71; Park, *Papal Protection and the Crusader*, pp. 12 and 49–51; Tyerman, *The World of the Crusades*, p. 10.

In a charter from around 1174, Agnes de Percy consented to her husband Jocelin de Louvain mortgaging her manor of Ludford (Lincolnshire) to the Priory of Sixle for a 100*l* to help cover the costs of Joscelin's crusade.[64] The money was expressly given to both Agnes and Jocelin, intimating her shared part in the transaction.[65] Ahead of the Third Crusade, Amphelisia of Rolleston consented to her husband Jollan II de Neville granting a tithe of her mill in Rolleston (Nottinghamshire) to Thurgarton Priory.[66] Like the case of William de Mandeville, this may have been done in exchange for an unstated cash payment toward Jollan's expenses. In 1249, a once independently wealthy woman named Christian, the widow of Walter le Tayllur, had fallen on hard times and attempted to regain some dower property she had once held. Entering a Salisbury court to press her case, Christian's claim was found wanting. She admitted that she had been present and agreed to the sale of her messuage (a dwelling and accompanying land), in order to fund her husband's journey to the Holy Land.[67] In a much more modest example, during the first half of the thirteenth century, a Matilda consented to her husband granting one and a half acres to Nostell Priory (West Yorkshire) for 14*s* toward his crusade costs.[68] Matilda's consent was crucial; she solidified the deal by vowing never to reclaim the property, possibly as a means to negotiate a higher price, and she later quitclaimed her right to any lands granted to the monks in the past, for an unspecified sum of money.[69]

These women directly assented to transactions that were described in the charters/court records as occurring in advance of a husband's crusade. There were probably many more women who did this during the Middle Ages. However, such explicit cases are quite uncommon in English cartularies. It is crucial to remember that medieval cartularies were formed from copies (sometimes just summaries) of charters that were drafted decades, or even hundreds of years, beforehand. Later scribes may well have removed details they considered extraneous, like the context in which a grant was made, or the sellers' plans regarding their profit. This silence on the crusading context of grants was not a uniquely English affair. Park has similarly observed that while countess Sybilla of Flanders was regent over her husband's lands during his crusade, Sybilla's surviving charters never acknowledged the context of her administration.[70]

---

[64] *EYC*, vol. 11, p. 66, no. 68, "concessu uxoris mee Agnetis de Perci".
[65] *EYC*, vol. 11, p. 67, no. 68.
[66] T. Foulds (ed.), *The Thurgarton Cartulary* (Stamford, 1994), p. 72, no. 111.
[67] M.T. Clanchy (ed.), *Civil Pleas of the Wiltshire Eyre, 1249* (Gloucester, 1971), p. 141, no. 483.
[68] J.A. Frost (ed.), 'An Edition of the Nostell Priory Cartulary, London, British Library, Cotton Vespasian E XIX', 2 vols (Unpublished PhD Thesis, University of York, 2006), at vol. 2, p. 780, no. 957.
[69] Frost, 'An Edition of the Nostell Priory Cartulary', vol. 2, pp. 780–1, nos. 957–8.
[70] Park, *Papal Protection and the Crusader*, p. 141.

The complexities and ambiguities of the surviving evidence at least highlight the potential for further examples to be uncovered with more prosopographical or archival research. To look at one example: in a deed drafted between 1188 and 1189, Agnes, the wife of Richard Lord of Little Windsor (Dorset), consented to her husband's gift of a virgate, a meadow and then, separately, of the western part of the manor of Little Windsor to Forde Abbey (Dorset).[71] It appears to be a simple *pro anima* gift, like thousands of others. But, if we delve deeper, in another charter dated to the same time (possibly days later), Richard granted the monks the entirety of the manor, specifying that he was about to go to Jerusalem.[72] When he returned, he confirmed the grant of the virgate and meadow that Agnes had consented to, and in this later deed, Richard explicitly affirmed that Agnes had consented and that this all happened just before he left for Jerusalem.[73] Those details, if true, are left out of the cartulary's version of the original grant.

In another case, dating between 1220 and 1230 – around the time of the Sixth Crusade (1227–9) – William, "son of Nigel the Dean", gave the canons of St Frideswide (Oxford) lands in return for 10*m*10*s* to: "make my pilgrimage to Jerusalem".[74] In a contemporary grant, William's wife Alice was guaranteed a quart (eight bushels) of the crop from twenty 'butts' of land given to the canons for another 6*m*.[75] Alice then expressly consented to William's act, confirming all their lands in Walton to the canons, so long as they provided her with clothing and a home for life.[76] Alice's actions cannot be definitively linked to her husband's crusade. However, the tenor of the arrangements and their proximity to one another make it likely there was a link. If so, it is perplexing that the cartulary's compiler deemed it unnecessary to add Alice's consent in the first charter and state the context. Perhaps he simply felt it was tiresome to repeat why William needed capital in each transcription of these charters. Whatever his reasoning, without these details, our grasp on medieval preparations for crusade slips further away. In a very similar case, Thomas Gansel granted lands to St Augustine's Abbey in Bristol for 8*m* toward his crusade. By 1258, Thomas was dead and his widow, Swanilda, drew up an agreement with the monks, relinquishing her right to claim any of her dower lands that Thomas had given to them. This may have been a

---

[71] Hobbs, *The Cartulary of Forde Abbey*, pp. 56–7, nos. 208 and 210. For the original Latin, see: Taunton, SHC, 'Liber Albus Abboticiae de Forde', Phillipps MS. 13823, ff. 88v–89v.
[72] Hobbs, *The Cartulary of Forde Abbey*, p. 56, no. 209.
[73] Hobbs, *The Cartulary of Forde Abbey*, p. 59, no. 222.
[74] *Frideswide*, vol. 1, p. 418, no. 594, "quibus feci peregrinacionem meam apud Ierosolimam".
[75] *Frideswide*, vol. 1, p. 419, no. 597.
[76] *Frideswide*, vol. 1, pp. 419–21, no. 598, at 420.

consequence of litigation, perhaps arising from clauses and details that, again, were not outlined in the cartulary's copy of Thomas's original grant.[77]

It is possible to distinguish other instances where women may have consented to financial arrangements for crusading, such as deals where they received compensation or security themselves. In the early 1230s, for example, Juliana Haringer was guaranteed her dower and a house for life in a conveyance of three messuages in Oxford to the Brothers of the Hospital of St John the Baptist ahead of her husband's crusade.[78] Similarly, around 1188, the unnamed wife of Ralph de Chall was guaranteed daily food and her dower (after three years had elapsed) in a grant of two bovates of land to Easby Abbey (Yorkshire). Ralph's charter states that these arrangements were made as he prepared to go to the Holy Land.[79] Sometime during King John's reign (1199–1216), the Prior of Westminster Abbey drew up a grant concerning a house. Within the deed, he explained how the property had come into his possession. The house had been pledged to him around the time of the Third Crusade, though he had not been able to gain full seisin until both owners – one Alice and her crusading husband – had died, because they had bought it together.[80] When Gerard de Furnevatt died on crusade in 1219 and his testament was executed, it revealed provisos for the security of his wife's dower, which had been pledged before he departed, probably for funding.[81] In a final example, sometime before 1249, a Wiltshire crusader pledged some lands and stipulated that, if he was killed, the creditor could only take full seisin of the land after paying 100*s* to the crusader's aunt, Loretta of Crundal.[82]

The examples discussed here show women with strong interests in properties used in crusade funding, and they received payments and securities in recognition of their stake in the lands. These situations indicate that these women were closely involved and sympathetic to the original transactions, rather than necessarily having these terms dictated to them. However, this was by no means the case for everyone.

Some husbands may have coerced or even forced their wives to consent to the disposal of their dower.[83] English court records are littered with examples of

---

[77] D. Walker (ed.), *The Cartulary of St Augustine's Abbey, Bristol* (Bristol, 1998), pp. 260–1, no. 408 and p. 269, no. 422.
[78] H.E. Salter (ed.), *The Cartulary of the Hospital of St. John the Baptist*, 3 vols (Oxford, 1914–17), at vol. 2, p. 135.
[79] *EYC*, vol. 5, Part II, p. 122, no. 215.
[80] E. Mason (ed.), *Westminster Abbey Charters 1066-c.1214* (Bath, 1988), p. 193, no. 347.
[81] T.D. Hardy (ed.), *Rotuli Litterarum Clausarum in Turri Londinensi Asservati: 1204–1224*, 2 vols (London, 1833), at vol. 1, p. 390.
[82] Clanchy, *Civil Pleas of the Wiltshire Eyre*, p. 46, no. 69.
[83] For discussions of wives pushed into selling land, see: R.M. Smith, 'Women's Property Rights under Customary Law: Some Developments in the Thirteenth and Fourteenth Centuries', *Transactions of the Royal Historical Society*, vol. 36 (1986), pp. 165–94, at 183–6; M. Howell, 'The Problem of Women's Agency in Late Medieval and Early

women (mostly widows) seeking dower property that had been sold/mortgaged to raise money for crusading. These lawsuits generally took place after the death or disappearance of the crusader in question.[84] In some of these cases, the women may have agreed to their lands being mortgaged for specific terms or under certain clauses, but their creditors refused to honour the contracts upon hearing of the crusaders' death. In other instances, the crusaders may have sold their wives' property without their consent at all. There is a wider array of legal records that reveal the bitter family squabbles that took place over the property of dead or missing crusaders. Plaintiffs and defendants often gave differing versions of the events leading up to a crusader's departure, as well as the funding arrangements that took place. With an eight-hundred-year gap, it is highly difficult to corroborate who was telling the truth. It has even been suggested that, given the number of court cases, many contemporises may not have fully comprehended the fiscal ramifications of crusade.[85] While some individuals undoubtedly did not account for all eventualities, or were simply cheated and therefore had to resort to legal action to regain their dower, this was probably not true of all contemporaries. Equally, it should not be assumed that all women who enabled crusaders typically lost control of their dower or were ignorant of the implications of selling it. In the end, court cases only provide a glimpse of the negative impact on English landholders, and so it can be hard to determine how representative these situations were for the majority of women who funded crusaders.[86]

One typical example of these squabbles can be seen in an inquest from 1234. A court determined that Nicholas of Greywell gave his wife Mabel's *maritagium* (land given to a woman upon her wedding) to Richard Cumin to hold for the duration of Nicholas's crusade, presumably for credit.[87] Nicholas died on his pilgrimage, but the land was never returned to Mabel despite the termination clause. Years later, Mabel's daughter Edith eventually regained the land, claiming it as her inheritance.[88] Whether Mabel agreed to the pledge or not, it seems she had been powerless to regain the land in her lifetime.

Court cases also reveal the complex and imaginative ways would-be crusaders and their families went about the funding process. To look at one well-recorded

---

Modern Europe', in S.J. Moran and A.C. Pipkin (eds), *Women and Gender in the Early Modern Low Countries, 1500–1750* (Leiden, 2019), pp. 21–31, at 22.

[84] For details of eleven cases, see: Clanchy, *Civil Pleas of the Wiltshire Eyre*, p. 141, no. 483; *CRR*, vol. 1, p. 69; p. 85, no. m4; vol. 8, p. 21; vol. 10, p. 268; vol. 11, p. 85, no. 452; p. 157, no. 785; p. 312, no. 1563; p. 446, no. 2231; vol. 13, p. 83, no. 364; vol. 14, p. 109, no. 552 (the identity of the husband in the former case as a crusader may be seen at pp. 280–1, no. 1322); vol. 16, p. 320, no. 1625; *CCR, 1231–34*, p. 510.

[85] Tyerman, *England and the Crusades*, p. 212.

[86] Riley-Smith, *The First Crusaders*, p. 98.

[87] *CCR, 1231–34*, p. 510.

[88] *CCR, 1231–34*, p. 511.

example, Emma, the widow of a crusader named Roger of Meauton (now Great Malton, Norfolk), made a series of pleas to regain her dower lands between 1223 and 1224. In three separate hearings, Emma claimed eleven different plots of land held by ten (or possibly nine) people:

Table 1: Dower lands sought by Emma of Meauton [Great Malton], 1223–4.

Defendants	Land and Location (Norfolk)
Robert Cutting	Half of a 7 or 6 acre plot in Hethersett*
Radulf of *Bauburg*	1 acre in Great Malton
Robert son of Alvin	Half of a 7 acre plot in Great Malton, and half of a 5 acre plot in Hethersett
Bertram Asar	Half of a 3 acre plot in Great Malton
Odo son of Robert	Half of 1 acre plot in Great Malton
Nicholas of *Bere*	Half of a 12 acre plot in Great Malton
Walter Chinke	Half of a 1 acre plot in Hethersett
Walter Gruk (it is possible this is the same man as the above)	Half of a 1 acre plot in Hethersett
Vincent of *Bec*	Half of a 30 acre plot in Hethersett
Matilda of Meauton [Great Malton]	Half of a 1 carucate plot in Great Malton

* The amount of property that Emma claimed from Robert Cutting varies between suits, either due to the confusion of the scribe who wrote them or because the legal action she took had changed.

Sources: *CRR*, vol. 11, p. 157, no. 785, p. 312, no. 1563, and p. 446, no. 2231.

The land that Emma of Meauton sought – equivalent to (very approximately) ninety-five acres – was her dower that she pledged to fund her husband's crusade, which was not returned after his death. This figure only accounts for land that Emma tried to recover through litigation; there may well have been more that was promptly returned to her. Moreover, if she was present and assented to all the transactions listed above, she must have had to engage in a large number of negotiations and taken a highly active role in her husband's preparations. Emma does not appear to be a person who sat on the periphery; she was at the heart of her husband's ability to go on crusade.

Enabling a person to participate in armed pilgrimage fits within the spirit of support that preachers extolled and *Quia maior* encouraged. As a practical means of raising capital, consenting to the disposal or mortgaging of dower was probably a crucial and typical means of equipping crusaders. There was undoubtedly a very large number of women who enabled crusaders in this way and, in all probability, perceived their assistance as adherence to an idealised form of sponsorship. When the French nobleman Jean de Joinville recalled his preparations in the 1240s ahead of the Seventh Crusade, he was somewhat bitter that his widowed mother had been so reluctant to sell her property, forcing Jean to pledge large amounts of his own land.[89] Clearly, he expected support to be more forthcoming, which may have been something he witnessed amongst his peers.

However we interpret Emma of Meauton's involvement, her litigation highlights another aspect of women's support: the individual that leased the largest amount of land, and presumably paid the most considerable amount toward Roger's enterprise, was a Matilda of Meauton. Matilda's appearance amongst the defendants raises a vital issue: was her purchase/lease perceived as a form of support? Our investigation must now shift toward examining how women directly sponsored crusaders.

---

[89] Smith, *Crusading in the Age of Joinville*, p. 174.

5

Backing the Expeditions

> A certain Frankish captive told me that he was his mother's only son. They possessed no worldly goods other than a house which she sold and used the purchase money to equip him and send him to free [Jerusalem] and that he was taken prisoner. This is an extreme example of the religious and spiritual motivation that the Franks had.
>
> (Ali Ibn al-Athīr [d.1233], historian from Mosul)[1]

This nameless mother, who may well have been a figment of Ibn al-Athīr's imagination, cuts a striking figure in his writings. Making oneself destitute and homeless for the sake of sending a son on a journey of thousands of miles to fight in a holy war? It sounds absurd, even farcical today. We cannot guess where she came from. The Arabic term *Ifranji* or 'Franks' was a generic word for western Europeans.[2] No name, no son's name, no whereabouts. We can approximate the timing of this figure's recklessly charitable (or coercive) gift to her son; she sent him to liberate Jerusalem sometime shortly after the city fell in 1187 to Saladin. How can we approach a person like this, and understand their motivations, their worldview?

For any crusade to materialise, or for an individual to plan a lengthy journey, a whole society had to offer up their wealth, knowledge and advice. The scene that Ibn al-Athīr depicts appears somewhat dramatic and may well have been an anecdote to amuse a Muslim readership with tales of haplessly grasping Latin Christians.[3] However, he was perceptive about one thing: parents, spouses, friends and more, all across Christendom, must have felt an overwhelming affinity with crusade despite never physically taking part. So much so, that they poured their time and money into sending their kin on the pilgrimage. As we have seen,

---

[1] Ibn al-Athir, *The Chronicle of Ibn al-Athir for the Crusading Period from al-Kamil fi'l-Ta'rikh*, 3 vols, D.S. Richards (ed. and trans.) (Farnham, 2005–8), at vol. 2, p. 364.

[2] P.M. Cobb, *The Race for Paradise, An Islamic History of the Crusades* (Oxford, 2014), p. 16.

[3] He also relied on the observations of his brother, see: Ibn al-Athir, *The Chronicle of Ibn al-Athir*, vol. 1, p. vii; Nicholson, 'Women on the Third Crusade', p. 339; J.D. Hosler, *The Siege of Acre, 1189–1191: Saladin, Richard the Lionheart, and the Battle that Decided the Third Crusade* (New Haven, 2018), p. 198, n. 22.

many women enabled crusaders. There was also a huge variety of ways people sponsored crusaders: offering gifts of cash, grants of land (to be exchanged for capital), purchasing crusaders' property, subsuming debts and more. This chapter will investigate how women showed their support for holy war by directly patronising the movement.

Giving Cash

We might imagine that in the days or even moments before crusaders and pilgrims left their homelands, friends and family thrust money or tokens into their hands. When Stephen of Blois wrote to his wife Adela while on campaign during the First Crusade, he proudly declared that he had acquired twice as much wealth as she had given him.[4] A charmingly simple mosaic in the Church of San Giovanni Evangelista in Ravenna shows a woman passing a gift to a man leaving for the Fourth Crusade (1202–4).[5] Jean de Joinville – the *Champenois* participant in the Seventh Crusade (1248–54), who we have encountered already – recalled that although his mother had not bankrolled his crusade, she had given him a fine cloak before he left for Egypt.[6] Although these sorts of *ad hoc* gifts and grants of cash were probably very common, they rarely necessitated any written record, so references to these close exchanges are rare.

In one tantalising case from around 1230, a laywoman named Rose Marnet leased a messuage to a chaplain of Carisbrooke Priory (Isle of Wight), named Simon son of Geoffrey de Bosco. Rose was a widow at the time and therefore in full control of her estate. She negotiated to receive an annuity of 3*d* and an upfront payment of 10*s*. Rose's charter states very plainly what she intended to use the money for: "and for this donation and concession to me, the said Simon gave me ten shillings of silver which I gave to the said Andrew, my son, for his journey to Jerusalem".[7] The fact that the scribe mentioned what Rose would do with the money, or that she asked that it be noted for posterity, is particularly

---

[4] Barber and Bate, *Letters from the East*, pp. 22–5, no. 5, at 22. Stephen's letters (if he did indeed draft them) were reworked by monastic scribes who committed them to posterity. Assuming that the passage referring to Adela's support is an interpolation, it would at least represent one clerical writer's notions of expected preparations. For detailed analysis of this source, see: S.T. Parsons, 'The Letters of Stephen of Blois Reconsidered', *Crusades*, vol. 17 (2018), pp. 1–29; Smith, *Rewriting the First Crusade*, pp. 67–82.

[5] A.E. Lester, 'Remembrance of Things Past: Memory and Material Objects in the Time of the Crusades, 1095–1291', in Cassidy-Welch, *Remembering the Crusades and Crusading*, pp. 73–94, at 77, fig 5.4.

[6] Monfrin, *Vie de Saint Louis*, p. 158, § 323.

[7] *Carisbrooke*, p. 85, no. 123, "Et pro hac donatione et concessione mea dedit michi dictus Symon decem solidos sterlingorum quos ego dedi predicto Andree filio meo proficiscenti Ierusalem".

thought-provoking. Comparatively few contemporary charters state if a party had an immediate purchase or donation in mind. This meant a lot to Rose.

There were likely many more instances like Rose's that simply were not recorded as fully. For example, also around 1230, Matilda of Edgefield transferred six acres to the monks of Binham Priory (Norfolk) and stipulated that if her nephew returned from Jerusalem, he should inherit the land along with a house and a further acre; otherwise the monks could retain the land after her death.[8] This does not appear to be a simple gift; rather the clause regarding the nephew's return intimates that some bargaining around this transaction took place, probably to gain a sum of money for the nephew's journey. Similarly, Evelyn, wife of Richard de *Baubaduu*, brought a suit against Henry de Percy in 1191, claiming half a knight's fee in Duncton (Sussex) – that is, half an area of land that produced enough rents/profits to support a knight. She did this while her husband was away on the Third Crusade. The court dismissed Evelyn's claims, after finding that she had quitclaimed the land to Henry for 37.5*m*.[9] It is possible that she had been offloading assets to raise money for her husband's crusade, but the court records offer no further context.

Giving Land

Finding buyers for property was a time-consuming affair. If a large-scale crusade was underway, the process of raising cash would have been far more complex. A land market could become saturated as hundreds, if not thousands, of landowners began desperately converting assets into cash before an embarkation date. Perhaps avoiding the hassle of selling property themselves, many women appear gifting assets to crusaders, which these pilgrims could then translate into capital in their own time.

Sometime before 1185, Matilda Baiarde gave her nephew, Robert Beche, some rents worth 10*s* a year. Robert then transferred these to the brothers of St Bartholomew's Hospital in London, just before his departed on crusade.[10] In one of the two charters detailing this gift, Robert stated that, even if he returned from his pilgrimage, the rent would remain with the brothers. This is a strong indication that the grants were a form of sale and that the monks gave him a lump sum of money.[11] Around 1220, Juliana – the widow of an alderman of London named Alan de Balon – gave Reynold de Wirham rents worth 20*s* annually. Similarly

---

[8] J. Margerum (ed.), *The Cartulary of Binham Priory* (Norfolk, 2016), p. 111, no. 144.
[9] M.J. Martin (ed.), *The Percy Chartulary* (Durham, 1911), p. 381, no. 891.
[10] N.J.M. Kerling (ed.), *Cartulary of St Bartholomew's Hospital, Founded 1123* (London, 1973), p. 146, nos. 1599–1600. See also: London, Saint Bartholomew's Hospital Archive (SBHA), 'Cok's Cartulary', MS HC/2/1, f. 573.
[11] N. Moore (ed.), *The History of St. Bartholomew's Hospital*, 2 vols (London, 1918), at vol. 1, p. 207, n. 2.

Laywomen and the Crusade in England, 1150–1300

to the previous case, Reynold subsequently left these rents to St Bartholomew's Hospital before leaving for Jerusalem (and probably gained some financing in the deal).[12] In another case, in 1237, Philip Clerk gave a rent worth 6s annually, a messuage and a virgate of land to the vicar of Walburton (Sussex) for a total of 12m upfront to help fund Philip's journey to Jerusalem.[13] Philip is clear in his charters that his mother Alice de Blakepaine gave him the rents, and that his uncle had given the dwelling and land to Alice. Philip's mother must have either given or bequeathed him all these assets.

Admittedly, it is uncertain how much time had elapsed between these three women's gifts and the later transfers. They could have given assets to these men before the latter took crusade vows. However, it is telling that all three men made sure to assert the provenance of their wealth. They perhaps felt a debt of gratitude that needed to be acknowledged. Juliana's grant to Reynold is particularly curious. Their exchange and Reynold's fund-raising for his crusade both occurred around the same year. It seems odd that he gave her a gold ring for her assets: a portable piece of wealth that a crusader would need. Either he was buying her property immediately before deciding to sell up and go on crusade (an interesting about-turn), or more likely the ring was a token gesture to solidify the deal and perhaps commemorate Juliana's support. A similar gesture can be seen a generation earlier, at the time of the Third Crusade. Gervase of Hampton – the founder of God's House Hospital in Southampton – gave Peter de Cosham 20m in return for some lands, so that Peter could make his journey to Jerusalem. Gervase also gave a gold ring with a sapphire to Peter's nephew, William de la More, in "recognition" of his assent to the transaction.[14]

Some land exchanges formed rather convoluted funding schemes in which each party tried to attain the best spiritual reward for their investment. Around 1240, Isabella Hacard gave the monks of Carisbrooke Priory a total of twelve acres in return for her admission as a sister of the house, as well as the monks' prayers for her and her ancestors.[15] Soon after this, possibly even the same day, Isabella's son Geoffrey Hacard confirmed his mother's grants, and the monks gave Geoffrey a total of 3.5m toward his crusade costs.[16] This is probably an instance where the parties wanted to avoid accusations of usury, and so the exchanges and confirmations were treated separately. It is conceivable that this was also done as

---

[12] Kerling, *Cartulary of St Bartholomew's Hospital*, p. 72, nos. 687–8. For original Latin, see: SBHA, MS HC/2/1, ff. 287–9.

[13] L. Fleming (ed.), *Chartulary of the Priory of Boxgrove* (Lewes, 1969), p. 122, no. 260 and pp. 124–5, no. 268.

[14] R. Bearman (ed.), *Charters of the Redvers Family and the Earldom of Devon, 1090–1217* (Exeter, 1994), pp. 191–2, no. 21, "recognitione".

[15] *Carisbrooke*, pp. 110–1, no. 161. For her donation of five acres see: pp. 111–2, no. 163.

[16] *Carisbrooke*, pp. 112–113, no. 164 and pp. 113–4, no. 166.

a means for Isabella and Geoffrey to bargain for more money for his expedition.[17] By entering the Church, Isabella would not have been able to personally hold on to property, and so, presumably, her assets were transferred to Geoffrey, helping fund him further.

Cartularies, court records and other documentary sources detail a huge variety of scenarios for medieval crusade preparations. Women not only appear in these records as patrons and sponsors, but also as crusaders: a reminder that women were omnipresent in the culture of holy war.[18] For instance, sometime in the 1230s, Joanna, daughter of Anketill, gave rents to the Hospital of St John the Evangelist in Cambridge for 4*m* toward her journey to Jerusalem.[19] Agnes, the widow of a certain John Sweyn, appointed attorneys and directed what was to be done with her property before she went to the Holy Land in 1269. She may have been joining the Lord Edward's Crusade, which departed the following year. Agnes was acutely aware of the "dangers" (*periculosa*) of her particular journey.[20] Juliana Guer and her husband John took out licences of protection and appointed an attorney just before they left on the same expedition.[21] In an undated charter, Henry of Glastonbury made a grant of a virgate of land in *Wryington*, but he noted that half of it belonged to his sister, Hawisa. Henry's charter included a clause stating that if Hawisa ever returned from the Holy Land, she should get her portion of the land back.[22] It seems as though Hawisa pledged her share to her brother and then went missing abroad, but no more is known of these people.

Passive Donations

Our discussion has, for obvious reasons, mostly focused on recorded examples of women's support. However, we should remain conscious that many people in medieval England would have helped propel crusade with meaningful, yet mundane, acts. Perhaps the most commonplace form of sponsorship that laypeople would have engaged in was to place alms in collection boxes for the Holy Land. Pope Innocent III's *Quia maior* mandated in 1213 that every church in Christendom had to have a chest for this exact purpose and, as we saw in Chapter 2, these

---

[17] See also: Lower, *The Barons' Crusade*, p. 142.
[18] For more women from England who joined the crusade, see: Hurlock, *Britain, Ireland and the Crusades*, pp. 84–5.
[19] M. Underwood (ed.), *The Cartulary of the Hospital of St John the Evangelist, Cambridge* (Cambridge, 2008), pp. 2–3, no. 4.
[20] Blake, *The Cartulary of the Priory of St Denys Near Southampton*, vol. 1, pp. 19–20, no. 31.
[21] *CCR*, 1268–72, pp. 288–9.
[22] A. Watkin (ed.), *The Great Chartulary of Glastonbury*, 3 vols (Frome, 1947–56), at vol. 2, p. 546, no. 1017.

objects were repeatedly placed in churches well into the fourteenth century.[23] The chests were to be constructed solidly, bound in iron and have three locks, with three separate people acting as key holders in case of malfeasance. So much wealth sat in these chests – from ecclesiastical contributions, laypeople's donations and crusade-vow redemptions – that there was a genuine fear that embezzlement was rife. In 1283, King Edward I felt obliged to send officials to audit the collection of crusade monies in Ely (Cambridgeshire), fearing corruption while he had been on campaign in Wales.[24]

Collection chests, or at least the practice of local alms-giving, would have formed a highly recognisable feature of crusade culture. Several chests from English churches are reputed to be extant crusade-collection boxes. Chichester Cathedral's treasury holds three supposed examples: one belonging to the cathedral itself, and two that once sat in the Sussex parish churches of Climping and Felpham.[25] There are around fifty other known chests in England that are stylistically similar to these three.[26] Dendrochronological analysis has shown that the wood used in the Chichester Cathedral chest was felled sometime between 1255 and 1277, and that used in the Climping example was felled after 1294 (see Figure 6).[27] Assuming these chests were used for crusade collections, they may have been constructed by local bishops or made in compliance with Pope Clement V's 1308 call for donations, or perhaps simply used to collect local ecclesiastical taxes in aid of the Holy Land.[28] However, ascribing a specific use to these particular objects is not possible without any epigraphical or decorative evidence. They may equally have just been used for storing documents or vestments. Many chests would have served multiple functions or have been repurposed at times when crusading fervour was not particularly high. In the 1270s, the bishop of York had to remind the archdeacon of Cleveland to commission collection boxes for his churches.[29] Evidently, some had gone astray. Nevertheless, the local memory of the usage of the Chichester examples is absorbing.

Parishioners may have deposited modest sums of money in chests much like these when they visited their local church, or possibly when redeeming their own

---

[23] See Chapter 2, p. 51.
[24] *CCR*, Edward I, vol. 2, p. 235.
[25] The Climping example was included in the following: J. Riley-Smith (ed.), *The Oxford Illustrated History of the Crusades* (Oxford, 1995) (reprinted: 2001), p. 58.
[26] C.G. Pickvance, 'The St. Mary's, Climping and Chichester Cathedral medieval chests: a dendrochronological and comparative study', *SAC*, vol. 157 (2019), pp. 173–87, at 173.
[27] Pickvance, 'The St. Mary's, Climping and Chichester Cathedral medieval chests', p. 180; C.G. Pickvance, 'The Canterbury Group of Arcaded Gothic Early Medieval Chests: A Dendrochronological and Comparative Study', *The Antiquaries Journal*, vol. 98 (2018), pp. 149–85.
[28] Menache, *Clement V*, p. 109.
[29] Brown, *The Register of Walter Giffard*, p. 277, no. 857.

Figure 6. A thirteenth-century 'Crusade Chest' originally from St Mary's Church, Climping (Sussex). (Photographed with kind permission of the Dean and Chapter of Chichester Cathedral, and Rev Richard Hayes and the parish of Climping – Photograph: Author).

crusade vows. Casual deposits in crusade chests did not necessitate any written record, however, and so details on who typically made donations, whether they were ritualised, or how common they were, have not come down to us.

The Military Orders

Rather than giving money to individual pilgrims or crusaders, laywomen could patronise the Military Orders. Two key groups, the Orders of the Knights Templar and Hospitaller, developed in the opening decades of the twelfth century. They had a presence in the Kingdom of Jerusalem and the wider Mediterranean, actively fought in holy wars, and used one-third of the profits they raised on their lands in the West to support their efforts in the Near East.[30] Other smaller militarised orders associated with crusade, such as the Order of Saint Lazarus and the Knights of St Thomas of Canterbury at Acre, as well as orders focused on aiding captured crusaders, like the Trinitarians, also had houses in England.[31] A layperson had a wealth of choices when considering who to patronise.

A sizeable number of women actively engaged with the Military Orders, not only through generous financial contributions but also by joining these institutions.[32] Defining people's motivations for giving gifts to the Military Orders, however, is not clear-cut. Many would have patronised a religious house simply because it was in their locality, they had a pre-existing relationship with members of the house or their family had a history of patronising that particular institution or religious order.[33] Nevertheless, contemporaries who gave gifts to the Military Orders would have done so with the knowledge that their money was going toward the crusading movement. Furthermore, a significant number of people who did

---

[30] D.M. Metcalf, 'The Templars as bankers and monetary transfers between West and East in the twelfth century', in P.W. Edbury and D.M. Metcalf (eds), *Coinage in the Latin East, The Fourth Oxford Symposium on Coinage and Monetary History* (Oxford, 1980), pp. 1–17, at 6; J. Prawer, *The Crusaders' Kingdom: European Colonialism in the Middle Ages* (London, 1972) (reprinted: 2001), p. 262.

[31] Marcombe, *Leper Knights*; J. Walker, 'Crusaders and Patrons: The Influence of the Crusades on the Patronage of the Order of St Lazarus in England', in Barber, *The Military Orders*, pp. 327–32; D. Pringle, 'The Order of St Thomas of Canterbury in Acre', in P.W. Edbury (ed.), *The Military Orders, Vol. 5: Politics and Power* (Farnham, 2012), pp. 75–82; J. Flannery, 'The Trinitarian Order and the Ransom of Christian Captives', *Al-Masaq*, vol. 23, no. 2 (2011), pp. 135–44, at 137.

[32] Sarnowsky, 'Gender-Aspekte in der Geschichte der geistlichen Ritterorden', pp. 168-88; Bom, *Women in the Military Orders*; Nicholson, 'Relations between Houses of the Order of the Temple in Britain and their Local Communities', pp. 195–207; Luttrell and Nicholson, *Hospitaller Women in the Middle Ages*.

[33] R. MacLellan, *Donations to the Knights Hospitaller in Britain and Ireland, 1291–1400* (London and New York, 2021), pp. 101–18.

Backing the Expeditions

so had familial links to other spheres of crusade, showing something of a wider pattern of behaviour and interests.[34]

Laywomen in England certainly showed interest in benefiting these orders from an early date. In the 1130s, Matilda of Boulogne (wife of Stephen of Blois, King of England r.1135–54) gave her manor at Cressing (Essex) and land in Cowley (Oxfordshire) to the Templars.[35] The Cressing site is particularly well known now because two timber-framed barns are still standing there which dates back to the time of the Templar's occupation. Similarly to Matilda, in 1156, Margaret countess of Warwick granted Llanmadoc (Gower) to the Knights Templar.[36] The Hospitaller's Godsfield and Baddesley cartulary contains seventeen grants made by women between 1180 and 1300.[37] In the same date range, there are 120 donations made by women or explicitly with their consent in the Hospitallers' *Prima* and *Secunda Camera* of their so-called Great Cartulary.[38] There was even a house of Hospitaller sisters established at Buckland Priory (Somerset) around 1180 and a Hospitaller nunnery was founded at Aconbury (Herefordshire) in 1216 by the noblewoman Margaret de Lacy.[39] During the thirteenth century, twenty grants were made to the Aconbury nuns either by women, with their consent or at their insistence.[40] Some of these charters' language shows a real conviction. Roger de Clifford gifted a rent of 8*s* to the nuns, "with the counsel and advice of his wife, lady Sybil de Ewias".[41] Lady Sybil had more than a passing interest. She personally made four other separate grants to the nuns between 1216 and 1236, including: rents, cash, tithes, and even the services of the miller (along with his holdings) who worked on her manor.[42]

---

[34] Schenk, *Templar Families*, pp. 203–49.
[35] Nicholson, 'Women's Writing and Cultural Patronage', in Bale, *The Cambridge Companion to the Literature of the Crusades*, pp. 72–84 at 80.
[36] Nicholson, *Women and the Crusades*, p. 119. See also the grants by various women to the Templars in England noted in: S. Tibble, *Templars: The Knights Who Made Britain* (New Haven, 2023), pp. 57, 68 and 166.
[37] Appendix 3.
[38] Appendix 3.
[39] The Aconbury house received papal permission to become an independent house of Augustinian canonesses in 1237, though it is uncertain when the house formally changed over, see: Hurlock, *Britain, Ireland and the Crusades*, pp. 151 and 156–7; M.E. Scott (ed.), 'A Herefordshire Nunnery: A Calendar, with introduction, of the Cartulary of Aconbury Nunnery' (Unpublished M.Phil. thesis, University of Southampton, 2001), p. 12; Bom, *Women in the Military Orders of the Crusades*, pp. 106–7 and 115; H.J. Nicholson, 'Margaret de Lacy and the Hospital of St John of Aconbury, Herefordshire', *Journal of Ecclesiastical History*, vol. 50, no. 4 (1999), pp. 629–51.
[40] Appendix 3.
[41] Scott, 'A Herefordshire Nunnery', p. 194, C27.
[42] Scott, 'A Herefordshire Nunnery', p. 197, C29; p. 198, C30; pp. 210–1, C41–2.

Individuals may have engaged these orders, as they did with other ecclesiastical institutions, to gain access to their liquid capital. Isabel Chilham, a noblewoman from Essex, and her husband David I of Strathbogie earl of Atholl decided to join the English contingents embarking on crusade in 1270. To do so, they acquired a royal licence to let Isabel's manor of Chingford (Essex). She and her husband then leased the property to the Knights Templar for 40*l*.[43] It is uncertain whether Isabel actually joined her husband on the expedition, but David is known to have died at King Louis IX of France's camp at Tunis in 1270.[44]

The Military Orders were not only responsible for transporting the proceeds of various crusade taxes and their own surplus revenue to the East; but they were also relied upon for safekeeping money and carrying goods, pilgrims and crusaders' funds to the Holy Land.[45] This was a particularly useful service for travellers, when there was every possibility that they could be robbed on the road while carrying all their necessaries. Around 1190–1200, an inquest was made into *crucesignati* residing in England who had not completed their vows. It found that an individual in Lincolnshire, Hubert son of Wido, had indeed been robbed in northern Italy. This probably left him without the money to pay for passage on a boat to the Holy Land, and so he was forced to turn around and walk all the way back to England, his vow unredeemed.[46] Women were able to send cash via Templar or Hospitaller messengers to mitigate these sorts of eventualities, and to top up the funds that a crusader might have while abroad.

Although we know that private individuals made use of the orders for international transfers, there are severe limitations to the source material from England. Investigations into English records of the Knights Templar have yielded no discernible pattern between money paid into their treasury in London and money taken out in the East.[47] These problems are compounded, because the Templar order was dissolved in the early fourteenth century. During this process, many of their records were subsequently destroyed, while most of the remainder

---

[43] *CPR, 1266–72*, pp. 422–3; M. Gervers (ed.), *The Cartulary of the Knights of St. John of Jerusalem in England, Part 2, Prima Camera, Essex* (Oxford, 1996), p. 18.

[44] MacQuarrie, *Scotland and the Crusades*, p. 57. For more on this crusade, see: M. Lower, *The Tunis Crusade of 1270: A Mediterranean History* (Oxford, 2018).

[45] Metcalf, 'The Templars as bankers', p. 6; Barber, 'Supplying the Crusader States', p. 326; H. Nicholson, *The Knights Templar, a New History* (Stroud, 2001) (reprinted: 2002), p. 188; T.W. Parker, *The Knights Templars in England* (Tucson, 1963), p. 58; L. Delisle, *Mémoire sur les Opérations Financières des Templiers* (Paris, 1889) (reprinted: Genève, 1975), pp. 20–4.

[46] HMC, *Report on Manuscripts in Various Collections*, vol. 1, pp. 235–6, no. 227, at 236.

[47] Parker, *The Knights Templars in England*, pp. 58–9. Agnes Sandys made a similar conclusion earlier, see: A. Sandys, 'The Financial and Administrative Importance of the London Temple in the Thirteenth Century', in A.G. Little and F.M. Powicke (eds), *Essays in Medieval History Presented to Thomas Frederick Tout* (Manchester, 1925), pp. 147–62, at 148.

were transferred to the Hospitallers, who preserved them in a sporadic fashion. Nevertheless, there are clear indications that contemporaries were familiar with using the Templars for private transfers of money. This is abundant in the legal records from a murder trial in the 1280s. A minor nobleman named William de Munchensy of Edwardstone (Suffolk) was found guilty of orchestrating the murder of Hugh Bukky at Castle Hedingham (Essex) and harbouring the assassins.[48] He was sentenced to exile in the Holy Land to serve as a crusader. William's family was instructed that they could raise 100*m* from his lands and send the proceeds on to him via messengers from the Military Orders.[49] The court's declaration shows a degree of assumption that William's family, and probably other contemporaries, would have been acquainted with the mechanics of this arrangement. Earlier in this book, we saw Hawisa de Nevill's letter to her son in Acre. This document again attests that sending money to the Holy Land via the Military Orders was fairly straightforward, or at least did not warrant much explanation on her part.

Custodianship and the Acquisition of Crusaders' Assets

When Pope Innocent III issued *Quia maior* in 1213, he called upon laypeople to offer up donations toward the recapture of the Holy Land out of *caritas*, "charity".[50] In return for their devotion, these people were to receive the spiritual reward of crusade. He was emphasising an ideal. But Innocent III was fully aware that the practicalities of mobilising a crusade were far more nuanced and often financially ruthless. Much of the backing that crusaders would receive could not easily fit within the parameters of *caritas*. Laywomen were conscious of this too. They were eager to support crusade, but not if it seriously ran a risk of causing them financial ruin akin to Ibn al-Athīr's anecdote. An obvious solution was to invest rather than donate. Many people appear to have bought or rented crusaders' property to furnish them with the monetary assets that they needed. Indeed, James Powell has noted that elite laywomen in the Italian state of Genoa tended to have more liquid capital on hand than their male counterparts. He suggested that women may have been more able to purchase crusaders' assets or donate money.[51]

There is good reason to interpret property acquisitions within this context as a move to aid holy war. Many crusaders may have found themselves needing cash with relatively short notice. This was especially true if they were not the main leader of their expedition, and therefore the date of departure was out of

---

[48] D. Richardson, *Plantagenet Ancestry: A Study in Colonial and Medieval Families*, 2nd edn (Salt Lake City, 2011), part 1, p. 336.
[49] *CPR, 1281–92*, pp. 247 and 422.
[50] T. Guard, '*Opus caritatium*: Crowdfunding the Later Crusades, The English Evidence', in G.E.M. Lippiatt and J.L. Bird (eds), *Crusading Europe: Essays in Honour of Christopher Tyerman* (Turnhout, 2019), pp. 211–33.
[51] Powell, 'The Role of Women in the Fifth Crusade', pp. 296–7.

their control. There could also be difficulty in finding buyers if the market was suddenly flooded with others' properties. This does not necessarily mean that all the women who bought/rented crusaders' lands did so entirely altruistically. It is possible that in these situations, some buyers tried to make quick and profitable acquisitions, disregarding the financial needs of the crusader.

Despite the opportunity to drive hard bargains, numerous willing buyers were perceived to have done the seller a favour. Some charters that detail women's purchases of property in England make special note of the crusading context for posterity, seemingly to emphasise the transaction's considerate nature. Around 1220, Alice Baskervill and her husband paid 30*s* for a curtilage in *Schotplace* and a piece of land in Castle Foregate (Shropshire) from Nicholas Brito. Nicholas stated in the charter records that this transaction was: "for my urgent need [of funds] to make my pilgrimage to the land of Jerusalem".[52] Given the principles of coverture, Alice's husband could have bought this property himself, without making any note of his wife's intention or consent. Therefore, a joint purchase like this one, where Alice was mentioned, is particularly noteworthy and may be an indication of her insistence on the transaction. In a very similar example, sometime after 1210, a woman named Eustacia and her husband bought her brother's tenement in Derby for 21*m*, specifically so her brother could travel to Jerusalem.[53] Just like Alice Baskervill's case, Eustacia's appearance in the record is significant and, given that it was her brother's crusade that she was funding, it is very plausible that she pressured her husband into buying the property.

Some women were far more determined and independent in purchasing assets. In a rather extreme example from 1202, a court case concluded that one Cecilia bought half a virgate of land in Flore (Northamptonshire) from a man for an unspecified amount of money to furnish him with cash to go on crusade. Cecilia, however, was married at the time and her husband was either unaware or did not approve of her acquisition. Attitudes towards married women's ability to dispose of chattels (such as money, as opposed to land) were somewhat mixed in this period. On the one hand, it simply was not possible for a person to operate in society without the ability to use money. Yet, theoretically, medieval Common Law judged that a married woman did not have legal rights over her family's moveable property while her husband lived. This was a deeply patriarchal system. Although a wife was certainly treated as having a legal interest in her family's chattels, she would have to have her husband's permission to make purchases,

---

[52] U. Rees (ed.), *The Cartulary of Haughmond Abbey* (Cardiff, 1985), p. 200, no. 1067, "pro urgenti necessitate mea ad peregrinacionem meam versus terram Jerosolituam proficiscendam".

[53] R.R. Darlington (ed.), *The Cartulary of Darley Abbey*, 2 vols (Kendal, 1945), at vol. 1, p. 44, no. Axxxix.

perhaps especially so in a conveyance.[54] In Cecilia's case, the jury decided that her actions were illegal.[55]

In a less controversial instance, in 1230, Gundreda, a Yorkshire landowner, paid 12m to a crusader named John de *Herdislawe* for all the land he held in Micklegate (York) and a few rents.[56] Despite seeming more straightforward, the language of this charter exposes some fascinating beliefs. In this case, both Gundreda and John are described as having "given" (*dedi* and *dederunt*) these assets to each other. Medieval charters used very formulaic phrasings and language for the actions taking place and, as we would expect of modern contracts, they are often very unambiguous if a sale was occurring. Rather than using the language of a sale, Gundreda and John's exchange emphasised the charitable nature of the deal. Gift-giving language is not uncommon in the records surrounding crusade financing. Christopher Tyerman highlighted this when drawing attention to the example of Walter le Nair. Walter granted the nuns of Swine Priory (East Riding, Yorkshire) two bovates of land with a toft (a house with adjoining land) before going on the Third Crusade. In return for the land, the nuns gave Walter 5m towards his journey to Jerusalem.[57] This charter recorded that Walter "gives" (*dedi*) the nuns the land, and they in turn "gave" (*dederunt*) him the money.[58] Such phrasing may have been used in an attempt (somewhat unimaginatively) to avoid accusations of usury. Alternatively, it may have echoed the parties' sense that they were not trading for commercial gain but were entering a contract within a perceived sacred context, that of holy war.

Not all charters and documentary sources that record crusaders offloading property state that they were paid (or given) money in return. There was a certain expectation that those departing for the Holy Land would provide for their family's wellbeing. Before departure, many pilgrims offered their lands to deserving family members, either as gifts, or for them to act as custodians until their return. Danielle Park's study of crusade-regencies in France and Flanders has shown how critical this was for the realisation of the crusading movement.[59] Take, for instance, the case of Lucy "daughter of William, son Roger de *Berhholte*". In 1270, a wealthy Suffolk crusader named Roger de Reymes entrusted Lucy to act as the guardian

---

[54] See especially: Hall and Clanchy, *Glanvill*, bk. 6, p. 60, cap. 3; Seabourne, *Women in the Medieval Common Law*, p. 39

[55] The scribe appears to have confused the names of the plaintiff and defendant, making a literal reading of the record incomprehensible. The editor offers the interpretation that Cecillia purchased the land, see: D.M. Stenton (ed.), *The Earliest Northamptonshire Assize Rolls, A.D. 1202 and A.D. 1203* (London, 1930), p. 57, no. 450.

[56] J.S. Purvis (ed.), *The Chartulary of the Augustinian Priory of St John the Evangelist of the Park of Healaugh* (Cambridge, 1936), pp. 156–7.

[57] *EYC*, vol. 3, p. 116, no. 1409.

[58] Tyerman, *England and the Crusades*, pp. 196–7.

[59] Park, *Papal Protection and the Crusader*.

of his young son William. On top of this, Lucy was to collect the annual rents totalling 40*l* from properties in Wherstead, Ipswich, Caldwell and Westerfield, and safeguard the money until William came of age. Finally, Lucy was also to have custody of some property which she could keep for life if Roger never returned from the Holy Land.[60] The latter clause obviously served as an inducement and reward for her integral help in looking after Roger's affairs.

Appendix 1 contains a further twelve inquests and charters from England, in which fourteen women were found to be holding the property of absent or deceased crusaders, or were expressly left property by a departing crusader for no stated payment. It is clear that some elite women took on positions of considerable power while their crusading kinsmen were away. To look at just one of these examples: a Northamptonshire court case from 1229 detailed an ugly legal battle between the family of the missing (and presumed dead) crusader, William of Stanford. Accusations of fraud and disseisin flew back and forth. However, there was one point that the parties agreed upon: before William left, he gave his seal matrix to his sister Matilda.[61] Seal matrices were used by individuals and institutions to validate and affirm documents, such as charters, or to sign (so to speak) correspondence.[62] William may have left his seal matrix behind, fearing that if it were lost or stolen on the march, an individual could make counterfeit documents in his name. Equally, however, he may have left it with Matilda so that she could operate on his behalf and endorse acts concerning his property. Regardless of the motivations, for Matilda, this represented a substantial endorsement of her integrity.[63]

It is not impossible that credit or donations changed hands when women were made custodians of property, despite the surviving documentary sources remaining silent on the matter. A good case can be made that Agnes de Vescy helped pay for her son's pilgrimage. Before departing on the Lord Edward's Crusade, John de Vescy enfeoffed his mother Agnes with the manors of Newson, Brende and Thornton (Yorkshire) for life.[64] In March 1271, at the time of this crusade's departure, Agnes was granted a royal protection for three years, potentially as a way of consolidating the lands she had just acquired.[65] When John returned from

---

[60] A.L. Raimes, 'The Family of Reymes of Wherstead in Suffolk', *Suffolk Institute of Archaeology and Natural History*, vol. 23 (1939), pp. 89–115, at 110–11, App. D, nos. 1–2.

[61] *CRR*, vol. 13, pp. 443–4, no. 2107.

[62] P.R. Schofield, 'Seals: Administration and Law', in Schofield, News, Johns and McEwan, *Seals and Society*, pp. 35–47.

[63] The plaintiff in the court case was Matilda's sister, Agnes. Dissatisfied with her portion of the inheritance after William died on crusade, she accused Matilda of forging grants in William's name to enrich herself.

[64] *CIPM*, vol. 2, pp. 445–7, no. 723.

[65] *CPR, 1266–72*, p. 524.

the crusade, he did not take these properties back; he had not simply left them in her care, nor had he leased them to his mother.[66] John was certainly in need of cash for this journey; in 1269, he had received a licence to lease his manors of Alnham and Alnmouth (Northumberland) for three years. The next year, he took out a licence to lease another manor, Winteringham (Lincolnshire), for four years.[67] Agnes may well have been sympathetic to John's need for money and bought the properties she was given. As Linda Mitchell has noted, Agnes de Vescy was already in the habit of lending funds to John's younger brother, William.[68]

Noble crusaders took months to settle their affairs and ensure that they were able to leave the kingdom. John de Vescy's case above is a clear example of that convoluted process. One major concern was ensuring that creditors were satisfied, and/or debts were settled. Wealthy crusaders with outstanding dues, such as taxes, could be barred from abjuring the realm by royal authorities. Occasionally this required guarantors to step in, or a patron to take on the debt. If a person assumed a crusaders' liabilities, this would have helped enable their journey, but it was not without risk. In September 1227, Alice Briwere agreed to help pay 60*m* that her husband, William Paynel, owed to the Exchequer, so he could acquire royal permission to leave the kingdom with Peter des Roches's expedition. Alice agreed, along with a Hugh de Samford, to render this in instalments of 20*m* yearly for three years. In return, William left them the manor of Bampton (Devon) as collateral.[69] Although Alice appears to have eagerly taken over management of Bampton, as well as her husband's manor of Uffculme, the idyll ended abruptly. William died *en route* to the Holy Land not long after he had left England. By June 1228, the Crown seized William's property, and in November a Herbert son of Matthew had been assigned the manors (and the responsibility of paying William's debts). Alice received her dower and her share of the crop that she had ordered to be planted on the land.[70]

This is not to say that every woman held responsible for their husband's crusading arrears intended for this to happen. A wife in medieval England could

---

[66] For more on this case, see: Lloyd, *English Society and the Crusade*, p. 174.

[67] *CPR, 1266–72*, pp. 371 and 439. Prince Edward took his vow to go on crusade in June 1268, so it is likely that John had also taken his vow by the time of this first licence. For Edward's vow, see: Lloyd, 'The Lord Edward's Crusade', p. 121.

[68] L.E. Mitchell, 'The Lady is a Lord: Noble Widows and Land in Thirteenth-Century Britain', *Historical Reflections*, vol. 18, no. 1 (1992), pp. 71–97, at 91.

[69] This document appears amongst rolls dated between February and March of 1228, yet it was marked as 27th September. Given that William was described as a living person in the document concerned, it is most probable that it was drafted in September of the preceding year but added into the rolls later. See: P. Dryburgh, B. Hartland, A. Ciula and J.M. Vieira (eds), *Calendar of Fine Rolls, Henry III, 1224–1234* (Woodbridge, 2008), p. 191, no. 92; Cf: *EYC*, vol. 6, pp. 54–5.

[70] Dryburgh, Hartland, Ciula and Vieira, *Calendar of Fine Rolls, Henry III, 1224–1234*, p. 207, no. 205 and p. 229, no. 36.

inherit their spouse's debts. Yet, this was only possible if a woman was her husband's designated executor, and that was not a common legal arrangement. In 1223, Joanna de Mares was, significantly, accused of being her husband's "heir" and asked to repay 39*s* he had borrowed before going on crusade. Joanna denied this and said she could not pay anyway, as her husband had sold (*vendidit*) everything they had.[71] Wives were not normally designated as their husbands' heirs in Common Law proceedings of this period. In the thirteenth century, widows inherited their designated third of the 'marriage portion' (as it was termed), and the rest was bequeathed to the deceased's heir and was at the mercy of creditors.[72] It is hard to say why the creditor, or court scribe, used this language in Joanna's case, but it may have been part of the creditor's tactics to claim legal rights to the wealth she had inherited.

From 1188 onwards, papal mandates stipulated that creditors could not charge interest on loans that they had previously given to *crucesignati*, nor could a moneylender demand outstanding payments from a crusader until they fulfilled their vow. This would have made for an awkward situation for many impetuous individuals who took a vow before considering how they would fund their journey. To circumvent the difficulties in gaining credit, some crusaders' spouses may have volunteered to take out loans themselves.

This may have been the situation when, in 1231, a creditor stated that Sybil of Icklesham (Sussex) owed 100*s* 25*d* that she had not settled within the agreed four-year term. Sybil contracted this debt around Easter 1227, not long before her husband, Nicholas Haringod lord of Icklesham, had left for the Holy Land.[73] Sybil argued before the court that her husband took out the debt alone and that she was not, much like Joanna de Mares's statement, her husband's "heir" (*heres*). There is evidence, however, that Sybil was more involved in her husband's venture than she intimated. Sybil was the heiress to the lordship of Icklesham, and Nicholas was only Lord by right of his wife. She therefore exerted considerable authority in dealings concerning these lands.[74] In 1226, probably during Nicholas's preparations for crusade, he and Sybil granted Icklesham Church to Battle Abbey (Sussex) as co-grantors (Figure 7).[75] They may have done this for credit, but almost certainly for spiritual intercession during Nicholas's journey. By Easter 1229, Sybil was involved in some litigation, in which the records state that Nicholas had died, presumably on crusade.[76] By the following year, Sybil

---

[71] *CRR*, vol. 11, p. 262. no. 1309, "Et Johanna venit et dicit quod non est heres domini sui".
[72] Mitchell, 'The Lady is a Lord', pp. 80–1; R.H. Helmholz, 'Bankruptcy and Probate Jurisdiction Before 1571', *Missouri Law Review*, vol. 48, no. 2 (1983), pp. 415–30, at 424–5.
[73] *CRR*, vol. 14, pp. 280–1, no. 1322.
[74] L.F. Salzmann, 'Some Sussex Domesday Tenants', *SAC*, vol. 58 (1916), pp. 171–89, at 181–5.
[75] T.T. Churchton, 'Icklesham Church', *SAC*, vol. 32 (1882), pp. 105–22, at 106.
[76] *CRR*, vol. 13, p. 372, no. 1772.

Figure 7. A charter drawn up by Sybil of Icklesham and her husband Nicholas Haringod around the time of crusade preparations, with both their seals attached. (Huntington Library, BA v.41/1236 – Reproduced by kind permission of the Huntington Library, San Marino, California).

was in court again, this time successfully regaining a third of a carucate of land in Ospringe (Kent) that was her dower, which she must have pledged not long before her husband left England.[77] In all likelihood, Sybil mortgaged this land during her husband's fund-raising. These actions, taken together, may indicate that Sybil was indeed supporting her husband.

In the end, the court presiding over the lawsuit of 1231 ordered Sybil to repay the creditor. They found her guilty of defaulting, in part, because they believed she had taken out the loan herself. More than that, in the months between contracting the debt and Nicholas's departure, Sybil left her husband.[78] By the early fourteenth century, English courts recognised that a husband might not be held responsible for his wife's debts if the wife, specifically, had left her husband: Sybil's case appears to be an early example of a similar ruling.[79]

---

[77] *CRR*, vol. 14, p. 109, no. 552.
[78] *CRR*, vol. 14, pp. 280–1, no. 1322.
[79] C. Beattie, 'Married Women, Contracts and Coverture in Late Medieval England', in Beattie and Stevens, *Married Women and the Law in Premodern Northwest Europe*, pp. 133–54, at 151–2.

Given that Sybil of Icklesham and Joanna de Mares, the wives of crusaders, both contested that they were not their husbands' heirs, there may be more to these cases than meets the eye. The language in these lawsuits suggests that other women may have been designating themselves as their crusading husband's heirs. It is possible that this was done to formally become the custodians of family property. As the cases above highlight, such a situation would, in turn, give creditors greater access to collateral in the event of the husband's death on crusade. If some crusaders' wives were indeed taking this risk, it could have been a means to negotiate for a larger loan.

Gaining credit was made more complicated from the mid-twelfth century, when the Papacy stipulated that *crucesignati* could only pledge assets to Christian lenders or the Church, to exclude private Jewish creditors.[80] This further meant that crusade supporters had more freedom of choice when it came to borrowing funds than the crusaders themselves.[81] Such a situation may have played out in mid-thirteenth-century Yorkshire. In 1268, Margaret, the widow of Thomas of Dreuton, came to a court settlement with a Jewish creditor concerning a debt of 50*m* that, supposedly, Thomas had contracted before he sailed for Jerusalem. The Crown intervened in this case to stipulate mutually agreeable terms for Margaret to make repayments, as her chattels were deemed insufficient to settle the debt.[82] This odd situation required mediation because either Thomas took out the loan before he was a crusader, or he must have forfeited his legal privileges as a *crucesignatus* at the time he borrowed. Alternatively, Margaret may well have been the debtor and, in a bid to default, convinced the court that it was Thomas's debt, but was still recognised as his executor. Whatever the truth of the matter, it seems logical that creditors would have stipulated terms or penalty clauses designed to deter debtors from evading their arrears by taking crusade vows. There may be a link here, regarding the crusaders who engaged in the antisemitic violence in York in 1190: they were incredibly calculating in destroying Jewish records of debts held in York Minster.[83]

As we saw in Part I, thirteenth-century preachers encouraged many laypeople to redeem their crusade vows by donating a sum to papal funds for the Holy Land or by personally arranging for a warrior to go in one's stead. This became an integral and consistent means of drumming up support for crusade. Considering how prevalent this practice was, it is worth reflecting upon whether any of the laywomen's sponsorship and support examined in this chapter constituted part of

---

[80] Tyerman, *England and the Crusades*, pp. 196–7.
[81] Tyerman, *England and the Crusades*, pp. 203–4.
[82] *CCR*, 1264–68, p. 479.
[83] Tyerman, *England and the Crusades*, p. 204; Watson, 'Introduction', p. 7; D.A. Irwin, 'Acknowledging Debt in Medieval England: A Study of the Records of Medieval Anglo-Jewish Moneylending Activities, 1194–1276' (Unpublished PhD Thesis, Canterbury Christ Church University, 2020), p. 29.

their own vow redemptions. Despite the likelihood that this was the case, none of the sponsored men (or women for that matter) discussed in this chapter were described as undertaking their mission at the behest of female benefactors. Isabel de Mauduit's son – who was described as a crusade-proxy for his (deceased) mother – may have been an exception, but whether he went or whether she organised his sponsorship is uncertain. There are distinct examples from England of men sending male crusade proxies, which makes the apparent lack of women benefiting from this practice all the more puzzling.[84]

It may simply be a quirk of the surviving English records, or the manipulation of later compilers, that so few men are identified as women's crusade proxies. Alternatively, the reasoning may lie in crusade's martial nature. There are notable exceptions, but women seldom participated in combat during this period.[85] It is conceivable, then, that there may have been some perception that, since women ideally did not engage in battle, men who went in their place could not be crusading on their behalf in quite the same manner as they would for a fellow layman.[86] If true, this could have been a consequence of the wider efforts to gender participation on crusade as a masculine activity and supportive roles as a feminine ideal.

The evidence that survives from crusade preparations highlights that many women were intertwined with the financial mechanisms of the movement. These records are, however, somewhat vague regarding supporters' timelines and motivations, as well as the negotiations and discussions that preceded their dealings. Given the nature of the sources, it is understandable that the women who remained in western Europe during the crusades have often been viewed as suffering the fiscal ramifications of their crusading kinsmen. This chapter, however, has offered an alternative reading of the evidence, considering laywomen as sponsors and patrons of crusading. In any of the cases discussed, it is possible that these benefactors encouraged their beneficiary to go on crusade. They may have made it clear that they were willing to fund would-be crusaders, as an inducement to inspire or comfort those considering taking up the cross. It is both historically plausible, as well as critical to our own view of the past, to grasp that crusaders

---

[84] E.g. Around 1190–1215, Roger of Poitou gave his brother Hugh all his land in Normanton to act as his crusade-proxy, see: *EYC*, vol. 3, p. 248, no. 1573; Evans, 'Commutation of Crusade Vows', pp. 219–28.

[85] For discussions of this topic with regard to crusade, see: Nicholson, 'Women on the Third Crusade', pp. 335–49; Christie, 'Fighting Women in the Crusading Period through Muslim Eyes', pp. 183–95; M. McLaughlin, 'The Woman Warrior: Gender, Warfare and Society in Medieval Europe', *Women's Studies*, vol. 17, no. 1 (1990), pp. 193–209.

[86] For a discussion of perceptions of combatants and non-combatants, see: A.V. Murray, 'Warriors and Civilians in the Crusade Movement. Military Identities and Status in the Liberation and Defence of the Holy Land (1096–1204)', *Millars: Espai I Historia*, vol. 43, no. 2 (2017), pp. 97–127.

did not appear out of thin air with divergent opinions and mindsets from their home communities. The unspeakable violence that characterised crusading was meted out by sponsors of the movement as much as those wielding the sword.

Sponsoring crusaders was undoubtedly expensive, but it would be a mistake to think that contemporaries were naïve to this. Many, who undoubtedly held an affinity with crusade and could have gone to the East, instead offered up money (sometimes huge sums), time and prayer rather than joining expeditions. It is clear that questions remain to be answered regarding laywomen's motivations to conform to the ideals that crusade preachers laboured: questions that the following chapters will address.

6

Trends and Motivations

And for this donation and grant the said Simon gave me ten shillings sterling, which I gave to the aforesaid Andrew, my son, for his journey to Jerusalem.

(Rose Marnet, in a charter, c.1230).[1]

Rose Marnet included the above details in her charter for Simon, the Carisbrooke Priory chaplain, around 1230. Her provision for her son's crusade had no effect on the transaction between herself and Simon; nevertheless, Rose, and indeed the scribe, felt it important to note it for posterity. In the last chapter, we saw that charters, as transcriptions in cartularies, often lack contextualising details. They do not always state why an individual was selling property or what prompted them to donate or transfer lands.[2] However, several examples noted that women were taking action in advance of a person's crusade. Contextualising the deal felt critical to those involved, and, significantly, these women wanted their contribution to be recognised and documented. The otherwise unknown Rose Marnet wanted recognition as a patron of crusade, but what did sponsoring crusade mean to her and women like her?

Those who went on crusade had numerous, perhaps sometimes contradictory, motivations for doing so.[3] There is no reason to doubt that crusade supporters were driven by any less varied goals. "Maddening" is how Simon Lloyd described his attempts to uncover medieval people's reasoning for joining holy war. The problem is, as he put it: "it is possible to postulate an almost limitless number of motives, most of them incapable of empirical proof or disproof, or dangerously dependent upon inference".[4] He could not have been more correct. Pinpointing any historic person's motivations for an action can only rely on informed speculation. In this chapter we will not see a catalogue of all the influences that could have driven women to support crusade. Rather, it will discuss the overarching trends seen in the evidence and three broad, likely stimuli: spiritual rewards, family traditions and personal prestige.

---

[1] *Carisbrooke*, p. 85, no. 123. For Latin, see Chapter 5, p. 102 n.7.
[2] D. Bates, 'Charters and Historians of Britain and Ireland: Problems and Possibilities', in Flanagan and Green, *Charters and Charter Scholarship*, pp. 1–14, at 1–2.
[3] T. Asbridge, *The First Crusade: A New History* (London, 2004), p. 41.
[4] Lloyd, *English Society and the Crusade*, p. 103.

Spiritual Reward as a Motivation

During the thirteenth century, Latin Christians understood that those who aided the crusade movement – whether financially, spiritually or sometimes even emotionally – received a proportionate indulgence. The spiritual remuneration that Pope Innocent III's encyclical *Quia maior* offered those who supported crusade may have lain at the heart of all the laity's donations and prayers for holy war in the subsequent decades (with the exception of crusade taxes). Some laypeople do appear to have been cognisant of the canon law that qualified them for a crusade indulgence, which might indicate that they were acting out of a desire for this reward. The case of Rose Marnet, quoted above, fits this category well. She gave her son Andrew money for his crusade, apparently asking nothing in return; this would have won her an indulgence for her sins. However, this is hardly conclusive. The intent of a donor can seldom be proven. There are a few examples, though, which highlight that some women who were unwilling or incapable of travelling to the Holy Land, nevertheless had a desire to capitalise on the divine rewards on offer in the age of the crusades.

In 1225, one Annora daughter of John, took two crusaders to court. She claimed that thirty acres of land in Hampshire were rightfully hers, which William of *Hokesour* and his wife Erneburge were holding, because: "the same Annora complains that the same William and Erneburge did not make their journey and were in the county of Southampton".[5] William came to court and explained that Erneburge was actually in the Holy Land, therefore stalling the suit: the case could not legally continue as Erneburge was named in the plea. William explained that he had not accompanied his wife. Instead, "the lord pope had absolved him of his journey because of his sickness".[6] William's "absolution" suggests he had made a crusade or possibly pilgrim's vow, a morally and legally binding oath.[7] It appears that Annora entered into a contract with William and Erneburge, whereby she gave the couple thirty acres – probably for them to sell or pledge for credit – dependent on them both going to the Holy Land. However, Annora considered William's decision to remain and Erneburge's lone departure to invalidate their deal.

A person could fund a male crusader, a warrior, and (by the thirteenth century) depending on the proportion of their wealth that they granted, the amount of the crusader's expenses they covered and the donor's sense of contrition, they would receive a proportionate absolution of their sins.[8] By funding William, Annora was owed recompense, but a financed crusader who did not actualise their crusade vow

---

[5] *CRR*, vol. 12, p. 12, no. 69, "eadem Annora questa fuit quod ipsi Willelmus et Erneburga iter non arripuerunt et quod fuerunt in comitatu Suht".

[6] *CRR*, vol. 12, p. 12, no. 69, "et quod dominus papa absolvit eum de illo itinere pro infirmitate sua".

[7] See: Brundage, "'*Cruce Signari*'", p. 289.

[8] 'Quia Maior', p. 92.

may have been perceived to be putting their sponsor's spiritual reward in jeopardy. Although Annora's funding had helped Erneburge to go to the East, perhaps even as a *crucesignata*, canonically, this would not have incurred any reciprocal spiritual benefits for Annora. In all likelihood, Annora funded the couple to gain absolution of her sins: by remaining in England, William undermined Annora's attempt to gain an indulgence, hence the lawsuit.

Ironically, people's desire for spiritual rewards is most evident in cases where the methods of their support did not clearly qualify them for an indulgence. We saw in the previous chapter that some supporters used the language of gift-giving when acquiring crusaders' property and, in turn, offering financial support. Instead of saying that they had bought or leased land, many instead 'gave' money and were 'given' land. It is also possible that laypeople who purchased crusaders' property employed this language to ensure that they qualified for an indulgence. Although these transactions were a practical necessity to support crusade, *Quia maior* offered no spiritual rewards for those who exchanged assets with a crusader; the earthly repayment undermined any notion of charitable support.[9] By emphasising that transactions were, in fact, an exchange of gifts, supporters attempted to gain indulgences while retaining as much wealth possible.

This language was deployed in two cases we have seen already. First, in the 1220s, Walter, son of Henry the Dean, gave (*dedi*) some property in Derby to his sister Eustacia and her husband for a gift of 21*m*. This clear sale was described as a donation (*donacione*).[10] Second, in 1230, John de *Herdislawe* granted all his property in Micklegate (York) to a Gundreda, "daughter of Richard the Priest", because of the 12*m* that Gundreda had given (*dedit*) him for his crusade.[11] It is not clear exactly when Gundreda gave John the money. They may have allowed some time to elapse between her donation and the transfer of the property, so she could claim a remittance of sin.

In a similar vein, in 1270, Hawisa Lestrange promised to hold her brother Hamo's manor for the duration of his crusade and to return it when he came back, presumably keeping the land's profits in the interim.[12] This was not necessarily an instance of a crusader looking to safeguard those he was leaving behind. Hawisa was a wealthy noblewoman and married; the deed even notes her husband's assent. Rather than offering custodianship, Hamo appears to have pledged his land to his sister, yet there is no mention of Hawisa paying him for it. The manuscript of this deed is admittedly badly damaged. However, if Hawisa gave Hamo money under-the-table, so to speak, and left this detail out of the charter, this again

---

[9] For more on medieval gift-giving, see: Bijsterveld, *Do ut Des*, p. 85.
[10] Darlington, *The Cartulary of Darley Abbey*, vol. 1, p. 44, no. Axxxix.
[11] Purvis, *The Chartulary of the Augustinian Priory of St John the Evangelist of the Park of Healaugh*, pp. 156–7.
[12] R.W. Eyton, *Antiquities of Shropshire*, 12 vols (London, 1853–60), at vol. 10, pp. 274–5.

could have been a very deliberate means of camouflaging the payment as a gift towards crusade.

This is not to say that all crusade sponsors subscribed to this gift-giving perspective or, perhaps, used these sorts of linguistic and record-keeping tactics to distort the circumstances of their patronage and remuneration. Alice Baskervill in 1220 and Cecilia de Flore in 1202 were both specifically "sold" (*vendedit*) people's property, and they did not shy away from that term.[13] This is not unique to laywomen patrons. At a similar time, Roger Gateles sold a toft in Blyth (Nottinghamshire) to Adam of Elton for 25*s*, "to pursue my pilgrimage toward to land of Jerusalem".[14]

The cases discussed so far in this section involved women who received some assets, and so it is fair to say that material reward played a part in their motivations for supporting crusaders, whether they were involved in gift-exchange or sale. However, without fuller details on the value of the lands exchanged and the amounts paid, particularly in the case of Hawisa Lestrange, it is hard to say whether any of these women made a profit.

There are other hints that people became preoccupied with their own salvation at times of crusading fervour. Isabella Hacard, for instance, whom we have seen earlier, helped raise money for her son around 1240 by gifting assets to Carisbrooke Priory. She was very particular in requesting that she be made a sister of the house and that prayers should be said for the salvation of her soul.[15] When Sybil of Icklesham and her husband, Nicholas Haringod, granted Icklesham Church to Battle Abbey in 1226 – not long before Nicholas departed on crusade – they used a telling phrasing in their preamble:

> I Nicholas Haringod and I Sybil of Icklesham, wife of said Nicholas, mindful of divine love and for the salvation of our souls, and those of our successors, give and concede this present charter.[16]

Before departing, knightly crusaders typically made donations to religious houses, especially those that their families had previously patronised. The donors often requested prayers for themselves, their ancestors and specific members of their living family, such as a spouse or children.[17] Spouses would undoubtedly

---

[13] See respectively: Rees, *The Cartulary of Haughmond Abbey*, p. 200, no. 1067; Stenton, *The Earliest Northamptonshire Assize Rolls*, p. 57, no. 450.

[14] R.T. Timson (ed.), *The Cartulary of Blyth Priory* (London, 1973), p. 40, no. 18, "ad perficiendam peregrinacionem meam uersus terram Jerusalem".

[15] *Carisbrooke*, pp. 110–1, no. 161. See also Chapter 5, p.

[16] Churchton, 'Icklesham Church', p. 106, "quod ego Nichs Harengod et ego Sibilla de Ikelsham uxor ejusdem Nichi intuitu divine caritatis et pro salute animarum nostrarum, et successorum nostrorum dedimus et concessimus et hac presenti carta".

[17] M.R. Evans, 'The Ferrers Earls of Derby and the Crusades', *Nottingham Medieval Studies*, vol. 44 (2000), pp. 69–81, at 73; Kaye, *Medieval English Conveyances*, p. 178.

Trends and Motivations

have voiced their concerns and interests at this time. It is certainly intriguing that so many documents survive, where crusaders made benefactions, while requesting prayers for their wives remaining behind in England.[18] It is important to stress, however, that the language of these charters is not unique. Donations to the Church in aid of family members' souls were common practice. What is important here is the timing of these donations, coinciding with high points in crusade preparations. This gives us some indication (from the perspective of the male donors) of what preoccupied the minds of women intimately associated with English crusading.

In the 1180s, for example, Walter de Scoteny and Robert Beche granted lands to Drax Priory (West Riding, Yorkshire) and St Bartholomew's Hospital (London) respectively. Both donations were specifically made at their departure for the Holy Land and partly for the benefit of their wives' souls.[19] As William I de Ferrers prepared to leave on the Third Crusade, he loaned the Canons of Breedon (Derbyshire) a church and three messuages in Breedon and a chapel in Worthington, amongst various other rents and lands in the area, to be held for the "duration of his journey to Jerusalem".[20] He requested prayers for himself, his wife Sybil de Braose, and his ancestors. As William passed through France to join the other crusaders, he also gifted lands to the Abbey of Saint-Denis for Sybil's salvation.[21] Robert de Beaumont, third earl of Leicester (d.1190), likewise made donations of wine and wheat to the Abbey of Evreux (duchy of Normandy) for the benefit of his wife Petronilla de Grandmesnil's soul before he left on the Third Crusade.[22] Between 1200 and 1218, Robert Marmion baron of Tamworth gave 500*l* and all his land in Checkendon and Littlestoke (Oxfordshire) to the monks of Barbéry (duchy of Normandy) to commute his crusade vow and for prayers for his and his wife Philipa's souls.[23] In the thirteenth century, William de Forda, bound for the Holy Land, gave some properties to the Priory of St Denys in Southampton in return for 6.5*m* towards his journey and prayers for his wife Juliana's salvation.[24] Between 1240 and 1247, Hamund de *Brocherste* (possibly Brockenhurst, New Forest) granted a messuage and croft, along with a total of twenty-six and a half acres, half of Whale Island (Portsmouth harbour), and yearly rents totalling

---

[18] Farmer, 'Persuasive Voices', pp. 540–2.

[19] *EYC*, vol. 6, pp. 167–8, no. 78; Moore, *The History of St. Bartholomew's Hospital*, vol. 1, p. 207, n. 2.

[20] Frost, 'An Edition of the Nostell Priory Cartulary', vol. 2, p. 763, no. 927, "que ipsi canonici tenuerunt quando Ierl'm profectus sum".

[21] W. Dugdale (ed.), *Monasticon Anglicanum*, 6 vols (London, 1814–30) (reprinted: 1848), vol. 6, part II, p. 1078, no. iii.

[22] J.H. Round (ed.), *Calendar of Documents Preserved in France Illustrative of the History of Great Britain and Ireland, vol. 1, 918–1206* (London, 1899), pp. 102–3, no. 306.

[23] N. Vincent (ed.), *Norman Charters from English Sources: Antiquaries, Archives and the Rediscovery of the Anglo-Norman Past* (London, 2013), pp. 196–7, no. 71.

[24] Blake, *The Cartulary of the Priory of St Denys Near Southampton*, vol. 2, p. 192, no. 328.

Laywomen and the Crusade in England, 1150–1300

nearly 56*d* to Southwick Priory (Southampton) for 20*m* towards his costs and prayers for his wife, Alice.[25] One retrospective case indicates some bargaining between spouses. In the mid-thirteenth century, Agatha and Walter Basset had to sell large amounts of property to the Priory of St Denys (Southampton) for 64*d*, possibly due to protracted costs incurred from Walter's past crusade.[26] Perhaps as compensation for the costs, this transaction also included a clause for prayers to be made for the benefit of Agatha's soul.[27]

It can be hard to gain clear insights into women's interests in crusade, compared to how loud the male voice is from the Middle Ages. In English sources this is often a symptom of the customs of coverture and the limited scope that married women were afforded to voice their ideas within charters. There are, nevertheless, some significant instances where women's intentions were clearly written. This is especially true of donations to the Military Orders. Around the time of the Third Crusade, Humbert de Munchensy made a grant to the Knights Hospitaller for his and his wife's souls, at the "counsel and request of my wife Antigone".[28] Lady Sybil de Ewias, likewise, requested that her husband make donations to the Hospitaller nuns at Aconbury (Herefordshire) between 1216 and 1227 (around the time of the Fifth and Sixth Crusades), for the benefit of their souls.[29] It is wholly plausible that the heightened enthusiasm for crusade at these particular points in time fuelled both Antigone and Sybil's demands.

Cleansing personal sin was not only a motivation behind crusading but was also perceived as a means to ensure its success. Crusaders routinely settled feuds, confessed sins and repented. They did this before embarking on their expeditions, as well as during campaigns themselves. There were frequently points when they felt the need to do penance, not just for their own salvation, but to ensure the progress of the mission at hand.[30] Crusaders' close family and supporters may

---

[25] K.A. Hanna (ed.), *The Cartularies of Southwick Priory*, 2 parts (Southampton, 1988–9), at part 2, pp. 95–8, no. iii, 279, 281 and 283.

[26] Blake, *The Cartulary of the Priory of St Denys Near Southampton*, vol. 2, p. 188, no. 317. See also: p. 193, no. 329n. For a charter drawn up in advance of Walter's crusade, see: vol. 2, pp. 192–3, no. 329.

[27] Blake, *The Cartulary of the Priory of St Denys Near Southampton*, vol. 2, p. 188, no. 317. Agatha further confirmed these gifts in 1253, after Walter's death, possibly for more money, see: vol. 2, p. 188, no. 318.

[28] M. Gervers (ed.), *The Hospital Cartulary in the British Library (Cotton MS Nero E VI), A Study of the Manuscript and its Composition with a Critical Edition of Two Fragments of Earlier Cartularies for Essex* (Toronto, 1981), pp. 316–7, "consilio et peticione uxoris mee Antigonie".

[29] Scott, 'A Herefordshire Nunnery', p. 194, no. 27. Ellen de Turbervill, likewise, requested that her husband make a grant to the nuns in 1263, but this may have been when the house had become an Augustinian site: p. 195, no. 28.

[30] Tessera, 'Philip Count of Flanders and Hildegard of Bingen', p. 84; G.M. Reynolds, 'Asking for Forgiveness as an Aspect of Crusade: Case Studies from 13th-century

well have followed in this spirit of contrition. Charters that detailed gifts made to the Church, which included terms guaranteeing prayers for wives or other female family members, offer some evidence that women remaining in England associated personal salvation with crusade preparation.

Correlations with Crusades

There are some apparent trends in, what may broadly be called, crusade-support activity. The cases that informed this book are arranged in chronological order in Appendix 1. However, they number just seventy-two in total. It is remarkable that something as prominent, and with as much cultural currency, as crusading leaves so little trace in the written record. Nevertheless, there appears to have been a definitive and significant peak in the numbers of women involved in crusade support around 1220–50. Whatever their personal situations, concerns or networks, these people's actions took place within a wider political context. Appreciating the developments in crusading, English involvement in holy war, as well as domestic politics between 1150 and 1300, opens new perspectives on the patterns in women's interest in sponsoring crusade. These trends can broadly be summarised in the following way.

Landholders in England joined crusades from their outset in the 1090s, through the twelfth century, particularly during the Second Crusade (1147–50). Numerous magnates from England like William de Warrene third earl of Surrey and Roger de Mowbray joined King Louis VII's army in the latter crusade, and many others joined the fleet that attacked Lisbon. However, there is, generally speaking, little surviving evidence of the preparations of crusaders from this time, or of the family who supported them. The picture becomes much clearer by the time of the Third Crusade. In 1189, King Richard I led a major contingent on this expedition, and large numbers of crusaders left the British Isles in his army.[31] During the same period there is evidence of women supporting crusaders; ten cases discussed in this study (nos. 5–14 in App 1) roughly corresponded to the era of this expedition. The next major voyage, the Fourth Crusade (1202–4), on the other hand, attracted very few participants from England. The papacy was successful in persuading King John to levy a tax to support the venture, and in 1201 he demanded a fortieth of his vassals' revenues. Royal officials certainly collected money in England, but the amount that this was gathered, and the numbers of people who paid, is obscure.[32]

The country was soon racked by the chaos of the First Barons' War (1215–7). Correspondingly, there is limited evidence of women becoming involved in

---

Scotland', *Proc Soc Antiq Scot*, vol. 152 (2023), pp. 135–46.

[31] For the English involvement in this crusade, see: Tyerman, *England and the Crusades*, pp. 57–84.

[32] Tyerman, *England and the Crusades*, p. 191; Edwards, *Finance and the Crusades*, pp. 36–8.

crusade preparations in the first decade of the thirteenth century (nos. 15–19 in App 1). In 1213, the encyclical *Quia maior* called for a new crusade, which materialised in 1217 as the so-called Fifth Crusade. This new expedition occurred as the First Barons' War concluded in England and, with the new peace, English recruits flocked to this venture. A succession of other English expeditions soon followed: Peter des Roches and William Briwere's voyage (1227–9), Richard of Cornwall and Simon de Montfort's contingents of the Barons' Crusade (1240–1) and William II Longéspee's following on the Seventh Crusade (1249–50).[33] Women's continuous and heightened involvement in preparations in the years following *Quia maior* mirrors this spate of English crusading expeditions (nos. 20–56 in App 1).

Steven Epstein made a similar observation in his study of wills from Genoa. He notes that there was a sharp increase in the number of women who made bequests in aid of the Holy Land in the period surrounding the Fifth Crusade (1217–21).[34] While reviewing this evidence, James Powell wrote that most of the testators redacted or edited their crusade-related bequests in later life.[35] He believed that the original wills were made following crusade preaching tours that whipped up people's enthusiasm, but only briefly. But why this crusade? Preaching required charismatic public speakers, and there surely had been no shortage of them in previous crusades. Perhaps it was not the preaching that was novel, but the message that the speakers were armed with. After *Quia maior*, in 1213, preachers emphasised that laypeople could win indulgences through sponsoring crusade and, crucially, that women should play a major part in this.

Although women continued to support crusade through the thirteenth century, there appears to have been a decline in the numbers after the 1250s (nos. 57–71 in App 1). It is possible that there were simply less crusaders leaving England for the Holy Land at this time. The protracted Second Barons' War racked the kingdom from 1264 to 1267, pitting rebel barons against the supporters of King Henry III. One Marcher lord and keen royalist, John II FitzAlan, took a crusade vow but was too entangled in the conflict to leave for the Holy Land. He drew up his testament in 1267, in which he left 20*l* "with my cross, in aid of the Holy Land" to Haughmond Abbey (Shropshire), seemingly to pay for a willing proxy to take his place in the future.[36] This civil war was followed by King Edward I's wars in Wales. From 1276 to 1295, Edward I was largely occupied with fighting Llywelyn ap Gruffydd, conquering Wales and then quelling of rebellions within the country. The internal pressure only rose, as a war of succession developed in Scotland and Edward I used the opportunity to pursue his conquest of the kingdom from 1296 onwards. This sparked the First War of Scottish Independence, lasting almost

---

33 Lloyd, *English Society and the Crusade*, pp. 84–6.
34 S. Epstein, *Wills and Wealth in Medieval Genoa, 1150–1250* (Cambridge, 1984), p. 189.
35 Powell, 'The Role of Women in the Fifth Crusade', p. 296.
36 Rees, *The Cartulary of Haughmond Abbey*, p. 157, no. 770, "cum cruce mea in subsidium terre sancta".

continuously until 1328.[37] These local conflicts sapped resources and troops from across England.[38] Some individuals were certainly unable to fulfil their crusade vows because of these wars. King Edward II took a crusade vow himself in 1313, but, four years later, with no sign of the Scottish conflict ending, he was advised by his chancellor and London council to delay departure until "the empeachments [*sic*] of your wars cease".[39] Therefore, it stands to reason that there were fewer people travelling to the Holy Land who were available for laywomen to sponsor.

However, it would be wrong to suggest that the numbers of those departing, and thus needing support, had dried up entirely: a minority went during the Second Baron's War itself. Around 1266, John of Arundel, for example, gave Boxgrove Priory (Sussex) some houses in return for 8*m* towards the costs of his pilgrimage to Jerusalem.[40] Court cases regarding deceased crusaders in the years on either side of the war highlight that others were leaving England.[41] Hawisa de Nevill sent money on to her son in Acre at the conclusion of the Second Barons' War.[42] Margaret, the widow of Thomas of Dreuton, was held responsible for crusade debts in 1268.[43] Crusaders also continued to depart during the Welsh wars. Between August 1272 and June 1291, the chancery Patent Rolls list thirty-nine individuals departing for the Holy Land, as well as two criminals sent as penance.[44] Likewise, the registers of Walter Giffard archbishop of York note five women who volunteered or were instructed to donate towards the recovery of the Holy Land in 1275.[45] Evidently, there was continued enthusiasm amongst laywomen during these periods of strife, and opportunities to support crusaders.

It is highly probable that women offered support in two English crusades in the second half of the thirteenth century: the Lord Edward's Crusade (1270–2) and Otto

---

[37] M. Prestwich, *Edward I* (New Haven, 1988) (reprinted: 1997).
[38] Hurlock, *Wales and the Crusades*, p. 178; Hurlock, 'Power, Preaching and the Crusades in Pura Wallia c.1180-c.1280', pp. 102–8; Tyerman, *England and the Crusades*, p. 231; Hurlock, Hurlock, *Britain, Ireland and the Crusades*, p. 48.
[39] Guard, *Chivalry, Kingship and Crusade*, pp. 30–1; R.C. Fowler, J.B.W. Chapman and R.L. Atkinson (eds), *Calendar of Chancery Warrants, A.D. 1244–1326* (London, 1927), p. 455.
[40] Fleming, *Chartulary of the Priory of Boxgrove*, p. 88, no. 152.
[41] E.g. W. Page (ed.), *Three Early Assize Rolls for the County of Northumberland* (Durham, 1891), p. 144; S. Stewart (ed.), *The 1263 Surrey Eyre* (Bristol, 2006), p. 88, no. 129; Hodgson, *Northumberland Pleas from the Curia Regis and Assize Rolls, 1198–1272*, p. 243, no. 725 and p. 254, no. 738; *CCR, 1264–68*, p. 479.
[42] Giuseppi, 'XIX – On the Testament of Sir Hugh de Nevill', pp. 351–70.
[43] *CCR, 1264–68*, p. 479.
[44] *CPR, 1266–72*, p. 674; Edward I, A.D. 1272–1281, pp. 209, 330, 437 and 445; Edward I, A.D. 1281–1292, pp. 30, 39, 78, 158, 167, 173, 234, 268, 297, 340, 345, 357, 362, 364–8, 371–4, 376, 381, 427, 429, 432 and 434. For the criminals sent abroad, see: *CPR*, Edward I, A.D. 1281–1292, pp. 194 and 247.
[45] Brown, *The Register of Walter Giffard*, pp. 281–2 and 284.

de Grandson's expedition (1290–1). As we have seen, Agnes de Vescy and Hawisa Lestrange probably sponsored family members during the Lord Edward's Crusade.[46] Isabel Chilham agreed to mortgage her property so that her husband could also join.[47] Other women displayed their enthusiasm by personally participating in these campaigns, like Agnes Sweyn and Juliana Guer.[48] Prince Edward's consort, Eleanor of Castile, also joined the 1270 crusade.[49] Otto de Grandson's expedition may have attracted some interest from women keen on sponsoring crusade. Eva Tibetot might have intended to join this expedition when she was asked to commute her crusade vow in 1291.[50] Otto himself probably went on his 1290 expedition, in part, so as to act as Eleanor of Castile's proxy.[51] Yet, it seems as though neither Edward I's nor Otto's ventures garnered the same reaction from women as the crusades of the first half of the century. This comparative decline in the evidence for support seems odd, especially considering the wealth of records that have survived, which illuminate how the Lord Edward's Crusade was organised.[52]

During the latter crusade, an unprecedented number of participants appear to have been contracted and subsidised.[53] Very few original copies of these contracts (and subcontracts) have survived, but hundreds must have been drafted. Unlike a deed for land, a person might not need to refer back to an old employment contract years or even generations later, and so they were probably discarded. It is clear that they were originally produced in large quantities. For instance, the Crown transferred one group of eighteen crusaders a total of 22,500m and asked them to muster 225 knights and pay each contractor at a rate of 100m each.[54] Historians once believed that this sudden appearance of mass contracting represented a new shift in the way crusades were organised. However, individuals had been contracted or paid to go on crusade since the eleventh century; the only novelty in the 1270s may have been that they began writing contracts down.[55]

---

[46] *CIPM*, vol. 2, pp. 445–7, no. 723; Eyton, *Antiquities of Shropshire*, vol. 10, pp. 274–5.
[47] *CPR, 1266–72*, pp. 422–3; Gervers, *Prima Camera*, p. 18.
[48] Blake, *The Cartulary of the Priory of St Denys Near Southampton*, vol. 1, pp. 19–20, no. 31; *CCR, 1268–72*, pp. 288–9.
[49] For her licence of royal protection to go on the expedition, see: *CPR, 1266–72*, pp. 479–80.
[50] Langlois, *Les Registres de Nicholas IV*, vol. 1, p. 650, no. 4490.
[51] Reynolds, 'Proxy over Pilgrimage', pp. 129–31; Clifford, *A Knight of Great Renown*, p. 126.
[52] Tyerman, *England and the Crusades*, p. 125.
[53] Lloyd, 'The Lord Edward's Crusade', p. 124–5; Tyerman, *England and the Crusades*, p. 130; Lunt, *Financial Relations of the Papacy with England to 1327*, pp. 446–8.
[54] Lloyd, 'The Lord Edward's Crusade', pp. 120–33, at 126. See also: Beebe, 'The English Baronage and the Crusade of 1270', pp. 143–8; *CCR, 1268–72*, pp. 281–3 and 288–9; *CPR, 1266–72*, pp. 411, 440, 464–5, 479–80, 484–5 and 587.
[55] Tyerman, *England and the Crusades*, p. 130; Richardson and Sayles, *The Governance of Mediaeval England*, p. 463.

Gathering enough liquid capital to pay these subsidies did require some novel action. From 1268–70, Henry III negotiated with Church officials and the barons to get permission to levy a national crusade tax. This would have been the first of its kind since 1201 and the first tax on the laity's moveable property since 1237.[56] Eventually, Edward was granted a twentieth of the kingdom's taxable assets. Seeing as Edward was not the leader of the Seventh Crusade, but joining the army of Louis IX of France, he needed these collections to move at pace. Daniel Edwards argues that this encouraged officials to be somewhat lenient, favouring getting money into royal coffers quickly, rather than extracting the proper figure from taxpayers.[57]

Despite these levies and subsidies, the need for private sources of money remained as strong as ever. Many of the participants on the Lord Edward's Crusade clearly struggled to get enough financial support.[58] John Lovel, for instance, obtained a licence in 1270 to let four of his manors for terms of ten years.[59] This was a heavy commitment. In all likelihood, John would have aimed to return home long before this term was finished, but his property would remain beyond his grasp. Walter of Wigginton (N. Yorkshire) was similarly driven to lease his entire estate for four years: a substantial gamble.[60] Eustace de Balliol received a licence to lease five manors.[61] Robert Charles sold all the property he owned. His dedication was so extreme (and piteous) that Henry III awarded him 400*m*.[62] Simon de *Henesale* granted all his land in Roecliff to Selby Abbey (N. Yorkshire), probably for cash.[63] One prominent nobleman who went on the expedition, John II of Brittany earl of Richmond, granted the village of Ainderby Quernhow (N. Yorkshire) to the monks of Fountains Abbey. His charter states that they gave him 40*l* out of "charity towards his journey to Jerusalem".[64] John also received a royal licence to lease his lands until he accrued 2000*m* because "he requires a great sum of money".[65]

There was undoubtedly a significant need for sponsors at this time and yet, bizarrely, there is little evidence of laywomen's support. This may represent a change in women's attitudes towards crusade itself. There had been little alteration

---

[56] Edwards, *Finance and the Crusades*, p. 38.
[57] Edwards, *Finance and the Crusades*, pp. 41–3.
[58] Beebe, 'The English Baronage and the Crusade of 1270', p. 131.
[59] *CCR, 1268–72*, p. 281; *CPR, 1266–72*, p. 425.
[60] *CPR, 1266–72*, p. 443.
[61] *CPR, 1266–72*, pp. 440 and 441.
[62] *CPR*, 1266–72, pp. 434–5; *CPR, 1272–81*, p. 170.
[63] J.T. Fowler (ed.), *The Coucher Book of Selby: From the Original MS. In the Possession of Thomas Brooke*, 2 vols (Cambridge, 1891–3), at vol. 2, p. 84, no. 2.
[64] W.T. Lancaster (ed.), *Abstracts of the Charters and other Documents Contained in the Chartulary of the Cistercian Abbey of Fountains in the West Riding of the County of York*, 2 vols (Leeds, 1915), at vol. 1, p. 11, no. 44.
[65] *CPR, 1266–72*, p. 314.

Laywomen and the Crusade in England, 1150–1300

in crusade-financing methods between the 1240s and the 1270s – aside from the tax of 1270 – making a change in outlook all the more probable as an explanation. However, this lack of records of laywomen's sponsorship is not a clear indication that they had lost interest in supporting crusade entirely. The majority of the leases and sales from the 1270s onwards might have involved buyers from the laity and these lands may have remained in secular hands, rather than religious institutions. Despite the high number of royal licences to dispose of manors, very few of the subsequent transactions appear to have involved religious houses or, at least, were not recorded in their cartularies. This is a critically important point because far fewer secular cartularies have survived compared with ecclesiastical ones, and so this may account for the lack of surviving records of women's support from the later thirteenth century.[66]

Interestingly, there is an almost identical fluctuation in laypeople's donations to the Military Orders. Patronage of the Templars' house at Sandford (Oxfordshire) dropped by more than two-thirds between the 1220s and the 1260s/70s.[67] When the Templars were being disbanded in England in 1308, accounts were rendered on the state of their mills. Many of these sites had apparently been in a state of disrepair, which suggests that there had been a period of some decline.[68] On a royal level, the Templars were close to the establishment until their dissolution.[69] Nevertheless, Agnes Sandys, Thomas Parker and Peter Slavin have noted that King Edward I relied on the Templars markedly less than his predecessors for depositing money or transferring cash.[70] This apparent decline in the Templars' popularity in England may, also, be a reflection of deficiencies with the extant source material. The Templars may have been consolidating their holdings and rearranging property, rather than accepting donations of disparate lands.[71] Also, and much more crucially, when their order was dissolved, their estates were handed over to the Hospitallers. This order preserved the Templars' records in

---

[66] A similar deduction was made in Bull, *Knightly Piety*, p. 268.

[67] H. Nicholson, *Templars, Hospitallers and Teutonic Knights, Images of the Military Orders, 1128–1291* (Leicester, 1993), p. 58, table 1. Nicholson also notes that similar trends are seen in the records in the Provins and Beauvoir Templar cartularies, see: p. 59.

[68] E. Gooder, *Temple Balsall, The Warwickshire Preceptory of the Templars and their Fate* (Chichester, 1995), p. 85; D.D. Andrews (ed.), *Cressing Temple. A Templar and Hospitaller Manor in Essex* (Chelmsford, 1993), p. 12.

[69] Tibble, *Templars*, pp. 214–28.

[70] Sandys, 'The Financial and Administrative Importance of the London Temple in the Thirteenth Century', p. 159; Parker, *The Knights Templars in England*, p. 63; P. Slavin, 'Landed Estates of the Knights Templar in England and Wales and their Management in the Early Fourteenth Century', *Journal of Historical Geography*, vol. 42 (2013), pp. 36–49, at 41.

[71] J.M. Jefferson, 'The Templar Lands in Lincolnshire in the Early Fourteenth Century' (Unpublished PhD Thesis, University of Nottingham, 2016), p. 85.

Trends and Motivations

a very haphazard fashion. For instance, the bulk of Hospitallers' holdings in Essex were obtained from the Templars after 1313. Yet, only 4% of surviving records concerning Essex in the Hospitallers' cartulary date from the period of the Templars' ownership.[72] The Hospitallers had such a clear mandate in taking over the Templars' lands that, to them, most of the transactions and deeds made prior to their tenure were simply irrelevant. This complicates scholars' attempts to understand the laity's interactions with the Templars in England across the thirteenth century.

With that caveat aside, it is important to note that the Hospitallers, similarly, seem to have experienced a rise in donations from women in the first half of the thirteenth century, followed by a sharp decline in the second half.[73] The remnants of the Crusader States in the Near East became profoundly weakened in the second half of the thirteenth century, as their territory was rolled back. With the Christians suffering repeated setbacks, the reputation of the Military Orders also began to suffer.[74] They had been founded explicitly to protect pilgrims and crusaders travelling around the Latin East. With less and less Latin East to protect, the Hospitallers and Templars may have seemed redundant. Even the round churches, that were a prominent monumental celebration of crusade in England, ceased to be built by the Military Orders or by private donors in England after the 1240s.[75] On balance, it does appear that the English laity's interest in crusade, roughly over the period 1250–1300, did not match the enthusiasm seen at the beginning of the century.

In England, elite laywomen's patronage of crusade saw something of a zenith in popularity around 1220–50. The apparent decline in the numbers of supporters in the later thirteenth century is intriguing but may represent a return to normality after a period of particular fervour (for both laywomen and the region's stake in crusade in general). These fluctuations were obviously influenced by a myriad of factors, and so explaining them may never be entirely feasible. A plausible interpretation is that the preaching of the Fifth Crusade – which emphasised the availability of indulgences for women – combined with the greater establishment

---

[72] Nicholson, H.J., 'Memories of the Templars in Britain: Templar Charters in Hospitaller records after the Dissolution of the Templars', paper presented at the 49th International Medieval Congress, Kalamazoo, 2014, pp. 1–13, Available Online, https://www.researchgate.net/deref/http%3A%2F%2Fdx.doi.org%2F10.13140%2F2.1.2765.1204 (accessed 19 Feb 2024), pp. 2–3; S. Philips, 'The Hospitallers' Acquisition of the Templar Lands in England', in H. Nicholson, P.F. Crawford and J. Burgtorf (eds), *The Debate on the Trial of the Templars (1307–1314)* (Farnham, 2010), pp. 233–42; Slavin, 'Landed Estates of the Knights Templar in England and Wales', pp. 36–49.

[73] Appendix 3. See also: J. Riley-Smith, *Hospitallers: The History of the Order of St John* (London, 1999), pp. 79–80.

[74] Siberry, *Criticism of Crusading*, p. 2; J. Riley-Smith, *The Knights Hospitaller in the Levant, c.1070–1309* (Basingstoke, 2012), p. 210.

[75] Hundley, 'The English Round Church Movement', p. 368.

of the mendicant orders, had a dramatic, if temporary, effect in England. Preachers, armed with new incentives – especially following papal encyclicals like *Quia maior* (1213) and *Rachel suum videns* (1234) – were able to rouse intense support. The steady departure of expeditions over these years gave women ample opportunity to capitalise on the preachers' spiritual offers. This period saw a perfect storm for medieval Christian society's interest in crusade.

Family and Regional Tradition

Crusade offered noble and gentry laywomen a powerful identity, in a religious and cultural sense, as well as within their kin groups. Those who went on crusade were seen as setting a precedent to be emulated amongst their family, peers, social class and region.[76] The prestige that could be won on crusade or pilgrimage certainly had practical clout. These were considered to be highly chivalric endeavours that could add to, or indeed make, a dynasty's prestige. As James Naus put it, crusade offered "a new economy of power".[77] Taking the cross – or sponsoring someone who did – could impact a person's reputation or *fama*, which was of immense importance to the nobility.[78] That sense of crusading identity could be felt for generations and across larger networks than simply direct patrilineal descendants, or 'immediate family' in the phrase's modern sense.[79] In England, numerous baronial families produced several crusaders over three or more generations within the twelfth and thirteenth centuries alone.[80] Whether that was happenstance or not, it must have fed into these people's sense of self.

Women certainly encouraged their male kin to follow family traditions of crusade; however, laywomen's involvement may have been more meaningful than that. Those who enabled crusaders were conforming to a societal and gendered expectation. By doing so, they did not simply facilitate others: laywomen exercised their authority within their dynasties and placed themselves firmly within traditions of crusading. That is to say, sponsoring crusaders was a way for women to demonstrate their largesse, prestige and influence. Similar arguments have been made

---

[76] Paul, *To Follow in Their Footsteps*; Paul and Schenk, 'Family Memory and the Crusades', pp. 177–82; Lloyd, *English Society and the Crusade*, pp. 108–9.

[77] J. Naus, *Constructing Kingship: The Capetian Monarchs of France and the Early Crusades* (Manchester, 2016), pp. 28 and 39.

[78] For more on *fama*, see: T. Fenster and D.L. Smail 'Conclusion', in T. Fenster and D.L. Smail (eds), *Fama: The Politics of Talk and Reputation in Medieval Europe* (Ithaca, 2003), pp. 210–4.

[79] Paul and Schenk, 'Family Memory and the Crusades', pp. 174–5. See also: David Crouch's discussion of the difference between *lineage* and *parage*: D. Crouch, *The Birth of Nobility: Constructing Aristocracy in England and France, 900–1300* (Harlow, 2005), pp. 124–55; Nicholson, *Women and the Crusades*, p. 40.

[80] Lloyd, *English Society and the Crusade*, pp. 102–3.

respecting women's benefaction of religious houses.[81] Take for instance, the family of William Marshal earl of Pembroke and Isabella de Clare: Linda Mitchell has commented on the distinct way in which this couple's daughters engaged in politics and benefactions that followed "family policy". [82] Attention to crusading probably featured in many families' identities in a comparable way.

One tantalising example may be seen in Agnes de Percy, who helped enable her husband, Jocelin de Louvain, to go on crusade in 1174.[83] Agnes's husband does not appear to have had any family connections to crusade, but Agnes was the heir to the Percy estate and a descendant of William I de Percy, a First Crusader.[84] A mid-twelfth-century memorial to William, written in Whitby Abbey's cartulary, describes him dying in sight of Jerusalem: "then the most noble William de Percy, on the approach to Jerusalem atop a place called Mont Joy, which is on the outskirts of Jerusalem, went to the Lord [i.e. died], and is honourably buried there".[85]

Given the contemporary awareness of William's exploits and Agnes's position as the head of the Percy estate, she may have wished to emulate her ancestor. But William de Percy was not Agnes's only crusade-positive forebear. Agnes's actions are perhaps more akin to those of William's wife, Emma de Porte. Before leaving on the First Crusade, William gifted lands to the monks at Whitby, in part, for prayers for his wife Emma, who also witnessed this charter: her name appears as one of the "witnesses and condoners" (*testes et concessores*).[86] This is a rare example of a charter that explicitly details crusade preparations from England that also names a laywoman as one of the witnesses. Emma's appearance here

---

[81] E.L. Jordan, *Women, Power and Religious Patronage in the Middle Ages* (New York, 2006), pp. 61–85; Jordan, 'Exploring the Limits of Female Largesse', pp. 149–69; C.H. Berman, 'Noble Women's Power as Reflected in the Foundations of Cistercian Houses for Nuns in Thirteenth-Century Northern France: Port-Royal, Les Clairets, Moncey, Lieu, and Eau-Les-Chartres', in K.A. Smith and S. Wells (eds), *Negotiating Community and Difference in Medieval Europe: Gender, Power, Patronage, and Authority of Religion in Latin Christendom* (Leiden, 2009), pp. 137–49.

[82] L.E. Mitchell, 'The Most Perfect Knight's Countess: Isabella de Clare, Her Daughters, and Women's Exercise of Power and Influence, 1190- ca.1250', in Tanner, *Medieval Elite Women and the Exercise of Power*, pp. 45–65, at 52–4.

[83] *EYC*, vol. 11, p. 66, no. 68.

[84] *EYC*, vol. 11, pp. 1–6; R. Lomas, *A Power in the Land: the Percys* (Phantassie, 1999), p. 2.

[85] J.C. Atkinson (ed.), *Cartularium Abbathiae de Whiteby*, 2 vols (Durham, 1879–81), at vol. 1, p. 2, "Denique nobilissimus Willielmus de Perci Ierosolimam petens, apud locum qui vocatur Mons Gaudii, qui est in provincia Ierosolimitana, migravit ad Dominum, ibique honorifice sepultus est." For the dating of the passage, see: vol. 1, pp. xxxii and 10–1, n. 4.

[86] *EYC*, vol. 2, p. 197–8, no. 855.

probably shows her blessing of her husband's undertaking.[87] Similar language was used by Adela of Blois, Emma's contemporary. Adela acted as a witness for her husband Stephen of Blois's charters before he went on the First Crusade, and she was highly invested in Stephen's venture.[88]

There may have been a pattern of pro-crusade attitudes circulating amongst the women of the Percy family. Agnes de Percy's sister, Matilda, married William de Beaumont earl of Warwick. He later became a crusader and died in 1184 *en route* to the Holy Land.[89] It is not clear, however, if Matilda helped sponsor her husband's expedition. But both sisters were certainly keen to show their adherence to family traditions by patronising religious houses that were founded or favoured by the Percy dynasty.[90] It may be that Agnes was not 'passing the torch', so to speak, to her husband when she helped initiate his crusade. Instead, we could interpret Agnes's actions as a means of confirming in her charters that she, like her ancestor Emma de Porte, was an enabler of crusade and an active participant in a female family tradition.

Another case that shares similarities can be seen in Margaret de Lacy and her foundation of the Hospitaller nunnery at Aconbury in 1216. Margaret may also have been partly inspired by crusade-positive women in her family. Her paternal aunt was Sybil de Braose who, as we have seen, benefitted spiritually from donations her husband made to the Church before he joined the Third Crusade.[91] In addition to this, Margaret's great-grandmother, Amirie, supported her husband Reginald of Saint Valéry's crusade in the 1160s.[92] Before departing, Reginald gave the monks of St Frideswide in Oxford various lands in Knighton (Berkshire) and, in return, the monks gave him a payment of 20*m* and then 13*m* for his journey. In both these charters, Amirie received 1*m*.[93] These lands were held by Reginald's father and so the payment to Amirie was not in recognition of her ancestral rights to the land, nor was the property her dower.[94] Instead, it seems as though she was paid

---

[87] For more on medieval witness lists, see: Clanchy, *From Memory to Written Record*, pp. 254–5 and 263; D. Broun, 'The Presence of Witnesses and the Writing of Charters', in D. Broun (ed.), *The Reality Behind Charter Diplomatic in Anglo-Norman Britain* (Glasgow, 2011), pp. 235–90 at 251–5.

[88] Park, *Papal Protection and the Crusader*, p. 51.

[89] Lomas, *A Power in the Land*, pp. 27–8.

[90] Ricketts, *High-Ranking Widows in Medieval Iceland and Yorkshire*, p. 226.

[91] Sybil de Braose was a daughter of a William de Braose, Lord of Bramber (d.1179), who was Margaret de Lacy's grandfather. For a history of the family, see: generally D.G.C. Elwes, *The Family of de Braose, 1066–1326* (Exeter, 1883).

[92] For Margaret's connection to the Saint Valéry family, through her mother, see: R.V. Turner, 'Briouze [Braose], William de (d. 1211)', in *Oxford Dictionary of National Biography*, https://doi.org/10.1093/ref:odnb/3283, Published Online 23 Sept 2004, Updated 28 Sept 2006 (accessed 10 Feb 2024).

[93] *Frideswide*, vol. 2, p. 299, no. 1073, p. 303, no. 1080.

[94] *Frideswide*, vol. 2, p. 297, nos. 1070–1.

as a form of recognition of her support and consent. Margaret de Lacy may also have wished to imitate these kinswomen's apparent positivity towards holy war.[95]

However, Margaret de Lacy had an array of crusading relatives from whom she could draw inspiration. Her Saint Valéry family included Walter and his sons, Eudon and Bernard: all three went on the First Crusade as companions of Robert Curthose.[96] Margaret's marital family, the Lacys, also had a history of crusade and an association with the Templars, which may have conditioned Margaret's choice of foundation.[97] The women of the Lacy family may well have felt the pressure of family tradition. For example, Petronilla de Lacy's dower property in Walthamstow (Essex) was used to fund her husband Ralph VI de Tosny's efforts in the Barons' Crusade (1239–41) and, as a widow, she went on pilgrimage to Santiago de Compestella.[98]

If we were in any doubt about Margaret de Lacy's family connections and personal interest in crusade, her sister, Loretta de Braose (d.1266), had remarkably similar concerns. Loretta married a veteran of the Third Crusade – Robert de Beaumont, fourth earl of Leicester (d.1204) – and in her widowhood in 1227, she made generous gifts to the house of Hospitaller sisters at Buckland Priory.[99] Other women hailing from crusading families similarly gravitated towards the Military Orders. Kathryn Hurlock has pointed out that Agnes d'Aubigny had a number of dynastic connections to crusading, and she, likewise, joined the Hospitallers' house at Buckland Priory in 1232.[100]

Agnes de Vescy, who enabled her son's crusade in 1270, also had a string of ancestors who had supported crusade.[101] She was a granddaughter of a notable crusader, William Marshal earl of Pembroke, and a great-granddaughter of the Third Crusader William I Earl de Ferrers and his wife Sybil de Braose, who featured conspicuously in William's grants to religious houses on the eve of

---

[95] For more on the influence of grandmothers within the medieval family dynamic, see: J.T. Rosenthal, 'Looking for Grandmother: The Pastons and their Counterparts in Late Medieval England', in J.C. Parsons and B. Wheeler (eds), *Medieval Mothering* (New York, 1996), pp. 259–77.

[96] For more on the Saint Valéry First Crusaders, see: Riley-Smith, *The First Crusaders*, pp. 202, 224, 234 and 248.

[97] Nicholson, 'Margaret de Lacy and the Hospital of St John at Aconbury', pp. 634–5; Scott, 'A Herefordshire Nunnery', p. 12. For more on the Lacy's and crusade, see the edited volume: P. Duffy, T. O'Keefe and J.M. Picard (eds), *From Carrickfergus to Carcassonne: The Epic Deeds of Hugh de Lacy during the Albigensian Crusade* (Turnhout, 2017).

[98] *CRR*, vol. 16, p. 320, no. 1625; *CPR, 1247–58*, p. 104.

[99] H.C. Maxwell Lyte (ed.), *Calendar of the Charter Rolls Preserved in the Public Record Office, Vol. 1: Henry III A.D. 1226–1257* (London, 1903), pp. 52–3.

[100] Hurlock, *Britain, Ireland and the Crusades*, p. 151.

[101] *CIPM*, vol. 2, pp. 445–7, no. 723.

crusade.[102] Hawisa Lestrange, who seems to have supported her brother's crusade in 1270, may have been inspired by a family interest in such patronage. Her father, John III Lestrange, had exhibited a deep respect for women's assistance in crusade when he made significant donations to the Hospitaller nunnery at Aconbury.[103] Likewise, Sybil of Icklesham helped drive her husband's preparations to take part in the Sixth Crusade; her paternal grandfather, Robert of Icklesham (d.c.1193) was a participant in the Third Crusade.[104] Another example can be seen in Eva Tibetot's case. She took a crusade vow sometime before February 1291 and was encouraged by Pope Nicholas IV to fund a warrior instead.[105] Eva's husband, Robert Tibetot, had been a participant in Lord Edward's Crusade twenty years previously. Robert's companion and co-contractor on that expedition, Payn de Chaworth, may also have been one of Eva's relatives.[106]

Wider kin networks or regional patterns in crusading may have influenced others. Isabella Hacard – who helped enable her son's crusade around 1240 – described herself as the daughter and heir of a Ranulf of Bashley.[107] Bashley was a relatively modest village in the New Forest in Hampshire. A certain Bosgerius of Bashley took the cross and gifted all his land in Bashley to the monks of Christchurch Priory around 1200.[108] Proving a hereditary connection between Bosgerius and Isabella is difficult, but their shared connections to the Bashley region and the religious house at Christchurch are intriguing. Perhaps their shared actions in crusading reflected a local community identity regarding lay piety and patronage. However, Isabella's motivations may not have been limited to honouring the convictions and/or prestige of her forebears. Isabella's son would have owed much of his crusading success to his mother's generosity, and contemporaries may have appreciated her influence. By sponsoring her crusading son, Isabella affirmed her own power.[109]

---

102 Agnes was a daughter of Sybil Marshal, the daughter of William Marshal. For the latter's participation in the Third Crusade, see: Crouch, *William Marshal*, pp. 67–8.

103 Eyton, *Antiquities of Shropshire*, vol. 10, pp. 275–6.

104 Salzmann, 'Some Sussex Domesday Tenants', pp. 180 and 189; J. Sayers, 'English Charters from the Third Crusade', in D. Greenway, C. Holdsworth and J. Sayers (eds), *Tradition and Change: Essays in Honour of Marjorie Chibnall Presented by her Friends on the Occasion of her Seventieth Birthday* (Cambridge, 1985), pp. 196–213, at 207–12.

105 Langlois, *Les Registres de Nicholas IV*, vol. 1, p. 650, no. 4490.

106 Beebe, 'The English Baronage and the Crusade of 1270', p. 132, table ii; Tyerman, *England and the Crusades*, p. 195; W.E. Rhodes, 'Tiptoft[Tivetot], Robert, Lord Tiptoft', in *Oxford Dictionary of National Biography*, https://doi.org/10.1093/ref:odnb/27472, Published Online 23 Sept 2004, Updated by R.R. Davis 22 Sept 2005 (accessed 12 Feb 2024).

107 *Carisbrooke*, p. 111, no. 163. For her case, see Chapter 5, p. 104.

108 Hanna, *The Christchurch Priory Cartulary*, p. 95, no. 277.

109 See also: Marjorie Chibnall's discussion of the relationship between Empress Matilda and her eldest son Henry; M. Chibnall, 'The Empress Matilda and Her Sons', in Parsons

Prestige in Patronage

Around 1230, the Icelandic writer Snorri Sturluson drafted his great work *Heimskringla*.[110] In it, he recounted an anecdote revolving around a heated argument between the co-kings of Norway, Sigurðr I Magnusson (d.1130) and Eystein I (d.1123).[111] Sigurðr had been the first European king to go on crusade, sailing from 1107–11. He had recently returned from his travels around the Mediterranean and Byzantine world, and was feasting with his brother.[112] The pair engaged in a game of wordplay and mockery over dinner that quickly got out of hand. While attempting to belittle his brother, Sigurðr boasted of his crusade:

> people have said that the journey that I took abroad was pretty princely, but you sat at home in the meantime like your father's daughter.[113]

Bristling, Eystein quickly retorted:

> Now you have touched on a sore spot. I would not have started this conversation if I had had no answer to give to this. I think it more to the point that I fitted you out as I would my sister before you were ready to set out on your journey.[114]

The cultural interplay of gender, power and largesse, mixed with crusade, is stark. Eystein's belief (according to Snorri at least) that he was the more superior ruler given his ability to actualise a crusade, rather than lead one, raises a crucial point: clearly a person who patronised another's crusade could do so to exert authority within a family or political dynamic.

We have seen how women's sponsorship of kinfolk could have been rooted in a sense of commitment to familial traditions. Equally, these women could have been asserting their dominance as patrons of crusade, as King Eystein saw himself. This notion is perhaps more visible, however, in instances where women patronised crusaders with whom they held no kinship. For instance, Alice Baskervill, along with her husband, bought property from Nicholas Britto around 1220, to provide him with money for his crusade.[115] Alice may have had some crusading forebears.

---

and Wheeler, *Medieval Mothering*, pp. 279–94, at 287–8.

[110] S. Bagge, *Society and Politics in Snorri Sturluson's Heimskringla* (Berkeley, 1991), pp. 23–5; Snorri Sturluson, *Heimskringla*, 3 vols, A. Finlay and A. Faulkes (eds and trans.) (London, 2011–5), at vol. 1, p. viii.

[111] J. Doherty, 'The Presentation of Crusader Masculinities in Old Norse Sagas', in Hodgson, Lewis and Mesley, *Crusading and Masculinities*, pp. 129–46, at 129.

[112] See: G.B. Doxey, 'Norwegian Crusaders and the Balearic Islands', *Scandinavian Studies*, vol. 68, no. 2 (1996), pp. 139–60, at 156.

[113] Snorri Sturluson, *Heimskringla*, vol. 3, p. 159, cpt. 21.

[114] Snorri Sturluson, *Heimskringla*, vol. 3, p. 159, cpt. 21.

[115] Rees, *The Cartulary of Haughmond Abbey*, p. 200, no. 1067.

In 1109, a Robert de Baskerville gave lands to the Church of St Peter in Gloucester after returning from Jerusalem.[116] Proving a link between Alice and this earlier Robert is difficult, but they do both appear to have been active in the Welsh March and were part of the wider Baskervill kin group: a wealthy family on the rise, conscious of society's perception of them. However, the crusader Nicholas Brito does not appear to have had any relationship with Alice or her husband's wider *familia*, nor do they appear to have had any prior dealings. Enabling Nicholas cannot be seen as facilitating a continuation of any Baskervill crusading tradition. However, Alice's support, like other women who sponsored crusaders from outside of their kin group, may have been an act to distinguish her personal stance as a patron of crusade.[117]

The influence of family on some women who sponsored crusade is clear. Patrons wished to aid crusaders so as to link themselves with family traditions, of both male and female ancestors, while others wished to demonstrate their own unique power within their family and perhaps initiate family traditions of crusade. We cannot assume, however, that this was a potent motivator for every crusade sponsor. Given the intervening centuries and the degradation of records, the origins of many women who financed crusaders has now become obscure. Very little is known about the family or networks of Matilda Baiarde (who gave assets to her nephew), Rose Marnet (who funded her son), the Matilda who bought land from a crusader in 1202, or the Annora who tried to reclaim the grants she made to a crusader.[118]

The families of women from higher social circles are far more visible in the written record, and so their connections to crusaders can more easily be identified. This does not necessarily mean that women with no provable connection to other crusaders did not act to enhance their own or their families' prestige through patronising *crucesignati*. The roles and actions of women from the lesser aristocracy of the Middle Ages often mirrored those from higher social strata.[119] The critical issue is that women's generosity towards crusaders was often specifically noted in cartularies for posterity. In doing so, it is clear that the significance

---

[116] W.H. Hart (ed.), *Historia et Cartularium Monasterii Sancti Petri Gloucestriae*, 3 vols (Cambridge, 1863–7), at vol. 1, p. 81.

[117] Likewise, Gundreda "daughter of Richard the Priest" – who bought property from a crusader around 1230 – had no apparent prior relationship with the man she helped sponsor. See: Purvis, *The Chartulary of the Augustinian Priory of St John the Evangelist of the Park of Healaugh*, pp. 156–7.

[118] For the charters and records of these women's grants, see respectively: Kerling, *Cartulary of St Bartholomew's Hospital*, p. 146, nos. 1599–1600; *Carisbrooke*, p. 85, no. 123; Stenton, *The Earliest Northamptonshire Assize Rolls*, p. 57, no. 450; *CRR*, vol. 12, p. 12, no. 69.

[119] Johns, *Noblewomen*, p. 153.

Trends and Motivations

of their patronage was recognised and considered noteworthy. These individuals had attained some level of distinction and perhaps that was their ultimate goal. Although it was not as daring as going to the Levant itself, patronising a crusader did involve some hardship. The emotional toll of sending family members on crusade, the financial burden of the costs, and the physical effort of prayer and penance must have all been prompted by strong motives. Some were driven by piety and a belief in the necessity of holy war, others by the desire to make shrewd acquisitions of property, and then others may have been compelled. Many troops went to the Holy Land out of obligation to their lord, and so it stands to reason that some supporters of crusade also acted under some level of coercion.[120] Yet, the best means for gauging the motivations of sponsors is to examine the climate within which they acted. Here, there are some telling correlations.

The evidence suggests that there was a peak in women's involvement in crusade preparations in the first half of the thirteenth century. This is especially striking given that the Third Crusade and the Lord Edward's Crusade – two large and culturally important English ventures – lie outside of this period. Perhaps the women who supported crusade had differing motives from their counterparts who travelled to the Holy Land. Equally, it would appear that women's support was not necessarily a foregone conclusion when large numbers of crusaders wished to depart England. Yet, it seems that laywomen within this kingdom became especially enamoured by crusade support in the wake of *Quia maior* and the establishment of regular preaching by the mendicant orders.

Numerous English knightly families produced crusaders, supporters and patrons of the Military Orders. All of these individuals, in some way, were conforming to gender and class expectations, as well as the political pressures of their day. Despite this, they would have been deeply aware of their family links to crusade. There can be little doubt that many aristocratic laywomen were raised in environments where they were taught about their crusading ancestors. This must have conditioned many people to view the movement favourably.[121] Indeed, as we have seen, numerous supporters had clear and direct links to crusading relatives. This adds a further, and substantial, dimension to the current theory that crusade was a family enterprise, pursued over generations and across community networks.[122] We can be sure that more individuals than simply the crusaders harboured an affinity with holy war, and sought out recognition for the role they played. With that in mind, it is important to examine supporters' perceptions of their own legacy and the specific actions they took to ensure that they were remembered within crusading traditions.

---

[120] Lloyd, *English Society and the Crusade*, pp. 111–2.
[121] Paul, *To Follow in Their Footsteps*, p. 201.
[122] Riley-Smith, 'Family Traditions', pp. 101–8; Riley-Smith, *The First Crusaders*, pp. 93–9; Lloyd, *English Society and the Crusade*, pp. 108–9; Paul, *To Follow in Their Footsteps*, pp. 55–89; Paul and Schenk, 'Family Memory and the Crusades', pp. 173–86.

PART III

Memory

7

Commemoration and Creating Identity

> Let it be known that if Robert Ruffus, my husband, returns from the Holy Land and wishes to break this concession and confirmation, then the said Robert, myself, and my heirs will return to the said James all his chattels.
>
> (Helewisa Ruffus, in a charter, c.1250)[1]

Charter language can be astoundingly dry and formulaic; not many other documents can offer such a bureaucratic nod at the prospect that a spouse might die hundreds of miles from home. Perhaps that is why Helewisa's trepidation might easily be glossed over. Her husband's absence certainly did not stop her from conducting business in Harmston (Lincolnshire). Nevertheless, his crusade occupied her thoughts for the future. We may be able to read a somewhat forlorn tone to her phrasing or, perhaps, boastful of her husband's status as a *crucesignatus*. This was a role that came with legal protections for her and their property, and a shrewd point to put in writing during a transaction. Whatever her perspective, Robert's crusade loomed large in Helewisa's mindset, and until she had knowledge of his return or death, there must have been huge uncertainty for the future. A charter produced sometime later, between 1250 and 1257, described Helewisa as a widow.[2] Whether Robert returned and died or failed to come back, or perhaps Helewisa simply gave up hope, we may never know. What is clear is that crusade formed a distinct aspect of Helewisa's life: it became a frame of reference and a point to be committed to writing in her dealings.

Whether a person helped enable their kinfolk's crusade or not, the absence of family members – and the alienation of property they once enjoyed – would have been an emotional disruption. It would not have been atypical for a person to live for years without a spouse or relative who had gone on crusade, and they would have been aware of that when preparations were underway. In the 1130s, Fulcher of Chartres recollected scenes of the First Crusaders leaving France thirty

---

[1] Foulds, *The Thurgarton Cartulary*, p. 405, no. 667. See also: p. 406, no. 668, "Sciendum quod si Robertus Ruffus maritus meus a terra sancta reveniat et velit hanc concessionem ac confirmacionem frangere dictus Robertus et ego heredes mei reddemus dicto Jacobo totum catallum suum".

[2] Foulds, *The Thurgarton Cartulary*, p. 407, no. 670.

years beforehand: "She, fearing that she would never see him again, not able to hold up, fell senseless to the ground; mourning her living beloved as though he were dead".[3] A remarkably similar scene was painted in one thirteenth-century French Bible (see Figure 8). In 1188, a Welsh nobleman named Gruffydd boasted while taking the cross that there could be nothing less desirable than to survive the crusade and live to return home.[4] These were events were written down as romanticised departure scenes, but long absences were common and must have been expected.

Some individuals may have questioned whether they could remarry when crusading husbands disappeared abroad and could not be located. One canonist, Tancredus (d.c.1236), may have been influenced by cases of missing crusaders when he proposed that wives should wait five years after the last communication from their husbands before remarrying.[5] English court records show that these situations were not unheard of. In 1229, Cecilia Luvel was taken to court and accused of adultery after she remarried. Her husband had gone missing in the Holy Land, and some family members disputed whether there was enough proof that he was dead.[6] Another awkward situation played out in an ecclesiastical court in Wells (Somerset) in 1248. An unnamed woman from Bishops Lydeard was alleged to have had a relationship with a vicar named Henry of *Mertok*. The court noted that the woman's husband had been away in the Holy Land for the past five years. Perhaps the court scribe mentioned this detail to intimate that the woman assumed her husband was dead.[7]

Crusading was obviously highly dangerous, and this was not lost on those who enabled their family to participate. Women who remained in England must have given thought to the aftermath of crusade funding and their own futures when expeditions set off. The effects of crusade on those who remained in western Europe, particularly women, have been a rich topic of discussion amongst

---

3   E. Peters (ed. and trans.), *The First Crusade, The Chronicle of Fulcher of Chartres and Other Source Materials*, 2nd edn (Philadelphia, 1998), p. 59, v.13.

4   Gerald of Wales, 'Itinerarium Kambriae, et Descriptio Kambriae', p. 15, cpt. 1.

5   Brundage, 'The Crusader's Wife Revisited', p. 246. See also: Lloyd, *English Society and the Crusade*, App. 1, pp. 248–52; Barber and Bate, *Letters from the East*, pp. 15–7, no. 1 and pp. 22–5, no. 5.

6   *CRR*, vol. 13, Henry III, p. 347, no. 1636. See also: Tyerman, *England and the Crusades*, p. 211. Cf: J. Murray, 'Individualism and Consensual Marriage Some Evidence from Medieval England', in C.M. Rousseau and J.T. Rosenthal (eds), *Women, Marriage and Family in Medieval Christendom, Essays in Memory of Michael M. Sheehan, C.S.B.* (Kalamazoo, 1998), pp. 125–37.

7   W.P. Baildon (ed.), *Calendar of the Manuscripts of the Dean of the Chapter of Wells*, 2 vols (London, 1907–14), vol. 1, p. 87. See also the similar case on: pp. 74–5. See also the case of Katherine le Marbeler, the widow of a crusader, who was defaulted while her husband was abroad (or recently dead): A.H. Hershey (ed.), *The 1258-9 Special Eyre of Surrey and Kent* (Woking, 2004), p. 85, no. 170.

Figure 8. A thirteenth-century imagining of a departure scene in which two women, an elderly man and two children look distraught as they bid farewell to a group of Crusaders. (Vienna, Österreichische Nationalbibliothek, Bible Moralisée, Codex Vindobonensis 2554, f.4r. – Reproduced by kind permission of Österreichische Nationalbibliothek).

scholars.[8] Indeed, the memory of crusade proved to be critically important to noble families and local communities.[9] This chapter will examine the ways in which women in England remembered crusade, both the acts of crusaders, as well

---

[8] Tyerman, *England and the Crusades*, pp. 208–15; Lloyd, *English Society and the Crusade*, pp. 174–5; Riley-Smith, *The First Crusaders*, p. 98.

[9] Paul, *To Follow in Their Footsteps*; Cassidy-Welch, *Remembering the Crusades and Crusading*; Cassidy-Welch, *War and Memory at the Time of the Fifth Crusade*; E. Brenner, M. Cohen and M. Franklin-Brown (eds), *Memory and Commemoration in Medieval Culture* (London, 2013); Siberry, *Tales of the Crusaders*.

as the commemoration of patrons of, and the support of, crusade. The personal recollections of individuals are not as important in this regard but rather the "social commemoration" that was so crucial in medieval displays of identity.[10] These acts highlight that many laywomen created lasting displays of personal association with holy war.

Creating Links

People who participated in medieval crusade were typically very keen for their peers to know about it. Ensuring that crusade was recognised and remembered was vitally important to contemporaries.[11] Numerous crusaders organised for religious houses to hold remembrance days after their deaths and intone prayers for their souls, or they committed their deeds to songs or epitaphs.[12] When Geoffrey of Dutton returned from crusade in 1220, he brought back a fragment of the True Cross and gifted the relic to Norton Priory (Cheshire), ensuring the monks would commemorate him and his pilgrimage. Later, he may have also adopted a palm frond on his seal, used to authenticate documents. Anyone so much as glancing at his letters or charters would appreciate his identity as a former crusader.[13] At another end of the social spectrum, King Louis IX of France was widely recognised as having undergone something of a transformation following his return from the East in 1254. He eschewed luxuries and became noticeably more pious.[14]

Many returned crusaders, both commoners and nobles, took on epithets that referenced their journey. Some used 'Jerusalemite', referencing their pilgrimage to the Holy City; others used 'Palmer', suggesting that they had collected a palm frond from the River Jordan. These epithets appear quite frequently within medieval cartularies. In Gloucestershire, palmers appear so frequently amongst medieval juries that it has been speculated that contemporaries considered them to be more trustworthy because of their pilgrimage.[15] Thirteenth-century records from Dublin frequently note people called 'palmer' accompanying merchants. As

---

[10] M. Innes, 'Keeping it in the Family: Women and Aristocratic Memory, 700–1200', in E. Van Houts (ed.), *Medieval Memories: Men, Women and the Past, 700–1300* (Abingdon, 2001, revised 2013), pp. 17–35, at 17; Paul, *To Follow in Their Footsteps*.

[11] Housley, *Fighting for the Cross*, pp. 264–89; Hurlock, 'A Transformed Life?', pp. 15–27. See also: J. Esra, 'Cornish Crusaders and Barbary Captives: Returns and Transformations', in M. Gibson, S. Trower and G. Tregidga (eds), *Mysticism, Myth and Celtic Identity* (Abingdon, 2013), pp. 155–70.

[12] Paul, *To Follow in Their Footsteps*, pp. 148–9; Hurlock, 'A Transformed Life?', p. 23.

[13] Hurlock, 'A Transformed Life?', pp. 15–27. See also: Reynolds, 'Battling the Lion', pp. 240–62.

[14] M.C. Gaposchkin, *The Making of Saint Louis: Kingship, Sanctity, and Crusade in the Later Middle Ages* (Ithaca, 2008), pp. 21 and 188.

[15] Stacy, *Surveys of the Estates of Glastonbury Abbey*, p. 65.

proven travellers and warriors, they may have been useful professional security.[16] The power of memory was such that even the rebellious son of William the Conqueror, Robert Curthose (d.1134) – who fell afoul of his brothers and spent nearly thirty years of his life imprisoned – was nevertheless widely respected for his part in leading the First Crusade.[17]

As medieval women supported crusade and associated themselves with holy war, it appears that they, too, wanted to be seen as part of the crusade movement. They wished to be remembered, much like their martial counterparts. Laywomen's desire to be upheld as sponsors is evident from the moment that they began supporting those bound for the Jerusalem pilgrimage. We have seen how clauses were added to charters that promised counter-gifts, prayers or future acknowledgement of women's crusade support. As well as signalling these women's consent to transactions, these promises would have marked women out as patrons of crusade in later years. These sorts of clauses could have formed an aspect of what Cassidy-Welch called "preparatory memory": the organisation of the remembrance of an event while that event was still unfolding.[18]

For example, in the 1180s, Easby Abbey's monks guaranteed Ralph de Chall's wife her dower and a daily delivery of food if her husband did not return.[19] In the early decades of the thirteenth century, the canons of St Frideswide (Oxford) guaranteed Alice, the wife of William "son of Nigel the Dean", the security of a house in Walton, 0.5*m* worth of clothing annually and a quart of the future crops harvested from twenty 'butts' of land given to the canons before William departed.[20] Sometime before 1249, Loretta of Crundal was promised a 100*s* from a creditor in the event of her nephew's death in the East.[21] Likewise, the clergy of Drax Priory, St Bartholomew's Hospital in London, Breedon Priory, St Denys in Southampton and Southwick Priory (to name a handful) all agreed to pray for the souls of crusaders' wives on the eve of departure. By offering women ongoing prayers or gifts, religious communities were able to continually pay respect to women who enabled crusade.[22] Some of these arrangements resemble provisions made by the elderly in light of their retirement, and that may well have been a

---

[16] C. Swift, '"Palmers" as ex-crusaders in Irish urban environments? The Evidence of the *Dublin Guild Merchant Roll*', in Coleman, Duffy and O'Keeffe, *Ireland and the Crusades*, pp. 70–6.

[17] Aird, *Robert Curthose*, pp. 191–244.

[18] Cassidy-Welch, *War and Memory at the Time of the Fifth Crusade*, pp. 18–41.

[19] *EYC*, vol. 5, p. 112, no. 215.

[20] *Frideswide*, vol. 1, p. 419, no. 597 and p. 420, no. 598.

[21] Clanchy, *Civil Pleas of the Wiltshire Eyre*, p. 46, no. 69. See also a similar case involving a crusader receiving a reduced rent if he survived: R. Ransford (ed.), *The Early Charters of the Augustinian Canons of Waltham Abbey, Essex, 1062–1230* (Woodbridge, 1989), p. 220, no. 329.

[22] For discussions of such commemoration, see: Bijsterveld, *Do ut Des*, p. 122; I.F. Silber, 'Gift-Giving in the Great Traditions: The Case of Donations to Monasteries in the

factor in their thinking. Nevertheless, the context of these provisions would have been well known to the communities providing food and care.[23] The giving of food during the Middle Ages, in particular, has been recognised as holding significance regarding women's piety, and it frequently formed part of recognition and reward for commendable behaviour.[24]

Women's preparations to enter religion on the eve of crusade may similarly have functioned as a means of security as well as a lasting display of their association with holy war.[25] Sally Thompson has highlighted the case of Gundreda, wife of Roger de Glanville, who founded the nunnery of Bungay (Suffolk) in 1183. Gundreda then joined the house as a nun around the time of Roger's death on the Third Crusade.[26] Thompson has also drawn attention to Wroxall Priory (Warwickshire), which was similarly founded by Hugh FitzRichard around the time of his participation in the Second Crusade. Hugh's wife and daughter both entered this foundation and became nuns.[27] Ela of Salisbury founded a nunnery at Lacock (Wiltshire) in 1229 and entered the house a decade later in 1239. She decided to become a nun at the exact time that she was gifting her properties to her son so he could join the Barons' Crusade.[28]

In neighbouring Scotland, Christiana de Brus founded a hospital of Trinitarian brothers in 1247 in Dunbar (East Lothian) with the assent of her stepson, Patrick II earl of Dunbar. She did this while Patrick was preparing to depart on the Seventh Crusade.[29] The Trinitarian Order were established to help pay the ransoms of Christian captives in the Holy Land; a third of their income was for this express purpose.[30] Christiana's timing and choice of foundation may show something

---

Medieval West', *European Journal of Sociology*, vol. 36, no. 2 (1995), pp. 209–43, at 218; Sweetinburgh, *The Role of the Hospital in Medieval England*, pp. 35–7.

[23] E. Clark, 'Social Welfare and Mutual Aid in the Medieval Countryside', *Journal of British Studies*, vol. 33, no. 4 (1994), pp. 381–406, at 393–4; E. Clark, 'Some Aspects of Social Security in Medieval England', *Journal of Family History*, vol. 7, no. 4 (1982), pp. 307–20, at 311–2.

[24] C.M. Woolgar, 'Gifts of Food in Late Medieval England', *Journal of Medieval History*, vol. 37, no. 1 (2011), pp. 6–18, at 8–9; C.W. Bynum, *Holy Feast and Holy Fast: The Religious Significance of Food to Medieval Women* (Berkeley, 1988), pp. 190–4.

[25] Lester, 'A Shared Imitation', pp. 356–7.

[26] In this period, wealthy and noblewomen could be pressured by their overlord or king to remarry. For more on Gundreda's case, see: S. Thompson, *Women Religious, The Founding of English Nunneries after the Norman conquest* (Oxford, 1991), p. 176.

[27] Thompson, *Women Religious*, p. 176.

[28] Reynolds, 'A Paragon of Support?', pp. 260–1.

[29] C.C. Harvey (ed.), *Calendar of Writs Preserved at Yester House, 1166–1503* (Edinburgh, 1916), pp. 8–9, no. 14; MacQuarrie, *Scotland and the Crusades*, pp. 47–8; A. Beam, J. Bradley, D. Broun, J.R. Davies, M. Hammond, N. Jakeman, M. Pasin, A. Taylor, *et al* (eds), *People of Medieval Scotland: 1093–1371* (Glasgow and London, 2019), no. 5989.

[30] Flannery, 'The Trinitarian Order and the Ransom of Christian Captives', p. 137.

of a lack of confidence in her stepson's military acumen. However, we should be conscious that her foundation would have been viewed as a celebration of family commitment to holy war. As a widowed stepmother, Christina may have felt that it was especially crucial to affirm and commemorate her support of, and links with, the earls of Dunbar and their newfound interest in crusade.[31] Further afield, Elizabeth of Thuringia/Hungary (d.1231) was famously canonised in 1235 for her reaction to her husband's death on crusade; she immediately took up a life of charity, founding hospitals and caring for the poor.[32] Those who founded, or entered, religious houses were perceived to be joining in a family commitment to benefit Christendom, and this was thought to reflect the martial efforts that their kin had made on crusade.[33]

Isabella Hacard's preparations in 1240 for her future may show a fusion of ideas, securing her livelihood, entering religion and permanently connecting herself and her legacy with her crusading son, Geoffrey.[34] Isabella made precise provisions for her own livelihood, asking that the monks accept her as a sister of the house and provide her with food, clothing and lodging for life. Her decision displayed a comparable sense of devotion to that which her son exercised by going to the Holy Land. Isabella's son agreed on similar terms in the event of his homecoming. Geoffrey would receive food from the monks and annually collect a robe, a tunic and an "over-tunic" for life.[35] It looks as though he, too, would take the habit, but his charter does not directly state this. Isabella's gifts to Carisbrooke Priory were intimately tied to her son's fund-raising, and it is plausible that she was also involved in the discussions over Geoffrey's return.[36] There is significance to the fact that this supporter and crusader would spend the rest of their lives working and living in the same priory that helped them actualise a crusading venture. This whole situation appears to have been a linked effort between the local religious and lay communities.

---

[31] For more on this group and crusade, see: Reynolds, 'Asking for Forgiveness as an Aspect of Crusade', pp. 137–9.

[32] For the testimony at her canonisation hearing and a study of her life see: K.B. Wolf (ed. and trans.), *The Life & Afterlife of St. Elizabeth of Hungary* (Oxford, 2011). See also: Paul, *To Follow in Their Footsteps*, pp. 166–70.

[33] See also: Bull, *Knightly Piety*, p. 286.

[34] *Carisbrooke*, pp. 110–14, nos. 161, 163–4 and 166.

[35] *Carisbrooke*, pp. 113–14, no. 166, "si rediero a peregrinatione mea habebo victum in domo de Caresbroc et unam robam annuatim scilicet tunicam cum supertunica quam diu vixero".

[36] It would not necessarily be unusual for a sponsor to take an interest in the homecoming of the crusader they supported, for example, see: Margerum, *The Cartulary of Binham Priory*, p. 111, no. 144.

Homecoming

Some individuals were set on ensuring that they would be recognised as pious patrons of crusade before those whom they financed had even left. Those who remained in England were deeply conscious of their own future as well as the eventual homecoming of their kin. So much so, that the return of a crusader may have been an occasion to celebrate the supporters who had patronised the venture as well as the safe return of the pilgrim; these enterprises were joint efforts after all.

Although the First Crusade established a series of states along the Levant, relatively few subsequent crusaders intended to remain in these Christian polities. The vast majority who went to the East intended to return to the West.[37] This attitude was one of the major contributing factors to the downfall of the Crusader States; they habitually suffered from a lack of manpower and troops. We can see individuals' intention, to go and then simply come back, being referenced when they vowed to go on crusade in the first place. An English document called the *Coventry Pontifical*, dated around 1200, contains rites that were read during the ceremony in which a person took the cross. The penitent would be given their scrip and staff – a practical travellers' satchel and walking stick – within a ceremony loaded with ritualistic references to pilgrimage. They would also be given a fabric cross to sew onto their clothing, to mark them out as a person 'signed with the cross'. The *Coventry Pontifical* highlights the expectation that a crusader would ideally return:

> …and may it [the sewn cross] be a guard throughout the outward journey and the return. When he has finished his journey may he be worthy to return to his own home with benefit to mind and body.[38]

Although many communities in England would, then, have welcomed their kin back when they returned, their emotions, attitudes and commemorations in the moment are mostly obscure. English court records offer some insight into the effects of crusaders' return home.[39] However, given that these sources' focus on quarrels and litigation, they only reveal exceptionally negative situations. Typically, they refer to situations where the crusader in question had been missing for an abnormal amount of time and had been assumed dead. There is no way of knowing what proportion of crusaders' families were drawn into litigation or

---

[37] Housley, *Fighting for the Cross*, p. 267.
[38] Riley-Smith and Riley-Smith, *The Crusades*, pp. 136–8, no. 31. For Latin, see: Brundage, "'*Cruce Signari*'", p. 307, "Contra omnia antiqui hostis temptamenta sit in uia defensio, in domo protectio, sit ubique presidium eundo et redeundo, ut cum tua gratia quo cupit pergat et peracto itinere cum commoditate mentis et corporis ad propria reuerti mereatur".
[39] Tyerman, *England and the Crusades*, pp. 209–11; Hurlock, *Britain, Ireland and the Crusades*, pp. 118–9.

financial straits; indeed, the legal protections bestowed on crusaders' families and property were so robust that this has been considered by historians to have been a powerful motivation for contemporaries to take crusade vows.[40]

Nevertheless, there are some revealing cases of upset when crusaders returned. For instance, a widow named Sybil was undoubtedly shocked when her rights to lands in Bourton-on-the-Water (Gloucestershire) were challenged by her brother-in-law in the 1220s, when he returned from crusade. He had seemingly gone missing decades before, perhaps on the Third or Fourth Crusades.[41] Another awkward homecoming happened sometime before 1229. One Alditha was confronted by her furious (*iratus*) father, Radulf de Hodeng, probably a Fifth Crusader. While her father was away, Alditha married Alwald "the Merchant", her father's villein, and she took some family land in Hedingham (Essex) to build a house.[42] The emotional (and legal) confrontations caused by these sorts of homecomings would have been felt for generations. Numerous later medieval English folk stories revolve around crusader protagonists who return home after years abroad, only to find some tragedy has occurred at home.[43] It is tempting to think that many of these tales have their roots in real arguments and misunderstandings.

Narrative sources, such as chronicles, typically did not discuss crusaders' return in much detail, if at all, as these events did not fit within chroniclers' focus on major religious and political events.[44] The emotion of departure scenes attracted far more comment from contemporaries, mostly because they could reconstruct the scenes for didactic purposes, offering moralising ideas.[45] When writers did discuss homecomings, they tended to focus on the *crucesignati* alone. There are a few exceptions that hint at the emotions of reunions. The return of William de Mandeville from the Holy Land in the 1170s is one such case. A monk at Walden Priory witnessed William's return (or at least was his contemporary), and he described the proceedings. In typical fashion for nobles, William made gifts of

---

[40] Park, *Papal Protection and the Crusader*, pp. 29 and 86. In an infamous example from France, Erard I of Ramerupt (d.1246) desired to marry Philippa of Champagne to lay claim to her (potential) inheritance: the county of Champagne. Philippa, however, was in the Kingdom of Jerusalem. So, Erard made a crusade vow, was ambiguous about his destination and used his legal status to counter officials sent to intercept him by royal and comital adversaries. See: G. Perry, *The Briennes: The Rise and Fall of a Champenois Dynasty in the Age of the Crusades, c.950–1356* (Cambridge, 2018), pp. 58–60; Power, 'Who Went on the Albigensian Crusade?', p. 1079.

[41] Stenton, *Rolls of the Justices in Eyre being the Rolls of Pleas and Assizes for Gloucestershire, Warwickshire and Staffordshire, 1221, 1222*, pp. 97–8, no. 232.

[42] *CRR*, vol. 13, p. 370, no. 1760 and p. 164, no. 730.

[43] K. Hurlock, 'Cheshire and the Crusades', *Transactions of the Historic Society of Lancashire and Cheshire*, vol. 159, no. 1 (2010), pp. 1–18, at 1–2.

[44] Housley, *Fighting for the Cross*, p. 268.

[45] S.J. Spencer, *Emotions in a Crusading Context, 1095–1291* (Oxford, 2019), pp. 160–4.

relics and luxury textiles to the Priory and churches nearby, and was treated to a reception of prayers and hymns by Walden's monks.[46] Following this:

> When they had enjoyed pleasant, friendly conversation, he was escorted to his lodging where a splendid banquet was sumptuously provided for him and his men. When he departed from here he visited some friends and relations who were delighted at his success.[47]

It is a brief comment on these people's reaction, but typical of our sources. The Gaelic poet, Muireadhach Albanach, similarly hinted at the importance of reunions. He composed a poem for Cathal Crobhdearg, king of Connacht (d.1224), while returning from the Fifth Crusade sometime between 1220 and 1224. Muireadhach emphasised his dedication to the ruler by saying that upon his return: "we will not linger with our women till we see Cathal of Cruachan".[48]

Commemorating the Fallen

There are far more abundant sources regarding women who associated themselves with crusade after incidents where their kinfolk either died abroad or disappeared without a trace. Although these were undoubtedly highly charged situations, these circumstances provided people in England with an opportunity to ensure their associations with crusade were remembered through the commemoration of the deceased. The evidence for these commemorations predominantly comes from grants made to religious houses.

Much of the interactions between lay and monastic communities rested on reciprocal relationships of patronage and commemoration. Lay donors typically gifted land or privileges to religious houses in exchange for monks' intercession on behalf of a deceased's soul.[49] These gifts were perceived to help assuage any punishment waiting for the dead in Purgatory and help move their soul to heaven. It is very telling that so many people anxiously paid clerics to pray for dead

---

[46] Greenway and Watkiss, *The Book of the Foundation of Walden Monastery*, bk ii, caps. 5–6, pp. 57–61. For more on the return of crusaders bearing relics and souvenirs, see: Paul, *To Follow in Their Footsteps*, pp. 90–133; Lester, 'What Remains', pp. 311–28; Tyerman, *The World of the Crusades*, pp. 252–5; Housley, *Fighting for the Cross*, p. 273.

[47] Greenway and Watkiss, *The Book of the Foundation of Walden Monastery*, bk ii, cap. 6, p. 59. For Latin, see p. 58, "Celebrato itaque dulcissime iocunditatis et familiaritatis colloquio, ducitur ad hospitium ubi sibi et suis est administrate splendide refectionis abundantia. Abiens inde consanguineous et familiares prosperitati eius congaudentes uisitauit".

[48] T.O. Clancy (ed.), *The Triumph Tree: Scotland's Earliest Poetry, AD 500–1350* (Edinburgh, 1998), p. 270.

[49] Silber, 'Gift-Giving in the Great Traditions', p. 214.

crusaders' souls. Despite dying in holy war as penitents – an event that supposedly cleansed them of sin, or temporal punishment – relatives at home were never wholly certain that their crusading loved ones fell as martyrs or died shriven. There was always some doubt about the spiritual value of crusade. That being said, many of the grants made to religious houses had dual purposes. They also helped preserve family memory, celebrate ancestors' deeds and affirm relations with the religious house.[50] Laywomen who participated in this, memorialised their crusading kin's efforts and emphasised their personal links to those who fell in the Holy Land.

Some women were selected directly to carry out these acts of remembrance. Agnes de la Mara, for example, was asked to organise her father's commemorations. On his return from the Third Crusade, Agnes's father, Robert de la Mara, fell fatally ill in Benevento in Italy and drew up some bequests.[51] He desired a "memorial for the benefit of my soul and those of my ancestors", stating that he would leave the village of Uffington (Shropshire), its people (*hominum*) and appurtenances to the Church.[52] However, Robert left the specifics, and indeed the deserving religious house, up to his heir, Agnes. She honoured the promise and decided to make the gift to Haughmond Abbey. Agnes specified that the gift was for the benefit of the souls of her father, mother, their ancestors and heirs, which included Agnes herself; she further stipulated that the monks should also pray for her own deceased husband's soul.[53] Agnes was intent that she and her whole family were considered in the remembrances for her father and the crusading context of his death. Agnes maintained a good relationship with Haughmond Abbey long after. In 1195, she made further quitclaims and a confirmation of her original gift, along with her new husband Ralph de Ardene.[54]

In a comparable example, a crusader asked a woman to make commemorations for him in the event he died. In the last decade of the twelfth century, one Ailiva received two bovates of land from Thomas of Cuckney (Nottinghamshire) as he was preparing to go to the Holy Land. The charter describes Thomas as the father of Ailiva's daughter, but the two do not appear to have been married. Alivia promised that if Thomas never returned, she would pay an increased rent to the

---

[50] These are actions that have been particularly associated with crusaders, see: Bull, *Knightly Piety*, p. 286; Paul, *To Follow in Their Footsteps*, pp. 69–74.

[51] Both this charter, and that of Robert's daughter, Agnes (which are described below), were transcribed in one document for Hubert Walter, archbishop of Canterbury. For Robert's description of the context of his gift, see: C.R. Cheney and E. John (eds), *English Episcopal Acta III, Canterbury 1193–1205* (Oxford, 1986), pp. 139–41, no. 488, at 140. See also: Rees, *The Cartulary of Haughmond Abbey*, p. 224, no. 1228.

[52] Cheney and John, *English Episcopal Acta III*, pp. 139–41, no. 488, at 140, "haberem memoriam pro remedio anime mee et antecessorum meorum".

[53] Cheney and John, *English Episcopal Acta III*, pp. 139–41, no. 488, at 140.

[54] Rees, *The Cartulary of Haughmond Abbey*, pp. 224–5, no. 1232.

Hospitallers for the benefit of Thomas's soul.[55] The choice of religious house, a Military Order, further stressed the crusading nature of this commemoration.

Another striking example, involving commemoration and the Military Orders, may be seen in the Quincy family. Saher IV de Quincy, an Anglo-Scottish nobleman and earl of Winchester, took the cross in advance of the Fifth Crusade around 1217.[56] Saher's three sons, Roger and two others both named Robert, followed suit. However, the eldest son Robert died before the group could set out on the journey. Crucially, he was still a *crucesignatus* when he died. Robert's wife, Hawisa of Chester, had him buried in the choir of the Hospitallers' house of Clerkenwell in London. She then gave the brothers a rent of 5*m* per year, a commemoration that, significantly, was recognised and added to by King Henry III.[57] It would appear, then, that Hawisa was very successful in displaying her and her family's connections to crusade.

Not all commemorations were prearranged, nor were they necessarily made hastily after hearing of the demise of a crusader abroad. Individuals would have carefully selected the appropriate religious house and, perhaps more importantly, which assets they wanted to use to pay for spiritual intercession. The timing was equally crucial. Some commemorations were deliberately set up during later periods of crusading fervour. In these instances, it appears that the people involved had either waited for an appropriate moment to honour their family and past crusades, and/or perceived a chance amid the prevailing political climate to bolster their dynasty's reputation. Matilda de Percy may have done this when, in March 1189, she leapt to the rescue of Sallay Abbey (Lancashire). This monastery had been in financial straits for forty years; theirs was not a new crisis. But at this time, Matilda gifted them Tadcaster's Church, Haselwood chapel, Newton Church's annual pension and a carucate of land in Catton. This series of properties would bring revenue and help steer Sallay to solvency.[58] Matilda made this grant on the eve of the Third Crusade and did so, in part, for the salvation of her husband William de Beaumont earl of Warwick. He had died five years earlier, while *en route* to the Holy Land.[59] The context of Matilda's donation may well have helped to amplify her family's crusading pedigree. Moreover, Matilda's sister, Agnes de

---

[55] W.H. Turner (ed.), *Calendar of Charters and Rolls Preserved in the Bodleian Library* (Oxford, 1878), pp. 274–5.

[56] Lloyd, *English Society and the Crusade*, p. 107.

[57] Wilkinson, *Women in Thirteenth-Century Lincolnshire*, p. 42.

[58] J. McNulty (ed.), *The Chartulary of the Cistercian Abbey of St. Mary of Sallay in Craven*, 2 vols (Wakefield, 1933–4), at vol. 2, pp. 128–9, no. 615.

[59] McNulty, *The Chartulary of the Cistercian Abbey of St. Mary of Sallay in Craven*, vol. 2, p. 129, no. 615.

Percy, immediately confirmed the grant. She, likewise, asked the monks to pray for her recently deceased husband, Jocelin de Louvain, another past crusader.[60]

The timing of Margaret de Lacy's foundation of the Hospitaller nunnery at Aconbury in 1216 had a similar context: it coincided with preparations for the Fifth Crusade.[61] She made her foundation for the benefit of all her ancestors, one of whom, as discussed, was a crusade supporter and numerous others were crusaders. However, her foundation charter has not survived, and so little can be said about the specifics of her family tribute.[62] In a comparable case, in 1227 – while many were readying for the Sixth Crusade – Loretta de Braose countess of Leicester (d.1266) gave large tracts of land to the Hospitaller sisters at Buckland Priory. Again, her charter asked for prayers for her husband's soul: Robert Beaumont (d.1204), a veteran of the Third Crusade.[63]

Following a person's death, the medieval elite typically confirmed the grants that the deceased had made with associates, institutions and religious houses. These confirmations acted as assurances that the deceased's family or heirs would not dispute previous transactions. Confirmations were a legal security for the beneficiaries of previous grants, for which they often paid a fee. When it came to ratifying these documents, however, this was an occasion for ritual and community bonding. It was a means for the parties to reaffirm their connections, show good faith and display a shared link with the dead.[64] These rituals could involve reciprocal counter-gifts for the donor, marking them out in the commemorations, much like the counter-gifts offered to some women who enabled crusaders.

In one interesting thirteenth-century example, Alice Querderay began confirming her husband, John's, grants to Fountains Abbey (Yorkshire) after hearing that he had died while travelling to Jerusalem. Alice even offered up her dower lands to the monks at this time, including a series of tofts, crofts, meadows and everything else belonging to the tenements.[65] Cistercian houses, like Fountains, were eager to commemorate deceased crusaders in their intercessions for the Holy Land, and so Alice's offer may have been an appealing opportunity to include John in their

---

[60] McNulty, *The Chartulary of the Cistercian Abbey of St. Mary of Sallay in Craven*, vol. 2, p. 131, no. 619.
[61] Nicholson, 'Margaret de Lacy and the Hospital of St John at Aconbury', pp. 635.
[62] Nicholson, 'Margaret de Lacy and the Hospital of St John at Aconbury', pp. 633–4.
[63] H.C. Maxwell Lyte (ed.), *Calendar of the Charter Rolls Preserved in the Public Record Office, Vol. 1: Henry III A.D. 1226–1257* (London, 1903), pp. 52–3.
[64] D. Carraz, 'Mémoire lignagère et archives monastiques: les Bourbouton et la commanderie de Richerenches', in M. Aurell (ed.), *Convaincre et persuader: communication et propaganda aux XIIe et XIIIe siècles* (Poiters, 2007), pp. 465–502; E. Cavell, 'The Burial of Noblewomen in Thirteenth-Century Shropshire', in Weiler, Burton, Schofield and Stöber, *Thirteenth Century England XI*, pp. 174–92, at 183.
[65] Lancaster, *Abstracts of the Charters and other Documents Contained in the Chartulary of the Cistercian Abbey of Fountains*, vol. 2, p. 777, nos. 35–6. For John Querderay's recorded donations to the abbey, see: vol. 2, pp. 775–6, nos. 23–32.

remembrances.[66] The monks, in turn, gave Alice some property that John had given to Fountain's for safekeeping until his heirs – the couple's children, Matilda and Juliana – reached their majority. Sometime later, when Matilda and Juliana both came of age, they confirmed all their ancestors' grants, with particular note of those their father, John, and their grandfather, Richer, had made to the abbey.[67] In recognition of their charity, the monks granted the security of a messuage and three acres in *Neusom* (possibly Newsham, Richmond), which Matilda and Juliana promptly gave to their mother. Alice's financial security may have been a point of concern in these confirmations. Nevertheless, these three women's confirmations of John's gifts helped in the commemoration of his death, cemented a family relationship with the monks of Fountains and ensured recognition of their association with this crusader through counter-gifts.

The act of confirmation may also have included a recital of the deceased's notable deeds. In the case of noblemen, this would have included discussion of chivalric and pious actions, and participation in holy war was certainly perceived to have fallen into these categories.[68] This sort of ritual probably formed an aspect of all these women's confirmations or commemorations of crusading kinsmen, allowing them to display and talk about their connections to holy war.

This is likely to have happened to a noble Sussex family during the twelfth century. Sometime between 1191 and 1192, Robert of Icklesham was with the armies of the Third Crusade at Jaffa. He felt he was "in danger of dying", and drew up a grant to Battle Abbey (Sussex), giving them an annual rent worth 0.5*m*.[69] Robert no doubt picked this monastery at this moment to ease his conscience; sometime before 1175, he had, quite literally, come to blows with Abbot Walter de Luci's men over a land dispute.[70] This was a powerful moment for Robert and his family to make peace with the monks. When the grant found its way back to England, Robert's wife Sybil of Dene made sure to confirm it, and she did so with the consent of their adult son Ralph.[71] Given the dramatic context of Robert's death, and the news arriving home along with his final wishes, it is

---

66 Maier, 'Crisis, Liturgy and Crusade', p. 633. B.M. Bolton, 'The Cistercians and the Aftermath of the Second Crusade', in Gervers, *The Second Crusade and the Cistercians*, pp. 131–40. Hurlock has noted the crusading imagery in the tiles of the Welsh Cistercian abbeys of Neath and Tintern, see: Hurlock, 'Welsh Pilgrims and Crusaders in the Middle Ages', p. 164.
67 Lancaster, *Abstracts of the Charters and other Documents Contained in the Chartulary of the Cistercian Abbey of Fountains*, vol. 2, pp. 776–7, no. 34.
68 Paul, *To Follow in Their Footsteps*, p. 29.
69 Sayers, 'English Charters from the Third Crusade', p. 213.
70 E. Searle (ed. and trans.), *The Chronicle of Battle Abbey* (Oxford, 1980), pp. 218–21. For more on the settling of scores within crusading contexts, see: Reynolds, 'Asking for Forgiveness as an Aspect of Crusade', pp. 135–46.
71 London, Lincoln's Inn, Hale MS 87, f.69v–r. My sincere thanks to Dunstan Speight for providing me with images of the manuscript. This gift built upon one of Robert's

hard to believe that the ritual of Sybil's confirmation could possibly have glossed over the context of crusade in the changing relationship between this family and this abbey. Robert and Sybil's descendants may have continued this relationship based on memorialisation. Decades later, in 1247, their granddaughter, Sybil of Icklesham – also a supporter of her husband's crusade – acknowledged Battle Abbey's rights to the advowson of the Church at Icklesham and a messuage in the same area, as well as sixty acres of land.[72] She did all this so that the monks would receive Sybil, along with her ancestors and heirs, into the house's prayers; surely they remembered Robert, too.[73]

But how would this ritual recitation of crusading deeds (or simply acknowledgement of them) have played out during the signing of confirmations? An early Norman example may offer some insight here. In 1105, Lancelin, son of Osmond, entered the chapter house of Troarn in Normandy and gave thanks for his safe return from crusade in front of a gathering of the local lay and ecclesiastic communities. He wished to celebrate his safe return, while also memorialising his brothers who had died on the crusade. To do this, he offered the monks the tithe of the monastery of Airam as well as three acres of land. However, the land was not his to give. The cartulary of Troarn describes the scene:

> [Lancelin] brought forward his wife Agnes of whose inheritance it was, and earnestly besought her to grant it of her own accord. And she raising her voice, said, in the hearing of all: "I gladly grant [it] to God and St Martin, and will cause it to be confirmed by my sons".[74]

This scene is reminiscent of the staged events in which nobles publicly took the cross, encouraging others to follow suit.[75] Agnes and Lancelin almost certainly prearranged this gift-giving ceremony, to demonstrate Agnes's links to these crusaders and celebrate their family enterprise before their local communities. It is especially interesting that Agnes used the occasion to affirm that she would have her sons confirm the grant. This clearly signals her focus on cementing a lasting crusading legacy. The whole scene neatly summarises how women who

---

concessions to Battle made 1175 x 1189, see: T. Thorpe (ed.), *Muniments of Battle Abbey* (London, 1835), p. 40.

[72] L.F. Salzmann (ed.), *An Abstract of Feet of Fines of the County of Sussex*, 2 vols (Lewes, 1903–8), vol. 1, no. 433.

[73] Sybil also asked the monks of Battle Abbey to accept her body for burial and did so by confirming a grant she and her husband had made to the monks just before Nicholas set out on crusade. Conspicuously, she omitted any mention of Nicholas in the later agreement: San Marino, Huntington Library, MSS. BA v.41/1236 and BA v.41/1111.

[74] Round, *Calendar of Documents Preserved in France*, p. 169, no. 476.

[75] Tyerman, *England and the Crusades*, pp. 66–7. For a much later example, see: J. Paviot, 'Burgundy and the Crusade', in N. Housley (ed.), *Crusading in the Fifteenth Century* (Basingstoke, 2004), pp. 70–80, at 73–4.

remained in the West could position themselves in family remembrances of holy war. Fortunately, this particular spectacle was committed to writing, as there are very few descriptions of the procedure by which people made these donations.

Patronising Literature

Noblewomen were keen patrons of literature and poetry during the Middle Ages. They commissioned works that explored the mood of their age, as well as their own personal worldviews.[76] Crusade formed the context behind many women's benefaction of literature and poetry, and also featured as a backdrop or focus in the works they commissioned. This, too, could act as a medium to champion family crusading history. Perhaps the most notable noblewoman who engaged in this was Marie of France countess of Champagne (d.1198). She famously patronised Chrétien de Troyes's romances and literature – which used many crusading themes – when her husband left for the Holy Land in 1169.[77] Later, in the fourteenth and fifteenth centuries, after the last Latin Christian outposts in the Near East had fallen, tales of crusade were frequently interwoven in family traditions. These aristocratic stories celebrated the distant past and figures who had become semi-legendary, while repurposing older narratives for the political atmosphere of their era.[78] Patronising literature, and steering the subject matter, became a useful means of augmenting dynastic identity.

There is evidence of noblewomen influencing the literature produced within monastic circles, for instance, ensuring that their crusading family was remembered for posterity as well as for prayer. William II Longespée – a veteran of the Barons' Crusade, who died during the Seventh Crusade – appears prominently in narrative texts produced at Barlings Abbey and Lacock Abbey. It has been suggested that his female family members lay behind this literary flattery.[79] William's wife, Idonea de Camville, had strong family connections to Barlings, and she outlived William by about two years. Likewise, William's mother, Ela of Salisbury (d.1261), was abbess of Lacock from 1239. The so-called Book of Lacock, the house's chronicle, is now in a fragmentary state, and what remains dates from the early fourteenth century. Nevertheless, the text placed Ela and her son in the centre of its retelling

---

[76] J. Ward, *Women in Medieval Europe, 1200–1500*, 2nd edn (London and New York, 2016), pp. 154–74.

[77] J.H. McCash, 'The Cultural Patronage of Medieval Women: an Overview', in J.H. McCash (ed.), *The Cultural Patronage of Medieval Women* (Athens, 1996), pp. 1–49, at 18–9.

[78] See: Hodgson, *Women, Crusading and the Holy Land in Historical Narrative*, p. 10.

[79] S. Lloyd and T. Hunt, 'William Longespee II: The Making of an English Crusading Hero, Part II', *Nottingham Medieval Studies*, vol. 36 (1992), pp. 79–125, at 86–7. See also: Nicholson, 'Women's Writing and Cultural Patronage', p. 78.

of the house's early years; its narrative was likely built upon earlier writings.[80] It was not unusual for monastic writers to use crusade as a moralising tool, or to link their house with crusade to claim some prestige on the international stage. Barlings and Lacock would, therefore, have been quite receptive to the notion of celebrating William II Longespée, a man whose death was heralded as martyrdom by English contemporaries without hesitation.[81]

Outside of the monastery's book collection, noble patrons, too, amassed literature that they enjoyed, read to their households and hoped would arouse later generations' concern for crusade. The personal interests of women, as readers and patrons, can tell us something of their perception of crusade, and how they felt their descendants should contemplate it. In England, an abundance of thirteenth-century illuminated manuscripts of the Apocalypse have survived. Many of these texts appear to have been owned or commissioned by noblewomen who either were crusaders, or had strong connections to crusading circles.[82] There are clear links between these two interests. The rhetoric, preaching and dialogue that surrounded crusading often played upon contemporary concerns that the End of Days was approaching, as well as the consequent need for individuals to strive for salvation. Apocalyptic literature might have served as a frame for ruminating upon Christendom's spiritual struggle within holy war.

There were several notable occasions when the crusade and the Apocalypse were closely conflated. In the early twelfth century, Bohemond of Taranto (d.1111) – one of the leaders of the First Crusade – attempted to gain fresh recruits for his campaigns in the East by undertaking a preaching tour. In his addresses, he harkened to the Old Testament Book of Daniel and Nebuchadnezzar II's prophetic dream of a huge statue that crumbled before him. In the biblical story, the statue symbolised the empires of the earth that would succeed each other until the End of Days. Bohemond, and many after him, interpreted the First Crusade's conquests as a series of victories over 'empires', fulfilling the prophecy and thus presaging the end of the world: the crusaders were acting in the interests of a Christian apocalypse.[83] By the time of the Third Crusade, individuals were being directly linked to apocalyptic prophecy. A Calabrian abbot named Joachim of Fiore encouraged Richard the Lionheart to battle

---

[80] London, British Library, Cotton MS Vitellius A VIII. William and Ela were mentioned on: ff. 128v–130v.

[81] K.A. Smith, 'Monastic Memories of the Early Crusading Movement', in Cassidy-Welch, *Remembering the Crusades and Crusading*, pp. 131–44; Lloyd and Hunt, 'William Longespee II: Part II', pp. 79–125.

[82] L.J. Whatley, 'Crusading for (Heavenly) Jerusalem: A Noble Woman, Devotion, and the Trinity Apocalypse (Cambridge Trinity College, MS R.16.2)', in E.A. Foster, J. Perratore and S. Rozenski (eds), *Devotional Interaction in Medieval England and its Afterlives* (Leiden, 2018), pp. 49–79.

[83] J. Rubenstein, *Nebuchadnezzar's Dream: The Crusades, Apocalyptic Prophecy, and the End of History* (Oxford, 2019).

Figure 9. The Seven-Headed Dragon of the Apocalypse battles with 'the Elect', including two women, in the *Trinity Apocalypse*. (Cambridge Trinity College, MS R.16.2, f.14r. By permission of the Master and Fellows of Trinity College, Cambridge).

Saladin, telling him that Saladin was, in fact, one of the 'heads' of the Seven-Headed Beast of the Apocalypse from the Book of Revelations.[84] Supposedly, once Saladin was defeated, only the Antichrist would be left for the Christians to overcome. The fact that the crusaders did not defeat Saladin may have caused no little consternation. Apocalypse and crusade reared one of its heads again during the Fifth Crusade. The leaders of this expedition were utterly galvanised after being shown an enigmatic Arabic book that prophesied their imminent conquest of Egypt. Furthermore, the text presaged the arrival of the Holy Roman Emperor, and (as the crusaders understood

---

[84] Phillips, *The Life and Legend of the Sultan Saladin*, pp. 316–7.

Commemoration and Creating Identity

it) Prester John – a mysterious Christian ruler of an empire somewhere beyond the known fringes of the world – all before the coming of the Antichrist.[85]

One surviving thirteenth-century English manuscript, known as the Trinity Apocalypse, focuses heavily on these entwined themes of holy war and the Day of Judgement. This manuscript was probably owned by a noble or royal female patron, in part, because an image of a noblewoman appears repeatedly in the manuscript, interacting in the illuminations and guiding the reader, as a "visual signpost".[86] It includes highly evocative depictions of scenes from the Book of Revelations, showing women battling the Seven-Headed Dragon and Beast of the Apocalypse (Figure 9).[87] The amount of money and time invested in producing artistry and scribal work of its quality could be staggering. This object, and others like it, were designed to last, to be cherished and to be passed down to friends or family. In doing so, they promulgated the ideals of Christendom's spiritual struggle within the crusading ethos and, as their original owners hoped, potentially instilled that vision in subsequent generations.[88]

Shared Spaces of Burial

Enduring and tangible forms of commemoration, honouring both crusaders and financiers, were erected across the English landscape, remaining visible for centuries. Shared spaces of memorial, notably family chapels, served as a touchstone for generations.[89] Within these spaces, crusaders' tombs, and the effigies that adorned them, were cherished and remodelled by their descendants. The tomb of the First Crusader Robert Curthose (d.1134), in Gloucester Cathedral, was reconstructed long after his death, sometime in the thirteenth century.[90] The Champagne knight Jean de Joinville similarly took pride in rebuilding his great-grandfather's tomb, adding epitaphs that celebrated his family's crusading record.[91] When the Scottish nobleman James "the Good" Douglas was killed on crusade in

---

[85] B. Hamilton, 'The Impact of Prester John on the Fifth Crusade', in E.J. Mylod, G. Perry, T. Smith and J. Vanderburie (eds), *The Fifth Crusade in Context* (London, 2016), pp. 53–67.

[86] Whatley, 'Crusading for (Heavenly) Jerusalem', p. 51.

[87] Whatley, 'Crusading for (Heavenly) Jerusalem', pp. 60–4.

[88] It is worth noting that another member of the crusade-enthusiastic Quincy family commissioned a similar manuscript: the Lambeth Apocalypse. Eleanor de Quincy – wife of the Fifth Crusader Roger de Quincy – had this object made around 1265, see: Whatley, 'Crusading for (Heavenly) Jerusalem', p. 57.

[89] M. Cassidy-Welch, *Monastic Spaces and Their Meanings: Thirteenth-Century English Cistercian Monasteries* (Turnhout, 2001), pp. 237–41; M. Boulton, 'Introduction: Place and Space', in M. Boulton, J. Hawkes and H. Stoner (eds), *Place and Space in the Medieval World* (London, 2018), pp. xv–xxv, at xix; C. Daniell, *Death and Burial in Medieval England 1066–1550* (London, 1997), pp. 92–3. See also: Evans, 'The Ferrers Earls of Derby and the Crusades', p. 69; Paul and Schenk, 'Family Memory and the Crusades', pp. 178–9.

[90] Aird, *Robert Curthose*, p. 282.

[91] Paul, *To Follow in Their Footsteps*, pp. 148–9.

Spain in 1330, his followers brought his body back home. An elaborate tomb was then constructed in St Bride's Kirk in Douglas (South Lanarkshire). This building became a mausoleum for James's descendants, playing a pivotal role in shaping the wider family identity.[92] Locating the dead, whether that meant knowing where they lay or repatriating a body to a family chapel, reinforced both noble families' and religious houses' sense of self.[93]

Women who patronised crusade appear to have taken especial pride in being buried alongside martial crusaders, perhaps even those they had supported. The positioning and timing of nobles' burials were often noted within religious houses' cartularies and accompanying chronicles. These texts often discussed the lives of their lay patrons in detail, both for posterity and to promote the virtues of their lineage. The gender, class, societal, dynastic or emotional associations that surrounded an individual's burial place and tomb signified aspects of their identity that they – or those who buried them – considered paramount.[94] Exactly which of those factors took precedence in any one burial is always open to interpretation. But, by situating their burials next to martial crusaders, elite women could exhibit their family links to the movement.

The importance of aligning the burials of certain elite women next to crusaders is evident amongst the Peverel family. A branch of this family patronised Barnwell Priory (Cambridgeshire). As such, some select members were allowed to be buried in Barnwell's chapel. However, each of the people chosen to be interred in this chapel had some connection to crusade. The first of the dynasty, Pagan Peverel, re-founded the priory and gave relics to the monks that he had acquired on the First Crusade. He was later buried at the high altar of their chapel around 1132.[95] Pagan's son William then became the monks' benefactor. He later died and was buried in the Holy Land during the Second Crusade. According to the Barnwell Priory's *Liber Memorandorum*, William had "followed his father's footsteps".[96] The family patrimony then passed to Alice Peverel, the wife of Hamo I Peche. Alice and Hamo I's son, Gilbert I Peche (d.1212), went on the Third Crusade and mortgaged vast amounts of property to do so. When he died, he was not initially buried in Barnwell.[97] Gilbert I's son, Hamo II Peche, then joined the

---

[92] M. Markus, 'St Bride's, Douglas – A Family Mausoleum', *Proc Soc Antiq Scot*, vol. 134 (2004), pp. 403–21, at 404–5.

[93] Paul, *To Follow in Their Footsteps*, pp. 74–7, 118 and 139.

[94] J. Barker, *Stone Fidelity: Marriage and Emotion in Medieval Tomb Sculpture* (Woodbridge, 2020), p. 86; J. Burton, *Monastic and Religious Orders in Britain, 1000–1300* (Cambridge, 1994) p. 218.

[95] J.W. Clark (ed.), *Liber Memorandorum Ecclesie de Bernewelle* (Cambridge, 1907), p. 46. See also: Paul, *To Follow in Their Footsteps*, p. 121; S. Edgington, 'Pagan Peverel: An Anglo-Norman Crusader', in Edbury, *Crusade and Settlement*, pp. 90–3; Tyerman, *England and the Crusades*, p. 25.

[96] Clark, *Liber Memorandorum Ecclesie de Bernewelle*, p. 47, "sequens uestigia patris".

[97] Tyerman, *England and the Crusades*, p. 216.

Commemoration and Creating Identity

Barons' Crusade and died in the Holy Land in 1241; his body was brought back to be buried within Barnwell's chapel.[98] Perhaps the arrival of Hamo II's body prompted the family to develop their burial tradition, as Hamo II's son, Gilbert II Peche, then had his great-grandmother Alice and grandfather Gilbert I's remains exhumed (from an unknown location) and re-entombed together alongside Pagan Peverel's burial in the chapel.[99] It seems that the common denominator between all the laymen buried in the chapel was their participation in crusade.[100] Alice's re-burial in the chapel is, therefore, highly conspicuous.

According to the *Liber Memorandorum*, one other woman was buried in the chapel around this time: Hamo II's wife Eva (d.1286). The Barnwell writer cryptically described Eva only as having been born *trans marinus* "overseas", possibly a translation of *Outremer*, a common name for the Holy Land during the thirteenth century.[101] However, little more is known about Eva's life or origins.

In the fourteenth century, an anonymous scribe compiled a text on the foundation of Newburgh Abbey (Yorkshire) which, likewise, highlights the contemporary fondness for crusade memorials.[102] The text closely detailed the career of the prolific twelfth-century crusader, Roger de Mowbray, who was also the founder of this abbey. Roger was something of an anomaly; a crusade obsessive, who joined the Second Crusade, the Count of Flanders's expedition of 1177, and he went to the Holy Land again in the 1180s where he was fatally wounded at the Battle of Hattin in 1188.[103] His body was never returned to England, rather he was buried in the Holy Land.[104] However, the Newburgh writer fancifully reminisced that

---

[98] Clark, *Liber Memorandorum Ecclesie de Bernewelle*, p. 48.

[99] It was not uncommon in the Middle Ages for significant amounts of time to elapse between the death of an individual and the erection of their funerary monument, see: D. Park, 'Medieval Burials and Monuments', in Griffith-Jones and Park, *The Temple Church in London*, pp. 67–91, at 80.

[100] William Peche was another patron buried in the chapel during the thirteenth century. The writer of the *Liber Memorandorum* only said that William was an esteemed warrior and that he died young, but his participation in crusade is not mentioned. This William may, however, be the man who identified himself as William Peverel, who left the manor of Sandford (Oxfordshire) to the Templars, when he lay dying during the Baron's Crusade. See: Clark, *Liber Memorandorum Ecclesie de Bernewelle*, p. 48; A.M. Leys (ed.), *The Sandford Cartulary*, 2 vols (Oxford, 1938–41), at vol. 1, pp. 6–7, no. 4; Dryburgh, Hartland, Ciula and Vieira, *Calendar of Fine Rolls, Henry III, 1234–1242*, p. 491, no. 53. Cf: Lloyd, *English Society and the Crusade*, p. 161.

[101] Clark, *Liber Memorandorum Ecclesie de Bernewelle*, p. 48.

[102] Dugdale, *Monasticon Anglicanum*, vol. 6, part I, pp. 320–1, no. 6. See also: Paul, *To Follow in Their Footsteps*, pp. 86 and 156.

[103] Greenway, *Charters of the Honour of Mowbray*, p. 185, no. 276 and p. 248, no. 388; Tyerman, *England and the Crusades*, p. 31.

[104] R. Gilyard-Beer, 'Byland Abbey and the Grave of Roger de Mowbray', *The Yorkshire Archaeological Journal*, vol. 55 (1983), pp. 61–6.

Laywomen and the Crusade in England, 1150–1300

Roger survived his final sojourn and returned home to later be buried in Byland Abbey beside his since-deceased mother, Gundreda de Gournay. The writer was very precise: "he is buried in Byland in a certain niche in the wall of the chapter house, just south of his mother Gundreda".[105]

As we have seen, Gundreda was an avid supporter of her son's crusading. The Newburgh writer may have been reworking understandings of this mother-and-son effort in crusade. Alternatively, he may have been addressing a desire amongst the descendants of the Mowbrays to commemorate their crusading forebears together. The family did not have the opportunity to create a chapel centred on crusade, like the descendants of Pagan Peverel. The Newburgh writer himself lamented that Roger de Mowbray's son, Nigel de Mowbray, had died during the Third Crusade and that his body had unbecomingly been buried at sea.[106]

The Percy family's burial practices also show crusade-related patterns. We saw how Agnes de Percy had helped her husband, Jocelin de Louvain, to go on crusade in the 1170s, and that she may have drawn inspiration from her crusading ancestor, William I de Percy. The latter's body was buried in sight of Jerusalem, but later generations believed that his heart had been brought back for burial at Whitby Abbey (Yorkshire).[107] This is not necessarily a fanciful claim. Numerous other crusaders, including William d'Aubigny (d.1221) and Saher IV de Quincy (d.1219), had their heart or body repatriated for burial.[108] It is interesting, then, that both Jocelin de Louvain (d.1189) and Agnes de Percy (d.1205) were interred in Whitby Abbey's church.[109] Their burial at Whitby diverged from wider family traditions; Agnes's father, son and grandson were all buried at Sawley Abbey and other family members were buried at Fountains Abbey (both Yorkshire).[110] It is plausible that Agnes and Jocelin wanted their respective support and participation in holy war to be commemorated in a shared space with a famous crusading forebear.

---

[105] Dugdale, *Monasticon Anglicanum*, vol. 6, part I, p. 320, no. 6, "et sepultus in Ballalanda in quadam fornace in muro capituli ex parte australi juxta matrem suam Gundredam". See also: Gilyard-Beer, 'Byland Abbey and the Grave of Roger de Mowbray', p. 62.

[106] Dugdale, *Monasticon Anglicanum*, vol. 6, part I, p. 320, For contemporaries' fear of loved ones being lost abroad or at sea, see: Paul, *To Follow in Their Footsteps*, pp. 156–65.

[107] Atkinson, *Cartularium Abbathiae de Whiteby*, vol. 1, p. 2, n. 1.

[108] For William d'Aubigny's heart burial at Wymondham, see: D. Preest and J.G. Clark (eds and trans.), *The Deeds of the Abbots of St Albans: Gesta Abbatum Monasterii Sancti Albani* (Woodbridge, 2019), p. 396; *Chronica Majora*, vol. 3, p. 67. For Saher de Quincy's burial, see: R.D. Oram, 'Quincy, Saer de, earl of Winchester', in *Oxford Dictionary of National Biography*, https://doi.org/10.1093/ref:odnb/22967, Published Online 22 Sept 2005 (accessed 28 Jan 2024).

[109] For her epitaph see: Atkinson, *Cartularium Abbathiae de Whiteby*, vol. 2, p. 689.

[110] M. Holford, 'Family, Lineage and Society: Medieval Pedigrees of the Percy Family', *Nottingham Medieval Studies*, vol. 52 (2008), pp. 165–90, at 170–1.

Commemoration and Creating Identity

The specific religious orders with which crusading families aligned themselves, or used for their burials, were chosen to project an identity rooted in crusade's chivalric ethos. Historians have recognised that Cistercian houses had an avid interest in holding remembrances for deceased crusaders.[111] Matilda de Percy and her husband, William de Beaumont earl of Warwick, associated themselves closely with the Cistercian house of Fountains Abbey. When William died on crusade in 1184, his body was repatriated and buried in the Abbey's galilee porch and, when Matilda died in 1203, she was interred alongside him.[112] Cistercians did not typically accept laywomen for burial until a decade after Matilda's death and, even then, few were granted the privilege.[113] As a patron of the house (and probably of crusade), Matilda may have more easily persuaded the monks to accommodate her burial. In a similar case, Saher IV de Quincy, who died on the Fifth Crusade, asked for his ashes to be brought home and interred at the Cistercian house of Garendon Abbey.[114] Like Matilda de Percy, Saher's wife Margaret de Beaumont (d.1235) made gifts to Garendon in her widowhood and was buried next to her husband's ashes.[115]

Eva and Robert Tibetot's burial at Greyfriars Church, Ipswich (Suffolk), a house that they founded, is another comparable example.[116] Eva very probably sponsored a crusade-proxy and her husband was a participant in the Lord Edward's Crusade. Their patronage and burial in a Franciscan house, an order that produced a huge number of professional preachers of the cross in England, is unlikely to have been coincidental. Those who chose to be buried with such mendicant orders would have considered their choice carefully, as this was known to occasionally conflict with the desires of local secular clergy who often wished for laypeople to be interred in their churches.[117] Eva and Robert Tibetot's choice of burial place may well have been a deliberate display of their crusading past.

It must be said that there was nothing wholly unusual about medieval spouses wishing to be buried next to each other. It was, nevertheless, a conscious choice and not necessarily the most common one. Only half of the thirteenth-century Shropshire noblewomen studied by Emma Cavell were buried with their marital

---

[111] Maier, 'Crisis, Liturgy and Crusade', p. 633.
[112] Cassidy-Welch, *Monastic Spaces and Their Meanings*, p. 233. For Matilda's gift of Gisburn Forest, "cum corpore", to Fountains Abbey in the 1190s, see: McNulty, *The Chartulary of the Cistercian Abbey of St. Mary of Sallay in Craven*, vol. 1, p. 16, no. 26.
[113] Cassidy-Welch, *Monastic Spaces and Their Meanings*, p. 232.
[114] Oram, 'Quincy, Saer de, earl of Winchester'; Luard, *Annales Monastici*, vol. 2, p. 292.
[115] Dugdale, *Monasticon Anglicanum*, vol. 5, p. 331, no. 2 and n. A.
[116] B.P. Grimsey, 'The Grey-Friars Monastery, Ipswich', *Proceedings of the Suffolk Institute of Archaeology*, vol. 9, no. 3 (1897), pp. 373–8, at 377.
[117] Burton, *Monastic and Religious Orders in Britain*, pp. 120–1.

Laywomen and the Crusade in England, 1150–1300

family.[118] Yet, that did not diminish the important symbolism implied by people's funerary arrangements. Choosing to be buried with particular religious orders and at specific houses, next to specific people, could all help emphasise shared ideals, identity and links, and crusading culture could surely feature in that connectivity.

The military religious orders were perhaps the most overtly linked with crusading, and so laypeople who were buried within Templar or Hospitaller houses were also likely to have sought to display an affinity with those ventures.[119] The laywomen of the Quincy family are an interesting example: a group that, as discussed, clearly held their crusading character dear. We have already seen that Hawisa of Chester commemorated and buried her husband Robert de Quincy, a *crucesignatus*, in the Hospitallers' house of Clerkenwell in the early thirteenth century.[120] Hawisa and Robert's daughter, Margaret de Quincy countess of Lincoln (d.1266), showed her affinity with her natal family's crusading past by being buried next to her father in Clerkenwell, rather than either of her deceased husbands: John de Lacy (d.1240), himself a Fifth Crusader, or Walter Marshall (d.1245).[121] Other thirteenth-century noblewomen who had long widowhoods, like Margaret, tended towards burial with their natal family.[122] That said, Margaret, or those who chose her burial place, could hardly have overlooked the significance of interment in a Hospitaller priory.

In most cases, it is not possible to uncover whether laywomen's burials, along with their crusading associations, had been organised by the deceased before their death, or if these decisions were made by their surviving heirs and executors. As the classic archaeological mantra goes: the dead do not bury themselves. Regardless of who arranged their entombment, when laywomen were buried in spaces of commemoration alongside martial crusaders, or with mendicant or Military Orders, this likely served, in part, to affirm the feminine crusading ideals promoted by clerics. It was undoubtedly crucial for the Peche-Peverel family to see some select women buried within their family chapel, with all its crusading connotations. Yet, it is hard to discern what that precisely meant to them and their descendants. Personal celebrations of crusading ideology are much clearer in physical memorials to the movement.

---

[118] Cavell, 'The Burial of Noblewomen in Thirteenth-Century Shropshire', pp. 175–6. See also: A. Livingstone, *Out of Love for my Kin: Aristocratic Family Life in the Lands of the Loire, 1000–1200* (Ithaca, 2010), pp. 162–5.

[119] The tombs of William Marshal (d.1219) and his eldest son (d.1231) in New Temple London are prime English examples, see: H.J. Nicholson, *The Everyday Life of the Templars: The Knights Templar at Home* (Fonthill, 2017), pp. 114–6; P.J. Lankester, 'The Thirteenth-Century Military Effigies in the Temple Church', in Griffith-Jones and Park, *The Temple Church in London*, pp. 93–134, at 111–2.

[120] Wilkinson, *Women in Thirteenth-Century Lincolnshire*, p. 42.

[121] Dugdale, *Monasticon Anglicanum*, vol. 6, part I, p. 316. For John de Lacy's involvement in the Fifth Crusade, see: Lloyd, *English Society and the Crusade*, p. 82. See also: Wilkinson, *Women in Thirteenth-Century Lincolnshire*, p. 65.

[122] Cavell, 'The Burial of Noblewomen in Thirteenth-Century Shropshire', p. 176.

Monumental Celebrations

Laywomen's expressions of their crusading identity were displayed in the fabric and decoration of funerary monuments themselves. Some elite women's tombs would have included ornamentation or sculpture such as an effigy, which helped to identify the deceased, celebrate their position in society and act as a focus for prayers.[123] Very few, if any, medieval memorial sculptures in England have survived entirely unscathed to the modern day. They frequently have lost their epitaphs, if they ever existed, as well as the polychrome that adorned them. These details degraded over the centuries, were damaged through the iconoclasm of the Reformation and were removed by overenthusiastic Victorians' attempting restorations. It is often difficult, therefore, to confirm whom particular effigies represented.[124] More to the point, it means that any programmatic symbols, objects or artistic schema used on tombs to denote some connections to crusade, if they were ever used, have disappeared.[125]

Despite these hard truths regarding stone sculpture, we can be certain that women commissioned memorials that celebrated crusade through the artistry of the object. Countess Blanche of Navarre, for example, was exceptionally keen to legitimise her son's claim to the county of Champagne. To help in doing so, Blanche commissioned an effigy of her husband, Theobald III of Champagne (d.1201), which depicted him as a pilgrim with figures of crusader kin surrounding him.[126] The effect was to broadcast the pious and noble ancestors from whom Blanche's son descended. The need to cement the family's links to crusade was perhaps felt especially necessary, as Theobald had died before he could lead the Fourth Crusade. Another striking and provocative example can be seen in the mid-twelfth-century Belval Priory (Lorraine) sculpture. This statue was probably commissioned by Countess Aigeline of Burgundy, and it depicts her embracing her husband, Hugh of Vaudémont, as he returned from the Second Crusade.[127] Also, in Täby (Sweden), a surviving late eleventh-century rune stone bears an inscription stating that it was raised by a woman named Astrid, in memory of

---

[123] R.A. Dressler, *Of Armor and Men in Medieval England, The Chivalric Rhetoric of Three English Knights' Effigies* (Aldershot, 2004), p. 60; H.A. Tummers, *Early Secular Effigies in England* (Leiden, 1980), p. 151, n. 88.

[124] B. Gittos and M. Gittos (eds), *Interpreting Medieval Effigies: A Regional Study in Archaeology and Potential, the Evidence from Yorkshire to 1400* (Oxford, 2019), pp. 7–21.

[125] Paul, *To Follow in Their Footsteps*, pp. 145–6.

[126] J. Doherty, 'Count Hugh of Troyes and the Prestige of Jerusalem', *History*, vol. 102, no. 353 (2017), pp. 874–88, at 874–5.

[127] N. Kenaan-Kedar and B.Z. Kedar, 'The Significance of a Twelfth-Century Sculptural Group: Le Retour de Croisé', in M. Balard, B.Z. Kedar and J. Riley-Smith (eds), *Dei Gesta per Francos: Etudes sur les croisades dédiées à Jean Richard, Crusade Studies in Honour of Jean Richard* (Aldershot, 2001), pp. 29–44, at 44.

Laywomen and the Crusade in England, 1150–1300

her husband, Eysteinn, who died while on his way to Jerusalem.[128] The latter may predate the First Crusade, but it nevertheless represents a desire to commemorate Holy Land pilgrimage.

These sculptures celebrated and championed the crusaders that these women held dear – in Aigeline's case, quite literally – and by extension, displayed their personal links to those men and their mission. Contemporaries were typically quite anxious to assert the connections between those who went on crusade and those who endorsed it. This feeling pervaded medieval societies, but our abilities to distinguish exactly how women like Blanche, Aigeline or Astrid conceptualised their position within that culture is somewhat limited.

One of the few insights we have here is on the tomb of Queen Eleanor of Castile (d.1290), consort of Edward I of England. This lavish tomb sits within Westminster Abbey and is decorated with subtle, yet highly significant, crusading motifs. Eleanor had a strong affiliation with the holy wars of the thirteenth century; she had personally gone on crusade in 1270 with her husband Edward, and her uncle John of Brienne (d.1237) had been king of Jerusalem itself.[129] Edward I made a second vow to go on crusade in 1287, and it has been suggested that Eleanor did the same.[130] She did not live to redeem this oath, however. Her tomb decorations indicate that her mind was resolutely fixed on that sacred promise.

One panel on the north-facing base of her Westminster tomb is covered with a painted frieze, depicting a group of pilgrims approaching the tomb of the Holy Sepulchre (Figure 10). A knight stands ahead of the pilgrims, and he can be identified by his heraldry as Otto de Grandson (d.1328).[131] This knight is shown kneeling in prayer before the Virgin Mary and infant Christ, who stand ahead of Jesus's resting place.[132] The image has been interpreted as an allegorical depiction of Otto praying at Christ's tomb in Holy Sepulchre Church, Jerusalem, after having

---

[128] C. Krötzl, 'Pilgrimage', in J. Glauser, P. Hermann and S.A. Mitchell (eds), *Handbook of Pre-Modern Nordic Memory Studies: Interdisciplinary Approaches* (Berlin, 2018), pp. 594–600, at 595.

[129] B. Hamilton, 'Eleanor of Castile and the Crusading Movement', *Mediterranean Historical Review*, vol. 10, nos. 1–2 (1995), pp. 92–103.

[130] Tyerman, *England and the Crusades*, pp. 237–8. Edward was pressured by the papacy to take part in a renewed crusade as early as 1273, while he was returning from crusade, see: P.B. Baldwin, *Pope Gregory X and the Crusades* (Woodbridge, 2014), pp. 188–9.

[131] J.C. Parsons, *Eleanor of Castile: Queen and Society in Thirteenth-Century England* (New York, 1995), p. 58; N. Coldstream, 'The Tomb of Queen Eleanor in Westminster Abbey: An Evaluation of the Documentary Evidence', in H. Beck and K. Hengevoss-Dürkop (eds), *Studien zur Geschichte der europäischen Skulptur im 12./13. Jarhundert* (Frankfurt, 1994), pp. 101–8, at 102.

[132] E.W. Tristram and M. Bardswell, *English Medieval Wall Painting: The Thirteenth Century, Text* (Oxford, 1950), p. 152; E.W. Tristram and M. Bardswell, *English Medieval Wall Painting: The Thirteenth Century, Plates* (Oxford, 1950), Supplementary Plate 7a; Clifford, *A Knight of Great Renown*, p. 126.

Figure 10. A reconstruction of the painted scene on the north base of Eleanor of Castile's tomb in Westminster Abbey. (London, Westminster Abbey Library, WA 3682. Reproduced here by kind permission of the Dean and Chapter. © Dean and Chapter of Westminster).

fulfilled Eleanor's crusade vow.[133] Otto travelled to the Holy Land the year that Eleanor died, and she left him many gifts in her will. It has been argued, therefore, that Otto was the dying queen's crusade-proxy.

Rather than memorialise her own pilgrimage to the Holy Land, Eleanor's tomb drew attention to her sponsorship of (and salvation via) a noble crusader. This imagery harnessed the ideals that clerical circles were championing at this time. The frieze also drew direct comparisons with the Virgin Mary, a key figure behind medieval concepts of model feminine power and rulership. These were potent themes to combine with references to Eleanor's supposed model behaviour in holy war.

For some elite women in England, having their connections with crusade recognised in later life and in death was incredibly important to them and their families. Noblewomen had a deep sense of pride in having enabled individuals to go on crusade, and these sponsors took pains to ensure that their associations were not forgotten. Without a doubt, there must have been huge upset when crusading kin died abroad, yet commemorating those who perished was a task that provided opportunities to display family crusading character. Some individuals were supremely calculating in their approach to this. So much so, that some began making plans for commemorations, and how they could be associated with the remembrances, before crusaders had even departed.

It is an intriguing challenge, interpretating how crusading families typically honoured the memory of the women who enabled holy war. Yet, from the array of sources available – artistic, textual and material culture – several clear patterns have emerged. It appears that, much like crusaders themselves, sponsors harboured a distinct aspiration for recognition and commemoration. These women, and their communities, knew they were integral to the crusading effort. With that in mind, they sought to enter the collective memory of the crusades. Indeed, it seems some were welcomed into wider remembrances through prayer and memorialisation. Their desire to be remembered reflects a profound understanding of the impact of their actions in financing holy war. Laywomen patrons wanted to be part of a wider crusading identity, and many saw them as such.

---

[133] Reynolds, 'Proxy over Pilgrimage', pp. 129–30; Clifford, *A Knight of Great Renown*, p. 126; Tyerman, *England and the Crusades*, pp. 237–8; A. Forey, 'Otto of Grandson and the Holy Land, Cyprus and Armenia', *Crusades*, vol. 16 (2017), pp. 79–93; Lloyd, *English Society and the Crusade*, p. 59.

Conclusion
Identities Beyond the Battlefield

> The Franks were much distressed. They answered the call in great numbers, even the women, for there were with them at Acre a number of women, competing with their fellows, as we shall narrate, God willing. Those that were unable to depart hired people to go in their place or they gave money according to their circumstances. There gathered around them more men and money than there would be any way of counting.
>
> (Ali Ibn al-Athīr [d.1233], historian from Mosul)[1]

In a few short sentences, Ibn al-Athīr summarised the seemingly all-encompassing way that Latin Christians connected with the news that Jerusalem had been captured in 1187. From his perspective, everyone in Christendom was, in some way, involving themselves in attempts to recapture the city – to achieve crusade. Ibn al-Athīr was trying to portray the insurmountable odds that faced the Muslim defenders at Acre; however, he was not far off the mark in capturing the essential way that medieval Christians felt touched by the crusading idiom. Even while sitting 'outside' of this eruption of crusading fervour – or rather, very much in the firing line – his words are a reminder that there was clearly no singular way in which these people participated in holy war. And yet, all these people contributed to the movement. Indeed, many women went "competing with their fellows", while others funded those fellows: there was no one monolithic ideal within crusade.

The cultural landscape in England fostered that diversity in approaches to holy war. The reminders of crusade were everywhere, incorporated into shared spaces and viewed by a broad audience. Even the more exclusive churches and halls of the Knights Templar – with all their architectural references to Jerusalem – were not entirely inaccessible to outsiders. Although there were a plethora of messages and types of messaging, as we have seen, crusading culture and propaganda expected certain gendered roles of the secular and ecclesiastical communities. The stance within this body of material regarding women was often vague and generalising. Still, in England, laywomen were typically entreated to remain in the kingdom and offer up their money, pressure their male kinfolk to go on crusade in their stead and pray for the triumph of Christendom. People absorbed this propaganda from all directions and reflected it back on their society. If anything,

---

[1] Ibn al-Athir, *The Chronicle of Ibn al-Athir*, vol. 2, p. 364.

it is unnerving to think how the crusading ethos coolly sat within the day-to-day of life in medieval England.

Despite the ubiquitous way that people must have engaged with this culture, we cannot always see how this worked in practical scenarios. It is a familiar problem: people rarely feel the need to record the things in life that they consider normal or self-explanatory. By that token, there is so much about the more casual elements of crusade that we will never fully grasp. The overwhelming number of wooden chests, for instance, that were assembled for every church in Christendom (if we are to believe the papal orders) must have been astonishing and (initially) created a buzz in even the most remote villages. We can well imagine a scene where parishioners filed in and out of their local church, while dropping donations into these collection boxes. Or, perhaps there were more formalised rituals associated with this, even simply amongst the laypeople themselves. However it worked, it must have been a daily occurrence across the board and sincerely informed on people's sense of place in a wider world. Still, we have no surviving descriptions of this parish norm. This practice is just one example, though an emblematic one, of the pervasive way crusade culture and organisation manifested in the West.

This book has attempted to cut to the core of what laywomen thought of crusade and how they interacted with the movement within England. By examining what has survived, women's appearance in all aspects of crusade is wholly apparent. Their efforts assenting to the disposal of land and dower property, or purchasing crusaders' assets, are all abundant: all done to fund "fellows" destined for the Holy Land. This body of evidence is not huge, but it shows a range of sources that may indicate women's approval of crusade; it certainly underscores their close involvement in it.

Not everyone in English society would necessarily have praised these women for supporting crusaders. Crusading, as an institution, would come under fire over the course of the twelfth and thirteenth centuries. Latin Christendom's habitual failure to retake Jerusalem ensured that crusading was never a wholly loved endeavour within the West. There were always critics who doubted that it was worth the physical or monetary sacrifice. Individuals who were dedicated to financing the enterprise did so with no small degree of effort, planning and premeditation. The main thrust of this book has been considering that the people who appear amongst records of crusade funding probably encouraged crusade itself. Their actions might have been counter to the mood of their immediate environment, again indicating how deliberate they were.

Medieval people were deeply pragmatic and forthright in that groundwork ahead of crusades or pilgrimages. This might sound illogical, given that many of the cases explored in this book are lifted from surviving legal records, which showed crusade supporters mired in court battles. Nevertheless, many of these cases may have come about because of changing or unforeseen circumstances, or the designs of opportunistic neighbours. Those records that orbit crusaders or their families make up a comparatively small portion of the total corpus of English

Conclusion

legal sources. It gives me cause to wonder: if people were careless in their support of long-distance pilgrimages and crusades, would we not also see a concurrent swathe of litigation over lands and property used to gain capital? It is critical to bear in mind that thousands of landholders seemingly went on crusade across the twelfth and thirteenth centuries. It strikes me that the people who financed crusade were undeniably calculating and often had considerable time to meditate on their decision-making. This only further highlights how these same people had time to consider their ideological reasoning and interest in what they were doing.

Asking how women supported *crucesignati* has been an important means for gaining perspective on the family-orientated nature of crusading, as well as considering new readings of our sources. But, it is perhaps more important to think about the motivations and reasonings behind laywomen's adherence to the ideals around them. The theme of identity has run through this book's inquiry. Charters and the cartularies that they were copied into detailed women's involvement as financiers, often in quite matter-of-fact terms. Yet, they were not simply a dull deed. Rather, they acted as a means for capturing and shaping the memory of the crusading movement. By ensuring that their names were added to these documents, many women took ownership and credit for having a hand in the mechanics of one of the most impactful events of their age. Subsequent generations of cartulary scribes, living a century or more later, may, on occasion, have removed details regarding the crusading context of some grants. Yet despite these alterations, we can still appreciate that, at the time many documents were drafted in the High Middle Ages, laywomen were eager to have their actions enshrined in the record.

These texts encourage the reader to notice a family's crusading lineage, just as the wax seal attached to that same charter might nod at the person's heraldry or social ties. Many households and communities developed generations of crusaders and supporters alike, all forming part of a dynastic memory. The commemorative acts that some English families engaged in suggest that there was a deep regard for a variety of identities within (and performances of) crusade. By sponsoring and enabling martial crusaders, women were not only ensuring the continuation of a family identity *per se* but also positioning themselves within it.

It is also worth taking stock, however, and considering some of the inherent shortcomings of a study like this one. Research that is limited to a specific group in society and to a specific idea, or action – crusading and laywomen – naturally has a limited scope. This study has not offered a means for calculating how important crusading was to women's lay piety in comparison to, say, patronising the Augustinian order, making pilgrimages to local shrines or having an interest in holy wells (just to name a few). The conclusions drawn in this work may not have applied to all regions within England; only a more detailed scrutiny of local archives can develop our view here. And, more than that, how much currency does this study have for interpretations of neighbouring kingdoms that equally engaged in the crusades of the Middle Ages? The regionality of medieval holy war is still being determined, and the more we inspect this, it becomes clearer that there were distinctive crusading cultures across Europe.

Historians have long been aware that medieval sources pointed out women's support for crusade, but this, too, warrants a more expansive look. In doing so, others will find new inroads to flesh out exactly what the crusades were, and what they meant to contemporaries. For my part, I am highly sceptical that I have exhausted the routes for questioning this topic. As a man, I am unlikely to have asked the same questions of the sources or drawn the same conclusions that a woman might. This book is surely only one step and one point of view in what I hope becomes a deepening stream of study for historians of the Middle Ages. Indeed, it has highlighted the value of numerous case studies and methods for interpreting the surviving evidence that may act as a foundation for others in developing our picture of life in the era of the crusades. After all, questioning this period of history, and our modern views of it, from all angles is fundamental to comprehending the traumas caused by the crusades across Europe, the Near East and Africa, which are still felt and still mean something.

The efforts of those who supported crusade were certainly not celebrated in surviving medieval Christian literature and poetry with the same relish and frequency as battle. Yet this research has shown that taking this viewpoint at face value occludes our understanding of the totality and complexity of crusade. Laywomen across England were not only conscious of the gendered models surrounding holy war, but many of them were eager to be seen to be conforming to those ideals. Those that enabled others to go on crusade also sought acknowledgement from their peers, superiors and, in many ways, from the future generations that they envisioned would read their charters. Crusade was an intrinsic and multifaceted part of high medieval England's culture and lay piety, not simply the work of lone zealots. Whole communities who never left their kingdom nonetheless found a lasting affinity with holy war.

Appendices

Appendix 1
Crusade-Support Activity

The following table is a chronological list of cases dating from the mid-twelfth till the late thirteenth century from which laywomen's involvement in crusade sponsorship may be inferred. This list represents the observable cases regarding landholders in England within the printed primary sources used in this book. Instances of women's fund-raising for their own ventures are not listed.

Years marked with an asterisk (*) indicate that the date given is that of the document's drafting, not the date at which the women's actions took place. For example, litigation over dower lands presumably took place months or years after those lands were originally pledged or sold to fund crusade.

#	Date Ranges	Name	Action	Source
1.	c.1147	Gundreda de Gournay	Made donations for the spiritual benefit of a crusader.	Greenway, *Charters of the Honour of Mowbray*, p. 116, no. 156; p. 197, no. 300.
2.	c.1174	Agnes de Percy	Consented to dower being pledged.	*EYC*, vol. 11, p. 66, no. 68.
3.	c.1185*	Matilda Baiarde	Granted her nephew assets.	Kerling, *Cartulary of St Bartholomew's Hospital*, p. 146, nos. 1599–1600.
4.	c. 1185	Wife of Robert Beche	Spiritual beneficiary of a crusader's donation.	Moore, *The History of St. Bartholomew's Hospital*, vol. 1, p. 207, no. 2.
5.	c. 1188	Wife of Ralph de Chall	Dower and livelihood guaranteed in conveyance.	*EYC*, vol. 5, p. 122, no. 215.
6.	1176 x 1200	Amphelisia of Rolleston	Consented to her dower being pledged.	Foulds, *The Thurgarton Cartulary*, p. 72, no. 111.
7.	1188 x 1189	Agnes lady of Little Windsor	Consented to land grants.	Hobbs, *The Cartulary of Forde Abbey*, pp. 56–7, nos. 208–10, p. 59, nos. 222–3.
8.	1189 x 1190	Matilda Touche	Received property from a crusader.	*EYC*, vol. 3, p. 375–6, no. 1748.

Appendix 1

#	Date Ranges	Name	Action	Source
9.	Before Oct 1190	Sybil de Braose	Spiritual beneficiary of a crusader's donations.	Frost, 'An Edition of the Nostell Priory Cartulary', vol. 2, p. 763, no. 927; Dugdale, *Monasticon Anglicanum*, vol. 6, Part II, p. 1078, no. iii.
10.	1189 x 1190	Petronilla de Grandmesnil	Spiritual beneficiary of a crusader's donations.	Round, *Calendar of Documents Preserved in France*, pp. 102–3, no. 306.
11.	1190 x 1200	Ailiva of Cuckney	Received property from a crusader.	Turner, *Calendar of Charters and Rolls Preserved in the Bodleian Library*, pp. 274–5.
12.	1191*	Evelyn, wife of Richard de Baubaduu	Sold her dower prior to husband's crusade.	Martin, *The Percy Chartulary*, p. 381, no. 891.
13.	1199*	Gunnore de Valunies	Dower pledged.	*CRR*, vol. 1, p. 69.
14.	1199*	Alice Briewer	Dower pledged.	*CRR*, vol. 1, p. 85, no. m.4.
15.	1202*	Cecilia de Flore	Bought property from a crusader.	Stenton, *The Earliest Northamptonshire Assize Rolls*, p. 57, no. 450.
16.	1203*	Matilda de Crevequer	Received property from a crusader.	*CRR*, vol. 2, p. 182.
17.	1203*	Alice de Ouvill	Received property from a crusader.	*CRR*, vol. 2, pp. 275–6.
18.	1200 x 1218	Philippa, wife of Robert Marmion	Spiritual beneficiary of a crusader's donation.	Vincent, *Norman Charters from English Sources*, pp. 196–7, no. 71.
19.	c.1210*	Alice, wife of Gilbert	Consented to a land grant.	Mason, *Westminster Abbey Charters*, pp. 193–4, no. 347.
20.	c.1210 or later	Eustacia, sister of Walter son of Henry the Dean	Bought property from a crusader.	Darlington, *The Cartulary of Darley Abbey*, vol. 1, p. 44, no. Axxxix.

Appendix 1

#	Date Ranges	Name	Action	Source
21.	1218*	Edith of Navenby	Received property from a crusader.	Stenton, *Rolls of the Justices in Eyre: Being the Rolls of Please and Assizes for Lincolnshire 1218–9 and Worcestershire 1221*, p. 70, no. 159.
22.	1219*	Wife of Gerard de Furnevatt	Dower pledged.	Hardy, *Rotuli Litterarum Clausarum in Turri Londinensi Asservati*, vol. 1, p. 390.
23.	1219*	Amabele, wife of Aunfrid Breton	Received property from a crusader.	*CRR*, vol. 8, p. 21.
24.	1211 x 1236*	Milda White	Received property from a crusader.	Farrer, *The Chartulary of Cockersand Abbey*, vol. 3, part I, pp. 887–8.
25.	c.1220	Juliana, widow of Alan de Balon	Gave assets to a crusader.	Kerling, *Cartulary of St Bartholomew's Hospital*, p. 72, nos. 687–8.
26.	c.1220	Alice Baskervill	Bought assets from a crusader.	Rees, *The Cartulary of Haughmond Abbey*, p. 200, no. 1067.
27.	1222*	Leticia, widow of Richard son of Richard	Dower pledged.	*CRR*, vol. 10, p. 268.
28.	1223*	Matilda, wife of Adam of London	Dower pledged.	*CRR*, vol. 11, p. 85. no. 452.
29.	1223*	Joanna de Mares	Held responsible for debts.	*CRR*, vol. 11, p. 262. no. 1309.
30.	1223–4*	Emma of Meauton	Dower pledged.	*CRR*, vol. 11, p. 157, no. 785; p. 312, no. 1563; p. 446, no. 2231.
31.	1224*	Matilda of Meauton	Received property from a crusader.	*CRR*, vol. 11, p. 312, no. 1563.
32.	1225*	Annora daughter of John	Gave assets to a crusader.	*CRR*, vol. 12, p. 12, no. 69.

Appendix 1

#	Date Ranges	Name	Action	Source
33.	1230 x 1230	Alice, wife of William son of Nigel the Dean	Consented to the disposal of land and had her livelihood guaranteed.	*Frideswide*, vol. 1, pp. 418–21, nos. 594, 597–8.
34.	1226 x 1227	Sybil of Icklesham	Spiritual beneficiary of a crusader's donation. Her dower was pledged and she was held responsible for debts.	Churchton, 'Icklesham Church', p. 106; *CRR*, vol. 14, p. 109, no. 552, and pp. 280–1, no. 1322.
35.	1227	Marie, wife of Robert le Norreys	Made heir of a crusader.	*CRR*, vol. 13, p. 64, no. 292.
36.	1227*	Matilda, widow of Henry de Scalar	Dower pledged and Received property from a crusader.	*CRR*, vol. 13, p. 25, no. 114, and p. 83, no. 364.
37.	1227*	Hawisa, daughter of Walter de Eure	Rented property from a crusader.	Maitland, *Bracton's Note Book*, vol. 3, pp. 598–9, no. 1770.
38.	1227	Alice Briwere (also known as de Paynel and de Mohun)	Subsumed a crusader's debts and received property from a crusader.	Dryburgh, Hartland, Ciula and Vieira, *Calendar of Fine Rolls, Henry III, 1224–1234*, p. 191, no. 92.
39.	1229*	Matilda, wife of Adam of Stanford	Claimed that she received property from a crusader.	*CRR*, vol. 13, pp. 443–4, no. 2107.
40.	c.1230	Rose Marnet	Granted money to a crusader.	*Carisbrooke*, p. 85, no. 123.
41.	1230	Gundreda, daughter of Richard the Priest	Bought assets from a crusader.	Purvis, *The Chartulary of the Augustinian Priory of St John the Evangelist of the Park of Healaugh*, pp. 156–7.
42.	1232 x 1233*	Juliana Haringer	Livelihood guaranteed in a conveyance.	Salter, *The Cartulary of the Hospital of St. John the Baptist*, vol. 2, pp. 134–5.

Appendix 1

#	Date Ranges	Name	Action	Source
43.	1234*	Mabel wife of Nicholas of Greywell	Dower pledged.	*CCR, 1231–34*, pp. 510–1.
44.	1236–1249	Ela of Salisbury	Granted assets to a crusader, absorbed their debts and spiritually blessed their venture.	Reynolds, 'A Paragon of Support?', pp. 247–66.
45.	c.1237*	Alice de Blakepaine	Granted assets to a crusader.	Fleming, *Chartulary of the Priory of Boxgrove*, 1969, p. 122, no. 260, and pp. 124–5, no. 268.
46.	1230 x 1250	Matilda of Edgefield	Pledged assets to the Church, and made a crusader the heir.	Margerum, *The Cartulary of Binham Priory*, p. 111, no. 144.
47.	c.1240	Isabella Hacard	Granted assets to the Church to raise money for a crusader.	*Carisbrooke*, pp. 110–1, no. 161; pp. 111–2, nos. 163–4, and pp. 113–4, no. 166.
48.	Before 1241	Matilda, wife of Eustace of Warwick	Consented to dower being pledged.	Frost, 'An Edition of the Nostell Priory Cartulary', vol. 2, p. 780, no. 957.
49.	1241*	Petronilla de Tosny (de Lacy)	Dower pledged.	*CRR*, vol. 16, p. 320, no. 1625.
50.	1242*	Avecia de Somery	Received property from a crusader.	*CRR*, vol. 16, pp. 408–9, no. 2003.
51.	1242*	Idonee, widow of Radulf of *Wrokesham*	Received property from a crusader.	*CRR*, vol. 16, pp. 446–7, no. 2234.
52.	1240 x 1247	Alice, wife of Hamund de Brochurste	Spiritual beneficiary of a crusader's donation.	Hanna, *The Cartularies of Southwick Priory*, part 2, p. 95, no. iii 279; pp. 96–7, no. iii 281, and p. 98, no. iii 283.
53.	c.1245*	Evelyn Joy	Received assets from a crusader.	Grevers, *The Cartulary of the Knights of St John of Jerusalem in England, Part One*, p. 70, no. 107.

Appendix 1

#	Date Ranges	Name	Action	Source
54.	1249*	Christian, wife of Walter le Tayllur	Consented to her dower being sold.	Clanchy, *Civil Pleas of the Wiltshire Eyre*, p. 141, no. 483.
55.	1249*	Loretta of Crundal	Livelihood guaranteed in a conveyance.	Clanchy, *Civil Pleas of the Wiltshire Eyre, 1249*, p. 46, no. 69.
56.	Before 1258	Swanilda Gansel	Dower pledged.	Walker, *The Cartulary of St Augustine's Abbey, Bristol*, pp. 260–1, no. 408, and p. 269, no. 422.
57.	1265 x 1266*	Matilda Martin	Received assets from a crusader.	Hodgson, *Northumberland Pleas from the Curia Regis and Assize Rolls, 1198–1272, vol. II*, p. 243, no. 725.
58.	1265 x 1266*	Matilda Mayden	Received assets from a crusader.	Hodgson, *Northumberland Pleas from the Curia Regis and Assize Rolls, 1198–1272, vol. II*, p. 243, no. 725.
59.	1266 x 1269	Hawisa de Nevill	Promised a crusader financial aid and received property from him.	Giuseppi, 'XIX – On the Testament of Sir Hugh de Nevill', p. 360; *CCR, 1264–68*, p. 254.
60.	1268*	Margaret, wife of Thomas of Dreuton	Held responsible for debts.	*CCR, 1264–68*, p. 479.
61.	1268	Isabel de Mauduit	Had a crusade-proxy.	Willis Bund, *Episcopal Registers, Diocese of Worcester*, part 1, pp. 7–9.
62.	1268 x 1271	Agnes de Vescy	Received property from a crusader.	*CIPM*, vol. 2, pp. 445–7, no. 723.
63.	1270	Hawisa Lestrange	Received property from a crusader for a specified period of time.	Eyton, *Antiquities of Shropshire*, vol. 10, pp. 274–5.

Appendix 1

#	Date Ranges	Name	Action	Source
64.	1270	Isabel Chilham	Pledged her dower to fund a crusader.	*CPR*, 1266–72, pp. 422–3; Gervers, *Prima Camera*, p. 18.
65.	1270	Lucy, daughter of William son of Roger de *Berhholte*	Received property from a crusader.	Raimes, 'The Family of Reymes of Wherstead in Suffolk', pp. 110–1, App. D, no. 2.
66.	1275	Beatrice of Blackburn	Asked to commute vow and contribute to recovery of the Holy Land.	Brown, *The Register of Walter Giffard*, p. 284.
67.	1275	Wife of Radulf Mitton	Asked to commute vow and contribute to recovery of the Holy Land.	Brown, *The Register of Walter Giffard*, p. 284.
68.	1275	Wife of Hugh of *Sestefeld*	Asked to commute vow and contribute to recovery of the Holy Land.	Brown, *The Register of Walter Giffard*, p. 284.
69.	1275	Heloise Palmer	Contributed to the recovery the Holy Land.	Brown, *The Register of Walter Giffard*, p. 284.
70.	1275	Isabel Palmer	Contributed to the recovery the Holy Land.	Brown, *The Register of Walter Giffard*, pp. 281–2.
71.	1291	Eva Tibetot	Asked to commute vow and pay a crusader's costs.	Langlois, *Les Registres de Nicholas IV*, vol. 1, p. 650, no. 4490.
72.	13th century	Juliana, wife of William de Forda	Spiritual beneficiary of a crusader's donation.	Blake, *The Cartulary of the Priory of St Denys Near Southampton*, vol. 2, p. 192, no. 328.

Appendix 2
Known Round Churches in England
(Extant and Archaeological)

#	Name	Location	Construction Date	Founder
1	Church of the Knights Hospitaller of Clerkenwell	London	c.1144	Hospitallers
2	New Temple	London	c.1161	Templars
3	Old Temple Chapel of Holborn	London	c.1130s–40s	Templars
4	Commandery Chapel of St Michael, Garway	Herefordshire	c.1170–80s	Templars and Lay Donors
5	St Giles' Hospital	Herefordshire	c.1130s–50s	Templars
6	Church of Aslackby	Lincolnshire	c.1164	Templars
7	Temple Bruer Preceptory	Lincolnshire	c.1150–60	Templars
8	Holy Cross (Temple Church) of Bristol	Bristol	c.1145	Templars
9	Commandery Chapel of Bradden, Dover	Kent	c.1130s	Templars
10	Commandery Chapel of Penhill	Yorkshire	Twelfth Century	Templars
11	Temple Church of West Thurrock	Essex	c.1120–40s	Templars
12	St John the Baptist Church of Little Maplestead	Essex	c.1240–45	Hospitallers
13	Chapel of St Mary Magdalene, Ludlow Castle	Shropshire	c.1120s–30s	Gilbert I de Lacy (?)[1]

---

[1] This individual joined the Templars c.1158. The round church built within his castle may predate this vocation, see: Coppack, 'The Round Chapel of St. Mary Magdalene', p. 150.

Appendix 2Known

#	Name	Location	Construction Date	Founder
14	Church of the Holy Sepulchre, Cambridge	Cambridgeshire	c.1100–30s	Fraternity of the Holy Sepulchre
15	Church of the Holy Sepulchre, Northampton	Northamptonshire	c.1100–15	Simon I de Senlis (?)
16	St Sepulchre and St Bartholomew, Chichester	Sussex	c.1150s	Unknown Lay Founder
17	Woodstock Palace Chapel	Oxfordshire	c.1100–35	King Henry I of England (?)
18	Preceptory Chapel of the Templars, Dunwich	Suffolk	c.1180s–90s	Templars

Sources: Hundley, 'The English Round Church Movement', pp. 371–5; Gervers, 'The Use and Meaning of Round Churches in England', p. 379; Sloane and Malcolm, *Excavations at the Priory of the Order of the Hospital of St John of Jerusalem*, pp. 5–6 and 27–32; N. Baker, J. Brett, and R. Jones, *Bristol, a Worshipful town and Famous City: An Archaeological Assessment* (Oxford, 2018), pp. 211–3; Nicholson, 'At the Heart of Medieval London', p. 1; Coppack, 'The Round Chapel of St. Mary Magdalene', p. 150; Morris, 'Picturing the Crusades', pp. 198 and 215, plate. 8; M. Strickland, 'Senlis, Simon de [Simon de St Liz], earl of Northampton and earl of Huntingdon', in *Oxford Dictionary of National Biography*, https://doi.org/10.1093/ref:odnb/25091, Published Online 23 September 2004 (accessed 15 Jan 2024). Further afield within the British Isles, the round church of Orphir in Orkney is also considered to have been inspired by the pilgrimages or crusades of local earls in the early twelfth century, see: C.D. Morris, 'Viking Orkney: A Survey', in C. Renfrew (ed.), *The Prehistory of Orkney* (Edinburgh, 1985), pp. 234–5.

Appendix 3
Patronage of English Hospitaller Houses

Dating medieval charters can be problematic. The date at which they were originally drafted can often only be approximated to within a few decades. I have placed the charters below in rows that cover the largest proportion of their potential date range.

The following table lists instances of where women made donations or are explicitly described as consenting or encouraging a donation to a Hospitaller house. The figures are taken from four English cartularies, which are numbered as follows:
1. *The Godsfield and Baddesley Cartulary*
2. The *Prima Camera*
3. The *Secunda Camera*
4. *The Aconbury Cartulary.*

Each cartulary is represented by these **bold** numbers in the final column.

Date Range	No. Grants	No. Women as Donors/ Assenters	Charter No. in Cartulary
Pre c.1230	57	45	**1.** 7, 135 and 145. **2.** 111, 114, 152 and 161. **3.** 53, 67, 93, 217, 218, 257, 259, 262, 266, 271, 273, 274, 279, 282, 290, 291, 293, 296, 304, 315, 322, 323, 324, 336, 341, 345, 358, 365, 374, 392, 394, 417, 533, 566, 608, 906 and 907. **4.** 3, 16, 18, 19, 25, 27, 29, 30, 37, 38, 41, 42 and 70.

Appendix 3

Date Range	No. Grants	No. Women as Donors/Assenters	Charter No. in Cartulary
c.1230–1260	75	62	**1.** 51, 69, 70, 74, 92, 93, 103, 111, 140, 152, 175 and 198. **2.** 73, 115, 116, 122, 123, 129, 131, 137, 140, 180 and 212. **3.** 124, 128, 141, 146, 147, 152, 190, 221, 225, 226, 227, 241, 328, 329, 348, 380, 431, 439, 451, 452, 453, 466, 478, 479, 483, 484, 486, 487, 501, 502, 520, 536, 537, 540, 591, 683, 702, 716, 745, 747, 762, 763, 771, 792, 934, 935, 943, 947, 948 and 949. **4.** 4 and 5.
c.1260–1300	24	22	**1.** 97 and 203. **2.** 128. **3.** 130, 131, 132, 162, 183, 184, 244, 397, 488, 489, 490, 558, 665, 671, 911, 916 and 929. **4.** 7, 14, 15 and 28.
Unable to be dated	1	1	**4.** 50.

Sources: F. Beard (ed.), *The Knights Hospitallers in Medieval Hampshire: A Calendar of the Godsfield and Baddesley Cartulary* (Winchester, 2012); Gervers, *Prima Camera*; Gervers, *Secunda Camera*; Scott, 'A Herefordshire Nunnery'.

Bibliography

Manuscript Sources

Canterbury

Canterbury Cathedral Archives, MS DCc/MSSB/A/7: List of Cornish crusaders.

London

British Library, Additional Charter 19829: Crusade contract of Robert Tibetot and Payn de Chaworth.
British Library, Cotton MS Vitellius A VIII: The Book of Lacock
Lincoln's Inn, Hale MS 87: Battle Abbey Cartulary
Saint Bartholomew's Hospital Archive, 'Cok's Cartulary', MS HC/2/1: Cartulary of St Bartholomew's Hospital

Taunton

Somerset Heritage Centre, 'Liber Albus Abboticiae de Forde', Phillipps MS. 13823: Cartulary of Forde Abbey.

Primary Printed Sources

Adams, N., and Donahue, C. (eds), *Select Cases from the Ecclesiastical Courts of the Province of Canterbury c.1200–1301* (London, 1981).
Alan of Lille, *Anticlaudianus: or The Good and Perfect Man*, J.J. Sheridan (ed. and trans.) (Toronto, 1973).
Ambroise, *L'Estoire de la Guerre Sainte: histoire en vers de la troisième croisade (1190–1192)*, G. Paris (ed.) (Paris, 1897).
Ambroise, *The History of the Holy War, Ambroise's Estoire de la Guerre Sainte*, M. Ailes (ed. and trans.) (Woodbridge, 2003).
Atkinson, J.C. (ed.), *Cartularium Abbathiae de Whiteby*, 2 vols (Durham, 1879–81).
Auvray, L. (ed.), *Les Registres de Grégoire IX*, 4 vols (Paris, 1896–1955).
Baildon, W.P. (ed.), *Calendar of the Manuscripts of the Dean of the Chapter of Wells*, 2 vols (London, 1907–14).
Barber, M., and Bate, K. (eds and trans.), *Letters from the East: Crusaders, Pilgrims and Settlers in the 12th-13th Centuries* (Farnham, 2013).
Beard, F. (ed.), *The Knights Hospitallers in Medieval Hampshire: A Calendar of the Godsfield and Baddesley Cartulary* (Winchester, 2012).
Bearman, R. (ed.), *Charters of the Redvers Family and the Earldom of Devon, 1090–1217* (Exeter, 1994).

Bibliography

Bentley, S. (ed.), *Excerpta Historica* (London, 1831).
Berger, E. (ed.), *Les Registres D'Innocent IV (1243–1254)*, 4 vols (Paris, 1881–1921).
Bird, J., Peters, E., and Powell, J.M. (eds and trans.), *Crusade and Christendom: Annotated Documents in Translation from Innocent III to the Fall of Acre, 1187–1291* (Philadelphia, 2013).
Blake, E.O. (ed.), *The Cartulary of the Priory of St Denys Near Southampton*, 2 vols (Southampton, 1981).
Bliss, W.H. (ed.), *Calendar of Papal Registers Relating to Great Britain and Ireland: Vol 1, 1198–1304* (London, 1893).
Brial, M.J.J. (ed.), *Recueil des Historiens des Gaules et de la France* (Paris, 1808), vol. 15.
Brown, W (ed.), *The Register of Walter Giffard, Lord Archbishop of York, 1266–1279* (Durham, 1904).
Burton, J. (ed.), *The Foundation History of the Abbeys of Byland and Jervaulx* (York, 2006).
Butler, H.E., Williams, C.H., and Gillingham, J. (eds), *The Autobiography of Gerald of Wales* (Woodbridge, 2005, Originally published 1937).
Calendar of Close Rolls, Henry III – Edward I, 1227–1302, 19 vols (London 1902–75).
Calendar of Inquisitions Post Mortem, Henry III – Edward II, 6 vols (London, 1904–10).
Calendar of Liberate Rolls, Henry III – Edward I, 1226–72, 6 vols (London, 1917–64).
Calendar of Patent Rolls, Henry III – Edward I, 1216–1301, 9 vols (London, 1893–1913).
Cheney, C.R., and John, E. (eds), *English Episcopal Acta III, Canterbury 1193–1205* (Oxford, 1986).
Cheney, C.R., and Cheney, M.G. (eds), *The Letters of Pope Innocent III (1198–1216) Concerning England and Wales* (Oxford, 1967).
Chroust, A. (ed.), *Monumenta Germaniae Historica, Scriptores rerum Germanicarum, Nova Series* (Berlin, 1928), vol. 5.
Clancy, T.O. (ed.), *The Triumph Tree: Scotland's Earliest Poetry, AD 500–1350* (Edinburgh, 1998).
Clanchy, M.T. (ed.), *Civil Pleas of the Wiltshire Eyre, 1249* (Gloucester, 1971).
Clark, J.W. (ed.), *Liber Memorandorum Ecclesie de Bernewelle* (Cambridge, 1907).
Curia Regis Rolls, 20 vols (London, 1922–1961).
Darlington, R.R. (ed.), *The Cartulary of Darley Abbey*, 2 vols (Kendal, 1945).
David, C.W. (ed. and trans.), *The Conquest of Lisbon: De Expugnatione Lyxbonensi*, foreword and bibliography by J. Phillips (New York, 2001).
Dryburgh, P., Hartland, B., Ciula, A., and Vieira, J.M. (eds), *Calendar of Fine Rolls, Henry III, 1234–1242* (Woodbridge, 2009).

Bibliography

Dugdale, W. (ed.), *Monasticon Anglicanum*, 6 vols (London, 1814–30) (reprinted: 1848).

Eyton, R.W., *Antiquities of Shropshire*, 12 vols (London, 1853–60).

Farrer, W. (ed.), *The Chartulary of Cockersand Abbey of the Premonstratensian Order*, 3 vols (Manchester, 1898–1905).

Farrer, W., and Clay, C.T. (eds), *Early Yorkshire Charters*, 14 vols (Edinburgh, 1914–65).

Fleming, L. (ed.), *Chartulary of the Priory of Boxgrove* (Lewes, 1969).

Foulds, T. (ed.), *The Thurgarton Cartulary* (Stamford, 1994).

Fowler, J.T. (ed.), *The Coucher Book of Selby: From the Original MS. In the Possession of Thomas Brooke*, 2 vols (Cambridge, 1891–3).

Fowler, R.C., Chapman, J.B.W., and Atkinson, R.L. (eds), *Calendar of Chancery Warrants, A.D. 1244–1326* (London, 1927).

Fulcheri Carnotensis, *Historia Hierosolymitana (1095–1127)*, H. Hagenmeyer (ed.) (Heidelberg, 1913).

Gerald of Wales, *Instruction for a Ruler, De Principis Instructione*, R. Bartlett (ed. and trans.) (Oxford, 2018).

Gerald of Wales, *Giraldi Cambrensis Opera*, 8 vols, J.S. Brewer, J.G. Dimock and G.F. Warner (eds) (London, 1861–91).

Gervers, M (ed.), *The Cartulary of the Knights of St. John of Jerusalem in England, Part 2, Prima Camera, Essex* (Oxford, 1996).

Gervers, M (ed.), *The Cartulary of the Knights of St. John of Jerusalem in England, Secunda Camera, Essex* (Oxford, 1982).

Gervers, M. (ed.), *The Hospital Cartulary in the British Library (Cotton MS Nero E VI), A Study of the Manuscript and its Composition with a Critical Edition of Two Fragments of Earlier Cartularies for Essex* (Toronto, 1981).

Geoffrey Chaucer, *The Canterbury Tales*, J. Mann (ed.) (London, 2005).

Greenway, D., and Watkiss, L. (eds and trans.), *The Book of the Foundation of Walden Monaster* (Oxford, 1999).

Greenway, D.E. (ed.), *Charters of the Honour of Mowbray, 1107–1191* (London, 1972).

Guillaume le Clerc, *Fergus of Galloway: Knight of King Arthur*, D.D.R. Owen (ed. and trans.) (Edinburgh, 2018).

Guillaume le Clerc, *The Romance of Fergus*, W. Frescoln (ed.) (Philadelphia, 1983).

Guiraud, M.J. (ed.), *Registres d'Urbain IV (1261–1264)* (Paris, 1901).

Hagenmeyer, H. (ed.), *Kreuzzugsbriefe aus den Jahren 1088–1100* (Innsbruck, 1901).

Hall, G.D.G., and Clanchy, M.T. (eds and trans.), *The Treatise on the Laws and Customs of the Realm of England Commonly Called Glanvill* (Oxford, 1993).

Hanna, K.A. (ed.), *The Cartularies of Southwick Priory*, 2 parts (Southampton, 1988–9).

Bibliography

Hardy, T.D. (ed.), *Rotuli Litterarum Clausarum in Turri Londinensi Asservati: 1204–1224*, 2 vols (London, 1833).

Hart, W.H. (ed.), *Historia et Cartularium Monasterii Sancti Petri Gloucestriae*, 3 vols (Cambridge, 1863–7).

Harvey, C.C. (ed.), *Calendar of Writs Preserved at Yester House, 1166–1503* (Edinburgh, 1916).

Hershey, A.H., (ed.), *The 1258–9 Special Eyre of Surrey and Kent* (Woking, 2004).

Historical Manuscripts Commission, *Report on Manuscripts in Various Collections, Volume 1* (London, 1901).

Hodgson, J.C. (ed.), *Northumberland Pleas from the Curia Regis and Assize Rolls, 1198–1272, Newcastle-upon-Tyne Records Committee, vol II* (Newcastle-upon-Tyne, 1922).

Hobbs, S. (ed.), *The Cartulary of Forde Abbey* (Taunton, 1998).

Hockey, S.F. (ed.), *The Cartulary of Carisbrooke Priory* (Southampton, 1981).

Holmes, R. (ed.), *The Chartulary of St. John of Pontefract*, 2 vols (Leeds, 1899–1902).

van Houts, E.M.C. (ed. and trans.), *Gesta Normannorum Ducum of William of Jumièges, Orderic Vitalis, and Robert of Torigni*, 2 vols (Oxford, 1992–5) (reprinted: 2003).

Humbert of Romans, *De Predicatione Crucis*, V. Portnykh and C. Vande Veire (eds) (Turnhout, 2018).

Humbert of Romans, 'Opus Tripartitum', in E. Brown (ed.), *Appendix ad Fasciculus Rerum Expetendarum et Fugiendum* (London, 1690), pp. 185–229.

Huygens, R.B.C. (ed.), *Lettres de Jacques de Vitry (1160/1170–1240) évêque de Saint-Jean-d'Acre, Edition Critique* (Leiden, 1960).

Ibn al-Athir, *The Chronicle of Ibn al-Athir for the Crusading Period from al-Kamil fi'l-Ta'rikh*, 3 vols, D.S. Richards (ed. and trans.) (Farnham, 2005–8).

Jackson, P. (ed.), *The Seventh Crusade, 1244–1254: Sources and Documents* (Farnham, 2009).

Jaffé, P. (ed.), *Regesta Pontificum Romanorum, ab Condita Ecclesiae ad annum post Christum Natum MCXCVIII*, 2 vols, 2nd edn (Lipsiae, 1885–8).

James, B.S., and Kienzle, B.M. (eds and trans.), *The Letters of St Bernard of Clairvaux* (reprinted: Guildford, 1998).

Jean de Joinville, 'The Life of Saint Louis', in C. Smith (ed. and trans.), *Joinville and Villehardouin: Chronicles of the Crusades* (London, 2008), pp. 147–336.

Johannis de Garlandia, *De Triumphis Ecclesiae Libri Octo*, T. Wright (ed.) (London, 1856).

John of Forde, *The Life of Wulfric of Haselbury, Anchorite*, P. Matarasso (ed. and trans.) (Trappist, 2011).

John of Hexham, 'Historia Regum', in T. Arnold (ed.), *Symeonis Monachi Opera Omnia*, 2 vols (London, 1882–5), at vol. 2, pp. 284–332.

Jones, W.R., and MacRay, W.D. (eds), *Charters and Documents Illustrating the*

Bibliography

History of the Cathedral, City, and Diocese of Salisbury in the Twelfth and Thirteenth Centuries (London, 1891).
Jones, W.H.R. (ed.), *Vetus Registrum Sarisberiense alias dictum Registrum S. Osmundi Episcopi*, 2 vols (London, 1883–4).
Kemp, B.R. (ed.), *English Episcopal Acta 18, Salisbury 1078–1217* (Oxford, 1999).
Kemp, B.R. (ed.), *English Episcopal Acta 19, Salisbury 1217–1228* (Oxford, 2000).
Kerling, N.J.M. (ed.), *Cartulary of St Bartholomew's Hospital, Founded 1123* (London, 1973).
Lancaster, W.T. (ed.), *Abstracts of the Charters and other Documents Contained in the Chartulary of the Cistercian Abbey of Fountains in the West Riding of the County of York*, 2 vols (Leeds, 1915).
Langlois, E. (ed.), *Les Registres de Nicholas IV*, 2 vols (Paris, 1886–91).
Larkin, P. (ed.), *Richard Coer de Lyon* (Kalamazoo, 2015).
Leclercq, J., Rochais, H., Talbot, C.H., and Duchet-Suchaux, M. (eds), *Bernard de Clairvaux, Lettres, Oeuvres completes*, 3 vols (Paris, 1997–2000).
Leys, A.M. (ed.), *The Sandford Cartulary*, 2 vols (Oxford, 1938–41).
London, V.C.M. (ed.), *The Cartulary of Bradenstoke Priory* (Stoke-on-Trent, 1979).
Luard, H.R. (ed.), *Annales Monastici*, 5 vols (London, 1864–9).
Luard, H.R. (ed.), *Flores Historiarum Vol. II A.D. 1067 – A.D. 1264* (London, 1890)
Maier, C.T., '*Brevis Ordinacio de Predicacione Sancte Crucis*: Edition, Translation and Commentary', *Crusades*, vol. 18 (2019), pp. 25–65.
Maitland, F.W. (ed.), *Bracton's Note Book. A Collection of Cases Decided in the King's Courts during the reign of Henry the Third*, 3 vols (London, 1887).
Margerum, J. (ed.), *The Cartulary of Binham Priory* (Norfolk, 2016).
Martin, M.J. (ed.), *The Percy Chartulary* (Durham, 1911).
Mason, E. (ed.), *The Beauchamp Cartulary Charters 1100–1268* (London, 1980).
Mason, E. (ed.), *Westminster Abbey Charters 1066-c.1214* (Bath, 1988).
Matthew Paris, *Chronica Majora*, 7 vols, H.R. Luard (ed.) (London, 1872–83).
Matthew Paris, *Historia Anglorum and Abbreviatio Chronicorum*, 3 vols, F. Madden (ed.) (London, 1866–9).
Matthew Paris, 'Vita Sancti Edmundi Auctore Matthaoe Parisiensi', in C.H. Lawrence (ed.), *St. Edmund of Abingdon, A Study in Hagiography and History* (Oxford, 1960), pp. 222–89.
Maxwell Lyte, H.C. (ed.), *Calendar of the Charter Rolls Preserved in the Public Record Office, Vol. 1: Henry III A.D. 1226–1257* (London, 1903).
McNulty, J. (ed.), *The Chartulary of the Cistercian Abbey of St. Mary of Sallay in Craven*, 2 vols (Wakefield, 1933–4).
Monfrin, J. (ed.), *Vie de Saint Louis* (Paris, 2010).
Moore, N. (ed.), *The History of St. Bartholomew's Hospital*, 2 vols (London, 1918).
Müller, U. (ed.), *Kreuzzugsdichtung* (Tübingen, 1969).
Nicholas Trevet, *Annals Sex Regum Angliae, Qui Comitibus Andegavensibus Originem Traxerunt*, T. Hog (ed.) (London, 1845).

Bibliography

Nicholson, H.J. (ed.), *The Chronicle of the Third Crusade: The Itinerarium Peregrinorum et Gesta Regis Ricardi* (Aldershot, 2001).

Orderic Vitalis, *The Ecclesiastical History of Orderic Vitalis*, 6 vols, M. Chibnall (ed. and trans.) (Oxford, 1969–80).

Page W. (ed.), *Three Early Assize Rolls for the County of Northumberland, Sæc XIII* (Durham, 1891).

Patrologiae Latinae cursus completus, 222 vols, J.P. Migne (ed.) (Paris, 1844–1903)

Peters, E. (ed.), *The First Crusade, The Chronicle of Fulcher of Chartres and Other Source Materials*, 2nd edn (Philadelphia, 1998).

Potthast, A. (ed.), *Regesta Pontificum Romanorum, inde ab a post Christum Natum MCXCVIII ad a. MCCCIV*, 2 vols (Berlin, 1873–5).

Powicke, F.W., and Cheney, C.R. (eds), *Councils & Synods with Other Documents Relating to The English Church, Vol. II, A.D. 1205–1313, Part I, 1205–1265* (Oxford, 1964).

Preest, D., and Clark, J.G. (eds and trans.), *The Deeds of the Abbots of St Albans: Gesta Abbatum Monasterii Sancti Albani* (Woodbridge, 2019).

Preest, D., and Webster, H.R. (eds and trans.), *The Annals of Dunstable Priory* (Woodbridge, 2018).

Pressutti, P. (ed.) *Regesta Honorii Papae III*, 2 vols (Rome, 1888–95).

Purvis, J.S. (ed.), *The Chartulary of the Augustinian Priory of St John the Evangelist of the Park of Healaugh* (Cambridge, 1936).

Raine, J. (ed.), *Historical Papers and Letters from the Northern Registers* (London, 1873).

Ransford, R. (ed.), *The Early Charters of the Augustinian Canons of Waltham Abbey, Essex, 1062–1230* (Woodbridge, 1989).

Rees, U. (ed.), *The Cartulary of Haughmond Abbey* (Cardiff, 1985).

Riley-Smith, L., and Riley-Smith, J. (eds and trans.), *The Crusades: Idea and Reality, 1095–1274* (London, 1981).

Roger of Howden, *Chronica Magistri Rogeri de Houedene*, 4 vols, W. Stubbs (ed.) (London, 1868–71).

Roger of Wendover, *Rogeri de Wendover liber qui dicitur Flores Historiarum ab anno domini MCLIV annoque Henrici Anglorum Regis Secundi Primo*, 3 vols, H.G. Hewlett (ed.) (Cambridge, 1886–9).

Rogers, K.H. (eds and trans.), *Lacock Abbey Charters* (Stoke-on-Trent, 1979).

Round, J.H. (ed.), *Calendar of Documents Preserved in France Illustrative of the History of Great Britain and Ireland, vol. 1, 918–1206* (London, 1899).

Salter, H.E. (ed.), *The Cartulary of the Hospital of St. John the Baptist*, 3 vols (Oxford, 1914–17)

Salzmann, L.F. (ed.), *An Abstract of Feet of Fines of the County of Sussex*, 2 vols (Lewes, 1903–8).

Searle, E. (ed. and trans.), *The Chronicle of Battle Abbey* (Oxford, 1980).

Snorri Sturluson, *Heimskringla*, 3 vols, A. Finlay and A. Faulkes (eds and trans.) (London, 2011–5).

Bibliography

Stacy, N.E. (ed.), *Surveys of the Estates of Glastonbury Abbey, c.1135–1201* (Oxford, 2001).
Stenton, D.M. (ed.), *The Earliest Northamptonshire Assize Rolls, A.D. 1202 and A.D. 1203* (London, 1930).
Stenton, D.M. (ed.) *Pleas Before the King or his Justices 1198–1202*, 4 vols (London, 1952–67).
Stenton, D.M. (ed.), *Rolls of the Justices in Eyre: Being the Rolls of Pleas and Assizes for Lincolnshire 1218–9 and Worcestershire 1221* (London, 1934).
Stenton, D.M. (ed.), *Rolls of the Justices in Eyre being the Rolls of Pleas and Assizes for Gloucestershire, Warwickshire and Staffordshire, 1221, 1222* (London, 1940).
Stevenson, J. (ed.), *Chronica de Mailros* (Edinburgh, 1835).
Stewart, S. (ed.), *The 1263 Surrey Eyre* (Bristol, 2006).
Stubbs, W. (ed.), *Itinerarium Peregrinorum et Gesta Regis Ricardi* (London, 1864).
Tangl, G. (ed.), *Studien zum Register Innocenz' III* (Weimar, 1929).
Thorpe, T. (ed.), *Muniments of Battle Abbey* (London, 1835).
Timson, R.T. (ed.), *The Cartulary of Blyth Priory* (London, 1973).
Tobin, F., Vivian, K., and Lawson, R.H. (eds and trans.), *Arthurian Romances, Tales, and Lyric Poetry: The Complete Works of Hartmann von Aue* (University Park, 2001).
Trimmer, R.D., and Crump, C.G. (eds), *Calendar of the Charter Rolls Preserved in the Public Record Office* (London, 1903), vol. 1.
Turner, W.H. (ed.), *Calendar of Charters and Rolls Preserved in the Bodleian Library* (Oxford, 1878).
Underwood, M. (ed.), *The Cartulary of the Hospital of St John the Evangelist, Cambridge* (Cambridge, 2008).
Usāma ibn Munqidh, *An Arab-Syrian Gentleman and Warrior in the Period of the Crusades: Memoirs of Usama ibn-Munqidh*, P.K. Hitti (ed. and trans.), 2nd edn (Princeton, 1987).
Vincent, N. (ed.), *English Episcopal Acta IX, Winchester 1205–1238* (Oxford, 1994).
Vincent, N. (ed.), *Norman Charters from English Sources: Antiquaries, Archives and the Rediscovery of the Anglo-Norman Past* (London, 2013).
'Vita Beati Edmundi Cantuariensis Archiepiscopi et Confessoris', in E. Martène and U. Durand (eds), *Thesaurus Novus Anecdotorum*, 5 vols (Paris, 1717), vol. 3, pp. 1775–1826.
Walker D. (ed.), *The Cartulary of St Augustine's Abbey, Bristol* (Bristol, 1998).
Walter Bower, *Scotichronicon*, 9 vols, D. Watt, *et al* (eds and trans.) (Aberdeen, 1993–8).
Watkin, A. (ed.), *The Great Chartulary of Glastonbury*, 3 vols (Frome, 1947–56).
Wigram, S.R. (ed.), *The Cartulary of the Monastery of St. Frideswide at Oxford*, 2 vols (Oxford, 1895–6).

Bibliography

William of Malmesbury, *Gesta Regum Anglorum*, 2 vols, R.A.B. Mynors, R.M. Thomson, and M. Winterbottom (eds and trans.) (Oxford, 1998–9).

William de Waude, 'Historia Translationis Veteris Ecclesiae Beatae Mariae Sarum ad Novum', in W.H. Rich Jones (ed.), *Vetus Registrum Sarisberiense alias dictum Registrum S. Osmundi Episcopi* (London, 1884), vol. 2, pp. 3–124.

Willis Bund, J.W. (ed.), *Episcopal Registers, Diocese of Worcester, Register of Bishop Godfrey Giffard*, 2 Parts. (Oxford, 1898–9).

Secondary Sources

Abulafia, D., 'Invented Italians in the Courtois Forgeries', in P.W. Edbury (ed.), *Crusade and Settlement, Papers Read at the First Conference of the Society for the Study of the Crusades and the Latin East and Presented to R.C. Smail* (Cardiff, 1985), pp. 135–47.

Aird, W.M., '"Many others, whose names I do not know, fled with them": Norman Courage and Cowardice on the First Crusade', in K. Hurlock and P. Oldfield (eds), *Crusading and Pilgrimage in the Norman World* (Woodbridge, 2015), pp. 13–29.

Aird, W.M., *Robert Curthose, Duke of Normandy, c.1050–1134* (Woodbridge, 2008).

Allen, S.J., *An Introduction to the Crusades* (Toronto, 2017).

Allmand, C., 'War and the Non-Combatant in the Middle Ages', in M. Keen (ed.), *Medieval Warfare: A History*, 2nd edn (Oxford, 2010), pp. 253–72.

Althoff, G., *Family, Friends and Followers: Political and Social Bonds in Medieval Europe*, C. Carroll (trans.) (Cambridge, 1990) (reprinted: 2004).

Ambrisco, A.S., 'Cannibalism and Cultural Encounters in *Richard Coeur de Lion*', *Journal of Medieval and Early Modern Studies*, vol. 29, no. 3 (1999), pp. 499–528.

Andrews, D.D. (ed.), *Cressing Temple. A Templar and Hospitaller Manor in Essex* (Chelmsford, 1993).

Appleby, J.T., *England Without Richard 1189–1199* (London, 1965).

Asbridge, T., *The First Crusade: A New History* (London, 2004).

Ashe, L., 'The Ideal of Knighthood in English and French Writing, 1100–1230: Crusade, Piety, Chivalry and Patriotism', in M. Bull and D. Kempf (eds), *Writing the Early Crusades: Text, Transmission and Memory* (Woodbridge, 2014), pp. 155–68.

Ashley, S., and Biddle, M., 'Recent Finds of Late Twelfth- or Early Thirteenth-Century Sword and Dagger Pommels Associated with the Crusades', *The Coat of Arms*, 3rd series, vol. 11 (2015), pp. 95–106.

Bachrach, D.S., *Religion and the Conduct of War, c.300–c.1215* (Woodbridge, 2003).

Bagge, S., *Society and Politics in Snorri Sturluson's Heimskringla* (Berkeley, 1991).

Bibliography

Baker, N., Brett, J., and Jones, R., *Bristol, a Worshipful town and Famous City: An Archaeological Assessment* (Oxford, 2018).

Baldwin, P.B., *Pope Gregory X and the Crusades* (Woodbridge, 2014).

Bandlien, B., 'Civil War as Holy War? Polyphonic Discourses on Warfare During the Internal Struggles in Norway in the Twelfth Century', in R. Kotecki, C.S. Jensen and S. Bennett (eds), *Christianity and War in Medieval East Central Europe and Scandinavia* (Leeds, 2021), pp. 227–43.

Barber, M., 'Supplying the Crusader States: The Role of the Templars', in B.Z. Kedar (ed.) *The Horns of Ḥaṭṭīn* (Jerusalem, 1992), pp. 314–26.

Barbieri, L., 'Crusade Songs and the Old French Literary Canon', in S.T. Parsons and L.M. Paterson (eds), *Literature of the Crusades* (Woodbridge, 2018), pp. 75–95.

Barker, J., *Stone Fidelity: Marriage and Emotion in Medieval Tomb Sculpture* (Woodbridge, 2020).

Barret, C., 'Roland and Crusade Imagery in an English Royal chapel: Early Thirteenth-Century Wall Paintings in Claverley Church, Shropshire', *The Antiquaries Journal*, vol. 92 (2012), pp. 129–68.

Bartlett, R., *Gerald of Wales, A Voice of the Middle Ages* (Stroud, 2006).

Bass, I.L., '"*Articuli Inquisicionis de crucesignatis*": Late Thirteenth-Century Inquiry into English Crusaders', *Crusades*, vol. 17 (2018), pp. 171–94.

Bates, D., 'Charters and Historians of Britain and Ireland: Problems and Possibilities', in M.T. Flanagan and J.A. Green (eds), *Charters and Charter Scholarship in Britain and Ireland* (London, 2005), pp. 1–14.

Baumgärtner, I., and Panse, M., 'Kreuzzüge aus der Perspektive der Genderforschung. Zielsetzung und Forschungsansätze', *Das Mittelalter*, vol. 21, no. 1 (2016), pp. 1–18.

Bautier, R.H., 'La collection de chartes de croisades dite "Collection Courtois"', *Comptes rendus des séances de l'Académie des Inscriptions et Belles-Lettres*, vol. 100, no. 3 (1956), pp. 382–6.

Beattie, C., 'Married Women, Contracts and Coverture in Late Medieval England', in C. Beattie and M.F. Stevens (eds), *Married Women and the Law in Premodern Northwest Europe* (Woodbridge, 2013), pp. 133–54.

Beattie, C. and Stevens, M.F., 'Introduction: Uncovering Married Women', in C. Beattie and M.F. Stevens (eds), *Married Women and the Law in Premodern Northwest Europe* (Woodbridge, 2013), pp. 1–10.

Beattie, C., *Medieval Single Women: The Politics of Social Classification in Late Medieval England* (Oxford, 2007).

Beebe, B., 'The English Baronage and the Crusade of 1270', *Bulletin of the Institute of Historical Research*, vol. 48, no. 118 (1975), pp. 127–48.

Bell, S.G., 'Medieval Women Book Owners: Arbiters of Lay Piety and Ambassadors of Culture', *Journal of Women in Culture and Society*, vol. 7, no. 4 (1982), pp. 742–68.

Bibliography

Bennett, J.M. and Karras, R.M. (eds), *The Oxford Handbook of Women and Gender in Medieval Europe* (Oxford, 2013).

Bennett, S., *Elite Participation in the Third Crusade* (Woodbridge, 2021).

Berkhofer III, R.F., *Forgeries and Historical Writing in England, France, and Flanders, 900–1200* (Woodbridge, 2022).

Berman, C.H., 'Noble Women's Power as Reflected in the Foundations of Cistercian Houses for Nuns in Thirteenth-Century Northern France: Port-Royal, Les Clairets, Moncey, Lieu, and Eau-Les-Chartres', in K.A. Smith and S. Wells (eds), *Negotiating Community and Difference in Medieval Europe: Gender, Power, Patronage, and Authority of Religion in Latin Christendom* (Leiden, 2009), pp. 137–49.

Biancalana, J., 'Widows at Common Law: The Development of Common Law Dower', *Irish Jurist*, New Series vol. 23, no. 2 (1988), pp. 255–329.

Bibby, M.A., 'Alexander's Arabian: Noble Steed or Fantastic Beast?', in M.A. Bibby and B.G. Scott (eds), *The Materiality of the Horse* (Budapest, 2020), pp. 175–202.

Bijsterveld, A.J., *Do ut Des: Gift Giving, Memoria, and Conflict Management in the Medieval Low Countries* (Hilversum, 2007).

Binski, P., *The Painted Chamber at Westminster* (London, 1986).

Bird, J., '"Far be it from me to Glory Save in the Cross of our Lord Jesus Christ" (Galatians 6:14): Crusade Preaching and Sermons for Good Friday and Holy Week', in M.E. Parker, B. Halliburton and A. Romine (eds), *Crusading in Art, Thought and Will* (Leiden, 2018), pp. 129–65.

Bird, J., 'James of Vitry's Sermons to Pilgrims', *Essays in Medieval Studies*, vol. 25, no. 1 (2008), pp. 81–113.

Bird, J., 'Preaching and Crusading Memory', in M. Cassidy-Welch (ed.), *Remembering the Crusades and Crusading* (London, 2016), pp. 14–33.

Bloss, C.A., *Heroines of the Crusades*, Auburn (Alden, 1853).

Bolton, B.M., 'The Cistercians and the Aftermath of the Second Crusade', in M. Gervers (ed.), *The Second Crusade and the Cistercians* (New York, 1992), pp. 131–40.

Bom, M.M., *Women in the Military Orders of the Crusades* (New York, 2012).

Booth, T., 'The Massacres of the Jews under Richard I (A.D. 1189–1190)', *Religions*, vol. 12 (2021), pp. 1–11.

Bouchard, C.B., *Holy Entrepreneurs, Cistercians, Knights and Economic Exchange in Twelfth-Century Burgundy* (Ithaca, 1991).

Bouchard, C.B., 'Monastic Cartularies: Organizing Eternity', in A.J. Kosto and A. Winroth (eds), *Charters, Cartularies, and Archives: The Preservation and Transmission of Documents in the Medieval West* (Toronto, 2002), pp. 22–32.

Bouchard, C.B., *Rewriting Saints and Ancestors: Memory and Forgetting in France, 500–1200* (Philadelphia, 2015).

Bouchard, C.B., *Sword, Mitre, and Cloister: Nobility and the Church in Burgundy, 980–1198* (Ithaca, 1987).

Bibliography

Boulton, M., 'Introduction: Place and Space', in M. Boulton, J. Hawkes and H. Stoner (eds), *Place and Space in the Medieval World* (London, 2018), pp. xv–xxv.

Bowles, W.L., and Nichols, J.G., *Annals and Antiquities of Lacock Abbey in the County of Wilts; with Memorials of the Foundress Ela Countess of Salisbury, and of the Earls of Salisbury of the Houses of Sarisbury and Longespe* (London, 1835).

Brace, S., *et al*, 'Genomes from a Medieval Mass burial Show Ashkenazi-associated Hereditary Diseases pre-date the 12th century', *Current Biology*, vol. 32 (2022), pp. 1–10.

Bradley, S., and Pevsner, N., *London: The City Churches* (New York, 2002).

Brenner, E., Cohen, M., and Franklin-Brown, M. (eds), *Memory and Commemoration in Medieval Culture* (London, 2013).

Bresc-Bautier, G., 'Les imitations du Saint-Sépulcre de Jérusalem (IXe-XVe siècles): Archéologie d'une dévotion', *Revue d'histoire la spiritualité*, vol. 50, no. 1 (1974), pp. 319–42.

Britton, J., *The History and Antiquities of the Cathedral Church of Salisbury* (London, 1814).

Broun, D., 'The Presence of Witnesses and the Writing of Charters', in D. Broun (ed.), *The Reality Behind Charter Diplomatic in Anglo-Norman Britain* (Glasgow, 2011), pp. 235–90.

Brown, E.A.R., and Cothren, M.W., 'The Twelfth-Century Crusading Window of the Abbey of Saint-Denis: *Praeteritorum Enim Recordatio Futurorum est Exhibitio*', *Journal of the Warburg and Courtauld Institutes*, vol. 49 (1986), pp. 1–40.

Brown, S., *Sumptuous and Richly Adorn'd: The Decoration of Salisbury Cathedral* (London, 1999).

Brundage, J.A. '"*Cruce Signari*": The Rite for Taking the Cross in England', *Traditio*, vol. 22 (1960), pp. 289–310.

Brundage, J.A., 'Crusaders and Jurists: The Legal Consequences of Crusader Status', in A. Vauchez (ed.), *Le Concile de Clermont de 1095 et l'appel à la Croisade* (Rome, 1997), pp. 141–54.

Brundage, J.A., 'The Crusader's Wife: a Canonistic Quandary', *Studia Gratiana*, vol. 12 (1967), pp. 425–41.

Brundage, J.A., 'The Crusader's Wife Revisited', *Studia Gratiana*, vol. 14 (1967), pp. 243–51.

Brundage, J.A., 'Humbert of Romans and the Legitimacy of Crusader Conquests', in B.Z. Kedar (ed.), *The Horns of Hattin* (Jerusalem, 1992), pp. 302–13.

Brundage, J.A., *Medieval Canon Law and the Crusader* (Madison, 1969).

Brundage, J.A., 'Prostitution, Miscegenation and Sexual Purity in the First Crusade', in P.W. Edbury (ed.), *Crusade and Settlement, Papers Read at the First Conference of the Society for the Study of the Crusades and the Latin East and Presented to R.C. Smail* (Cardiff, 1985), pp. 57–65.

Bibliography

Brundage, J.A., 'Widows and Remarriage: Moral Conflicts and Their Resolution in Classical Canon Law', in Sue Sheridan Walker (ed.), *Wife and Widow in Medieval England* (Ann Arbor, 1993), pp. 17–31.

Bull, M., *Knightly Piety and the Lay Response to the First Crusade: The Limousin and Gascony, c. 970–1130* (Oxford, 1993).

Burton, J., *Monastic and Religious Orders in Britain, 1000–1300* (Cambridge, 1994).

Bynum, C.W., *Holy Feast and Holy Fast: The Religious Significance of Food to Medieval Women* (Berkeley, 1988).

Bysted, A.L., *The Crusade Indulgence: Spiritual Rewards and the Theology of the Crusades, c. 1095–1216* (Leiden, 2015).

Calkin, S.B., *Saracens and the Making of English Identity: The Auchinleck Manuscript* (New York and London, 2005).

Callan, M.B., 'Conquest as Crusade: Ireland's Invasion and a Colonial Plea to the Papacy', in E. Coleman, P. Duffy and T. O'Keeffe (eds), *Ireland and the Crusades* (Dublin, 2022), pp. 52–69.

Callan, M.B., *The Templars, The Witch, and the Wild Irish: Vengeance and Heresy in Medieval Ireland* (Ithaca, 2014).

Carpenter, D., 'The English Royal Chancery in the Thirteenth Century', in A. Jobson (ed.), *English Government in the Thirteenth Century* (Woodbridge, 2004), pp. 49–69.

Carraz, D., 'Mémoire lignagère et archives monastiques: les Bourbouton et la commanderie de Richerenches', in M. Aurell (ed.), *Convaincre et persuader: communication et propaganda aux XIIe et XIIIe siècles* (Poiters, 2007), pp. 465–502.

Cassidy-Welch, M., *Monastic Spaces and Their Meanings: Thirteenth-Century English Cistercian Monasteries* (Turnhout, 2001).

Cassidy-Welch, M., *War and Memory at the Time of the Fifth Crusade* (Pennsylvania, 2019).

Caspi-Reisfeld, K., 'Women Warriors During the Crusades, 1095–1254', in S. Edgington and S. Lambert (eds), *Gendering the Crusades* (Cardiff, 2001), pp. 94–107.

Catlos, B.A., *Muslims of Medieval Latin Christendom, c.1050–1614* (Boulder, 2014).

Cavell, E., 'The Burial of Noblewomen in Thirteenth-Century Shropshire', in B. Weiler, J. Burton, P. Schofield and K. Stöber (eds), *Thirteenth Century England XI: Proceedings of the Gregynog Conference 2005* (Woodbridge, 2007), pp. 174–92.

Cazel Jr., F.A., 'Financing the Crusades', in H.W. Hazard and N.P. Zacour (eds), *A History of the Crusades: Vol. VI, The Impact of the Crusades on Europe* (Madison, 1989), pp. 116- 49.

Chazan, R., *God, Humanity, and History: The Hebrew First Crusade Narratives* (Berkeley, 2000).

Bibliography

Chibnall, M., 'The Empress Matilda and Her Sons', in J.C. Parsons and B. Wheeler (eds), *Medieval Mothering* (New York, 1996), pp. 279–94.

Chrissis, N.G., 'A Diversion That Never Was: Thibaut IV of Champagne, Richard of Cornwall and Pope Gregory IX's Crusading Plans for Constantinople, 1235–1239', *Crusades*, vol. 9 (2010), pp. 123–45.

Christie, N., 'Fighting Women in the Crusading Period through Muslim Eyes', in N.R. Hodgson, K.J. Lewis and M.M. Mesley (eds), *Crusading and Masculinities* (London, 2019), pp. 183–95.

Churchton, T.T., 'Icklesham Church', *SAC*, vol. 32 (1882), pp. 105–22.

Clanchy, M.T., *From Memory to Written Record: England 1066 – 1307*, 2nd edn (Oxford, 1993).

Clark, E., 'Social Welfare and Mutual Aid in the Medieval Countryside', *Journal of British Studies*, vol. 33, no. 4 (1994), pp. 381–406.

Clark, E., 'Some Aspects of Social Security in Medieval England', *Journal of Family History*, vol. 7, no. 4 (1982), pp. 307–20.

Clark-Maxwell, W.G., 'The Earliest Charters of the Abbey of Lacock', in *The Wiltshire Archaeological and Natural History Magazine vol. 35, 1907–1908* (Devizes, 1908), pp. 191–209.

Claverie, P.V., *Honorius III et l'Orient (1216–1227)* (Leiden, 2013).

Clifford, E.R., *A Knight of Great Renown, The Life and Times of Othon de Grandson* (Chicago, 1961).

Coakley, J.W., *Women, Men, and Spiritual Power: Female Saints and their Male Collaborators* (New York, 2006).

Cobb, P.M., *The Race for Paradise, An Islamic History of the Crusades* (Oxford, 2014).

Cohen, J., *Sanctifying the Name of God: Jewish Martyrs and Jewish Memories of the First Crusade* (Philadelphia, 2004).

Coldsteam, N., 'The Tomb of Queen Eleanor in Westminster Abbey: An Evaluation of the Documentary Evidence', in H. Beck and K. Hengevoss-Dürkop (eds), *Studien zur Geschichte der europäischen Skulptur im 12./13. Jarhundert* (Frankfurt, 1994), pp. 101–8.

Cole, P.J., 'Humbert of Romans and the Crusade', in M. Bull and N. Housley (eds), *The Experience of Crusading: Volume 1, Western Approaches* (Cambridge, 2003), pp. 157–74.

Cole, P.J., *The Preaching of the Crusades to the Holy Land, 1095–1270* (Cambridge, 1991).

Collinson, J., *The History of Somersetshire*, 3 vols (London, 1791).

Colvin, H.M. (ed.), *The History of the King's Work*, 6 vols (London, 1963–82).

Constable, G., *Crusaders and Crusading in the Twelfth Century* (Farnham, 2008).

Constable, G., 'The Financing of the Crusade in the Twelfth Century', in B.Z. Kedar, H.E. Mayer and R.C. Smail (eds), *Outremer: Studies in the History of the Crusading Kingdom of Jerusalem* (Jerusalem, 1982), pp. 64–88.

Constable, G., 'The Historiography of the Crusades', in A.E. Laiou and R.T.

Mottahedeh (eds), *The Crusades from the Perspective of Byzantium and the Muslim World* (Washington DC, 2001), pp. 1–22.

Constable, G., 'Medieval Charters as a Source for the History of the Crusades', in P.W. Edbury (ed.), *Crusade and Settlement, Papers Read at the First Conference of the Society for the Study of the Crusades and the Latin East and Presented to R.C. Smail* (Cardiff, 1985), pp. 73–89.

Constable, G., 'The Second Crusade as Seen by Contemporaries', *Traditio*, vol. 9 (1953), pp. 213–79.

Coppack, G., 'The Round Chapel of St. Mary Magdalene', in R. Shoesmith and A. Johnson (eds), *Ludlow Castle: Its History & Buildings* (Logaston, 2000), pp. 145–54.

Cosgrove, W.R., '*Crucesignatus*: A Refinement or Merely One More Term among Many?', in T.F. Madden, J.L. Naus and V. Ryan (eds), *Crusades – Medieval Worlds in Conflict* (London, 2010), pp. 95–107

Coss, P., *The Foundations of Gentry Life: The Multons of Frampton and their World 1270–1370* (Oxford, 2010).

Coss, P., *The Lady in Medieval England 1000–1500* (Stroud, 1998).

Coss, P., *The Origins of the English Gentry* (Cambridge, 2003).

Cotts, J.D., 'The Exegesis of Violence in the Crusade Writings of Ralph Niger and Peter of Blois', in E. Lapina and N. Morton (eds), *The Uses of the Bible in Crusader Sources* (Leiden, 2017), pp. 273–95.

Crouch, D., *The Birth of Nobility: Constructing Aristocracy in England and France, 900–1300* (Harlow, 2005).

Crouch, D., *The English Aristocracy 1070–1272, a Social Transformation* (New Haven, 2011).

Curbet, J., 'Two-Faced Eloquence. A Brief Note Towards Re-Evaluating the Troubadour Crusade Corpus, 1187–1200', *Medievalia*, vol. 16 (2013), pp. 47–53.

Crouch, D., *William Marshal*, 3rd edn (Abingdon, 2016).

Daniell, C., *Death and Burial in Medieval England 1066–1550* (London, 1997).

Davies, R.R., *Domination and Conquest: The Experience of Ireland, Scotland and Wales, 1100–1300* (Cambridge, 1990).

Davis, G.R.C., *Medieval Cartularies of Great Britain and Ireland* (London, 2010).

Day, K., 'Sorrow, Masculinity and Papal Authority in the Writing of Pope Innocent III (1198–1216) and his *curia*', *Journal of Medieval History*, vol. 49, no. 2 (2023), pp. 201–26.

Dean, R.J., and Boulton, M.B.M., *Anglo-Norman Literature, A Guide to Texts and Manuscripts* (London, 1999).

DeAragon, R.C., 'Power and Agency in Post-Conquest England: Elite Women and the Transformations of the Twelfth Century', in H.J. Tanner (ed.), *Medieval Elite Women and the Exercise of Power, 1100–1400: Moving Beyond the Exceptionalist Debate* (New York, 2019), pp. 19–43.

Delisle, L., *Mémoire sur les Opérations Financières des Templiers* (Paris, 1889) (reprinted: Genève, 1975).

Bibliography

Derbes, A., 'A Crusading Fresco Cycle at the Cathedral of Le Puy', *The Art Bulletin*, vol. 73, no. 4 (1991), pp. 561–76.

Derbes, A., 'Crusading Ideology and the Frescoes of S. Maria in Cosmedin', *The Art Bulletin*, vol. 77, no. 3 (1995), pp. 460–78.

Dernbecher C., *Deus et virum suum diligens. Zur rolle und Bedeutung der Frau im Umfeld der Kreuzzüge* (St. Ingbert, 2003).

Díaz, E.C., 'Maria Balteira, a Woman Crusader to Outremer', in C.A. González-Pas (ed.), *Women and Pilgrimage in Medieval Galicia* (Farnham, 2015), pp. 67–80.

Dickson, G., *The Children's Crusade: Medieval History, Modern Mythistory* (Basingstoke, 2008).

Dijkstra, C., 'Troubadours, Trouvères and Crusade Lyrics', in A.H. Touber (ed.), *Le Rayonnement des troubadours: actes du colloque de l'AIEO, Association Internationale d'Etudes Occitanes, Amsterdam, 16–18 Octobre 1995* (Amsterdam, 1998), pp. 173–84.

Doherty, J., 'Count Hugh of Troyes and the Prestige of Jerusalem', *History*, vol. 102, no. 353 (2017), pp. 874–88.

Doherty, J., 'The Presentation of Crusader Masculinities in Old Norse Sagas', in N.R. Hodgson, K.J. Lewis and M.M. Mesley (eds), *Crusading and Masculinities* (London, 2019), pp. 129–46.

Doxey, G.B., 'Norwegian Crusaders and the Balearic Islands', *Scandinavian Studies*, vol. 68, no. 2 (1996), pp. 139–60.

Drell, J., 'Norman Italy and the Crusades, Thoughts on the "Homefront"', in K. Hurlock and P. Oldfield (eds), *Crusading and Pilgrimage in the Norman World* (Woodbridge, 2015), pp. 51–63.

Dressler, R.A., *Of Armor and Men in Medieval England, The Chivalric Rhetoric of Three English Knights' Effigies* (Aldershot, 2004).

Duffy, M., *Royal Tombs of Medieval England* (Stroud, 2003).

Duffy, P., O'Keefe, T., and Picard, J.M. (eds), *From Carrickfergus to Carcassonne: The Epic Deeds of Hugh de Lacy during the Albigensian Crusade* (Turnhout, 2017).

Duggan, A.J., '*Totius christianitatis caput.* The Pope and the Princes', in B. Bolton and A.J. Duggan (eds), *Adrian IV The English Pope (1154–1159)* (Aldershot, 2003), pp.105–55.

Dunn, C., *Stolen Women in Medieval England: Rape, Abduction, and Adultery, 1100–1500* (Cambridge, 2013).

Edbury, P.W., 'Preaching the Crusade in Wales', in A. Haverkamp and H. Vollrath (eds), *England and Germany in the High Middle Ages* (Oxford, 1996), pp. 221–33.

Edgington, S.B., 'A Female Physician on the Fourth Crusade? Laurette de Saint-Valéry', in N. Housley (ed.), *Knighthoods of Christ, Essays on the History of the Crusades and the Knights Templar, Presented to Malcolm Barber* (Aldershot, 2007), pp. 77–85.

Bibliography

Edgington, S., 'Pagan Peverel: An Anglo-Norman Crusader', in P.W. Edbury (ed.), *Crusade and Settlement, Papers Read at the First Conference of the Society for the Study of the Crusades and the Latin East and Presented to R.C. Smail* (Cardiff, 1985), pp. 90–3.

Edgington, S., and Lambert, S. (eds), *Gendering the Crusades* (Cardiff, 2001).

Edwards, D., *Finance and the Crusades: England, c.1213–1337* (Abingdon, 2022).

Elias, M., 'Violence, Excess, and the Composite Emotional Rhetoric of *Richard Coeur de Lion*', *Studies in Philology*, vol. 114, no. 1 (2017), pp. 1–38.

Ellis, R.H., *Catalogue of Seals in the Public Record Office, Personal Seals*, 2 vols (London, 1978).

Elwes, D.G.C., *The Family of de Braose, 1066–1326* (Exeter, 1883).

Epstein, S., *Wills and Wealth in Medieval Genoa, 1150–1250* (Cambridge, 1984).

Esra, J., 'Cornish Crusaders and Barbary Captives: Returns and Transformations', in M. Gibson, S. Trower and G. Tregidga (eds), *Mysticism, Myth and Celtic Identity* (Abingdon, 2013), pp. 155–70.

L'Estrange, E., 'Gazing at Gawain: Considering Tournaments, Courtly Love, and the Lady Who Looks', *Medieval Feminist Forum*, vol. 44, no. 2 (2008), pp. 74–96.

Evans, G.R., *Bernard of Clairvaux* (Oxford, 2000).

Evans, M.R., 'Commutation of Crusade Vows, Some Examples for the English Midlands', in A.V. Murray (ed.), *From Clermont to Jerusalem: The Crusades and Crusader Societies, 1095–1500* (Turnhout, 1998), pp. 219–28.

Evans, M.R., 'The Ferrers Earls of Derby and the Crusades', *Nottingham Medieval Studies*, vol. 44 (2000), pp. 69–81.

Evans, M.R., *Inventing Eleanor: The Medieval and Post-Medieval Image of Eleanor of Aquitaine* (London, 2014).

Farmer, S., 'Persuasive Voices: Clerical Images of Medieval Wives', *Speculum*, vol. 61, no. 3 (1986), pp. 517–54.

Fenster, T., and Smail, D.L., 'Conclusion' in T. Fenster and D.L. Smail (eds), *Fama: The Politics of Talk and Reputation in Medieval Europe* (Ithaca, 2003), pp. 210–4.

Finlayson, J., '"Richard, Coer de Lyon": Romance, History or Something in Between?', *Studies in Philology*, vol. 87, no. 2 (1990), pp. 156–80.

Finucane, R.C., *Soldiers of the Faith: Crusaders and Moslems at War* (London, 1983).

Flannery, J., 'The Trinitarian Order and the Ransom of Christian Captives', *Al-Masaq*, vol. 23, no. 2 (2011), pp. 135–44.

Folda, J., *Crusader Art in the Holy Land, From the Third Crusade to the Fall of Acre, 1187–1291* (Cambridge, 2005).

Forey, A., 'Otto of Grandson and the Holy Land, Cyprus and Armenia', *Crusades*, vol. 16 (2017), pp. 79–93.

Fort, G., 'Suffering Another's Sin: Proxy Penance in the Thirteenth Century', *Journal of Medieval History*, vol. 44, no. 2 (2018), pp. 202–30.

France, J., *The Crusades and the Expansion of Catholic Christendom, 1000–1714* (London and New York, 2005).
France, J., *Western Warfare in the Age of the Crusades, 1000–1300* (London, 1999) (reprinted: 2007).
French, K.L., 'Medieval Women's history: Sources and issues', in J.T. Rosenthal (ed.), *Understanding Medieval Primary Sources: Using Historical Sources to Discover Medieval Europe* (London, 2012), pp. 196–209.
French, K.L., *The People of the Parish: Community Life in a Late Medieval English Diocese* (Philadelphia, 2001).
Galvez, M., *The Subject of Crusade: Lyric, Romance and Materials, 1150–1500* (Chicago, 2020).
Gaposchkin, M.C., *Invisible Weapons: Liturgy and the Making of Crusade Ideology* (Ithaca, 2017).
Gaposchkin, M.C., 'The Liturgical Memory of July 15, 1099: Between History, Memory and Eschatology', in M. Cassidy-Welch (ed.), *Remembering the Crusades and Crusading* (London, 2016), pp. 34–48.
Gaposchkin, M.C., *The Making of Saint Louis: Kingship, Sanctity, and Crusade in the Later Middle Ages* (Ithaca, 2008).
Gaposchkin, M.C., 'The Pre-Battle Processions of the First Crusade and the Creation of Militant Christian *Communitas*', *Material Religion*, vol. 14, no. 4 (2018), pp. 454–68.
Guard, T., *Chivalry, Kingship and Crusade: The English Experience in the Fourteenth Century* (Woodbridge, 2013).
Geary, P.J., *Phantoms of Remembrance: Memory and Oblivion at the End of the First Millennium* (Princeton, 1994).
Gee, L.L., *Women, Art, and Patronage from Henry III to Edward III: 1216–1377* (Woodbridge, 2002).
Geldsetzer, S., *Frauen auf Kreuzzügen* (Darmstadt, 2003).
Gerish, D., 'Gender Theory', in H.J. Nicholson (ed.), *Palgrave Advances in the Crusades* (Basingstoke, 2005), pp. 130–47.
Gervers, M., 'Rotundae Anglicanae', in *Actes du XXII congrès International d'Histoire de l'Art, Budapest 1969: Évolution génerale et développements régionaux en histoire de l'art* (Budapest, 1972), pp. 359–76.
Gervers, M., 'The Use and Meaning of the Twelfth- and Thirteenth-Century Round Churches of England', in R. Griffith-Jones and E. Fernie (eds), *Tomb and Temple: Re-Imagining the Sacred Buildings of Jerusalem* (Woodbridge, 2018), pp. 376–86.
Gillingham, J., *Richard I* (New Haven and London, 2002).
Gilyard-Beer, R., 'Byland Abbey and the Grave of Roger de Mowbray', *The Yorkshire Archaeological Journal*, vol. 55 (1983), pp. 61–6.
Gittos, B., and Gittos, M. (eds), *Interpreting Medieval Effigies: A Regional Study in Archaeology and Potential, the Evidence from Yorkshire to 1400* (Oxford, 2019).

Bibliography

Giuseppi, M.S., 'XIX – On the Testament of Sir Hugh de Nevill Written at Acre, 1267', *Archaeologia*, vol. 56 (1899), pp. 351–70.

Glass, D.F., *Portals, Pilgrimage, and Crusade in Western Tuscany* (New Jersey, 1997).

Goldy, C.N., 'Muriel, a Jew of Oxford: Using the Dramatic to Understand the Mundane in Anglo-Norman Towns', in C.N. Goldy and A. Livingstone (eds), *Writing Medieval Women's Lives* (New York, 2012), pp. 227–45.

Gooder, E., *Temple Balsall, The Warwickshire Preceptory of the Templars and their Fate* (Chichester, 1995).

Greasley, N., 'Revisiting the Compilation of Matthew Paris's *Chronica majora*: New Textual and Manuscript Evidence', *Journal of Medieval History*, vol. 47 (2021), pp. 1–27.

Grimsey, P.B., 'The Grey-Friars Monastery, Ipswich', *Proceedings of the Suffolk Institute of Archaeology*, vol. 9, no. 3 (1897), pp. 373–8.

Guard, T., *Chivalry, Kingship and Crusade: The English Experience in the Fourteenth Century* (Woodbridge, 2013).

Guard, T., '*Opus caritatium*: Crowdfunding the Later Crusades, The English Evidence', in G.E.M. Lippiatt and J.L. Bird (eds), *Crusading Europe: Essays in Honour of Christopher Tyerman* (Turnhout, 2019), pp. 211–33.

Guyotjeannin, O., Pycke, J., and Tock, B.N., *Diplomatique médiévale* (Turnhout, 1993).

Haines, J., 'The Songbook for William of Villehardouin, Prince of the Morea (Paris, Bibliothèque nationale de France, fonds français 844): A Crucial Case in the History of Vernacular Song Collections', in S.E.J. Gerstel (ed.), *Viewing the Morea: Land and People in the Late Medieval Peloponnese* (Washington DC, 2013), pp. 57–109.

Hamilton, B., 'Eleanor of Castile and the Crusading Movement', *Mediterranean Historical Review*, vol. 10, nos. 1–2 (1995), pp. 92–103.

Hamilton, B., 'The Impact of Prester John on the Fifth Crusade', in E.J. Mylod, G. Perry, T. Smith and J. Vanderburie (eds), *The Fifth Crusade in Context* (London, 2016), pp. 53–67.

Harwood, S., *Medieval Women and War: Female Roles in the Old French Tradition* (London, 2020).

Hechelhammer, B., '*Frauen auf dem Kreuzzug*', in H.J. Kotzur, B. Klein and W. Wilhelmy (eds), *Die Kreuzzüge: Kein Krieg ist Heilig* (Mainz am Rhein, 2004), pp. 205–11.

Heller, S.G., 'Surprisingly Historical Women in the Old French Crusade Cycle', in S.S. Poor and J.K. Schulman (eds), *Women and Medieval Epic: Gender, Genre, and the Limits of Epic Masculinity* (Basingstoke, 2007), pp. 41- 66.

Helmholz, R.H., 'Bankruptcy and Probate Jurisdiction Before 1571', *Missouri Law Review*, vol. 48, no. 2 (1983), pp. 415–30.

de Hemptinne, T., 'Les épouses de croisés et pèlerins flamands aux XIe et XIIe siècles: l'example des comtesses de Flandre Clémence et Sibylle', in M. Balard

Bibliography

(ed.), *Autour de la Première Croisade: Actes du Colloque de la Society for the Study of the Crusades and the Latin East (Clermont-Ferrand, 22–25 juin 1995)* (Paris, 1996), pp. 83–95.

Herlihy, D., 'Land, Family and Women in Continental Europe, 701–1200', *Traditio*, vol. 18, no. 18 (1962), pp. 89–120.

Heyman, A., 'The Representation of the Holy Sepulchre in Auvergnat Romanesque Sculpture: a Reflection of Crusader Patrons?', in M. Balard (ed.), *Autour de la Première Croisade. Actes du Colloque de le Society for the Study of the Crusades and the Latin East* (Paris, 1996), pp. 632–42.

Hill, F., *Excommunication in Thirteenth-Century England: Communities, Politics, and Publicity* (Oxford, 2022).

Hodgson, N., 'Honour, Shame and the Fourth Crusade', *Journal of Medieval History*, vol. 39, no. 2 (2018), pp. 220–39.

Hodgson, N.R., *Women, Crusading and the Holy Land in Historical Narrative* (Woodbridge, 2007).

Holford, M., 'Family, Lineage and Society: Medieval Pedigrees of the Percy Family', *Nottingham Medieval Studies*, vol. 52 (2008), pp. 165–90.

Hooper, N., 'Edgar the Aetheling: Anglo-Saxon Prince, Rebel and Crusader', *Anglo-Saxon England*, vol. 14 (1985), pp. 197–214.

Hosler, J.D., 'Knightly Ideals at the Siege of Acre, 1189–1191', in D. Crouch and J. Deploige (eds), *Knighthood and Society in the High Middle Ages* (Leuven, 2020), pp. 145–66.

Hosler, J.D., *The Siege of Acre, 1189–1191: Saladin, Richard the Lionheart, and the Battle that Decided the Third Crusade* (New Haven, 2018).

Housley, N., *Contesting the Crusades* (Oxford, 2006).

Housley, N., 'Crusades Against Christians: Their Origins and Early Development, c.1000–1216', in P.W. Edbury (ed.), *Crusade and Settlement, Papers Read at the First Conference of the Society for the Study of the Crusades and the Latin East and Presented to R.C. Smail* (Cardiff, 1985), pp. 17–36.

Housley, N., *Fighting for the Cross: Crusading to the Holy Land* (New Haven, 2008).

Housley, N. (ed.), *Knighthoods of Christ, Essays on the History of the Crusades and the Knights Templar, Presented to Malcolm Barber* (Aldershot, 2007).

van Houts, E., *Memory and Gender in Medieval Europe, 900–1200* (Basingstoke, 1999).

Howell, M., 'The Problem of Women's Agency in Late Medieval and Early Modern Europe', in S.J. Moran and A.C. Pipkin (eds), *Women and Gender in the Early Modern Low Countries, 1500–1750* (Leiden, 2019), pp. 21–31.

Hudson, J., *The Oxford History of Laws in England: Volume II, 871–1216* (Oxford, 2012).

Hundley, C.E., 'The English Round Church Movement', in R. Griffith-Jones and E. Fernie (eds), *Tomb and Temple: Re-Imagining the Sacred Buildings of Jerusalem* (Woodbridge, 2018), pp. 352–75.

Bibliography

Hurlock, K., *Britain, Ireland and the Crusades, c. 1000–1300* (Basingstoke, 2013).
Hurlock, K., 'Cheshire and the Crusades', *Transactions of the Historic Society of Lancashire and Cheshire*, vol. 159, no. 1 (2010), pp. 1–18.
Hurlock, K., 'Power, Preaching and the Crusades in Pura Wallia c.1180-c.1280', in B. Weiler, J. Burton, P. Schofield and K. Stöber (eds), *Thirteenth Century England XI: Proceedings of the Gregynog Conference 2005* (Woodbridge, 2007), pp. 95–108.
Hurlock, K., 'A Transformed Life? Geoffrey of Dutton, the Fifth Crusade, and the Holy Cross of Norton', *Northern History*, vol. 54, no. 1 (2017), pp. 15–27.
Hurlock, K., *Wales and the Crusades, c.1095–1291* (Cardiff, 2011).
Hurlock, K., 'Welsh Pilgrims and Crusaders in the Middle Ages', in P. Skinner (ed.), *The Welsh and the Medieval World: Travel, Migration and Exile* (Cardiff, 2018), pp. 157–74.
Innes, M., 'Keeping it in the Family: Women and Aristocratic Memory, 700–1200', in E. van Houts (ed.), *Medieval Memories: Men, Women and the Past, 700–1300* (Abingdon, 2001, revised 2013), pp. 17–35.
Jackson, W.E., *Ardent Complaints and Equivocal Piety: The Portrayal of the Crusader in Medieval German Poetry* (Lanham, 2003).
Jackson, W.E., 'Poet, Woman, and Crusade in Songs of Marcabru, Guiot de Dijon, and Albrecht von Johansdorf', *Mediaevalia*, vol. 22, no. 2 (1999), pp. 265–89.
Jacoby, D., 'Cypriot Gold Thread in Late Medieval Silk Weaving and Embroidery', in S.B. Edgington and H.J. Nicholson (eds), *Deeds Done Beyond the Sea: Essays on William of Tyre, Cyprus and the Military Orders Presented to Peter Edbury* (Farnham, 2014), pp. 101–14.
Jamroziak, E., *Rievaulx Abbey and its Social Context, 1132–1300: Memory, Locality, and Networks* (Turnhout, 2005).
Johns, S.M., *Noblewomen, Aristocracy and Power in the Twelfth-Century Anglo-Norman Realm* (Manchester, 2003).
Jones, A.W., 'Fulk of Neuilly, Innocent III, and the Preaching of the Fourth Crusade', *Comitatus*, vol. 41 (2010), pp. 119–48.
Jordan, E.L., 'Exploring the Limits of Female Largesse: The Power of Female Patrons in Thirteenth-Century Flanders and Hainaut', in T. Earenfight (ed.), *Women and Wealth in Late Medieval Europe* (New York, 2010), pp. 149–69.
Jordan, E.L., *Women, Power and Religious Patronage in the Middle Ages* (New York, 2006).
Jordan, W.C., *The Apple of His Eye: Converts from Islam in the Reign of Louis IX* (Princeton, 2019).
Jordan, W.C., 'The Rituals of War: Departure for Crusade in Thirteenth-Century France', in W. Noel and D. Weiss (eds), *The Book of Kings: Art, War, and The Morgan Library's Medieval Picture Bible* (London, 2002), pp. 98–105.
Kaeuper, R.W., 'Exempla, Crusade, and Chivalry', in J.D. Hosler and S. Isaac (eds), *Military Cultures and Martial Enterprises in the Middle Ages: Essays in Honour of Richard P. Abels* (Woodbridge, 2020), pp. 211–22.

Bibliography

Katzenellenbogen, A., 'The Central Tympanum at Vézelay: Its Encyclopaedic Meaning and its Relation to the First Crusade', *The Art Bulletin*, vol. 26, no. 3 (1944), pp. 141–51.

Kaye, J.M., *Medieval English Conveyances* (Cambridge, 2009).

Kedar, B.Z. (ed.), *The Horns of Hattin* (Jerusalem, 1992).

Kedar, B.Z., 'The Passenger List of a Crusader Ship, 1250: Towards the History of the Popular Element on the Seventh Crusade', *Studi Medievali*, vol. 13, no. 1 (1972), pp. 267–79.

Kemp, B., 'Family Identity: The Seals of the Longespées', in P.R. Schofield (ed.), *Seals and their Context in the Middle Ages* (Oxford, 2015), pp. 137–50.

Kenaan-Kedar, N., and Kedar, B.Z., 'The Significance of a Twelfth-Century Sculptural Group: *Le Retour de Croisé*', in M. Balard, B.Z. Kedar and J. Riley-Smith (eds), *Dei Gesta per Francos: Etudes sur les croisades dédiées à Jean Richard, Crusade Studies in Honour of Jean Richard* (Aldershot, 2001), pp. 29–44.

Krötzl, C., 'Pilgrimage', in J. Glauser, P. Hermann and S.A. Mitchell (eds), *Handbook of Pre-Modern Nordic Memory Studies: Interdisciplinary Approaches* (Berlin, 2018), pp. 594–600.

Labarge, M.W., *A Medieval Miscellany* (Ottawa, 1997).

Lambert, É., *L'Architecture des Templiers* (Paris, 1978).

Lambert, S., 'Crusading or Spinning', in S. Edgington and S. Lambert (eds), *Gendering the Crusades* (Cardiff, 2001), pp. 1–15.

Lankester, P.J., 'The Thirteenth-Century Military Effigies in the Temple Church', in R. Griffith-Jones and D. Park (eds), *The Temple Church in London: History, Architecture, Art* (Woodbridge, 2010), pp. 93–134.

Lapina, E., 'Crusades, Memory and Visual Culture: Representations of the Miracle of Intervention of Saints in Battle', in M. Cassidy-Welch (ed.), *Remembering the Crusades and Crusading* (London, 2016), pp. 49–72.

Lapina, E., 'The Mural Paintings of Berzé-la-Ville in the Context of the First Crusade and the *Reconquista*', *Journal of Medieval History*, vol. 31, no. 4 (2005), pp. 309–26.

Lapina, E., *Warfare and the Miraculous in the chronicles of the First Crusade* (Philadelphia, 2015).

Lawrence, C.H., *The Friars: The Impact of the Early Mendicant Movement on Western Society*, 2nd edn (London and New York, 2013).

Lawrence, C.H. (ed.), *The Life of St Edmund by Matthew Paris* (Stroud, 1996; repr. 1999).

Legge, M.D., *Anglo-Norman in the Cloisters: The Influence of the Orders upon Anglo-Norman Literature* (Edinburgh, 1950).

Lester, A.E., 'A Shared Imitation: Cistercian Convents and Crusader Families in Thirteenth-Century Champagne', *Journal of Medieval History*, vol. 34, no. 4 (2009), pp. 353–70.

Lester, A.E., 'Remembrance of Things Past: Memory and Material Objects in the

Bibliography

Time of the Crusades, 1095–1291', in M. Cassidy-Welch (ed.), *Remembering the Crusades and Crusading* (London, 2016), pp. 73–94.

Lester, A.E., 'What Remains: Women, Relics, and Remembrance in the Aftermath of the Fourth Crusade', *Journal of Medieval History*, vol. 40, no. 3 (2014), pp. 311–28.

Lethaby, W.R., 'Master Walter of Durham, King's Painter c. 1230–1305', *Burlington Magazine*, vol. 33, no. 184 (1918), pp. 3–8.

Leyser, H., *Medieval Women: a Social History of Women in England 450–1500* (London, 1996).

Libertini, C., 'Practical Crusading: The Transformation of Crusading Practice 1095–1221', in M. Balard (ed.), *Autour de le Première Croisade. Actes du Colloque de le Society for the Study of the Crusades and the Latin East* (Paris, 1996), pp. 281–91.

Linder, A., *Raising Arms: Liturgy in the Struggle to Liberate Jerusalem in the Late Middle Ages* (Turnhout, 2003).

Livingstone, A., *Out of Love for my Kin: Aristocratic Family Life in the Lands of the Loire, 1000–1200* (Ithaca, 2010).

Lloyd, S., *English Society and the Crusade, 1216–1307* (Oxford, 1988).

Lloyd, S., 'The Lord Edward's Crusade, 1270–2: its setting and significance', in J. Gillingham and J.C. Holt (eds), *War and Government in the Middle Ages* (Woodbridge, 1984), pp. 120–33.

Lloyd, S., '"Political Crusades" in England, c.1215–17 and c.1263–5', in P.W. Edbury (ed.), *Crusade and Settlement, Papers Read at the First Conference of the Society for the Study of the Crusades and the Latin East and Presented to R.C. Smail* (Cardiff, 1985), pp. 113–20.

Lloyd, S., 'William Longespee II: The Making of an English Hero – Part I', *Nottingham Medieval Studies*, vol. 35 (1991), pp. 41–69.

Lloyd, S. and Hunt, T., 'William Longespee II: The Making of an English Crusading Hero, Part II', *Nottingham Medieval Studies*, vol. 36 (1992), pp. 79–125.

Loengard, J., 'What is a Nice (Thirteenth-Century) English Woman Doing in the King's Courts?', in L.E. Mitchell, K.L. French and D.L. Biggs (eds), *The Ties that Bind: Essays in Medieval British History in Honor of Barbara Hanawalt* (Oxford, 2011), pp. 57–70.

Lomas, R., *A Power in the Land: the Percys* (Phantassie, 1999).

Loomis, R.S., 'Richard Cœur de Lion and the *Pas Saladin* in Medieval Art', *PMLA*, vol. 30, no. 3 (1915), pp. 509–28.

LoPrete, K.A., *Adela of Blois, Countess and Lord (c.1067–1137)* (Dublin, 2007).

Lower, M., *The Barons' Crusade, A Call to Arms and its Consequences* (Philadelphia, 2005).

Lower, M., *The Tunis Crusade of 1270: A Mediterranean History* (Oxford, 2018).

Lunt, W.E., *Financial Relations of the Papacy with England to 1327* (Cambridge, 1939).

Bibliography

Luttrell, A., 'English Levantine Crusaders, 1363–1367', *Renaissance Studies*, vol. 2, no. 1 (1988), pp. 143–53.

Luttrell, A. and Nicholson, H.J. (eds), *Hospitaller Women in the Middle Ages* (Aldershot, 2006).

Luyster, A., *The Chertsey Tiles, the Crusades, and Global Textile Motifs* (Cambridge, 2023).

Luyster, A., 'Fragmented Tile, Fragmented Text: Richard the Lionheart on Crusade and the Lost Latin Texts of the Chertsey Combat Tiles (c.1250)', *Digital Philology*, vol. 11, no. 1 (2022), pp. 86–120.

MacEvit, C., 'Processing Together, Celebrating Apart: Shared Procession in the Latin East', *Journal of Medieval History*, vol. 43, no. 4 (2017), pp. 455–69.

MacLellan, R., 'An Egyptian Jew in King Edward's Court: Jewish Conversion, Edward II, and Roger de Stanegrave', *Crusades*, vol. 19 (2020), pp. 143–53.

MacLellan, R., *Donations to the Knights Hospitaller in Britain and Ireland, 1291–1400* (London and New York, 2021).

MacQuarrie, A., *Scotland and the Crusades, 1095–1560* (Edinburgh, 1985).

Maddicott, J.R., *Simon de Montfort* (Cambridge, 1994).

Maier, C.T., 'The Bible Moralisée and the Crusades', in M. Bull and N. Housley (eds), *The Experience of Crusading, Volume One, Western Approaches* (Cambridge, 2003), pp. 209–22.

Maier, C.T., 'Crisis, Liturgy and Crusade in the Twelfth and Thirteenth Centuries', *Journal of Ecclesiastical History*, vol. 48, no. 4 (1997), pp. 628–57.

Maier, C.T., *Crusade Propaganda and Ideology, Model Sermons for the Preaching of the Cross* (Cambridge, 2000).

Maier, C.T., 'Mass, the Eucharist and the Cross: Innocent III and the Relocation of the Crusade', in J.C. Moore (ed.), *Pope Innocent III and His World* (Aldershot, 1999), pp. 351–60.

Maier, C.T., 'Papal Crusade Propaganda and Attacks Against Jews in France in the 1230s: a Breakdown of Communication?', *Journal of Medieval History*, vol. 49, no. 3 (2023), pp. 339–52.

Maier, C.T., *Preaching the Crusades: Mendicant Friars and the Cross in the thirteenth Century* (Cambridge, 1994).

Maier, C.T., 'Propaganda and Masculinity: Gendering the Crusades in Thirteenth-Century Sermons', in N.R. Hodgson, K.J. Lewis and M.M. Mesley (eds), *Crusading and Masculinities* (London, 2019), pp. 21–35.

Maier, C.T., 'The Roles of Women in the Crusade Movement: a Survey', *Journal of Medieval History*, vol. 30, no. 1 (2004), pp. 61–82.

Manion, L., 'The Crusading Romance in Britain: Religious Violence and the Transformation of Popular Chivalric Narratives', in R.L. Krueger (ed.), *A New Cambridge Companion to Medieval Romance* (Cambridge, 2023), pp. 101–18.

Marcombe, D., *Leper Knights: The Order of St Lazarus of Jerusalem in England, 1150–1544* (Woodbridge, 2003).

Markowski, M., '*Crucesignatus*: Its Origins and Early Usage', *Journal of Medieval History*, vol. 10, no. 3 (1984), pp. 157–65.

Markus, M., 'St Bride's, Douglas – A Family Mausoleum', *Proc Soc Antiq Scot*, vol. 134 (2004), pp. 403–21.

Marx, A., 'The *Passio Raginaldi* of Peter of Blois: Martyrdom and Eschatology in the Preaching of the Third Crusade', *Viator*, vol. 50, no. 3 (2019), pp. 197–232.

Mason, E., 'Fact and Fiction in the English Crusading Tradition: The Earls of Warwick in the Twelfth Century', *Journal of Medieval History*, vol. 14, no. 2 (1988), pp. 81–95.

Mazeika, R., '"Nowhere was the Fragility of their Sex Apparent" Women Warriors in the Baltic Crusade Chronicles', in A.V. Murray (ed.), *From Clermont to Jerusalem: The Crusades and Crusader Societies 1095–1500* (Turnhout, 1998), pp. 229–48.

McCash, J.H., 'The Cultural Patronage of Medieval Women: an Overview', in J.H. McCash (ed.), *The Cultural Patronage of Medieval Women* (Athens, 1996).

McCormick, M., 'The Liturgy of War in the Early Middle Ages: Crisis, Litanies, and the Carolingian Monarchy', *Viator*, vol. 15 (1984), pp. 1–24.

McGrath, K., 'The "Zeal of God": The Representation of Anger in the Latin Crusade Accounts of the 1096 Rhineland Massacres', in K.T. Utterback and M.L. Price (eds), *Jews in Medieval Christendom: Slay Them Not* (Leiden, 2013), pp. 25–44.

McLaughlin, M., 'Looking for Medieval Women: An Interim Report on the Project "Women's Religious Life and Communities, A.D. 500–1500"', *Medieval Prosopography*, vol. 8, no. 1 (1987), pp. 61–91.

McLaughlin, M., 'The Woman Warrior: Gender, Warfare and Society in Medieval Europe', *Women's Studies*, vol. 17, no. 1 (1990), pp. 193–209.

McLennan, G., *Women Crusaders: Women and the Holy Land 1095–1195* (Hawker, 1997).

Menache, S., *Clement V* (Cambridge, 1998) (reprinted: 2002).

Metcalf, D.M., 'The Templars as bankers and monetary transfers between West and East in the twelfth century', in P.W. Edbury and D.M. Metcalf (eds), *Coinage in the Latin East, The Fourth Oxford Symposium on Coinage and Monetary History* (Oxford, 1980), pp. 1–17.

Mitchell, L.E., 'The Lady is a Lord: Noble Widows and Land in Thirteenth-Century Britain', *Historical Reflections*, vol. 18, no. 1 (1992), pp. 71–97.

Mitchell, L.E., 'The Most Perfect Knight's Countess: Isabella de Clare, Her Daughters, and Women's Exercise of Power and Influence, 1190- ca.1250', in H.J. Tanner (ed.), *Medieval Elite Women and the Exercise of Power, 1100–1400: Moving Beyond the Exceptionalist Debate* (New York, 2019), pp. 45–65.

Mitchell, L.E., *Portraits of Medieval Women: Family, Marriage, and Politics in England 1225–1350* (New York, 2003).

Mitchell, P.D., Nagar, Y., and Ellenblum, R., 'Weapon Injuries in the 12th Century

Crusader Garrison of Vadum Iacob Castle, Galilee', *International Journal of Osteoarchaeology*, vol. 16 (2006), pp. 145–55.

Moore, J.S., 'Who was "Mahumet"? Arabs in Angevin England', *Prosopon*, vol. 11 (2000), pp. 1–7.

Morris, C., 'Martyrs on the Field of Battle Before and During the First Crusade', in D. Wood (ed.), *Martyrs and Martyrologies* (Oxford, 1993), pp. 93–104.

Morris, C., 'Picturing the Crusades: The Uses of Visual Propaganda, c. 1095–1250', in J. France and W.G. Zajac (eds), *The Crusades and Their Sources, Essays Presented to Bernard Hamilton* (Aldershot, 1998) (reprinted: Abingdon, 2016), pp. 195–215.

Morris, C., *The Sepulchre of Christ and the Medieval West* (Oxford, 2005).

Morris, C.D., 'Viking Orkney: A Survey', in C. Renfrew (ed.), *The Prehistory of Orkney* (Edinburgh, 1985), pp. 210–42.

Morris, J.E., *The Welsh Wars of Edward I* (Oxford, 1901) (reprinted: Guernsey, 1998).

Morton, N., 'The Defence of the Holy Land and the Memory of the Maccabees', *Journal of Medieval History*, vol. 36 (2010), pp. 275–93.

Morton, N., *Encountering Islam on the First Crusade* (Cambridge, 2016).

Morton, N., *The Mongol Storm: Making and Breaking Empires in the Medieval Near East* (New York, 2022).

Mulder-Bakker, A.B., King, M.H., Feiss, H., Bolton, B., and Folkerts, S. (eds and trans.), *Mary of Oignies, Mother of Salvation* (Turnhout, 2006).

Murray, A.V., 'Finance and Logistics of the Crusade of Frederick Barbarossa', in I. Shagrir, R. Ellenblum and J. Riley-Smith (eds), *In Laudem Hierosolymitani, Studies in Crusades and Medieval Culture in Honour of Benjamin Z. Kedar* (Aldershot, 2007), pp. 357–68.

Murray, A.V., 'Friedrich von Hausen on the Third Crusade and the Performance of Middle High German Crusading Songs', in S. John and N. Morton (eds), *Crusading and Warfare in the Middle Ages, Realities and Representations, Essays in Honour of John France* (Farnham, 2014), pp. 119–28.

Murray, A.V., 'The Middle Ground: The Passage of Crusade Armies to the Holy Land by Land and Sea, 1096–1204', in G. Theotokis and A. Yildiz (eds), *A Military History of the Mediterranean Sea: Aspects of War, Diplomacy and Military Elites* (Leiden, 2018), pp. 185–201.

Murray, A.V., 'Money and Logistics in the forces of the First Crusade: Coinage, Bullion, Service and Supply, 1096–99', in J.H. Pryor (ed.), *Logistics of Warfare in the Age of the Crusades* (Aldershot, 2006), pp. 229–50.

Murray, A.V., 'Roads, Bridges and Shipping in the Passage of Crusade Armies by Overland Routes to the Bosporus 1096–1190', in K. Holzner-Tobisch, T. Kühtreiber and G. Blaschitz (eds), *Die Vielschichtigkeit der Straße: Kontinuität und Wandel in Mittelalter und Früher Neuzeit* (Vienna, 2012), vol. 826, pp. 183–207.

Murray, A.V., 'Warriors and Civilians in the Crusade Movement. Military Identities

Bibliography

and Status in the Liberation and Defence of the Holy Land (1096–1204)', *Millars: Espai I Historia*, vol. 43, no. 2 (2017), pp. 97–127.

Murray, J., 'Individualism and Consensual Marriage: Some Evidence from Medieval England', in C.M. Rousseau and J.T. Rosenthal (eds), *Women, Marriage and Family in Medieval Christendom, Essays in Memory of Michael M. Sheehan, C.S.B.* (Kalamazoo, 1998), pp. 125–37.

Naus, J., *Constructing Kingship: The Capetian Monarchs of France and the Early Crusades* (Manchester, 2016).

Ng, J., 'Women of the Crusades: The Constructedness of the Female Other, 1100–1200', *Al-Masāq*, vol. 31, no. 3 (2019), pp. 303–22.

Nicholson, H.J., 'At the Heart of Medieval London: The New Temple in the Middle Ages', in R. Griffith-Jones and D. Park (eds), *The Temple Church in London: History, Architecture, Art* (Woodbridge, 2010), pp. 1–18.

Nicholson, H.J., *The Everyday Life of the Templars: The Knights Templar at Home* (Fonthill, 2017).

Nicholson, H.J., 'The Head of St. Euphemia: Templar Devotion to Female Saints', in S. Edgington and S. Lambert (eds), *Gendering the Crusades* (Cardiff, 2001), pp. 108–20.

Nicholson, H.J., 'How Secret was the Templar Admission Ceremony? Evidence from the Proceedings in Britain and Ireland', in S. Sammarco (ed.), *Commilitones Christi: Miscellanea di studi per il Centro Italiano di Documentazione sull'Ordine del Tempio, MMXI-MMXVI* (Rome, 2016), pp. 85–98.

Nicholson, H.J, *The Knights Templar, a New History* (Stroud, 2001) (reprinted: 2002).

Nicholson, H.J., 'Margaret de Lacy and the Hospital of St John of Aconbury, Herefordshire', *Journal of Ecclesiastical History*, vol. 50, no. 4 (1999), pp. 629–51.

Nicholson, H.J., 'The Military Religious Orders in the Towns of the British Isles', in D. Carraz (ed.), *Les Orderes Militaires dans la Ville Médiévale (1100–1350)* (Clermont-Ferrand, 2013), pp. 113–26.

Nicholson, H.J., 'Relations between Houses of the Order of the Temple in Britain and their Local Communities, as Indicated during the Trial of the Templars, 1307–12', in N. Housley (ed.), *Knighthoods of Christ, Essays on the History of the Crusades and the Knights Templar, Presented to Malcolm Barber* (Aldershot, 2007), pp. 195–207.

Nicholson, H.J, *Templars, Hospitallers and Teutonic Knights, Images of the Military Orders, 1128–1291* (Leicester, 1993).

Nicholson, H.J., *Women and the Crusades* (Oxford, 2023).

Nicholson, H.J., 'Women's Involvement in the Crusades', in A. Boas (ed.), *The Crusader World* (London, 2016), pp. 54–67.

Nicholson, H.J., 'Women on the Third Crusade', *Journal of Medieval History*, vol. 23, no. 4 (1997), pp. 335–49.

Nicholson, H.J., 'Women's Writing and Cultural Patronage', in A. Bale (ed.),

Bibliography

The Cambridge Companion to the Literature of the Crusades (Cambridge, 2019), pp. 72–84.
Norman, J.S., *Metamorphoses of an Allegory: The Iconography of the Psychomachia in Medieval Art* (New York, 1988).
Orme, N., and Padel, O.J., 'Cornwall and the Third Crusade', *Journal of the Royal Institution of Cornwall* (2005), pp. 71–7.
Ousterhout, R.G., 'The Church of Santo Stefano: A "Jerusalem" in Bologna', *Gesta*, vol. 20, no. 2 (1981), pp. 311–21.
Owens, C., 'Noblewomen and Political Activity', in L.E. Mitchell (ed.), *Women in Medieval Western European Culture* (London, 1999), pp. 209–19.
Paetow, L.J., 'The Crusading Ardour of John of Garland', in L.J. Paetow (ed.), *The Crusades and Other Historical Essays Presented to Dana C. Munro by his Former Students* (New York, 1928) (reprinted: 1968) pp. 207–22.
Park, D., 'Medieval Burials and Monuments', in R. Griffith-Jones and D. Park (eds), *The Temple Church in London: History, Architecture, Art* (Woodbridge, 2010), pp. 67–91.
Park, D., 'The Wall Paintings of the Holy Sepulchre Chapel', in T.A. Heslop and V.A. Sekules (eds), *Medieval Art and Architecture at Winchester Cathedral* (Leeds, 1983), pp. 38–62.
Park, D.E.A., *Papal Protection and the Crusader: Flanders, Champagne, and the Kingdom of France 1095–1222* (Woodbridge, 2018).
Park, D.E.A., 'The Power of Crusaders' Wives in Narrative and Diplomatic Sources, c.1096–1149', *The Reading Medievalist*, vol. 1, no. 2 (2014), pp. 18–31.
Parker, M.E., '*Papa et pecunia:* Innocent III's Combination of Reform and Fiscal Policy to Finance the Crusades', *Mediterranean Historical Review*, vol. 32, no. 1 (2017), pp. 1–23.
Parker, T.W., *The Knights Templars in England* (Tucson, 1963).
Parsons, J.C., *Eleanor of Castile: Queen and Society in Thirteenth-Century England* (New York, 1995).
Parsons, S.T. 'The Inhabitants of the British Isles on the First Crusade: Medieval Perceptions and the Invention of a Pan-Angevin Crusading Heritage', *English Historical Review*, vol. 134 (2019), pp. 273–301.
Parsons, S.T., 'The Letters of Stephen of Blois Reconsidered', *Crusades*, vol. 17 (2018), pp. 1–29.
Paterson, L., *Singing the Crusades: French and Occitan Lyric Responses to the Crusading Movements, 1137–1336* (Cambridge, 2018).
Paul, N.L, and Schenk, J.G., 'Family Memory and the Crusades', in M. Cassidy-Welch (ed.), *Remembering the Crusades and Crusading* (London, 2016), pp. 173–86.
Paul, N.L., *To Follow in Their Footsteps: The Crusades and Family Memory in the High Middle Ages* (Ithaca, 2012).
Paul, N.L., 'Writing the Knight, Staging the Crusade: Manasses of Hierges and

the Monks of Brogne', in D. Crouch and J. Deploige (eds), *Knighthood and Society in the High Middle Ages* (Leuven, 2020), pp. 167–92.

Paviot, J., 'Burgundy and the Crusade', in N. Housley (ed.), *Crusading in the Fifteenth Century* (Basingstoke, 2004), pp. 70–80.

Pernoud, R., *Femme au temps des Croisades* (Paris, 1990).

Perry, G., *The Briennes: The Rise and Fall of a Champenois Dynasty in the Age of the Crusades, c.950–1356* (Cambridge, 2018).

Pfaff, R.W., *The Liturgy in Medieval England, A History* (Cambridge, 2009).

Phair, R.W., 'William Longespée, Ralph Bigod, and Countess Ida', *The American Genealogist*, vol. 77, no. 308 (2002), pp. 279–81.

Phillips, J., *The Life and Legend of the Sultan Saladin* (London, 2019).

Phillips, J., *The Second Crusade: Extending the Frontiers of Christendom* (London and New Haven, 2007).

Philips, S., 'The Hospitallers' Acquisition of the Templar Lands in England', in H. Nicholson, P.F. Crawford and J. Burgtorf (eds), *The Debate on the Trial of the Templars (1307–1314)* (Farnham, 2010), pp. 233–42.

Pickvance, C.G., 'The Canterbury Group of Arcaded Gothic Early Medieval Chests: A Dendrochronological and Comparative Study', *The Antiquaries Journal*, vol. 98 (2018), pp. 149–85.

Pickvance, C.G., 'The St. Mary's, Climping and Chichester Cathedral medieval chests: a dendrochronological and comparative study', *SAC*, vol. 157 (2019), pp. 173–87.

Pollock, F., and Maitland, F.W., *The History of English Law Before the Time of Edward I*, 2 vols (Cambridge, 1898).

Powell, J.M., *Anatomy of a Crusade, 1213–1221* (Philadelphia, 1986).

Powell, J.M., *The Crusades, The Kingdom of Sicily, and The Mediterranean* (Farnham, 2007).

Powell, J.M., 'Preface', in S. Edgington and S. Lambert (eds), *Gendering the Crusades* (Cardiff, 2001), pp. vii–ix.

Powell, J.M., 'The Role of Women in the Fifth Crusade', in B.Z. Kedar (ed.), *The Horns of Hattīn* (Jerusalem, 1992), pp. 294–313.

Power, D., *The Norman Frontier in the Twelfth and Early Thirteenth Centuries* (Cambridge, 2004).

Power, D., 'The Preparations of Count John I of Sées for the Third Crusade', in S. John and N. Morton (eds), *Crusading and Warfare in the Middle Ages, Realities and Representations: Essays in Honour of John France* (Farnham, 2014), pp. 143–66.

Power, D., 'Who Went on the Albigensian Crusade?', *English Historical Review*, vol. 128, no. 534 (2013), pp. 1047–85.

Powicke, F.M., 'The Saracen Mercenaries of Richard I', *Scottish Historical Review*, vol. 8, no. 9 (1910), pp. 104–5.

Prawer, J., *The Crusaders' Kingdom: European Colonialism in the Middle Ages* (London, 1972) (reprinted: 2001).

Bibliography

Prestwich, M., *Edward I* (New Haven, 1988) (reprinted: 1997).

Pridgeon, E., and Sharp, S., 'Patronage and Function: The Medieval Wall Paintings at Lacock Abbey in Wiltshire', *The Journal of Medieval Monastic Studies*, vol. 5 (2016), pp. 113–37.

Pringle, D., *The Churches of the Crusader Kingdom of Jerusalem, A Corpus*, 4 vols (Cambridge, 1993–2009).

Pringle, D., 'The Order of St Thomas of Canterbury in Acre', in P.W. Edbury (ed.), *The Military Orders, Vol. 5: Politics and Power* (Farnham, 2012), pp. 75–82.

Pugh, R.B., and Crittall, E. (eds), *A History of Wiltshire* (Oxford, 1956), vol. 3.

Purcell, M., *Papal Crusading Policy, 1244–1291* (Leiden, 1975).

Purcell, M., 'Women Crusaders: a Temporary Canonical Aberration?', in L.O. Frappell (ed.), *Principalities, Powers and Estates: Studies in Medieval and Early Modern Government and Society* (Adelaide, 1979), pp. 57–64.

Radaelli, A., '"*Voil ma chançun a la gent fere oïr*", An Anglo-Norman Crusade Appeal (London, BL Harley 1717, fol. 251^v)', in S.T. Parsons and L.M. Paterson (eds), *Literature of the Crusades* (Woodbridge, 2018), pp. 109–33.

Raimes, A.L., 'The Family of Reymes of Wherstead in Suffolk', *Suffolk Institute of Archaeology and Natural History*, vol. 23 (1939), pp. 89–115.

Ramsey, L., 'Orientalism and the "Saracen"', in A. Bale (ed.), *The Cambridge Companion to the Literature of the Crusades* (Cambridge, 2019), pp.136–45.

Ray, M., 'A Black Slave on the Run in Thirteenth-Century England', *Nottingham Medieval Studies*, vol. 51 (2007), pp. 111–20.

Razi, Z., and Smith, R.M., 'The Origins of the English Manorial Court as a Written Record: A Puzzle', in Z. Razi and R.M. Smith (eds), *Medieval Society and the Manor Court* (Oxford, 1996), pp. 36–68.

RCHM, *An Inventory of the Historical Monuments in the County of Northampton, Vol. 5, Archaeological Sites and churches in Northampton* (London, 1985).

Reader, R., 'Matthew Paris and Women', in M. Prestwich, R. Britnell and R. Frame (eds), *Thirteenth Century England VII* (Woodbridge, 1999), pp. 153–9.

Reed, P.C., 'Countess Ida, Mother of William Longespée, Illegitimate son of Henry II', *The American Genealogist*, vol. 77, no. 306 (2002), pp. 137–49.

Reeve, M.M., 'The Painted Chamber at Westminster, Edward I, and the Crusade', *Viator*, vol. 37 (2006), pp. 189–221.

Reynolds, B.W., 'The Prehistory of the Crusades: Toward a Developmental Taxonomy', *History Compass*, vol. 6, no. 3 (2008), pp. 884–97.

Reynolds, G.M., 'A Paragon of Support? Ela of Salisbury, Martyrdom, and the Ideals of Sponsoring Crusade', *Crusades*, vol. 20 (2021), pp. 247–66.

Reynolds, G.M., 'Asking for Forgiveness as an Aspect of Crusade: Case Studies from 13th-century Scotland', *Proc Soc Antiq Scot*, vol. 152 (2023), pp. 135–46.

Reynolds, G.M., 'Battling the Lion: Visual Commemorations of Crusade in Twelfth- and Thirteenth-Century Seals from the British Isles', *The Antiquaries Journal*, vol. 103 (2023), pp. 240–62.

Reynolds, G.M., 'Proxy over Pilgrimage: Queen Eleanor of Castile and the

Celebration of Crusade upon her Funerary Monument(s)', *Peregrinations*, vol. 8, no. 4 (2023), pp. 117–39.

Richardson, D., *Plantagenet Ancestry: A Study in Colonial and Medieval Families*, 2nd edn (Salt Lake City, 2011).

Richardson, H.G., and Sayles, G.O., *The Governance of Mediaeval England, from the Conquest to Magna Carta* (Edinburgh, 1963).

Ricketts, P., *High-Ranking Widows in Medieval Iceland and Yorkshire: Property, Power, Marriage and Identity in the Twelfth and Thirteenth Centuries* (Leiden, 2010).

Riley-Smith, J., 'Early Crusaders to the East and the Costs of Crusading 1095–1130', in M. Goodich, S. Menanche and S. Schein (eds), *Cross Cultural Convergences in the Crusader Period, Essays Presented to Aryeh Grabois on his Sixty-Fifth Birthday* (New York, 1995), pp. 237–57.

Riley-Smith, J., 'Family Traditions and Participation in the Second Crusade', in M. Gervers (ed.), *The Second Crusade and the Cistercians* (New York, 1992), pp. 101–8.

Riley-Smith, J., *The First Crusade and the Idea of Crusading* (London, 1993) (reprinted: London, 2003).

Riley-Smith, J., 'Frauen auf Kreuzzügen, 1096–1291, by Sabine Geldsetzer', *The English Historical Review*, vol. 119, no. 484 (2004), pp. 1386–7.

Riley-Smith, J., *The First Crusaders, 1095–1131* (Cambridge, 1997).

Riley-Smith, J., *Hospitallers: The History of the Order of St John* (London, 1999).

Riley-Smith, J., *The Knights Hospitaller in the Levant, c.1070–1309* (Basingstoke, 2012).

Riley-Smith, J., 'The Idea of Crusading in the Charters of Early Crusaders, 1095–1102', in A. Vauchez (ed.), *Le Concile de Clermont de 1095 et l'appel à la Croisade* (Rome, 1997), pp. 155–66.

Riley-Smith, J. (ed.), *The Oxford Illustrated History of the Crusades* (Oxford, 1995) (reprinted: 2001).

Riley-Smith, J., and Throop, S.A., *The Crusades: A History*, 4th edn (London, 2023).

Ritoók, P., 'The Architecture of the Knights Templars in England', in M. Barber (ed.), *The Military Orders: Fighting for the Faith and Caring for the Sick* (Aldershot, 1994), pp. 167–78.

Rosenthal, J.T., 'Looking for Grandmother: The Pastons and their Counterparts in Late Medieval England', in J.C. Parsons and B. Wheeler (eds), *Medieval Mothering* (New York, 1996), pp. 259–77.

Rosenwein, B.H., *To Be the Neighbor of Saint Peter: The Social Meaning of Cluny's Property, 909–1049* (Ithaca, 1989).

Rosewell, R., *Medieval Wall Paintings in English and Welsh Churches* (Woodbridge, 2008).

Rousseau, C.M., 'Home Front and Battlefield: The Gendering of Papal Crusading

Bibliography

Policy (1095–1221)', in S. Edgington and S. Lambert (eds), *Gendering the Crusades* (Cardiff, 2001), pp. 31–44.

Rubenstein, J., *Nebuchadnezzar's Dream: The Crusades, Apocalyptic Prophecy, and the End of History* (Oxford, 2019).

Salzmann, L.F., 'Some Sussex Domesday Tenants', *SAC*, vol. 58 (1916), pp. 171–89.

Sandys, A., 'The Financial and Administrative Importance of the London Temple in the Thirteenth Century', in A.G. Little and F.M. Powicke (eds), *Essays in Medieval History Presented to Thomas Frederick Tout* (Manchester, 1925), pp. 147–62.

Sarnowsky, J., 'Gender-Aspekte in der Geschichte der geistlichen Ritterorden', in R. Hering (ed.), *Lebendige Sozialgeschichte, Gedenkschrift für Peter Borowsky* (Wiesbaden, 2003), pp. 168- 88.

Sarnowsky, J., 'Regional Problems in the History of the Mendicant and Military Orders', in J. Sarnowsky (ed.), *Mendicants, Military Orders, and Regionalism in Medieval Europe* (Aldershot, 1999), pp. 1–15.

Sayers, J., 'English Charters from the Third Crusade', in D. Greenway, C. Holdsworth and J. Sayers (eds), *Tradition and Change: Essays in Honour of Marjorie Chibnall Presented by her Friends on the Occasion of her Seventieth Birthday* (Cambridge, 1985), pp. 196–213.

Seabourne, G., *Women in the Medieval Common Law c.1200–1500* (London, 2021).

Schenk, J., *Templar Families: Landowning Families and the Order of the Temple in France, c. 1120–1307* (Cambridge, 2012).

Schmidt, P.G., '"*Peregrinatio Periculosa*". Thomas von Froidmont über die Jerusalemfahrten seiner schwester Margareta', in U.J. Stache, W. Maaz and F. Wagner (eds), *Kontinuität und Wandel: Lateinische Poesie von Naevius bis Baudelaire* (Hildesheim, 1986), pp. 461–85.

Schofield, P.R., 'Seals: Administration and Law', in P.R. Schofield, E.A. News, S.M. Johns and J.A. McEwan (eds), *Seals and Society: Medieval Wales, the Welsh Marches and their English Border* Region (Cardiff, 2016), pp. 35–47.

Schofield, P.R., News, E.A., Johns, S.M., and McEwan, J.A. (eds), *Seals and Society: Medieval Wales, the Welsh Marches and their English Border* Region (Cardiff, 2016).

Seidel, L., 'Images of the Crusades in Western Art: Models and Metaphors', in V.P. Goss and C.V. Bernstein (eds), *The Meeting of Two Worlds: Cultural Exchange between East and West during the Period of the Crusades* (Kalamazoo, 1986), pp. 377–91.

Setton, K.M., *The Papacy and the Levant: 1204–1571*, 4 vols (Philadelphia, 1976–84).

Shagrir, I., 'The "Holy Women" in the Liturgy and Art of the Church of the Holy Sepulchre in Twelfth-Century Jerusalem', in E. Lapina and N. Morton (eds), *The Uses of the Bible in Crusader Sources* (Leiden, 2017), pp. 455–75.

Shagrir, I., and Gaposchkin, C., 'Liturgy and Devotion in the Crusader States: Introduction', *Journal of Medieval History*, vol. 43, no. 4 (2017), pp. 359–66.

Bibliography

Shahar, S., *The Fourth Estate: A History of Women in the Middle Ages, Revised Edition*, C. Galai (ed. and trans.) (London, 2003).
Sharpe, R., 'Address and Delivery in Anglo-Norman Writs and Writ Charters', in M.T. Flanagan and J.A. Green (eds), *Charters and Charter Scholarship in Britain and Ireland* (London, 2005), pp. 32–52.
Sheingorn, P., *The Easter Sepulchre in England* (Kalamazoo, 1987).
Siberry, E., 'The Crusader's Departure and Return: A Much Later Perspective', in S. Edgington and S. Lambert (eds), *Gendering the Crusades* (Cardiff, 2001), pp. 177–90.
Siberry, E., *Criticism of Crusading 1095–1274* (Oxford, 1985).
Siberry, E., *Tales of the Crusaders: Remembering the Crusades in Britain* (London, 2021).
Siedschlag, B., *English Participation in the Crusades, 1150–1220* (Privately Published, 1939).
Silber, I.F., 'Gift-Giving in the Great Traditions: The Case of Donations to Monasteries in the Medieval West', *European Journal of Sociology*, vol. 36, no. 2 (1995), pp. 209–43.
Slack, C.K., and Feiss, H.B. (eds and trans.), *Crusade Charters 1138–1270* (Tempe, 2001).
Slater, L., 'Finding Jerusalem in Medieval Pontefract', *Northern History*, vol. 51, no. 2 (2014), pp. 211–20.
Slavin, P., 'Landed Estates of the Knights Templar in England and Wales and their Management in the Early Fourteenth Century', *Journal of Historical Geography*, vol. 42 (2013), pp. 36–49.
Sloane, B., and Malcolm, G., *Excavations at the Priory of the Order of the Hospital of St John of Jerusalem, Clerkenwell, London* (London, 2004).
Smalley, B., 'John Russel O.F.M.', *Recherches de théologie ancienne et médiévale*, vol. 23 (1956), pp. 277–320.
Smith, C., *Crusading in the Age of Joinville* (Aldershot, 2006).
Smith, C., 'Martyrdom and Crusading in the Thirteenth Century: Remembering the Dead of Louis IX's Crusades', *Al-Masāq*, vol. 15, no. 2 (2003), pp. 189–96.
Smith, D.J., 'The Abbot-Crusader: Nicholas Breakspear in Catalonia', in B. Bolton and A.J. Duggan (eds), *Adrian IV The English Pope (1154–1159)* (Aldershot, 2003), pp 29–39.
Smith, J.Z., *To Take Place: Toward Theory in Ritual* (Chicago, 1987) (reprinted: 1992).
Smith, K.A., 'Monastic Memories of the Early Crusading Movement', in M. Cassidy-Welch (ed.), *Remembering the Crusades and Crusading* (London, 2017), pp. 131–44.
Smith, K.A., *War and the Making of Medieval Monastic Culture* (Woodbridge, 2011).
Smith, R.M., 'Women's Property Rights under Customary Law: Some

Bibliography

Developments in the Thirteenth and Fourteenth Centuries', *Transactions of the Royal Historical Society*, vol. 36 (1986), pp. 165–94.

Smith, T.W., *Curia and Crusade: Pope Honorius III and the Recovery of the Holy Land: 1216–1227* (Turnhout, 2017).

Smith, T.W., 'How to Craft a Crusade Call: Pope Innocent III and *Quia Maior* (1213)', *Historical Research*, vol. 92, no. 255 (2019), pp. 2–23.

Smith, T.W., *Rewriting the First Crusade: Epistolary Culture in the Middle Ages* (Woodbridge, 2024).

Spacey, B.C., 'Martyrdom as Masculinity in the *Itinerarium Peregrinorum et Gesta Regis Ricardi*', in N.R. Hodgson, K.J. Lewis and M.M. Mesley (eds), *Crusading and Masculinities* (London, 2019), pp. 222–36.

Spacey, B.C., *The Miraculous and the Writing of Crusade Narrative* (Woodbridge, 2020).

Sparrow Simpson, W., 'Two Inventories of the Cathedral Church of St. Paul, London, dated respectively 1245 and 1402', *Archaeologia*, vol. 1, no. 2 (1887), pp. 439–524.

Spear, V.G., *Leadership in Medieval English Nunneries* (Woodbridge, 2005).

Spencer, S.J., *Emotions in a Crusading Context, 1095–1291* (Oxford, 2019).

Staunton, M., *The Historians of Angevin England* (Oxford, 2017).

Stenton, F.M., 'Early Manumissions at Staunton, Nottinghamshire', *English Historical Review*, vol. 26, no. 101 (1911), pp. 93–7.

Strickland, D.H., *Saracens, Demons, & Jews: Making Monsters in Medieval Art* (Princeton, 2003).

Sumption, J., *Pilgrimage: an Image of Mediaeval Religion* (London, 1975).

Sweetinburgh, S., *The Role of the Hospital in Medieval England: Gift-giving and the Spiritual Economy* (Dublin, 2004).

Swift, C., '"Palmers" as ex-crusaders in Irish urban environments? The Evidence of the *Dublin Guild Merchant Roll*', in E. Coleman, P. Duffy and T. O'Keeffe (eds), *Ireland and the Crusades* (Dublin, 2022), pp. 70–6.

Tamminen, M., *Crusade Preaching and the Ideal Crusader* (Turnhout, 2018).

Tamminen, M., 'Crusading in the Margins? Women and Children in the Crusade Model Sermons of the Thirteenth Century', in S. Katajala-Peltomaa and V. Vuolanto (eds), *Religious Participation in Ancient and Medieval Societies: Rituals, Interaction and Identity* (Rome, 2013), pp. 145–58.

Tanner, H.J. (ed.), *Medieval Elite Women and the Exercise of Power, 1100–1400: Moving Beyond the Exceptionalist Debate* (New York, 2019).

Tessera, M.R., 'Philip Count of Flanders and Hildegard of Bingen: Crusading Against the Saracens or Crusading Against Deadly Sin?', in S. Edgington and S. Lambert (eds), *Gendering the Crusades* (Cardiff, 2001), pp. 77–93.

Thiolier-Méjean, S., 'Croisade et registre courtois chez les troubadours', in J.M. d'Heur and N. Cherubini (eds), *Études de philologie romane et d'histoire littéraire offertes à Jules Horrent à l'occasion de son soixantième anniversaire* (Liege, 1980), pp. 295–307.

Bibliography

Thomson, R.M., Dolmans, E., and Winkler, E.A. (eds), *Discovering William of Malmesbury* (Woodbridge, 2017).

Thompson, S., *Women Religious, The Founding of English Nunneries after the Norman Conquest* (Oxford, 1991).

Throop, S.A., *Crusading as an Act of Vengeance, 1095–1216* (Farnham, 2011).

Tibble, S., *Templars: The Knights Who Made Britain* (New Haven, 2023).

Tristram, E.W., and Bardswell, M., *English Medieval Wall Painting: The Thirteenth Century, Plates* (Oxford, 1950).

Tristram, E.W., and Bardswell, M., *English Medieval Wall Painting: The Thirteenth Century, Text* (Oxford, 1950).

Tristram, E.W., and Constable, W.G., *English Medieval Wall Painting: The Twelfth Century* (Oxford, 1944).

Tucker, J., *Reading and Shaping Medieval Cartularies: Multi-Scribe Manuscripts and their Patterns of Growth* (Woodbridge, 2020).

Tummers, H.A., *Early Secular Effigies in England* (Leiden, 1980).

Tyerman, C., *England and the Crusades, 1095–1588* (Chicago, 1988).

Tyerman, C., *Fighting for Christendom: Holy War and the Crusades* (Oxford, 2004).

Tyerman, C., *God's War: A New History of the Crusades* (Cambridge, 2006).

Tyerman, C., *How to Plan a Crusade: Reason and Religious War in the High Middle Ages* (London, 2015).

Tyerman, C., *The Invention of the Crusades* (Basingstoke, 1998).

Tyerman, C., 'Some English Evidence of Attitudes to Crusading in the Thirteenth Century', in P.R. Coss and S.D. Lloyd (eds), *Thirteenth Century England I: Proceedings of the Newcastle-upon-Tyne Conference 1985* (Woodbridge, 1986), pp. 168–74.

Tyerman, C., 'Were There Any Crusades in the Twelfth Century?', *The English Historical Review*, vol. 110, no. 437 (1995), pp. 553–77.

Tyerman, C., *The World of the Crusades* (New Haven, 2019).

Vander Elst, S., *The Knight, the Cross, and the Song: Crusade Propaganda and Chivalric Literature, 1100–1400* (Philadelphia, 2017).

Vandeburie, J., 'The Preacher and the Pope: Jacques de Vitry and Honorius III at the Time of the Fifth Crusade (1216–27)', in J.L. Bird (ed.), *Papacy, Crusade, and Christian-Muslim Relations* (Amsterdam, 2018), pp. 131–54.

de Vasselot de Régné, C., 'A Crusader Lineage from Spain to the Throne of Jerusalem: The Lusignans', *Crusades*, vol. 16 (2017), pp. 95–114.

Veach, C., 'Henry II and the Ideological Foundations of Angevin Rule in Ireland', *Irish Historical Studies*, vol. 42, no. 161 (2018), pp. 1–25.

Vincent, N., *Peter des Roches: An Alien in English Politics, 1205–1238* (Cambridge, 1996) (reprinted: 2002).

Walker, J., 'Crusaders and Patrons: The Influence of the Crusades on the Patronage of the Order of St Lazarus in England', in M. Barber (ed.), *The Military Orders: Fighting for the Faith and Caring for the Sick* (Aldershot, 1994), pp. 327–32.

Bibliography

Walker, K.C., *The Profession of Widowhood: Widows, Pastoral Care & Medieval Models of Holiness* (Washington D.C., 2018).

Walker, S.S., 'Litigation as Personal Quest: Suing for Dower in the Royal Courts, circa 1272–1350', in S.S. Walker (ed.), *Wife and Widow in Medieval England* (Ann Arbor, 1993), pp. 81–108.

Ward, J., *Women in Medieval Europe, 1200–1500*, 2nd edn (London and New York, 2016).

Ward, J. (ed. and trans.), *Women of the English Nobility and Gentry, 1066–1500* (Manchester, 1995).

Watson, S., 'Introduction: The Moment and Memory of the York Massacre of 1190', in S. R. Jones and S. Watson (eds), *Christians and Jews in Angevin England: The York Massacre of 1190, Narratives and Contexts* (York, 2013), pp. 1–14.

Webb, D., *Medieval European Pilgrimage, c.700–1500* (Basingstoke, 2002).

Weikert, K., *Authority, Gender and Space in the Anglo-Norman World, 900–1200* (Woodbridge, 2020).

Weiler, B, 'History, Prophecy and the Apocalypse in the Chronicles of Matthew Paris', *English Historical Review*, vol. 133, no. 561 (2018), pp. 253–83.

Weiler, B., 'Matthew Paris on the Writing of History', *Journal of Medieval History*, vol. 35 (2009), pp. 254–78.

Weiss, D.H., *Art and Crusade in the Age of Saint Louis* (Cambridge, 1998).

Weiss, D.H., 'Biblical History and Medieval Historiography: Rationalizing Strategies in Crusader Art', *MLN*, vol. 108, no. 4 (1993), pp. 710–37.

Whatley, L.J., 'Crusading for (Heavenly) Jerusalem: A Noble Woman, Devotion, and the Trinity Apocalypse (Cambridge Trinity College, MS R.16.2)', in E.A. Foster, J. Perratore and S. Rozenski (eds), *Devotional Interaction in Medieval England and its Afterlives* (Leiden, 2018).

Whatley, L.J., 'Romance, Crusade, and the Orient in King Henry III of England's Royal Chambers', *Viator*, vol. 44, no. 2 (2013), pp. 175–98.

Willard, C.C., 'Isabel of Portugal and the Fifteenth-Century Burgundian Crusade', in B.N. Sargent-Baur (ed.), *Journeys Toward God: Pilgrimage and Crusade* (Kalamazoo, 1992), pp. 205–14.

Wilkinson, L.J., 'Women as Sheriffs in Early Thirteenth-Century England', in A. Jobson (ed.), *English Government in the Thirteenth Century* (Woodbridge, 2004), pp. 111–24.

Wilkinson, L.J., *Women in Thirteenth-Century Lincolnshire* (Woodbridge, 2007).

Wolf, K.B. (ed. and trans.), *The Life & Afterlife of St. Elizabeth of Hungary* (Oxford, 2011).

Woolgar, C.M., 'Gifts of Food in Late Medieval England', *Journal of Medieval History*, vol. 37, no. 1 (2011), pp. 6–18.

Yeager, S.M., *Jerusalem in Medieval Narrative* (Cambridge, 2008).

Yolles, J., 'The Maccabees in the Lord's Temple: Biblical Imagery and Latin

Poetry in Frankish Jerusalem', in E. Lapina and N. Morton (eds), *The Uses of the Bible in Crusader Sources* (Leiden, 2017), pp. 421–39.

Young, C.R., *The Making of the Neville Family in England, 1166–1400* (Woodbridge, 1996).

Unpublished Sources

Adair, P.A., '"Ego et mea uxor...": Countess Clemence and her Role in the Comital Family and in Flanders (1092–1133)' (Unpublished PhD Thesis, University of California, 1993).

Bass, I.L., 'The Crozier and the Cross: Crusading and the English Episcopate, c.1170–1313' (Unpublished PhD Thesis, Manchester Metropolitan University, 2019).

Blincoe, M.E., 'Angevin Society and the Early Crusades, 1095–1145', 3 vols (Unpublished PhD Thesis, University of Minnesota, 2008).

Frost, J.A. (ed.), 'An Edition of the Nostell Priory Cartulary, London, British Library, Cotton Vespasian E XIX', 2 vols (Unpublished PhD Thesis, University of York, 2006).

Haluska-Rausch, E.A., 'Family, Property, and Power: Women in Medieval Montpellier, 985–1213' (Unpublished PhD Thesis, Harvard University, 1998).

Irwin, D.A., 'Acknowledging Debt in Medieval England: A Study of the Records of Medieval Anglo-Jewish Moneylending Activities, 1194–1276' (Unpublished PhD Thesis, Canterbury Christ Church University, 2020).

Jefferson, J.M., 'The Templar Lands in Lincolnshire in the Early Fourteenth Century'. (Unpublished PhD Thesis, University of Nottingham, 2016).

McGrath, R.L., 'The Romance of the Maccabees in Mediaeval Art and Literature' (Unpublished PhD Thesis, University of Princeton, 1963).

Park, D.E.A., '"Under Our Protection, that of the Church and their own": Papal and Secular Protection for the Families and Properties the Crusaders Left Behind, c. 1095–1226' (Unpublished PhD Thesis, Royal Holloway University of London, 2013).

Scott, M.E. (ed.), 'A Herefordshire Nunnery: A Calendar, with introduction, of the Cartulary of Aconbury Nunnery' (Unpublished M.Phil. Thesis, University of Southampton, 2001).

Whatley, L.J., 'Localizing the Holy Land: Visual Culture of Crusade in England, Circa 1140–1307' (Unpublished PhD Thesis, University of Illinois at Urbana-Champaign, 2010).

Online Sources

'Henry de Lacy/Walter de Bibbesworth, *Sire Gauter, dire vos voil* (RS 1780a)', https://warwick.ac.uk/fac/arts/modernlanguages/research/french/crusades/texts/of/rs1780a/#page1 Published Online 27 Apr 2018 (accessed 20 Feb 2024).

'The Independent Crusaders Mapping Project', hosted by Fordham University, https://independentcrusadersproject.ace.fordham.edu (accessed 4 Dec 2023).

Bibliography

Nicholson, H.J., 'Memories of the Templars in Britain: Templar Charters in Hospitaller records after the Dissolution of the Templars', paper presented at the 49th International Medieval Congress, Kalamazoo, 2014, pp. 1–13, Available Online, https://www.researchgate.net/deref/http%3A%2F%2Fdx.doi.org%2F10.13140%2F2.1.2765.1204 (accessed 19 Feb 2024).

Oram, R.D., 'Quincy, Saer de, earl of Winchester', in *Oxford Dictionary of National Biography*, https://doi.org/10.1093/ref:odnb/22967, Published Online 22 September 2005 (accessed 28 Jan 2024).

Beam, A., Bradley, J., Broun, D., Davies, J.R., Hammond, M., Jakeman, N., Pasin, M., Taylor, A., *et al* (eds), *People of Medieval Scotland: 1093–1371* (Glasgow and London, 2019), no. 5989, https://www.poms.ac.uk/record/person/5989/ (accessed 25 Jan 2024).

Rhodes, W.E., 'Tiptoft [Tivetot], Robert, Lord Tiptoft', in *Oxford Dictionary of National Biography*, https://doi.org/10.1093/ref:odnb/27472, Published Online 23 Sept 2004, Updated by R.R. Davis 22 September 2005 (accessed 14 Feb 2024).

Strickland, M., 'Senlis, Simon de [Simon de St Liz], earl of Northampton and earl of Huntingdon', in *Oxford Dictionary of National Biography*, https://doi.org/10.1093/ref:odnb/25091, Published Online 23 September 2004 (accessed 15 Jan 2024).

Turner, R.V., 'Briouze [Braose], William de (d. 1211)', in *Oxford Dictionary of National Biography*, https://doi.org/10.1093/ref:odnb/3283, Published Online 23 Sept 2004, Updated 28 September 2006 (accessed 10 Feb 2024).

Acknowledgements

The research behind this book would never have been possible without encouragement, insights and waymarking from a number of people. Friends and colleagues have, in so many ways, shaped my thinking on the medieval world, challenged my preconceptions and supported my work. Had I not had the opportunity to air my thoughts and quandaries with them, this book would have been a different beast altogether. I am hugely appreciative of William "Bill" Aird, Cordelia Beattie, Gianluca Raccagni, Mike Carr and Natasha Hodgson in particular, who have been no end of help in developing this study.

While working on this book and other related projects, I came to rely on the sound advice and keen eyes of a couple friends who undeniably deserve their own paragraph of acclaim: Tamsin Prideaux and Emma Trivett – two scholars of immense integrity and passion. They have guided my rationale in academia and beyond, inspiring and pushing me in producing this book. I will always be grateful for them lending me an ear when I had petty quibbles that simply had to be discussed in microbial detail.

Others have been kind enough to simply share their knowledge and enthusiasm for their own topics of research. An unassuming gesture, but sometimes an impactful one all the same. I have seen that camaraderie and critique at brilliant sessions and talks through the International Medieval Congress in Leeds and the Society for the Study of the Crusades and the Latin East, and learned more about the Middle Ages through trivial conversation than I care to admit. I am especially thankful to Jonathan Phillips, Amanda Luyster, Richard Leson and Simon John who were happy to take time to explain aspects of their own research or work – giving me an introduction to elements of medieval culture that had eluded me. In the same vein, I must thank the anonymous reader of the initial draft of this book, as well as Caroline Palmer, who teased out numerous points that needed a rethink, useful cases and notes. Their efforts have done a huge amount to transform this text.

In a slightly more introspective sense, I am equally grateful for the many historians who wrote books that shaped the way I saw the past and thought about this project. The impact they have left is intangible and hard to convey. Yet, while reading this book, you will notice that I refer to figures such as Jonathan Riley-Smith, Christopher Tyerman, Simon Lloyd, Marcus Bull, William Chester Jordan, Helen Nicholson, Nicholas Paul, Katherine Lewis, Nicholas Morton and Kathryn Hurlock. Some are mentioned more often, some less. But, I think these individuals' work has left an indelible mark on the way I approach historical research, medieval sources and the paradigms and perspectives that have so often governed our thoughts on the distant past.

Acknowledgements

Numerous institutions and their staff gave up their precious time to assist me in tracing manuscripts, retrieving source material, and photographing objects and art that were invaluable to the book and to my own education on the topic of crusade. Thanks are especially owed to the staff and good people of: Centre for Research Collections of Edinburgh University Library, National Library of Scotland, Canterbury Cathedral Archives, British Library, John Rylands Library, Huntington Library (California), Musée de Cluny, The National Archives (Kew), Berkshire Record Office, Saint Bartholomew's Hospital Archive, Wiltshire and Swindon Archives, Somerset Heritage Centre, Westminster Abbey Library, Trinity College Cambridge, Österreichische Nationalbibliothek, Chichester Cathedral, The Round Church (Cambridge), Holy Sepulchre (Northampton), as well as the parishes of Damerham, Claverley, Climping and Hardham.

Ultimately, I owe most to the support and belief of my faultless parents, Karen and Paul, and my inspiring wife, Anna. My life is charmed for having these talismanic characters nearby. They have always nurtured my obsession with the past and, without them, I would not be who I am.

Index

Abergavenny 65
Aconbury, *see* Hospital
Acre xii, 1–2, 8, 88, 108, 111, 129, 173
Adam of Elton 124
Adam de Jesmond 91
Adela of Blois 36 n.55, 83, 84, 136
Africa 8, 93, 176
Agatha Basset 126, 126 n.27
Agnes widow of John Sweyn 105, 130
Agnes 159
    Lancelin son of Osmond, husband of 159
Agnes d'Aubigny 137
Agnes lady of Little Windsor 96
Agnes de la Mara 155
Agnes de Percy 95, 135–6, 156–7, 166
Agnes de Vescy 114–15, 130, 137
Aigeline of Burgundy 169–70
Ailiva of Cuckney 155
Ainderby Quernhow (Yorkshire) 131
Airam 159
al Mansurah, Battle of 24, 55, 57
Alditha 153
Aleppo xi
Alexander Golde 90
Alexander I of Scotland 43
Alfonso VIII of Castile 52
Alfred of Lincoln 24
Ali Ibn al-Athīr 101, 101 n.3, 111, 173
Alice wife of Gilbert 97
Alice 126
    Hamund de *Brochurste,* husband of 125
Alice 96, 149
    William son of Nigel the Dean, husband of 96, 149
Alice Baskervill 112, 124, 139–40
Alice de Blakepaine 104
Alice Briewer 180 no.14
Alice Briwere (otherwise known as de Paynel and de Mohun) 115
Alice de Montmorency 84
Alice de Ouvill 180 no.17
Alice Peverel 164–5
Alice Querderay 157–8
    John, husband of 157–8

Almohad Caliphate 52
Alnham (Northumberland) 115
Alnmouth (Northumberland) 115
Alwald the Merchant 153
Amabele wife Aunfrid Breton 181 no.23
Amaury de Montfort 84
Ambroise 66
Amirie Saint Valéry 136
Amphelisia of Rolleston 95
Anatolia 5
Annandale xxi, 80
Annora daughter of John 122–3, 140
Antigone 126
    Humbert de Munchesny, husband of 126
Antioch, Battle of 30–2, 83
Arabic
    language 44, 101, 162
Armenia xii
Arthenus 65, 83
Astrid 169–70
Audita Tremendi 49
Augustinian Order 109 n.39, 126 n.29, 175
Avecia de Somery 183 no.50

Baldwin of Forde 49–50, 60, 63, 65, 68
Bampton (Devon) 115
Bangor Cathedral 64
Bashley (Hampshire) 138
Battle Abbey 116, 124, 158, 159 n.73
Barbéry Abbey 125
Barlings Abbey 160–1
Barnwell Priory 164–5
Beatrice of Blackburn 72
Belval Priory 169
Benevento 155
Bernard de Nimphia 67
Bernard of Saint Valéry 137
Bertram Asar 99
Bertrand de la Tour 73
Bible 31–2, 146
Binham Priory 103
Bishops Lydeard (Somerset) 146
Blanche of Navarre 169–70
Blyth (Nottinghamshire) 124

231

Index

Bohemond of Taranto 161
Bosgerius of Bashley 138
Boso of La Chèze 94
Bourton-on-the-Water
   (Gloucestershire) 153
Boxgrove Priory 129
Bradenstoke Priory 71
Brecon (Powys) 64
Breedon Priory 125, 149
Brende (Yorkshire) 114
Bridlington (Yorkshire) 92
Bristol 96
Bromholm Priory 44
Buckland Priory 109, 137, 157
Bungay Priory 150
Bury St Edmonds 77
Byzantine
   architecture 39
   army 50
   empire x, 89, 139

Cador 68
Caldwell 114
Canterbury Abbey 72, 85
Cardigan 65
Carisbrooke Priory 102, 104, 121, 124, 151
Castle Foregate (Shropshire) 112
Castle Hedingham (Essex) 111
Cathal Crobhdearg 154
Catton (Yorkshire) 156
Cecilia de Flore 112, 124
Cecilia Luvel 146
Champagne 24, 169
Checkendon (Oxfordshire) 125
Chertsey Tiles 30–1
Chichester Cathedral 106
Chingford (Essex) 110
Chrétien de Troyes 160
Christchurch Priory 138
Christian widow of Walter le Tayllur 95
Christiana de Brus 150–1
Cistercian Order 157, 167
Claverley (Shropshire) 35–6
Clerkenwell Priory x, 29, 156, 168
Cleeve Abbey 31
Clermont x, 45
Cleveland 106
Clifford's Tower (York) 77
Climping (Sussex) 106
commemorations
   physical memorials 30–44, 162–3, 169–72

prayers 29, 87, 92, 104, 124–7, 135, 148–9, 157, 159, 169
song/literature 27–9, 160–2
Cornwall 67
countergifts
   cash 92–3, 95, 102–5, 112–13, 123–4, 149
   food and drink 97, 149–50, 151
   housing 97, 114, 149–51, 158
   objects 104
Courtenay Family 11, 86
Cowley (Oxfordshire) 109
Cressing (Essex) 109
crusades
   Albigensian Crusades 5, 84
   Baltic Crusades 5
   Barons' Crusade xi, 43, 55, 128, 137, 150, 160, 165
   Children's Crusade 50
   Count of Flanders' Crusade xi, 84 n.5, 93, 95, 165
   Fifth Crusade xi, 42, 44, 51, 53, 70, 128, 133, 154, 156–7, 162, 167
   First Crusade x, 3, 8 n.27, 23, 32, 39, 45, 46, 74, 76, 86, 102, 135, 136, 137, 149, 152, 161, 164, 170
   Fourth Crusade xi, 89, 102, 127, 169
   Lord Edward's Crusade xii, 28, 89, 91, 110, 129–31, 138, 141, 167
   Louis IX's Second Crusade xii, 75, 110
   Nicopolis Crusade 8
   Norwegian Crusade 139
   Otto de Grandson's Crusade xii, 85, 129–30, 170–2
   Second Crusade x, 8, 24, 87, 127, 150, 164–5, 169
   Seventh Crusade xi, 24, 25, 57, 100, 102, 128, 131, 150, 160
   Sixth Crusade xi, 70, 91, 96, 115, 138, 157
   Third Crusade xi, 30–1, 42, 49–50, 60, 63–8, 84, 89, 95, 97, 103, 104, 113, 125–7, 136–8, 141, 150, 155–8, 161, 164, 166
crusade chests 51, 105–8
Crusader States, *see* Jerusalem, Kingdom of

Dafydd ap Gruffydd 79
Damascus xi
Damerham (Hampshire) 35

232

Index

Damietta xi
Dartmouth x
David I of Strathbogie 110
Deheubarth 65
Demetrius, St 32
Derby 112, 123
Dionisia 89
   Hubert, husband of 89
donations toward crusade
   alms giving 75, 102–8
   enforced contributions x–xi, 69, 72, 88, 127, 131–2
   penalty clauses 118
Douglas (South Lanarkshire) 164
dower 115
   disputed 95–7, 98–100, 117
   pledged 93–4, 97, 117, 137, 149, 174
   sold 94, 98, 157
Dominican Order, *see* Mendicant Orders
Drax Priory 125, 149
Dunbar (Lothian) 150–1
Duncton (Sussex) 103
Durham 56

Easby Abbey 97, 149
Edessa x
Edgar Ætheling x
Edith of Navenby 181 no.21
Edmund of Abingdon 70–1, 71 n.64
Edward I of England xii, 40, 42, 77, 79–80, 85, 106, 128, 130–2, 170
Edward II of England 129
Edwardstone 111
Egypt xi, 162
Ela of Salisbury xi, 57, 150, 160
Eleanor of Castile xii, 85, 130, 170–2
Eleanor of Provence 30
Eleanor de Quincy 162 n.88
Ellis Gold 90
Ely (Cambridgeshire) 56, 106
Elizabeth of Thuringia/Hungary 151
Emerias de Alteias 47
Emma of Meauton 99–100
Emma de Porte 135–6
Erard I of Ramerupt 153 n.40
Erneburge 122–3
   William of *Hokesour*, husband of 122
Essex 1, 43, 110, 133
Eudes of Châteauroux 71, 73
Eudon of Saint Valéry 137
Eustace de Balliol 131
Eustace III of Boulogne 74

Eustace of Fly 52
Eustacia 112, 123
   Walter son of Henry the Dean, brother of 112, 123
   husband of 112, 123
Eva 165
   Hamo II Peche, husband of 164–5
Eva Tibetot 85, 130, 138, 167
Evelyn 103
   Richard de *Baubaduu*, husband of 103
Evelyn Joy 183 no.53
Evreux Abbey 125
Eystein I of Norway 139
Eysteinn 170
Ex multa xi, 24, 53, 84

Felpham (Sussex) 106
Fergus of Galloway 26–7
Ferrybridge (Yorkshire) 91
First Barons' War xi, 8, 78, 127–8
Flanders 113
Flore (Northamptonshire) 112
Forde Abbey 96
Fordington (Dorset) 35
Fountains Abbey 131, 157–8, 166–7
France x, xii, 5, 7, 10, 11, 17, 24, 25, 52, 68, 83–4, 94, 113, 125, 145, 152 n.40
Franciscan Order, *see* Mendicant Orders
Fulcher of Chartres 145
Fulk V of Anjou 5 n.15
Fulk of Neuilly 52

Galloway xii, 80
Garendon Abbey 87, 167
Geddington (Northamptonshire) 60
Genoa 70, 111, 128
Geoffrey Chaucer 44
Geoffrey of Dutton 44, 148
Geoffrey Hacard 104, 124, 138
George, St 32
Gerald of Wales 63–9, 71, 74, 83
Gerard de Furnevatt 97
   wife of 97
Germany 49
Gervase of Hampton 104
Gilbert 67
Gilbert I Peche 164–5
Gilbert II Peche 165
Gilbert of Tournai 73
Gisburn Forest 167 n.112
Glamorgan 43

233

Index

Glastonbury Abbey   31
Gloucester Cathedral   140, 163
Godfrey of Bouillon   74
Goxhill (Lincolnshire)   92
Great Malton (Norfolk)   99
Gundreda daughter of Richard the
    Priest   123, 140 n.117
Gundreda   150
    Roger de Glanville, husband of   150
Gundreda de Gournay   86–7, 166
Gunnore de Valunies   180 no.13
Guy de Lusignan   48, 90
Gwenllian   65
    Rhys ap Gruffydd, husband of   65
Gwynedd   79

Hamo Lestrange   123
Hamo I Peche   164
Hamo II Peche   164–5
Hamund de *Brocherste*   125
Hardham (Sussex)   35
Harmston (Lincolnshire)   145
Hartmann von Aue   57–8
Haselwood   156
Hattin, Battle of   48, 165
Haughmond Abbey   128, 155
Hawisa daughter of Walter de Eure   182
    no.37
Hawisa   105
    Henry of Glastonbury, brother of   105
Hawisa Lestrange   123–4, 130, 138
Hawisa de Nevill   1–2, 4, 26, 111, 129
Hawisa of Chester   156, 168
Hawisa of *Trevisac*   67
Hay-on-Wye   65
Helewisa Ruffus   145
Heloise Palmer   72
Henry II of England   x–xi, 69, 77, 85
Henry III of England   xi, 25, 30, 42,
    55–6, 78–9, 128, 131, 156
Henry of Glastonbury   105
Henry of Goxhill   92
Henry de Lacy   28
Henry of *Mertok*   146
Henry de Percy   103
Henry the Young King   x, 85
Herbert son of Matthew   115
Hethersett (Norfolk)   99
Hildegard von Bingen   84 n.5
Hinton (Wiltshire)   71
Holborn   x
hospital

St Bartholomew, London   103–4, 125,
    149
Dunbar   150
God's House, Southampton   104
Goxhill   92
St John the Baptist, Aconbury   xi,
    109, 109 n.39, 126, 136, 138, 157
St John the Baptist, Oxford   97
St John the Evangelist,
    Cambridge   105
St Leonard, York   87
Hospitallers, *see* Knights Hospitaller
Howden (Yorkshire)   61
Hubert son of Wido   110
Humbert de Munchensy   111, 126
Hugh Bukky   111
Hugh FitzRichard   150
Hugh de Nevill (d.c.1269)   1–2, 26
Hugh de Nevill (d.1234)   42
Hugh de Payns   x
Hugh de Samford   115
Hugh of *Sestefeld*   72
    wife of   72
Hugh Travers   89
Hugh of Vaudémont   169
Humbert of Romans   23, 35, 73, 75

Icklesham (Sussex)   116, 124, 159
Idonea de Camville   160
Idonee   183 no.51
    Radulf of *Wrokesham*, husband
        of   183 no.51
Inchcolm Abbey   48
Ingram de Umfravile   1
Ipswich (Suffolk)   114, 167
Isaac   26
Isabel Chilham   110, 130
Isabel de Mauduit   85
Isabel Palmer   72
Isabella de Clare   135
Isabella Hacard   104, 124, 138
Italy   110, 155
Ireland   77–8

Jacob's Ford   48
Jacques de Vitry   53, 69–70
Jaffa   158
James   145
James "the Good" Douglas   163–4
Jean de Joinville   24, 100, 102, 163
Jerusalem
    architecture   39, 170, 173

Index

celestial   40, 42, 57
crusades to recover   7–8, 79, 174
   depictions in art   32
   Kingdom of   x, xii   42, 48, 60, 68, 90, 108, 133, 152, 153 n.40, 170
   pilgrimage to   6, 42, 68, 90, 96, 101–5, 112–13, 118, 121, 124–5, 129, 131, 135, 140, 149, 157, 166, 170
   Siege of (70)   32
   Siege of (1099)   x, 23, 32, 39
   Siege of (1187)   xi, 8, 28, 42, 48–9, 68, 101, 173
   Siege of (1244)   xi
Joachim of Fiore   161–2
Joanna daughter of Anketill   105
Joanna de Mares   116, 118
Jocelin de Louvain   95, 135, 157, 166
John, vicar of Potterne   85
John of Abbeville   73
John of Arundel   129
John of Brienne   170
John II of Brittany   131
John Collinson   89
John of England   xi, 78, 97, 127
John II FitzAlan   128
John of Forde   24
John Gold   89–90
John Guer   105
John de *Herdislawe*   113, 123
John of Hexham   87 n.24
John de Lacy   42, 168
John III Lestrange   138
John Lovel   131
John II de Nesle   24
John Palmer   90
John Pecham   79
John le Romeyn   60–1, 75
John Russel   59, 74
John Sweyn   105
John de Vescy   114–5
Jollan II de Neville   95
Joseph   66
Juliana   103
   Alan de Balon, husband of   103
Juliana   125
   William de Forda, husband of   125
Juliana Guer   105, 130
Juliana Haringer   97
Juliana Querderay   158

Katherine le Marveler   146 n.7
Kerbogha   32

Knighton (Berkshire)   136
Knights Hospitaller   x–xii, 39, 87, 108–10, 126, 136–8, 157, 168
Knights of St Lazarus   108
Knights of St Thomas of Canterbury at Acre   108
Knights Templar   x, xii, 4, 39, 48, 108–10, 168, 173

Lacock Abbey   57, 83, 150, 160–1
Las Navas de Tolosa, Battle of   52
Latin East, *see* Jerusalem, Kingdom of
Leonard, St   87
Leticia   181 no. 27
   Richard son of Richard, husband of   181 no.27
Levant   8, 43, 58, 88, 141, 152
Lincoln   77
Lisbon   x, 8, 127
Little Windsor (Dorset)   96
Littlestoke (Oxfordshire)   125
Llanmadoc (Gower)   109
Llywelyn ap Gruffydd   128
London   x, 29, 31, 77, 103, 110, 125, 129, 149, 156
Loretta de Braose   137, 157
Loretta of Crundal   97, 149
Louis VII of France   127
Louis IX of France   xii, 25, 55, 75, 79, 110, 131, 148
Lucy daughter of William son of Roger de *Berhholte*   113–14
Ludford (Lincolnshire)   95
Lynn   77

Mabel   98
   Edith, daughter of   98
   Nicholas of Greywell, husband of   98
Mabelle of Bonville   43–4
Maccabees   31, 36
Mamluks   xii
Margaret   118, 129
   Thomas of Dreuton, husband of   118
Margaret de Beaumont   167
Margaret of Beverley   68
Margaret countess of Warwick   109
Margaret de Lacy   xi, 109, 136–7
Margaret de Perche   86
Margaret de Quincy   168
Marie wife of Robert le Norreys   182 no.35
Marie of France   160

Index

Master Hubert   70
Matilda wife of Adam of London   181 no.28
Matilda wife of Adam of Stanford   182 no.39
Matilda wife of Eustace of Warwick   183 no.48
Matilda wife of Henry de Scalar   182 no.36
Matilda Baiarde   103, 140
Matilda of Boulogne   109
Matilda de Crevequer   180 no.16
Matilda of Edgefield   103
Matilda Martin   184 no.57
Matilda Mayden   184 no.58
Matilda of Meauton   99–100
Matilda de Percy   136, 156, 167
Matilda Querderay   158
Matilda Touche   179 no.8
Matthew Paris   29, 57, 61, 71, 73, 83
Mendicant Orders   61, 134, 141, 167–8
   Dominican   35, 61
   Franciscan   59, 61, 72–3, 167
   Trinitarian   150
Mercurius, St   32
Micklegate (York)   113, 123
Milda White   181 no.24
Monopods   32
Monthléry Family   11, 86
Muireadhach Albanach   154
Muhammad, individual in Wiltshire   25
Muhammad Saracen   25

Neath Abbey   31, 158 n.66
Nebuchadnezzar II   161
Neusom   158
Newburgh Abbey   165
Newson (Yorkshire)   114
Newton (Yorkshire)   156
Nicholas of *Bere*   99
Nicholas Brito   112, 140
Nicholas of Greywell   98
Nicholas Haringod   116–17, 124
Nigel d'Aubigny   86–7
Nigel de Mowbray   166
Norton Priory   44, 148
Norwich   77
Nostell Priory   95

Odo son of Robert   99
Odo of Cheriton   73
Oliver Sutton   72

Orderic Vitalis   83
Ospringe (Kent)   117
Otto de Grandson   xii, 85, 129–30, 170, 172
Ottobueno, papal legate   79
Oxford   74, 96, 97, 136, 149

Pagan Peverel   164–6
palmers   72, 90, 148
Patrick II earl of Dunbar   150
Payn de Chaworth   91, 138
Peter of Blois   62
Peter de Cosham   104
Peter the Hermit   50
Peter des Roches   xi, 70, 91, 115, 128
Petronilla de Grandmesnil   125
Petronilla de Tosny (de Lacy)   137
Philip Clerk   104
Philip I Count of Flanders   85 n.5, 93
Philippa   125
   Robert Marmion, husband of   125
Philippa of Champagne   154 n.40
Philomelion   89
Pilia   67
Pocklington (Yorkshire)   61
Pontefract (Yorkshire)   42
Popes
   Adrian IV   x, 47–8
   Alexander III   77–8
   Clement III   49–50, 69
   Clement V   51, 106
   Gregory VIII   48–50, 60
   Gregory IX   11, 54–5
   Gregory X   75
   Honorius III   54
   Innocent III   xi, 11, 24, 45, 50–3, 60, 84, 105, 111, 122
   Innocent IV   55–7
   Nicholas IV   85, 138
   Urban II   x, 45
   Urban III   47–8
   Urban IV   60, 79
Potiphar   66
   wife of   66
Portsmouth   125
Prester John   162
Le Puiset family   11, 86

Quia maior   xi, 45, 51, 54, 62, 69, 75, 99, 105, 111, 122–3, 128, 134, 141

Rachel suum videns   54, 84, 134

Index

Radulf of *Bauburg* 99
Radulf de Hodeng 153
Radulf Mitton 72
   wife of 72
Ralph de Ardene 155
Ralph Niger 28
Ralph VI de Tosny 137
Ralph de Vaux 89
Ranulf of Bashley 138
Ralph de Chall 97
   Wife of 97
Ravenna 102
Reginald of Saint Valéry 136
Reynold de Wirham 103
Rhineland 76
Rhodes xii
Rhys ap Gruffydd, *see* Gwenllian
Richard of Cornwall xi, 40, 128
Richard Cumin 98
Richard "the Lionheart" of England xi, 25, 30, 66, 77, 127, 161
Richard Poore 70, 92
Richard "Strongbow" FitzGilbert 78
Richard of Swinfield 72
Richer 158
Robert son of Alvin 99
Robert de Beaumont, fourth earl of Leicester 137, 147
Robert de Beaumont, third earl of Leicester 125
Robert Beche 103, 125
   Wife of 125
Robert Charles 131
Robert Courçon 60
Robert Cutting 99
Robert Curthose 137, 149, 163
Robert of Icklesham 138, 158, 158 n.71
Robert de la Mara 155
Robert de Marisco 90–1
Robert Marmion 125
Robert de Quincy (the Elder) 156, 168
Robert de Quincy (the Younger) 156
Robert Ruffus 145
Robert of Sproatley 92
Robert Tibetot 91, 138, 167
Roecliff (Yorkshire) 131
Roger de Beaumont 86
Roger de Clifford 109
Roger Gateles 124
Roger de Glanville 150
Roger of Howden 52
Roger of Meauton 99

Roger de Mowbray 86–7, 127
Roger of Poitou 119 n.84
   Hugh, brother of 119 n.84
Roger de Quincy 156, 162 n.88
Roger de Reymes 113
   William, son of 114
Roger of Salisbury 73
Roger of Stanegrave 25
Roger of Wendover 52, 54, 70
   Roland 36
Rolleston (Nottinghamshire) 95
Rome 52
Rose Marnet 102–3, 121–2, 140
Round Churches x, 39–40, 133

Saher IV de Quincy 156, 166–7
St Albans Abbey 29, 83
St Andrews Cathedral 43
St Augustine's Abbey 96
St Denys Priory 125, 126, 149
St Frideswide's Priory 96, 136, 149
St Paul's Cathedral 43
Saladin xi, 28, 30, 42, 48, 101, 162
Saladin Tithe xi, 8, 69
Salisbury 95
Salisbury Cathedral 70
Sallay Abbey 156
Samson of Mauvoisin 47
Sandford (Oxfordshire) 132, 165 n.100
Santiago de Compostela 72, 137
Sawley Abbey 166
Schotplace 112
Scotland 43, 48, 67, 79–80, 128, 150
Seaborough (Somerset) 89–90
Second Barons' War xii, 8, 78–9, 129
Selby (Yorkshire) 61
Selby Abbey 131
Seleucid Empire 31
Sigurðr I Magnusson 139
Simon son of Geoffrey de Bosco 102
Simon de *Henesale* 131
Simon de Montfort, fifth earl of Leicester 84
Simon de Montfort, sixth earl of Leicester xi, 78
Simon I de Senlis x
Sixle Priory 95
Snorri Sturluson 139
Southampton 104, 122, 125–6, 149
Southwick Priory 126, 149
Stamford 77
Stephen of Blois 83–4, 102

237

Index

Stephen of Blois, King of England   x, 109
Sybil, from Bourton-on-the-Water   153
Sybil de Braose   125, 136, 137
Sybil of Dene   158–9
   Ralph, son of   158
Sybil de Ewias   109, 126
Sybil of Icklesham   116–18, 124, 138, 159, 159 n.73
Sybilla of Flanders   95
Symkyn's wife   44
Synocephali   32
Swanilda Gansel   96
Swine Priory   113

Täby (Sweden)   169
Tadcaster   156
Tancredus   146
taxes
   church tax   88
   crusade tax   x, 127, 131
   general tax   x, 131, 132
   see also Saladin Tithe
Templars, *see* Knights Templar
Temple (London)   x, 1
Thames   x, 29
Theobald III of Champagne   169
Theoderic, Prior of the Hospitallers   29
Thomas of Cuckney   155
Thomas of Froidmont   68
Thomas Gansel   96
Thornton (Yorkshire)   114
Thurgarton Priory   95
Tintern Abbey   31
Troarn (Normandy)   159
Tyre   68

Uffculme (Devon)   115
Uffington (Shropshire)   155
Usāma ibn Munqidh   25

Versailles   17
Vincent of *Bec*   99
vow redemptions   47, 54, 69–73, 106, 119, 125, 130

Walburton (Sussex)   104
Walden Priory   43, 92, 153
Wales   63–6, 69, 79, 106, 128
Walter Basset   126
Walter de Beauchamp   85
Walter of Bibbesworth   28
Walter Bower   48
Walter Chinke   99
Walter Giffard   51, 72, 129
Walter Gruk   99
Walter de Luci   158
Walter Marshall   168
Walter le Nair   113
Walter of Saint Valéry   137
Walter de Scoteny   125
Walter of Wigginton   131
Walthamstow (Essex)   137
Walton (Oxfordshire)   96, 149
Wells (Somerset)   146
Westerfield (Suffolk)   114
Westminster Abbey   85, 170
Westminster Palace   30–1
Whale Island (Hampshire)   125
Wherstead (Suffolk)   114
Whitby Abbey   135, 166
Wido of Creon   89
Wife *Porttejoie*   67
William III de Beauchamp   85
William de Beaumont   136, 156
William de Braose, lord of Bramber   136 n.91
William Briwere   xi, 91, 128
William the Conqueror   149
William I de Ferrers   125, 137
William FitzSimon   2, 26
William de Forda   125
William of *Hokesour*   122
William the Huntsman   5 n.15
William II Longespée   xi, 43, 57, 83, 160–1
William of Malmesbury   2–3
William de Mandeville   43, 92, 95, 153–4
William Marshall   85, 135, 137, 138 n.102, 168 n.119
William de la More   104
William de Munchensy   111
William de Muntford   6
William Paynel   115
William I de Percy   135, 166
William Peverel, Second Crusader   164
William Peverel, patron of the Templars   165 n.100
William of Stanford   114
William de Vescy   115

238

Index

William de Warrene   127
Winchester   31
Winchester Cathedral   40
Winteringham (Lincolnshire)   115
Worthington (Leicestershire)   125
Wroxall Priory   150

Wryington   105
Wulfric of Haselbury   24

York   77, 87, 113, 118, 123
Zara (Zadar)   89

Crusading in Context

*Eyewitness and Crusade Narrative: Perception and Narration in
Accounts of the Second, Third and Fourth Crusades*
Marcus Bull

*Baldric of Bourgueil: "History of the Jerusalemites":
A Translation of the* Historia Ierosolimitana
Translated by Susan B. Edgington with an
introduction by Steven J. Biddlecombe

The Miraculous and the Writing of Crusade Narrative
Beth C. Spacey

The Bible and Crusade Narrative in the Twelfth Century
Katherine Allen Smith

*Crusade, Settlement and Historical Writing in the
Latin East and Latin West, c.1100–c.1300*
Edited by Andrew D. Buck, James H. Kane and Stephen J. Spencer

Rewriting the First Crusade: Epistolary Culture in the Middle Ages
Thomas W. Smith

Printed and bound by CPI Group (UK) Ltd, Croydon, CR0 4YY
02/12/2024
14603683-0004